FREE TRADE AND ITS RECEPTION
1815–1960

The repeal of the Corn Laws in 1846 was a crucial, formative moment in the development of the modern world order. From that point on Britain, then the world's leading economic power, was committed to the path of free (or freer) trade. This path in turn had a major impact on the development of a more open and integrated world economy.

This book is Volume I of *Freedom and Trade*, a three-volume project to mark the 150th anniversary of the Corn Laws' repeal which originated at a major 1996 Manchester conference of international scholars. *Free Trade and its Reception* examines the Corn Laws and their repeal, and explores the development of free trade ideas in Britain and around the world.

The contributors to this volume, from Britain, Europe and the United States, include many of the leading international experts working in the field. Their contributions range widely over the history, politics and economics of free trade and protectionism in the nineteenth and twentieth centuries; together they provide a landmark study of a vitally important subject, and one which remains at the top of today's international agenda.

Andrew Marrison is a Senior Lecturer in Economic History at the University of Manchester. He is author of *British Business and Protection, 1903–1932* and is currently working on a study of Britain and Free Trade, 1815–1939.

ROUTLEDGE EXPLORATIONS IN ECONOMIC HISTORY

FREE TRADE AND ITS RECEPTION 1815–1960

Freedom and Trade
Volume I

Edited by
Andrew Marrison

Proceedings of a conference to
commemorate the 150th anniversary
of the repeal of the Corn Laws

General editors
Geraint Parry and Hillel Steiner

London and New York

First published 1998
by Routledge
11 New Fetter Lane, London EC4P 4EE

Simultaneously published in the USA and Canada
by Routledge
29 West 35th Street, New York, NY 10001

Typeset in Garamond by RefineCatch Limited, Bungay, Suffolk
Printed and bound in Great Britain by
Redwood Books, Trowbridge, Wiltshire

British Library Cataloguing in Publication Data
A catalogue record for this book is available from the British Library

Library of Congress Cataloguing in Publication Data
A catalogue record for this book has been requested.

ISBN 0–415–15527–4

CONTENTS

CONTENTS

CONTENTS

FIGURES AND TABLES

Figures

Tables

NOTES ON CONTRIBUTORS

John Breuilly is Professor of Modern History at the University of Birmingham. His previous publications include *Nationalism and the State* (Manchester University Press, 2nd edn, 1993) and *Labour and Liberalism in Nineteenth-Century Europe: Essays in Comparative History* (Manchester University Press, 1992). His principal current research interest is a comparative cultural history of the bourgeois elite in mid-nineteenth-century Hamburg, Lyon and Manchester.

Peter Cain is Research Professor in Modern History, Sheffield Hallam University. His research interests have recently centred on the economic foundations of British imperialism and the history of imperial thought, especially in the Edwardian period. He is author of *British Imperialism* (with A.G. Hopkins, Longman, 2 vols, 1993), which won the American Historical Association's Forkosch Prize in 1995. Among his many articles in leading journals are several on the protectionist movement before 1914, and he has edited *The Political and Economic Works of Richard Cobden* (6 vols, Routledge, 1995). He is currently working on an intellectual biography of J.A. Hobson.

Forrest Capie is Professor of Economic History in the Department of Banking and Finance at City University Business School. He has authored, co-authored or edited sixteen books and over a hundred articles on monetary, banking and trade topics. His publications include *Depression and Protectionism: Britain between the Wars* (George Allen & Unwin, 1983); *Tariffs and Growth: Some Insights from the World Economy, 1850–1940* (Manchester University Press, 1994), *The Future of Central Banking* (with Charles Goodhart and Stanley Fischer, Cambridge University Press, 1995), and *Asset Prices and the Real Economy* (with G.E. Wood, Macmillan, 1997). He is editor of *Economic History Review*.

Patricia Clavin is Senior Lecturer in Modern History in the Department of History at Keele University, where she has taught since 1990. Her research has lain in the economic and diplomatic relations of western

Europe and the USA and, more recently, in the role of historians in shaping government policy and national identity. She is author of *The Failure of Economic Diplomacy: Britain, France, Germany and the United States, 1931–1936* (Macmillan, 1996) and has published widely on international economic relations in the interwar period.

James Foreman-Peck has a doctorate from the London School of Economics. He has been Visiting Associate Professor in the Economics Department at the University of California, Davis, and Professor of Economic History at the University of Hull. At present he teaches economics and economic history at the University of Oxford and is Fellow of St Antony's College. His publications include *European Telecommunications Organisations* (Nomos, 1988), *A History of the World Economy* (Harvester Press, 2nd edn, 1994), *Public and Private Ownership of British Industry, 1820–1990* (Clarendon Press, 1994), *The Motor Industry* (Manchester University Press, 1995) and *Smith & Nephew in the Health Care Industry* (Elgar, 1995). His research interests include industrial policy and international economic relations; he has published widely on the effects of tariffs in the interwar period.

Andrew Hughes Hallett is Jean Monnet Professor of Economics in the University of Strathclyde, and a Research Fellow in the Centre for Economic Policy Research, London. His publications and research interests lie primarily in the areas of European integration and German unification, with particular reference to fiscal issues and labour markets. He has also worked on China and Vietnam and has published widely in leading journals such as *Economic Journal, American Economic Review, Journal of Economic Dynamics and Control, European Economic Review* and *Oxford Economic Papers*.

Boyd Hilton is University Reader in Modern British History and Fellow of Trinity College, Cambridge. He is interested in the political, intellectual and religious history of nineteenth-century Britain, and is author of *Corn, Cash, Commerce: The Economic Policies of the Tory Governments, 1815–1830* (Clarendon Press, 1977) and *The Age of Atonement: The Impact of Evangelicalism on Social and Economic Thought, 1785–1865* (Clarendon Press, 1988). He is currently working on the 1783–1846 volume of the *New Oxford History of England*.

Anthony Howe is Senior Lecturer in International History in the Department of International History at the London School of Economics and Political Science. His research interests centre upon the business-orientated Victorian middle classes, especially the cotton masters of Lancashire and the financiers of the City of London, and upon the international history of Free Trade since 1776. He is author of *The Cotton Masters, 1830–1860* (Clarendon Press, 1984) and *Free Trade and Liberal England, 1846–1946* (Clarendon Press, 1997).

Douglas A. Irwin is Professor of Economics at Dartmouth College and a Faculty Research Fellow with the National Bureau of Economic Research, having previously taught in the University of Chicago Graduate School of Business. He is author of *Against the Tide: An Intellectual History of Free Trade* (Princeton University Press, 1996), as well as many articles on the economic and political history of US and British trade policy in the nineteenth and twentieth centuries.

Alon Kadish is Associate Professor in the History Department at the Hebrew University of Jerusalem. He has published extensively on late-nineteenth-century English economics and is currently working on the economic ideology and methods of the Anti-Corn Law League. He is author of *The Oxford Economists in the Late Nineteenth Century* (Clarendon Press, 1982), *Apostle Arnold: The Life and Death of Arnold Toynbee, 1852–1883* (Duke University Press, 1986) and *Historians, Economists and Economic History* (Routledge, 1989). He edited *The Market for Political Economy: The Advent of Economics in British University Culture, 1850–1905* (with Keith Tribe, Routledge, 1993) and *The Corn Laws: The Formation of Popular Economics in Britain* (6 vols, Pickering, 1996).

Christine Kinealy is a graduate of Trinity College Dublin and a Fellow of the Institute of Irish Studies, University of Liverpool. She has written extensively on nineteenth-century Irish history, especially on the interplay between economy, ideology and policy formulation. Her publications include *This Great Calamity: The Irish Famine, 1845–52* (Gill and Macmillan, 1994), winner of the *Irish Post* Award in 1995, and *A Death-Dealing Famine: The Great Hunger in Ireland* (Pluto Press, 1997). She edited *The Famine in Ulster* (with Trevor Parkhill, Ulster Historical Foundation, 1997) and is currently extending her researches on Ulster in the famine and post-famine periods.

Roger Lloyd-Jones is Reader in Modern Economic and Business History at Sheffield Hallam University. His primary research interests and publications are in business structure and strategy in the cotton, metal and engineering industries; Schumpeterian long waves and the evolution of British industrial capitalism; and the use of computers in industrial and business history. He is author of *Manchester and the Age of the Factory: The Business Structure of Cottonopolis in the Industrial Revolution* (with M.J. Lewis, Croom Helm, 1988) and *Industrial Capitalism in Britain since the Industrial Revolution* (with M.J. Lewis, UCL Press, 1997). He is currently working on a study of Raleigh Industries Ltd.

Norman McCord is Emeritus Professor of Social History in the University of Newcastle-upon-Tyne, having spent most of his working life in the Department of History in that university. His research and writing have been concentrated on modern British history, with a particular interest in the history of his native region, north-east England, although his first major project was a history of the Anti-Corn Law League. For many years he also pursued a secondary research interest in archaeological aerial photography. His books include *The Anti-Corn Law League* (George Allen & Unwin, 1958), *North East England: The Region's Development, 1760–1960* (1979), *North East History from the Air* (1991) and *British History 1815–1906* (Clarendon Press, 1991).

Yue Ma is Reader in Economics at the University of Stirling. His research interests lie in international macroeconomics, rational expectations and policy economics, and international financial economics. He has published widely in leading journals, including *Economic Journal, Journal of Economic Dynamics and Control, Oxford Economic Papers*, and *European Economics Review*.

Lars Magnusson is Professor and Chair in Economic History in the Department of Economic History, Uppsala University, Sweden. He has written extensively on Swedish and European economic history, especially on proto-industrialization and industrial and social change in the nineteenth century, as well as on mercantilism and the history of economic ideas. He is author of *Proto-industrialisation in Scandinavia* (Berg, 1987), *The Contest for Control: Metal Industries in Sheffield, Solingen, Remscheid and Eskilstuna during Industrialisation* (Ixford, 1994), *Mercantilism: The Shaping of an Economic Language* (Routledge, 1994) and *Mercantilist Economics* (Kluwer, 1994). He edited *Mercantilism and Free Trade* (4 vols, Routledge, 1996).

John Maloney is Senior Lecturer in Economics in the School of Business and Economics at the University of Exeter. His publications and research interests centre upon the history of economic thought, the philosophy of economics, nineteenth-century public finance, political business cycles and optimum currency area theory. He is author of *Marshall, Orthodoxy and the Professionalisation of Economics* (Cambridge University Press, 1985) and *What's New in Economics* (Manchester University Press, 1992).

Andrew Marrison is Senior Lecturer in Economic History in the History Department, University of Manchester. His publications and research interests include British overseas trade in the nineteenth and twentieth centuries, the British cotton industry, tariffs and commercial policy, agricultural politics, the business community, and industry–government relations. He is author of *British Business and Protection, 1903–1932* (Clarendon Press, 1996) and is currently working on a study of Britain and Free Trade, 1815–1939.

Tim Rooth is Principal Lecturer in the Department of Economics at the University of Portsmouth. His research and publications have so far centred upon British international trade policy between the wars, particularly on economic relations with the Empire, Scandinavia, and Argentina.

He is now extending his studies in these areas into the post-1945 period. He is author of *British Protectionism and the International Economy: Overseas Commercial Policy in the 1930s* (Cambridge, 1993).

Cheryl Schonhardt-Bailey is Lecturer in Government in the Government Department, London School of Economics and Political Science. Her research interests and article publications concentrate upon modelling ideology and economic interests in trade policy, roll-call voting analysis, and nineteenth-century British and German trade policy. She is editor of *Free Trade: The Repeal of the Corn Laws* (Thoemmes Press, 1996) and *The Rise of Free Trade* (Routledge, 4 vols, 1997), the latter being a massive compilation of contemporary sources and scholarly articles on British trade policy between 1815 and 1914.

Alan Sykes is Lecturer in Modern History in the Department of Modern History, University of St Andrews. His principal field of research is Edwardian politics, both British and imperial. He is author of the standard work on the politics of the Edwardian fiscal controversy, *Tariff Reform in British Politics, 1903–1913* (Clarendon Press, 1979) and of *The Rise and Fall of British Liberalism, 1776–1988* (Addison Wesley Longman, 1997). He is currently writing a study of the radical right in twentieth-century Britain.

Keith Tribe is Reader in Economics at Keele University. His main research interests lie in the history of economic thought, particularly in the area of comparison between its Anglo-American and European formulations. His recent publications include *Governing Economy: The Reformation of Economic Discourse, 1750–1830* (Cambridge University Press, 1995), and *Strategies of Economic Order: German Economic Discourse, 1750–1950* (Cambridge University Press, 1995). He edited *The Market for Political Economy: The Advent of Economics in British University Culture, 1850–1905* (with Alon Kadish, Routledge, 1993) and a collection of interviews with senior British economists, *Economic Careers* (Routledge, 1997). He is currently completing a monograph on the development of the discipline of economics in Britain, 1870–1970.

GENERAL EDITORS' PREFACE

Geraint Parry and Hillel Steiner

The three volumes of *Freedom and Trade* consist of papers arising from a multidisciplinary international conference held at the University of Manchester in 1996 to commemorate the 150th anniversary of the repeal of the Corn Laws in 1846. The papers, along with commentaries, are published in three volumes, each self-contained and each devoted to one or more of the disciplines represented at the conference. One volume, edited by Andrew Marrison, is devoted to *Free Trade and its Reception 1815–1960*, a second, edited by Gary Cook, to *The Economics and Politics of International Trade* and the third to *The Legal and Moral Aspects of International Trade*, for which the editors are Asif Qureshi, Hillel Steiner and Geraint Parry. Professor Frank Hahn's plenary address to the conference appears in the volume on *Economics and Politics of International Trade*. The volume on *Legal and Moral Aspects of International Trade* also includes the papers of a panel of distinguished scholars representing, each of the major disciplines involved, who were invited to speak on 'The Feasibility and Desirability of Global Free Trade'.

The repeal of the Corn Laws in 1846 was an event of enormous significance in the history of international trade, in the development of institutions of international regulation, in the realignment of political parties and interests in Britain, and in the emergence of new modes of political action through mass politics and single-issue interest groups. It remains an event which promptly conjures up the economic, political and moral sentiments surrounding the idea of free trade and its confrontation with the policy of protection. This significance can safely be affirmed even though, as so many chapters in these volumes attest, the nature of this significance remains hotly debated by leading world scholars in every intellectual discipline which is touched by this still controversial measure. Was the real impact of the repeal substantive or symbolic? It would clearly be mistaken to dismiss it as *merely* symbolic, since symbols can be of the utmost importance not merely in history and politics but also in economics. No measure to regulate trade has ever given rise to so much contention at the time and since. It is also a suggestive indicator of the geopolitical situation at the time that this was not an international accord such as the General Agreement on Tariffs and Trade (GATT) but a unilateral legislative action by one economically hegemonic state.

A return to the subject of 'Freedom and Trade' in 1996, 150 years after the repeal and as the new world economic order faces the uncertainties of the twenty-first century, is an intriguing experience. History never exactly repeats itself, either as tragedy or farce. Nevertheless many of the claims and counter-claims of the repeal period can readily be recognized in new guises in the present era. The campaign for free trade stemmed in part from a recognition of the growing interdependence of nations and the emergence of an ever more global market. This has now become the phenomenon which dominates not only international politics but also the domestic politics and economies of nations large and small. The international and the domestic are intertwined as never before. Within this new order economic liberalization may be the dominant ideology but many arguments, familiar from debates surrounding the repeal, make a reappearance. Is liberalization a policy which in reality is designed to promote the interests of the present-day economic hegemon? Is free trade of genuinely mutual benefit or is it a cloak for exploitation of various kinds? Will the new trading blocs and the new political communities which they have begun to create seek to revert to forms of protection? A distinctively new concern, not at the forefront of minds in the optimistic period of the repeal, is whether free trade is compatible with protection of the global environment.

These concerns have given new urgency to the search for authoritative institutions of international regulation. The emergence and influence since the Second World War of such institutions and agencies as the World Bank, International Monetary Fund (IMF), and GATT must be counted among the most striking developments in the history of international politics and international law. The range and scope of these bodies have steadily grown and they have increasingly assumed political responsibilities in promoting policies which are of considerable future significance. It is not surprising therefore that, alongside these developments, there has been a growing interest among political theorists in the moral underpinnings of international economic and political policies. Many have turned from discussing the justice of domestic policy to examining the issues of fairness between nations, the legitimacy of interventions in the affairs of foreign countries and the proper limits to free international exchange.

The conference, which was entitled *1846 Freedom and Trade 1996: A Commemoration of the 150th Anniversary of the Repeal of the Corn Laws,* and these volumes of papers sought to address this range of issues from the perspective of economic and political historians, international economists, international lawyers and political theorists. While the repeal itself is the subject of many of the chapters, in others it serves as the peg upon which to hang discussions of the contemporary state of the international political economy. Moreover the conference was, it should be noted, a 'commemoration' and not a 'celebration' of the repeal. As many contributions indicate, the event still engenders strong views as to its intentions and its consequences. In each of the disciplines represented, there have been important developments in the ways in which the repeal and later issues of freedom and trade are analysed. Innovations in the study of political parties and interests have permitted new examinations of the coalitions of groupings behind the repeal. Subsequent experience of mass politics allows scholars to see the campaigns of the Anti-Corn Law League as forerunners of the techniques of contemporary single-issue politics. In international economics we are, as Gary Cook says in the introduction to the volume on *Economics and Politics of International Trade*, still experiencing 'Corn Laws' debates, which may be conducted in different economic languages but which can produce results just as paradoxical in terms of winners and losers as occurred 150 years ago. The remarkable revival in political theory since the mid-1960s is now bringing new insights to questions of international justice, while lawyers are refining the instruments of international regulation in an arena traditionally dominated by the interplay of power politics. Finally, 150 years which have experienced decades of imperial rivalry, two world wars and 40 years of Cold War tension have inevitably increased scepticism about the cherished beliefs of Richard Cobden and other campaigners that free trade would usher in an unprecedented era of world peace and harmony. Cobden was President of the International Education Society, which sought to promote the cause of European peace by establishing international schools in Britain, France and Germany. His views on trade were inextricably linked to his ideas on morality and on education. Cobden and the free-traders might therefore take some comfort if they could learn that, despite the intervening periods of scepticism and disillusionment, scholars are rediscovering the Cobdenite thesis and beginning to explore whether there is indeed a link between liberalization, democratization and peace between nations.

The conference and the volumes of *Freedom and Trade* have sought to address the range of issues which the original repeal of the Corn Laws raised, not only for its own time but also in ways which have seemed of continuing interest and relevance. The conference was initiated and convened by Hillel Steiner and Geraint Parry of the Department of Government of the University of Manchester, which was the main sponsor of the event. Andrew Marrison of the Department of History, Asif Qureshi of the Faculty of Law of the University of Manchester, and Gary Cook, initially of the Manchester Business School and currently at the University of Derby, were the convenors of the academic specialisms into which the conference and these volumes were divided. Professor Michael Rose of the Department of History at the University of Manchester and Professor Keith Tribe of the University of Keele made major contributions to the conference steering committee. The editorial team is also grateful to Routledge for its support and, in particular, to Alan Jarvis, whose involvement extended to active participation in the conference.

That Manchester was the most appropriate venue for this event can hardly be doubted. The 'Cottonopolis' was where the Anti-Corn Law League was founded. The ideology and the interests of the major manufacturing interests of the city entirely coincided. Indeed the statues of Richard Cobden and John Bright still prominently adorn the city centre. The movement's salience has been perpetuated in the name of the Free Trade Hall, which has been Manchester's chief venue for political and cultural events until, somewhat ironically, it closed in 1996, to reopen as an hotel and conference centre. Perhaps this too has its symbolic quality, since the closure and reopening can be seen as part of the city's reinvention of itself as a different kind of commercial centre, responding to new terms of international trade in a global economy more complex than existed in 1846 but still one exercised by fundamental issues of freedom and protection.

ACKNOWLEDGEMENTS

During the gestation and organization of the conference *1846 Freedom and Trade 1996* and the preparation of the three volumes of *Freedom and Trade* we have incurred many obligations. There is space only to acknowledge some of these debts. The Department of Government of the University of Manchester and its Manchester Centre for Political Thought sponsored the event. We are grateful for their support. The Dean of the Faculty of Economic and Social Studies, the Department of Economics, and Professor Martin Harris, Vice-Chancellor of the University of Manchester, were instrumental in arranging for the crucial seed money to enable the conference to be organized. The Faculty of Law and the Department of History at Manchester provided funds and administrative facilities, as did the University of Derby. On behalf of the History and Policy Section, Andrew Marrison gratefully acknowledges the support of the Conferences and Initiatives Fund of the Economic History Society for a grant towards administrative and travel costs.

Mrs Rebecca Naidoo was an outstanding administrator in the preparatory period leading up to the organization of the conference. Ms Bernadette McLoughlin of the Department of Government provided invaluable administrative backing at all stages and particularly during the immediate conference period.

Hillel Steiner acknowledges the support of the Economic and Social Research Council and the Nuffield Foundation for the award of grants to study issues of international justice which formed one of the conference's prime themes. Geraint Parry acknowledges the support of the Leverhulme Trust for an award to undertake research into nineteenth- and twentieth-century political thought.

Geraint Parry and Hillel Steiner
Department of Government, University of Manchester
February 1997

EDITOR'S INTRODUCTION

Andrew Marrison

The fiftieth anniversary of the repeal of the Corn Laws was essentially a
political affair, and indeed one conducted in an atmosphere where growing
doubts about Britain's economic and political hegemony and the correlative
attractions and imperatives of Empire had the effect of muting the air of
celebration. The hundredth anniversary was even less celebrated. Though the
occasion of a lecture before the Manchester Statistical Society by Sir John
Clapham, and marked in the press by his fellow economic historian Thomas
Ashton, it otherwise took place in conditions of austerity and dollar scarcity
when the nation's mind was occupied with other and more pressing matters.[1]
On both occasions, the truly scholarly literature available to establish an
accurate perspective on repeal was limited. The anniversary of 1996 offers the
first occasion when retrospect can be informed by a substantial body of high-
quality research conducted by professional historians and economic historians. Indeed, the occasion has itself prompted considerable activity among
academic publishers and scholars. Pickering and Chatto have issued a six-
volume collection of scarce tracts on the Corn Laws edited by Alon Kadish,
one of the contributors to this volume.[2] Routledge has published a six-
volume edition of Cobden's political and economic writings, edited by Peter
Cain, whose essay on J.A. Hobson is included in this volume,[3] as well as a
four-volume collection of contemporary and scholarly articles on free trade
edited by Cheryl Schonhardt-Bailey, another contributor here.[4] Beyond these
collections, interest in the Corn Laws, free trade, and commercial policy is at
present intense. Routledge has issued a new edition of Heckscher's classic
work on mercantilism, edited by Lars Magnusson, author of an important
monograph on the same subject and also of a chapter in this volume, as well
as an iconoclastic study of British import controls in the 1950s, written by
Alan Milward and George Brennan.[5] Oxford University Press has published
Anthony Howe's monograph on the free-traders in Victorian Britain, amaz-
ingly the first in which this group has received the scholarly attention it
deserves, and has issued the first full-scale study of the participation of businessmen in the protectionist reaction after 1900.[6] The works mentioned

above do not comprise an exhaustive list: indeed, the cluster of paper around the anniversary is testimony not only to an academic interest in repeal and its consequences which has continued unabated since the Second World War, but also to an academic recognition of its unique importance in British society and in the shaping of the British economy.

Whether viewed in terms of intellectual or political change, the transition in Britain's external economic policy from a conventional mercantilism to a precocious economic liberalism was a long process. Even in strictly formal, legislative terms, the repeal of the Corn Laws in 1846 was only one step on a long road to free trade that is perhaps best dated from Huskisson's rationalizations of the tariff in 1823–5 to Lowe's removal of the vestigial Corn Registration Duty in 1869. It did not even mark the completion of the substantive process, which had to await the dismantling of the Navigation Acts and Gladstone's budgets of 1853 and 1860. Nor, probably, was it the most important enactment in terms of its practical economic effect; on that count, the tariff reductions of 1842 are a strong contender.

Recognition of the long continuum into which repeal must be placed does not, however, destroy its significance. It is true that, even in that most immediate world of politics, the dramatic vote of 15 May 1846 can be understood only with the use of a long lens. Much earlier, Huskisson, Peel, and others in the Tory governments of 1815–30 had come to recognize that social stability was best served by moderate food prices and a tariff regime which kept the British market sufficiently open to European supplies to ensure some availability in times of dearth,[7] and it would perhaps be unwise to attribute too much significance to the Whig hesitations of the 1830s. It has even been suggested that 'free trade was probably something inevitable'.[8] But it would be illegitimate, too teleological, to argue that the real question of the politics of the previous quarter-century had not been whether to repeal the Corn Laws, but how and when to do it. For agricultural protectionists, and for supporters of the old Tory party, 1846 was a real watershed, and in one sense they were clearly correct. Repeal remains, in Britain's move to free trade, the most dramatic and agonized parliamentary decision of all, requiring conversion and imagination in a sequence still not fully understood in spite of the great advances made in recent scholarship. And, even in a longer context, it was still the Great Betrayal, the recognition that the new Tory party had to shed the skin of the old. For free-traders, too, the Corn Laws remained the citadel, the last fastness of the old regime, and their ideological descendants instinctively turned towards explanations couched in terms of assault from without rather than disintegration from within. From both these perspectives, repeal correctly remains in the memory as the symbol, the defining moment of the process.

For generations of British writers, especially from the political, professional, and literary middle classes, that symbol counted. For them, the romance of free trade lay not least in the way the enlightened self-interest of

businessmen showed such an easy symbiosis with the higher ideals of Cobdenism, in stark contrast to the feudal insularities and tyrannies of an ancient
landed class. In that process, Manchester became something fine among the
business centres of the world, was permeated by a cosmopolitanism that still
marks it out as unusual among English provincial cities. Even in its incep-
tion, the Free Trade Hall was remarkable: how many pressure groups not
only achieve their objective but also have so much money left over that such
a monument would absorb only a third of it?[9] But it became much more in
the 150 years that followed. Advertisement of the venue of every concert,
every public meeting, every political speech (even those which preached
Chamberlainite apostasy in the opening years of the new century) served only
to remind of progress, the path to greatness, and the rewards of freedom,
morality, and virtue.

Of course, the reality was less sublime. The association of Cobdenite
internationalism with mainstream business opinion, and even perhaps with
its more exotic Manchester variety, was overdrawn. As Searle has shown, free
trade was, for Cobden and his kind, part of a larger project for reform and
entrepreneurial radicalism, the weaknesses of which were exposed by the
Crimean War: 'thereafter the claims of Cobden and Bright to represent the
industrial and commercial classes lacked all credibility.'[10] Yet in many ways,
and for a long time, such incompletenesses, such awkward marriages, could
be ignored. The prosperous quarter-century after 1846 allowed the crudest
assertion of the success of free trade to pass for a serious examination of its
distributional effects, effects which have only recently begun to be examined.[11] Forgotten were the fears of the Chartists; indeed, free-trade ideology
established a remarkably sound base within the working class and the nascent labour movement.[12] On an even wider political basis, the reintroduction
of income tax in 1842 and the later Liberal–Peelite alignment provided the
foundation for a structure of taxation that was fundamental to the age of
Gladstonian finance and was to endure until the New Liberal adoption of
progressivity in the Edwardian period.[13] From abroad might come Listian
snipings that here was merely the crass self-interest of a nation which had
achieved world hegemony through protectionism and imperialism, accusations which only partly hit home given Britain's self-confessed search for her
own advantage through unilateral tariff reductions when prospects of European reciprocity were poor.[14] Some far-seeing contemporaries might even
discern what historians much later would recognize as an 'imperialism of
Free Trade'.[15] But most linked the higher motives of internationalism with
the progress of economy and society. Few cared to notice, and even fewer to
publicize, how Manchester's devotion to economic liberalism depended on
its illiberal denial to the Indian subcontinent of any vestige of economic self-
determination. When, under such dramatic circumstances, Manchester's own
'principled' belief in free trade evaporated in the interwar period, on account
of India's newfound freedom in tariff policy, there were few remaining to

3

share the *Manchester Guardian's* sense of shame.[16] In 1932, for right or wrong, Britain's commercial policy turned in the direction that those of its trading partners had always taken – a direction based on relativistism, pragmatism, and contingency. For the increasingly beleaguered defenders of free trade in the interwar years, it was not a new direction, but rather a return to the old in a 'new mercantilism'.

Was this the end of free trade in British culture? As a 'secular religion', perhaps.[17] There is a small irony in the closing of the doors of the Free Trade Hall in 1996, almost to the month in which, 150 years earlier, 348 MPs had marched through the lobbies in support of the third reading of Peel's bill.[18] Yet a certain exceptionalism has endured and I think will continue to, perhaps because of a vestigial pride lurking deep within the bosom of a commercial nation. In William Scammell's words, 'While economists generally have preached the virtues of Free Trade, only Britain, amongst the major trading nations of the world, has tried it.'[19] During its reign free trade played a major part in stamping an indelible cosmopolitanism on British society, a cosmopolitanism which has never yet disappeared, which shapes a distinctive British unconcern over the balance between manufacturing and services, and which underpins Britain's market-orientated rather than statist-orientated conception of the European Community. Though a British public, entrenched in the populist belief that Britain 'obeys the rules' while others do not, has become understandably wary of 'one-sided' arrangements,[20] there remains in the Thatcherite vision of a free-trading Europe a glimpse of the survival of mid-Victorian optimism and confidence. It remains to be seen whether 'globalization' of the world economy will result in the long-term diffusion throughout the world of values so long associated most particularly and most steadfastly with Britain.

Indeed, the chapters in this volume testify to the strong, continuing, and evolving interest in Britain's adoption of free trade and its subsequent commercial policy regime. Though preceded by important and still valuable studies,[21] there appeared in 1958 three works which in many ways laid the foundation for modern analysis – Norman McCord's *The Anti-Corn Law League, 1838–1846* (London); Lucy Brown's *The Board of Trade and the Free Trade Movement, 1830–1842* (Oxford); and Albert Imlah's *Economic Elements in the Pax Britannica* (Cambridge, Mass.). Since then, our understanding has increased at a pace which has if anything accelerated over time. The excessive disciplinary specialization and fragmentation which have sometimes slowed academic advance elsewhere have thankfully been absent in this area: economic historians, political scientists and historians of economic thought have been pleasingly aware of each other's methodologies and perspectives.

Thus there is much progress to report. Early analyses which skipped whiggishly from Adam Smith through Huskisson's reforms of the 1820s to the activities of the Anti-Corn Law League in the 1840s have not been exploded so much as transformed by a new understanding of the depth and subtlety of the process of change.[22] The very effects of the Corn Laws themselves continue to fascinate economic historians.[23] Though modern historians of economic thought have fairly stable views on the theoretical presumptions of the classical economists in favour of free trade, there is less unity over their application of their theories to economic policy, and their influence within Parliament and government.[24] Furthermore, it has been recognized that the precise influence of the classical economists is to be set alongside the development of a Christian – more precisely, a moderate Evangelical – free trade which, some would argue, was even more important in changing social and political values.[25] Gone are explanations resting on the pivotal importance of the Anti-Corn Law League, and which all too often associated policy change with a single-faceted and unilinear pressure exerted by a business community at the vanguard of economic and social transformation.[26] Just as historians have learned a new respect for the understanding of politicians in both economic doctrine and the pragmatic constraints on policy,[27] so too they have been disillusioned in the belief in a monolithic and atavistically protectionist landed interest.[28] But with recent advances has come a recognition of new uncertainties, new research frontiers. The precise weighting of ideological influences, changes in economic structure, business pressure, political manoeuvring, and ministerial autonomy still causes controversy. The difficulty of relating votes in Parliament to the specific economic interests of its members (MPs) and the broad economic interests of their constituencies has been illuminated by techniques of rational choice analysis imported duty free from the discipline of political science,[29] yet the issue has still not been resolved. Huge advances have been made in our understanding of the continuities and shifts in Peel's thinking[30] and of the parliamentary manoeuvres of 1841–6 and the changing economic background against which they took place. Nevertheless, historians still struggle to balance conviction against political self-interest in formulating a convincing explanation of Peel's decision, and the problem of explaining the precise context and circumstances in which the Peelites gave their support to the third reading of Peel's bill still remains.

The aftermath of repeal, indeed the whole of Britain's 'free-trade century', also continues to fuel the historian's interest. Easy associations of free trade with mid-Victorian prosperity are now doubted, the economic effects of the reintroduction of protection in 1932 have been vigorously debated, and doubts have even been expressed over the unalloyed benefits of unilateral free trade in the years before 1914.[31] Study of Joseph Chamberlain's Tariff Reform movement, scarcely beyond its infancy in the mid-1960s, has blossomed beyond an early concentration on high politics, particularly the immediate crisis in Balfour's cabinet. It now spreads its shadow over issues such as Empire radicalism and 'social imperialism', popular and populist politics, the radical right and Edwardian nationalism,[32] the emergence of Labour and the eclipse of the Liberal party, public finance and welfare reform, and the development of business politics under threat of an alleged 'modernization crisis'.[33] Even the free-traders, viewed for long as an unproblematic, homogeneous and unevolving survival from the politics of the 1840s, have begun to attract the historians' attention that they deserve,[34] while parallel developments in the study of foreign investment, the service sector, and 'gentlemanly capitalism' have deepened our understanding of British cosmopolitanism.[35] Considerable advance has also been made in the field of international comparison. Earlier, insular tariff histories of foreign nations have been widened, and historians and political scientists have re-examined trade policy in the light of changes in world economic hegemony long lurking implicit in the older literature.[36] The tariff issue is no longer regarded as an arcane subject left politely in the hands of specialists, but rather as an issue central to British politics and British political culture.

These and other related concerns are reflected in the chapters appearing in this volume. Alon Kadish's Chapter 1 brings us straight into a central issue permeating the debate over repeal – the free-traders' handling of accusations that their policy would result in a fall in real wages. He shows how the free traders grappled with the less supportive elements of Ricardian theory. Interestingly, there was what historians of a later period would term 'corporatist' elements in the attitude of both the League writers and their Whig antecedents to the relations between agriculture and industry, but in the interest of class tactics the language of aggression and confrontation was put to the fore in League pamphlets.

John Maloney in Chapter 2 deepens and extends our knowledge about the relationship between Gladstone's and Peel's thinking on the corn question, and in consequence yields new insights on the path to repeal. Especially in their careful reasoning on the best morphology of a sliding scale to stabilize prices, ensure supply, and diminish the effects of harmful speculation while not deterring price-smoothing speculation, both Peel and Gladstone are shown to have been 'more impressive at working out their own ideas than at discussing those of greater economists'. Indeed, in a sense, their conviction that corn was a special case ensured that their emphasis was pragmatic.

Christine Kinealy in Chapter 4 strips away the mythology which surrounds the connection between repeal and an Irish agriculture which, by 1830, supplied 80 per cent of Britain's imports of corn, as well as restoring the magnificent potato to its due place in the hierarchy of foods. Placing short-term relief needs and strategies in the context of long-term policy-objectives at Westminster, she also makes explicit just how far the motives of politicians can diverge from public perceptions.

Ideology can sometimes be forgotten in 'rational choice' analyses seeking to test votes against economic interest through techniques of statistical inference. Refining concepts of the interplay between ideology and economic interest originating in the discipline of political science in Chapter 5, Cheryl Schonhardt-Bailey develops a model to demonstrate the links between the two. Her particular argument that, both in Britain's move to free trade and in Germany's decision for protection in the late nineteenth century, economic interest groups '"nationalize the interest", and that ideology shapes and forms notions of self-interest' reminds us that economists can too readily assume that economic interests are given and unambiguous.

Roger Lloyd-Jones in Chapter 7 shows the ambiguities, inconsistencies and divisions that prevent us from constructing a simple and linear 'Manchester strategy' in favour of free trade. In stressing the volatility of the industry that underpinned the growth of 'Cottonopolis', he shows well the curious mixture of confidence and insecurity which pervaded the mushrooming business community. Even at height of the mid-1830s boom there were wide anxieties over foreign competition in textiles, especially from the Zollverein. Realization that diplomatic pressure against the Zollverein would not be forthcoming underlined Manchester's need to stand unaided: it was 'just as much fear as bravado which pushed the Manchester business community into the free trade camp'. Only then, in the turbulent conditions of 1837–42, could the classic dimensions of Manchester's agitation against the Corn Laws emerge fully.

In his *tour de force* Chapter 8 on the differences between Cobdenite and Hamburg versions of liberalism, John Breuilly tackles a subject too long ignored by a British historiography underlain by the precepts of 'English–American' economic thinking. On one level, there existed in Hamburg a dualism between an ethic of free exchange and a continued survival of regulations on personal mobility and institutional organization that can be traced to a contradiction between the city's entrepôt economy and its need for social control. But at a deeper level, even Hamburg's free-trade perceptions were based upon a static division of labour coupled with a certain antipathy towards industrial development, rather than upon dynamic implications for growth. Hamburg did not share Cobden's vision of free trade as a metaphor for, and a cause of, personal freedoms and a wider liberalism.

Douglas Irwin, earlier the author of one of the two pioneer analyses on the welfare effects of Britain's move towards unilateral free trade after 1846, takes in Chapter 10 the related issue of the 'terms of trade effect' further in his study of the pre-1846 House of Commons. Concentrating on the sophistications introduced into the classical theory of international trade by Robert Torrens, he shows the high quality of the tariff debate in Parliament. In this he reinforces the verdict of Maloney's chapter, yet his analysis of the extent to which politicians read and assimilated the latest writings of the political economists, and could debate their relative merits, suggests intriguing differences between Peel and Gladstone and their parliamentary colleagues.

In his careful examination of Swedish economic writers in Chapter 11, Lars Magnusson refutes Heckscher's argument that the influence of Smithian ideas in Sweden before the 1850s was small and, when it did come, largely indirect, through Bastiat and the 'harmony economists'. Furthermore, his chapter also contains themes concerning the complexity of transmission of ideas and their adaptation to local needs and conditions similar to those explored by Breuilly. In showing how Swedish economists combined such influences with a more positivist view of the state and state intervention, he separates the Swedish product not only from the English but from the Hamburg as well, hence underlining the point made by both writers.

Anthony Howe in Chapter 13 charts the tremendous consolidation of free trade in British politics and society after 1846. He demonstrates the iron grip that Peel's acceptance of unilateral as opposed to Huskissonite free trade established upon the Tory party. He dismisses the idea of the previously timid Whigs as 'bourbons of the fisc', for instance by examining their approach to imperial preference and their refusal to countenance tariff bargaining. Most provocatively, he uncovers the emergence of a rift between a 'rights view' of free trade and a 'market view' of free trade in the 1880s, the victory of the latter within the Liberal party leading to an ability to reconcile free trade with the New Liberalism.

In an analysis which demonstrates why Chamberlainite Tariff Reform continues to fascinate scholars from such a wide variety of disciplines, Alan Sykes (Chapter 14) places the economic objectives of the movement at a heavy discount. Concentrating on the political imperatives of the Tariff Reformers, he outlines the 'variety of meanings that [Tariff Reform] embraced as a result of political necessities and the logical confusions introduced by those necessities.' Chamberlain's own motives, moreover, relegated economic motives to the sidelines: his real concern was imperial consolidation in a Social-Darwinist struggle between great, integrated empires. Without Tariff Reform, in Chamberlain's nightmare, the 'weary Titan' could not endure.

Peter Cain explores in Chapter 16 the complex evolution of J.A. Hobson's economic thinking on protection. The protectionist implications of his early-career rejection of Say's law were susequently rejected because of his detestation of imperialism, resulting in an intellectual fusion of underconsumption with a theory of imperialism. Free trade might promote imperialism, but Chamberlain's schemes would if anything intensify it: only the removal of oversaving would reduce Britain's overseas lending and export-orientation. But, as Chamberlain's crusade erupted, Hobson retreated from this position back towards a more orthodox Cobdenism in which trade raised living standards and even free trade imperialism was broadly acceptable, allowing an ultimate reconciliation with orthodox Liberalism. If Hobson can be accused of contradiction, it may be that he was deeply concerned about poverty and imperialism, rather than just making the ritual obeisances that economists customarily make before diving head first into a more elegant world.

Andrew Marrison examines in Chapter 17 the effectiveness of the most-favoured-nation clause and the vulnerability of a Chamberlainite tariff to foreign retaliation during the period 1880–1914, an interlude somewhere between a mid-Victorian period where Britain could have exploited its 'large-player' status in international trade and an interwar period where it perhaps could not have done, concluding that the contemporary free-traders' fear of retaliation was probably exaggerated.

Forrest Capie in Chapter 19 searches for the fundamental explanations for Britain's return to protection in 1931–2. Arguing that political-economy models originating out of US experience are less suited to British conditions, he produces a multifaceted explanation embracing the effects of war, the appeal of Empire, the effectiveness of pressure groups and protectionist propaganda, and changing moods, which can result in policy shifts far more quickly than economic interests can be expected to change.

Developing a sophisticated economic model in Chapter 21, James Foreman-Peck, Andrew Hughes Hallett and Yue Ma offer an innovative argument that a temporary British tariff early in 1930 could have saved the gold standard and limited the spread of tariff barriers in the Great Depression. Raising the 'counterfactual' in this direct way is always likely to be provocative, yet we should remember that, as well as Keynes, much informed contemporary banking opinion was heading the same way. Of course, without the theoretical apparatus employed by Foreman-Peck *et al.*, the thinking was much more intuitive, but nevertheless the 'bankers' manifesto' of July 1930, and Henry Clay's later Bank of England memorandum, suggest some contemporary awareness of the plausibility of such a move. It might also be observed that some historians today question the traditional belief that bankers were trenchantly opposed to protection, believing rather that they might have willingly sacrificed free trade if this would have ensured the survival of gold.

Patricia Clavin's Chapter 22 shows the difficulties faced by US negotiators in their attempts to promote an Anglo-American trade agreement in the 1930s and 1940s. Their confusion was perhaps understandable. Britain's long adherence to internationalism, even in the increasingly adverse world economic context of the 1920s, and the depth of popular support at general elections that lay behind this, must have made 1931–2 look like an aberration. Against American difficulties in defining the basis on which US leadership of the international economy should be based, later British propagandists at the wartime Ministry of Information sought to further a 'doctrine of responsibility' that they hoped would have corollary benefits in Anglo-American relations, but which was urged in such a way as to leave the Americans with an exaggerated impression of British economic strength. By the same token, the British did not find it easy to deal with an administration unclear in its aims and dependent upon a Congress hostile to liberalization.

It is slightly ironic that Clavin quotes Hegel's remark that 'we learn from history that we do not learn from history', for in some ways her chapter acts as a bridge between the contributions in this volume and the discussion of post-1945 issues and current concerns that appear in its companion volumes.

The lessons from history may be misleading, but there are leitmotivs, the similarity and continuity of themes, the recurrence of problems, even if study of the history of international trade relations does not yield programmatic historical solutions. Predictably, and as the chapters collected in this and its companion volumes demonstrate, there is as yet no universally accepted intepretation of the causes, effects, and significance of Britain's move to free trade. Economists, especially of the more Anglo-American tradition, tend to embark upon studies of trade and trade policy with an outlook conditioned heavily by the elegance and theoretical completeness of ideal free trade. Even those who have developed the new 'strategic trade theory' tend to disclaim any motive of trying to undermine the general welfare superiority of the free-trade position. Some political scientists point to an alternative perspective, suggesting that while free trade might maximise *absolute* welfare or growth, protectionism can maximise *relative* welfare or growth. This approach is grounded in an uncomfortable aspect often overlooked by the theoreticians: trade policy can be as much about rivalry, power, prestige, self-respect – indeed simply about 'winning' – as it can be about exchange values, welfare, and growth. Historians, or at least those who do not come to their subject laden with presumptions learned in those other disciplines, have to live within both these traditions. For the historian of British free trade, this can cause particular difficulties. The tensions created exist less because historians differ fundamentally on the costs and benefits of universal free trade, but because of the particular historical context of a free trade nation in a protectionist world. Ironically, however, this only serves to fuel the historian's continued fascination with that certain nobility of purpose that was, and is still, associated with Britain's historic adoption of free trade.

Notes

1 Anthony Howe, *Free Trade and Liberal England, 1846–1946* (Oxford, 1997). Ironically, after being avoided throughout the war, bread rationing was introduced the day after the centenary of the repeal of the Corn Laws.
2 A. Kadish (ed.) *The Corn Laws: The Formation of Popular Economics in Britain*, (Pickering and Chatto, London, 6 vols, 1996).
3 P.J. Cain (ed.) *The Political and Economic Works of Richard Cobden* (Routledge, London, 6 vols, 1995).
4 Cheryl Schonhardt-Bailey (ed.) *The Rise of Free Trade* (Routledge, London, 4 vols, 1997).
5 E.F. Heckscher, *Mercantilism* (1st Eng. edn, 1935; new edn with introduction by Lars Magnusson, Routledge, London, 2 vols, 1994); Lars Magnusson, *Mercantilism: The Shaping of an Economic Language*, (Routledge, London, 1994); A. Milward and G. Brennan, *Britain's Place in the World: A Historical Enquiry into Import Controls, 1945–60* (Routledge, London, 1996).
6 Howe, *Free Trade and Liberal England*; Andrew Marrison, *British Business and Protection, 1903–1932* (Oxford, 1996).

7 Boyd Hilton, *Corn, Cash, Commerce: The Economic Policies of the Tory Governments, 1815–1830* (Oxford, 1977).

8 R. Stewart, *The Politics of Protection: Lord Derby and the Protectionist Party, 1841–1852* (Cambridge, 1971), p. 48.

9 N. McCord, *The Anti-Corn Law League, 1838–1846* (London, 1958).

10 G.R. Searle, *Entrepreneurial Politics in Mid-Victorian Britain* (Oxford, 1993), p. 291. See also N. McCord, 'Cobden and Bright in Politics, 1846–1857', in R. Robson (ed.) *Ideas and Institutions of Victorian Britain* (London, 1967).

11 J.G. Williamson, 'The Impact of the Corn Laws Just Prior to Repeal', *Explorations in Economic History*, 27, 1990.

12 E.F. Biagini, *Liberty, Retrenchment and Reform: Popular Liberalism in the Age of Gladstone, 1860–1880* (Cambridge, 1992).

13 N. Gash, *Sir Robert Peel: The Life of Sir Robert Peel after 1830* (London, 2nd edn, 1986); H.V. Emy, 'The Impact of Financial Policy on English Party Politics before 1914', *Historical Journal*, 15, 1972.

14 L. Brown, *The Board of Trade and the Free Trade Movement, 1830–1842* (Oxford, 1958).

15 B. Semmel, *The Rise of Free Trade Imperialism: Classical Political Economy, the Empire of Free Trade and Imperialism, 1750–1850* (Cambridge, 1970).

16 B. Chatterji, *Trade, Tariffs, and Empire: Lancashire and British Policy in India, 1919–1939* (Delhi, 1992); A.J. Robertson, 'Lancashire and the Rise of Japan, 1910–1937', *Business History*, 32, 1990.

17 F. Trentman, 'The Strange Death of Free Trade: The Erosion of "Liberal Consensus" in Great Britain, c. 1903–1932', in E.F. Biagini (ed.) *Citizenship and Community: Liberals, Radicals and Collective Identities in the British Isles, 1865–1931* (Cambridge, 1996), pp. 219–20.

18 In the hands of its new owners, the Hall will survive as a hotel and conference centre, but not, as some would have wished, as a centre for community affairs and local culture.

19 W.M. Scammell, *The International Economy since 1945* (London, 1980), p. 39.

20 See Patricia Clavin, Chapter 22 in this volume, for the early stages of Britain's retreat from unilateralism.

21 Esp. D.G. Barnes, *A History of the English Corn Laws from 1660–1846* (London, 1930); C.R. Fay, *The Corn Laws and Social England* (Cambridge, 1932); F.E. Hyde, *Mr. Gladstone at the Board of Trade* (London, 1934); R.L. Schuyler, *The Fall of the Old Colonial System: A Study in British Free Trade, 1770–1870* (New York, 1945).

22 For the 'new orthodoxy', see Hilton, *Corn, Cash, Commerce*, op. cit.

23 S. Fairlie, 'The Nineteenth-Century Corn Laws Revisited', *Economic History Review*, 2nd ser., 18, 1965; *idem*, 'The Corn Laws and British Wheat Production, 1829–76', *Economic History Review*, 2nd ser., 22, 1969; W. Vamplew, 'The Protection of English Cereal Producers: The Corn Laws Reassessed', *Economic History Review*, 2nd ser., 33, 1980; W.E. Van Vugt, 'Running from Ruin? The Emigration of British Farmers to the U.S.A. in the Wake of the Repeal of the Corn Laws', *Economic History Review*, 2nd ser., 41, 1988; J.G. Williamson, 'The Impact of the Corn Laws Just Prior to Repeal', *Explorations in Economic History*, 27, 1990; J. Prest, 'A Large Amount or a Small? Revenue and the Nineteenth-Century Corn Laws', *Historical Journal*, 39, 1996.

24 L. Robbins, *The Theory of Economic Policy in English Classical Political Economy* (London, 1952); D.A. Irwin, *Against the Tide: An Intellectual History of Free Trade* (Princeton, NJ, 1996); D.P. O'Brien, *The Classical Economists* (Oxford, 1975); W.D. Grampp, *The Manchester School of Economics* (Stanford, CA, 1960); *idem*,

'Economic Opinion When Britain Turned to Free Trade', *History of Political Economy*, 14, 1982; Hilton, *Corn, Cash, Commerce*; Gash, *Sir Robert Peel*.

25 Boyd Hilton, *The Age of Atonement: The Influence of Evangelicalism on Social and Economic Thought, 1795–1865* (Oxford, 1988).

26 M.J. Turner, 'Before the Manchester School: Economic Theory in Early Nineteenth-Century Manchester', *History*, 79, 1994; A.C. Howe, 'Free Trade and the City of London, *c.*1820–1870', *History*, 77, 1992; Roger Lloyd-Jones, Chapter 7 in this volume.

27 N. Gash, *Sir Robert Peel*; Douglas Irwin, 'Political Economy and Peel's Repeal of the Corn Laws', *Economics and Politics*, 1, 1989; John Maloney, 'Gladstone, Free Trade and Political Economy, 1841–6', *History of Economic Ideas*, 3, 1995; John Maloney and Douglas Irwin, Chapters 2 and 10 in this volume.

28 D.C. Moore, 'The Corn Laws and High Farming', *Economic History Review*, 2nd ser., 18, 1965. But, on agricultural protectionism, see Stewart, *The Politics of Protection*; T.L. Crosby, *English Farmers and the Politics of Protection, 1815–1852*, (Hassocks, 1977).

29 W.O. Aydelotte, 'The Country Gentleman and the Repeal of the Corn Laws', *English Historical Review*, 82, 1967; *idem*, 'The Disintegration of the Conservative Party in the 1840s: A Study of Political Attitudes', in W.O. Aydelotte, A.G. Bogue and R. Fogel (eds) *The Dimension of Quantitative Research in History* (Princeton, NJ, 1972).T.J. McKeown, 'The Politics of Corn Law Repeal and Theories of Commercial Policy', *British Journal of Political Science*, 19, 1989; C. Schonhardt-Bailey, 'Lessons in Lobbying for Free Trade in 19th-Century Britain: To Concentrate or Not', *American Political Science Review*, 85, 1991; *idem*, 'Specific Factors, Capital Markets, Portfolio Diversification, and Free Trade: Domestic Determinants of the Repeal of the Corn Laws', *World Politics*, 43, 1991; *idem*, 'Linking Constituency Interests to Legislative Voting Behaviour: The Rôle of District Economic and Electoral Composition in the Repeal of the Corn Laws', in J.A. Phillips (ed.) *Computing Parliamentary History: George III to Victoria* (Edinburgh, 1994).

30 Gash, *Sir Robert Peel*; Boyd Hilton, 'Peel: A Reappraisal', *Historical Journal*, 22, 1979; D.A. Irwin, 'Political Economy and Peel's Repeal of the Corn Laws', *Economics and Politics*, 1, 1989; John Maloney, Chapter 2 in this volume.

31 D.N. McCloskey, 'Magnanimous Albion: Free Trade and British National Income, 1841–1881', *Explorations in Economic History,* 17, 1980; P. Cain, 'Professor McCloskey on British Free Trade, 1841–1881: Some Comments', *Explorations in Economic History*, 19, 1982; D.A. Irwin, 'Welfare Effects of British Free Trade: Debate and Evidence from the 1840s', *Journal of Political Economy*, 96, 1988; F. Capie, 'The British Tariff and Industrial Protection in the 1930s', *Economic History Review*, 2nd ser., 31, 1978; J. Foreman-Peck, 'Tariff Protection and Economies of Scale: The British Motor Industry before 1939', *Oxford Economic Papers*, 31, 1979; J. Foreman-Peck, 'The British Tariff and Industrial Protection in the 1930s: An Alternative Model', *Economic History Review*, 2nd ser., 34, 1981; F. Capie, *Depression and Protectionism: Britain between the Wars*, (London, 1983); M. Kitson and S. Solomou, *Protectionism and Economic Revival: The British Interwar Economy* (Cambridge, 1990); M. Thomas, 'An Input-Output Approach to the British Economy, 1890–1914', *Journal of Economic History*, 45, 1985; Andrew Marrison, Chapter 17 in this volume.

32 B. Semmel, *Imperialism and Social Reform: English Social-Imperial Thought, 1895–1914* (London, 1960); Alan Sykes, *Tariff Reform in British Politics, 1903–1913* (Oxford, 1979); A. Summers, 'The Character of Edwardian Nationalism: Three Popular Leagues', in P. Kennedy and A Nicholls (eds) *Nationalist and Racialist*

Movements in Britain and Germany before 1914 (London, 1981); F. Coetzee, *For Party or Country: Nationalism and the Dilemmas of Popular Conservatism in Edwardian England* (New York, 1990); E.H.H. Green, *The Crisis of Conservatism: The Politics, Economics and Ideology of the British Conservative Party, 1880–1914* (London, 1995); P. Cain, 'The Conservative Party and "Radical Conservatism", 1880–1914: Incubus or Necessity?', *Twentieth Century British History*, 7, 1996; *idem*, 'The Economic Philosophy of Constructive Imperialism', in C. Navari (ed.) *British Politics and the Spirit of the Age* (Keele, 1996); Alan Sykes, Chapter 14 in this volume.

33 See esp. P.F. Clarke, *Lancashire and the New Liberalism* (Cambridge, 1971); *idem*, 'The End of Laissez-Faire and the Politics of Cotton', *Historical Journal*, 15, 1972; H.V. Emy, 'The Impact of Financial Policy on English Party Politics before 1914', *Historical Journal*, 15, 1972; S. Newton and D. Porter, *Modernization Frustrated: The Politics of Industrial Decline in Britain since 1900* (London, 1988); Marrison, *British Business and Protection*; F. Trentmann, 'The Transformation of Fiscal Reform: Reciprocity, Modernization, and the Fiscal Debate within the Business Community in Early Twentieth-Century Britain', *Historical Journal*, 39, 1996.

34 Anthony Howe, 'Towards the "Hungry Forties": Free Trade in Britain, *c.*1880–1906'; and F. Trentman, 'The Strange Death of Free Trade: The Erosion of "Liberal Consensus" in Great Britain, *c.*1903–1932', both in E.F. Biagini (ed.) *Citizenship and Community: Liberals, Radicals and Collective Identities in the British Isles, 1865–1931* (Cambridge, 1996). See also Anthony Howe and Peter Cain, Chapters 13 and 16 in this volume.

35 See esp. P.J. Cain and A.G. Hopkins, *British Imperialism: Innovation and Expansion, 1688–1914* (London, 1993).

36 The literature is too extensive for reference here. For studies with particular significance for Britain, see T.J. McKeown, 'Hegemonic Stability Theory and Nineteenth-Century Tariff Levels in Europe', *International Organization*, 37, 1983; P.M. Kennedy, *The Rise of the Anglo-German Antagonism, 1860–1914* (London, 1980); A.L. Friedberg, *The Weary Titan: Britain and the Experience of Relative Decline, 1895–1905* (Princeton, NJ, 1988); D.A. Lake, *Power, Protection, and Free Trade: International Sources of U.S. Commercial Strategy, 1887–1939* (Ithaca, NY, 1988); D. Verdier, *Democracy and International Trade: Britain, France, and the United States, 1860–1990* (Princeton, NJ, 1994); B. Simmons, *Who Adjusts? Domestic Sources of Foreign Economic Policy during the Inter-War Years* (Princeton, NJ, 1994). See also John Breuilly, Lars Magnusson and Patricia Clavin, Chapters 8, 11 and 22 in this volume.

1

FREE TRADE AND HIGH WAGES

The economics of the Anti-Corn Law League

Alon Kadish

Roger Lloyd-Jones in Chapter 7, ' "Merchant City": The Manchester business community, the trade cycle and commercial policy *c*.1820–1846' has shown the importance of free trade for the economic survival and prosperity of the Manchester business community. Indeed the question of the role of self-interest featured prominently in the campaign for free trade. A common accusation levelled against the Anti-Corn Law League was that it consisted of manufacturers who sought to repeal the Corn Laws in order to reduce wages and, thereby, improve their competitiveness in foreign markets. The League's critics assumed the iron law of wages, whereby cheap bread would result in a diminution of nominal wages following the reduction in the price of necessaries while real wages remained the same, so tending towards the minimum necessary for survival.

> the inevitable consequence of Free Trade would be the reduction of wages. In fact, the only way under Heaven, that a repeal of the Corn and Provision Laws could benefit [the manufacturers], would be by enabling them to obtain cheaper labour, to reduce the means of production, to lower wages, so as to enable them to compete with foreigners.[1]

The criticism was not only of the League's economic arguments. Free trade was often presented as a class issue, a typical example of the industrialists' egotism, whereby class interests were to be forced on the nation at the expense of all others. The differences between the manufacturers and the rest of society, especially the landed classes, went well beyond abstract economic reasoning.

> The capital invested in land, and the wealth arising from it, are estimated at more than those appertaining to manufacture. The

wealth of land is intrinsically permanent; its productions are essentially necessary for the support of life; its occupation conduces to health; its occupiers are peaceable and orderly subjects, and, looking *only* to this country for employment, they are nationalized.

But, on the contrary, manufacture varying with the change of fashion, or caprice; or affected by advantages of locality, by over trading, foreign competition, or high duties on importation, is not endued with the quality of permanency; and the health and morals of its operatives are injured by confinement and the density of population, which last circumstance renders its masses easy victims to designing demagogues.[2]

However, Manchester's businessmen also regarded themselves as leaders of the communities they had helped to create and sustain, and guardians of the moral and material welfare of the working classes placed in their charge by virtue of their economic and social position. An institutional expression of the concern felt by Manchester businessmen for the state of the working classes may be found in the foundation and early work of the Statistical Society of Manchester, established in the autumn of 1833 following the meeting of the British Association for the Advancement of Science in Cambridge and the creation of its statistical section – Section F.[3] The founders of the Manchester Society, described by the Society's historian, 'consisted of a small group of friends, all under forty years of age, all men of philanthropic and literary taste, and all connected in some degree with local industry or banking.'[4] They included William Langton (1803–81) and James Phillips Kay (1804–77, from 1842 Kay-Shuttleworth), co-secretaries of the Manchester and Salford District Provident Society, and Kay's friends Samuel and William Rathbone Greg. The latter's older brother Robert Hyde Greg joined the Society in 1834.

Manchester Statistical Society's initial purpose was not the collection of facts for its own sake but as a means of 'effecting improvement in the state of the people among whom [the members] lived', by using the information gathered to demand practical reforms.[5] The Society's early investigations focused largely on the moral and economic conditions of the working classes in Manchester and Salford compared with other urban (industrial and non-industrial) communities such as Liverpool, Hull, Bury, Ashton, Bolton, York, etc. and rural districts (Rutland). Its work followed in its general concerns and method Kay's well-known study, *The Moral and Physical Condition of the Working Classes Employed in the Cotton Manufacture in Manchester*, published in 1832, and written while Kay served as secretary to the Manchester Board of Health, set up to combat the cholera epidemic. 'The operative population', Kay wrote in the pamphlet's concluding paragraph, constitutes one of the most important elements of society; and when numerical considered, the magnitude of its interests and the extent of its power assume such vast proportions, that the folly which neglects them is allied to madness.[6]

Kay, the son of a Rochdale cotton manufacturer, regarded his investigation as reflecting the manufacturers' unique position in industrial society. In an introductory letter to the Revd Thomas Chalmers (1780–1847), the Scottish theologian and political economist, Kay stated that whereas the aristocracy had moved away from the large provincial towns, and the 'pure' merchants were 'seldom in immediate contact with the people',[7] it was the 'enlightened manufacturers of the country' who were

acutely sensible of the miseries of large masses of the operative body [and] are to be ranked amongst the foremost advocates of every measure which can remove the pressure of the public burdens from the people, and the most active promoters of every plan which can conduce to their physical improvement, or their moral elevation.[8]

Kay's words may be seen as reflecting the accusations, often made in the course of the Factory Movement's campaign and later in the public debate on the repeal of the Corn Laws, of the industrialists as responsible for the appalling conditions of the industrial urban working classes. The industrialists and their defenders produced in response a number of answers. The situation was not as bad or as common as widely supposed. Where working and living conditions were irrefutably awful, they were largely the result of external factors such as the landowners' Corn Laws. Conditions in non-industrial rural districts were worse (an argument not always borne out by the investigations of the Manchester Society). And the industrialists, acutely aware of the problem, were the first to try and solve it. But beyond the rhetoric of the often bitter public debate, Kay's work reveals a number of serious and genuine concerns.

In dealing with the particular problem of cholera, Kay found that the disease 'can only be eradicated by raising the physical and moral condition of the community, in such a degree as to remove the predisposition to its reception and propagation, which is created by poverty and immorality.'[9] Indeed poverty and immorality were two symptoms of the same disease – 'The sources of vice and physical degradation are allied with the causes of pauperism. Amongst the poor, the most destitute are too frequently the most demoralized – virtue is the surest economy – vice is haunted by profligacy and want.'[10] Accordingly Kay's research revealed that

those among the operatives of the mills, who are employed *in the process of spinning*, and especially of fine spinning, (who receive a high rate of

wages and who are elevated on account of their skill) are more atten-
tive to their domestic arrangements, have better furnished houses, are
consequently more regular in their habits, and more observant of their
duties than those engaged in other branches of the manufacture.[11]

The moral and physical well-being of the working classes was a source of
concern not only for religious or philanthropic reasons. It was the only safe
means of ensuring the very survival of society in general. The most immediate threat was to the industrial communities themselves:

a turbulent population, which, rendered reckless by dissipation and
want, – misled by the secret intrigues, and excited by the inflamma-
tory harangues of demagogues, has frequently committed daring
assaults on the liberty of the more peaceful portions of the working
classes, and the most frightful devastations on the property of their
masters. Machines have been broken, and factories gutted and
burned at mid-day.[12]

But the danger from a growing, ignorant working class, maddened by want
and incited by unscrupulous agitators, was not confined to its immediate
environment.

The wealth and splendour, the refinement and luxury of the superior
classes, might provoke the wild inroads of a marauding force, before
whose desolating invasion, every institution which science has erect-
ed, or humanity devised, might fall, and beneath whose feet all the
arts and ornaments of civilized life might be trampled with ruthless
violence.[13]

Appropriately Kay suggested two general solutions, education and free trade.
He condemned the Corn Laws

chiefly because they lessen the wages of the lower classes, increase the
price of food, and prevent the reduction of the hours of labour:–
because they will retard the application of a general and efficient
system of education, and thus not merely depress the health, but
debase the morals of the poor.[14]

In a state of free trade the increase in the employers' profits would enable
them to reduce the hours of labour thereby providing time for 'the education
and religious and moral instruction of the people.'[15]

Not surprisingly the League insisted on high wages as an inevitable result
of free trade, an issue of political and social as well as economic importance.
However, while the League's position on high wages might seem a

propaganda necessity, it had been employed earlier, in the 1820s and 1830s, by free trade Whig landowners. In 1826 James Robert George Graham (1792–1861), then a Whig owner of a large debt-ridden estate in Cumberland, and the future Home Secretary in Peel's 1841 government, published a pamphlet in which he identified the Corn Laws as one of the causes of economic, and consequent social, instability. The Corn Laws encouraged speculation and caused artificial and extreme price fluctuations and should be replaced by a fixed duty of 15s. a quarter and a general policy of free trade.[16]

Graham subscribed to the traditional physiocratic belief that the well-being of agriculture reflected on the economy as a whole. By the 1820s Liverpool's government had changed its position on the matter, placing commerce and industry before agriculture as the prime guarantors of the nation's prosperity.[17] The change is reflected in a pamphlet by Graham's Cumbrian friend John Rooke (1780–1865) from 1828, in which Rooke argued that the prosperity of agriculture depended on commerce. Rooke maintained that prices were solely determined by the amount of money in circulation. Commerce increased the supply of money thereby creating full employment, resulting in higher wages, higher effective demand, and higher prices. Free trade would have a similar effect abroad of raising prices, enabling England to maintain its competitiveness despite high wages. Trade, Rooke found, 'carries its own multiplying powers along with it, reduces the wilderness to the highest state of culture, civilizes society, and places a multitude of new products at the command of human desire.'[18]

According to Rooke, trade also allowed for an increase in the size of the population without the economy suffering from diminishing returns. Every additional pair of hands would mean a proportionate addition of wealth, and a further increase in effective demand for agricultural produce. Furthermore, the expansion of trade would raise the demand for land for urban and industrial development, thereby further increasing the landlords' profits.

The most prominent Whig landowner and politician to embrace the cause of free trade in the years preceding the League's formation was Charles William Wentworth Fitzwilliam, fifth Earl Fitzwilliam (1786–1857). Fitzwilliam sat in the House of Commons from 1806 to 1833, when he became the fifth Earl and was elevated to the Lords.[19] He was converted to free trade in the mid-1820s and published his first pamphlet on the subject in 1831.

Unlike Rooke, Fitzwilliam blamed the uneven harvests, whose effect was aggravated by the Corn Laws, for the fluctuations in the price of corn during the period 1815–22. But like Rooke he believed that the key to the state of the economy in general, and agriculture in particular, was in the prosperity of trade and industry. The price of provisions affected the cost of production, and thereby the competitiveness of British manufacturers.

> if they cannot compete with foreigners, our export trade is diminished – if our export trade be diminished, the prosperity of our

manufacturing population is undermined – if their prosperity be undermined, they will consume fewer provisions; the demand for agricultural produce in the manufacturing counties will be restricted – the surplus produce will remain in the hands of the farmer, and the ultimate result will be the fall of rents, occasioned, be it remembered, by an attempt to raise them.[20]

A high and regular level of urban consumption would ensure rural prosperity in the form of steady, but not high, prices of agricultural products.

The subject of consumption was further elaborated in Fitzwilliam's second free trade pamphlet of 1835. The nature of consumption, he argued, was determined by its marginal utility.

> Take the case of the person who spends the whole of his income, and let his expenditure consist of any given number of items varying in the degrees of utility. Let the numbers of these items be twenty, and let five of them be of indispensable necessity, while the remaining fifteen may vary in their degree of importance either to his comfort or his luxury. If the price of any of the latter class be enhanced, he will either give up or retrench the use of it, or of some other article in the same class, thereby diminishing his enjoyment and his demand for the article upon which he chooses to economise. If the articles of prime necessity are generally increased in cost, his entire consumption of those of secondary importance will be diminished; and *vice versa*, if their cost is lowered; a diminution, therefore, in the price of necessaries, and especially of bread, as the one which calls for the largest expenditure, will occasion an increased demand for and consumption of what are comparative luxuries, and thereby invigorate all those branches of industry which are exercised in the production and preparation of such articles of consumption.[21]

In his first pamphlet Fitzwilliam had left open the problem of how low wages, the result of cheaper bread, and essential for England's manufacturers' foreign competitiveness, would increase home consumption. In the second pamphlet Fitzwillaim explained that low wages under free trade were temporary. The immediate benefits to the capitalist from free trade would encourage him to extend his production, and consequently increase his demand for labour, hence raising wages, which were determined by the supply of and demand for labour, rather than the cost of provisions, as Fitzwilliam had stated in the first pamphlet. Fitzwilliam did not explain how the eventual high wages would affect competitiveness, but an answer to that had already been provided by Rooke. High wages, by changing the nature of consumption, would offer the farmer profitable alternatives to corn growing such as cattle breeding.

In his third pamphlet, signed January 1839, Fitzwilliam further developed his position on the importance of working-class consumption, that is high real wages.

> If any one imagines that the high profits and the high rents, the latter of which *are*, and the former of which *may be*, occasionally, the result of dear corn, enable the agricultural districts to take off the commodities of the manufacturers, let him observe that it is not the half dozen lords and squires who own a given district, or even the hundred or two hundred farmers, who occupy it, who are the purchasers and consumers, but the thousands and ten thousands of people, *properly so called*, by whose manual labour the earth is tilled, and who are in various ways engaged in the service of the wealthier, but less numerous classes. Among these we must look for the great source of consumption of manufactural commodities, and among these, that consumption can never be rapid or great, while they are called upon for a large outlay upon provisions.
>
> A high price of provisions is, therefore, injurious to the home demand for our manufactures.[22]

The issue, Fitzwilliam added, had also a moral dimension. The ruling class had always assumed responsibility for society's less fortunate members now suffering from the high price of bread. What simpler and more effective way to alleviate their distress than by reducing the price of corn? Doing so, he argued in a pamphlet from 1840, would be more than an act of charity, since the Corn Laws contravened God's design. Does not the law 'refuse the gifts which God in his mercy proffers? Does it not reject the beneficence of the Creator? and shut the gates of the Divine mercy on your countrymen?'[23] God has constructed the world so that each creature was provided for, whereas 'the pride of man leads him to think that he can *a priori* devise expedients for all contingencies – new contingencies arise, his ingenuity is vain, his contrivances are baffled – a just retribution upon his pride.' Instead of trying to intervene, man should allow the price of corn to be determined 'by supply and demand in a free unfettered market, in which the entire bounty of God is opened to the enjoyment of all his creatures.'[24]

Fitzwilliam and the other Whig free traders were primarily concerned with devising a strategy that would ensure the survival of their class. The prosperity of industry and commerce, and high wages, were means to that end. Fearful of the social and political consequences of the Corn Laws, Fitzwilliam wrote in 1839:

> What propositions may now be made by the people of England cannot as yet be foreseen, but they have got active leaders in the great seats of commerce, manufacture and population, and when men feel

the justice of their cause, and are urged to the prosecution of it by the fear of approaching disaster, it is not impossible that they will push their demands to a very great extent. . . . their efforts will be directed against the nuisance, and to abate the nuisance, they will pull down the house.[25]

Similarly, another Whig free trader, David Salomons (1792–1873), Jewish Lord Mayor of London, founder, in 1832, of the London and Westminster Bank, and owner of a small estate in Kent, wrote in 1839:

Party feeling is introduced with the view of awakening popular prejudice, and attempts are made to incite the multitude against the agricultural body, who are represented as being determined, from base and selfish motives, to resist every change, and anxious to enrich themselves at the expense of the rest of the people. . . . I cannot, therefore, but lament the agitation now in progress for the purpose of creating animosity between the manufacturing and rural population, – a course of conduct which appears to me to deserve the severest reprobation.[26]

The League's leaders, on the other hand, sought confrontation as the only means of achieving repeal. For instance Robert Hyde Greg (1795–1875), cotton manufacturer and Liberal MP for Manchester, stated in the Commons' debate in 1840 on Villiers' annual motion to discuss the Corn Laws:

On so hackneyed a subject as the Corn-laws, it is not easy to produce any new argument, . . . and indeed, when I see the determination of a small, but powerful party, interested in the continuance of these Laws . . . I am inclined to doubt the efficacy of any argument but one, which is, that of AGITATION.
Agitation prevailed in procuring freedom for the Negroes; *agitation* gave emancipation to the Catholics; *agitation* gave us the Reform Bill; and I much fear that a Repeal of the Corn-laws will be yielded to no other argument.[27]

In a letter to J.B. Smith earlier in 1840 Greg wrote from the House of Commons: 'to be *discreet*, and yet to convince others that you *feel* & are *angry* & *alarmed*, is not an easy task.'[28] Free trade, as described by the League's speakers, might be in the interests of the whole community, but the Corn Laws were clearly the result of selfish class legislation. The 'lords of the soil' were likened by a speaker in the Manchester Chamber of Commerce in 1838 to vampires, who 'lived upon the blood of the nation, and were solely interested in keeping up the monopoly.'[29] The League adopted the Whig theory of free trade and high wages but its tone was totally different.

One of the League's early pamphlets signed 'Anglus' stated:

> The price of labour is regulated wholly by the supply and demand. If there be an advantageous field for the employment of capital, and the master-manufacturer have many orders to execute, he will, in fear of being outbid, give wages up to the very highest limit that will afford him a profit on his capital, and this he will do, however cheap may be the price of provisions.[30]

There existed, then, a sufficiently wide margin of profitability which made it possible to increase wages without undermining either profitability or competitiveness. The employer's willingness to reduce his margin of profit by increasing wages was associated by 'Anglus' with the anticipation of increased profits through greater demand. 'Anglus' was not the only repealer to argue that contrary to the wages fund theory the amount of capital available at any given time for the payment of wages was flexible, depending on the general economic climate and the anticipation of profits, or, in other words, on credit. Revd Andrew Somerville (1800–77) of the Scottish Secession Church, in an 'Address to the People of Scotland' adopted by the conference of Scottish dissenting ministers opposed to the Corn Laws, held in Edinburgh in January 1842, as its position on the economics of free trade, stated:

> The law of wages is regulated by the proportion which the supply [of labour] bears to the demand, and by the rate of profit. If the demand is greater than the supply, and there exists a good prospect for the remuneration for the capital employed, there is a loud call for additional workmen, and wages by the competition for them rise, and this rise continues so long as the supply falls short of the demand.[31]

The League did not possess a cut and dried formal theory of wages. Many repealers had read Adam Smith's *The Wealth of Nations* but were otherwise ignorant of formal economic theory, or else rejected it. 'The question of the Corn Laws', wrote 'Anglus', 'is simply a law of injustice! and the less men's minds are puzzled about it by Political Economists the better.'[32] On the other hand there were repealers who had read and accepted the doctrines of Ricardo, McCulloch, *et al*. For instance a Yorkshire 'Manufacturer', author of the pamphlet *Reciprocity*, who stated in his preface that his intention was to 'furnish some who are not deeply read in the science of political economy, especially my brother manufacturers, whose avocations engross their attention, with more correct notions of Free Trade and RECIPROCITY.'[33] Another example is Edward Baines Jr (1800–90), editor of the *Leeds Mercury* and MP for Leeds 1859–74, who tried to reconcile Ricardian economics with the League's faith in high wages by arguing that classical theory applied to only parts of the economy.

It may be argued that a tax on Bread raises wages, and, therefore, does not really fall upon the labourer, but upon consumers of the commodities which he produces. It is true that a tax on Bread raises wages in those departments of industry which can afford it, and where the supply of labour is not too large; but in our principle manufactures there is a controlling power, namely, *foreign competition*, which *limits* the possible advance of wages; and there is also another limit in the limited *power of consumption* both at home and abroad. If, however, a tax on Bread makes wages artificially high, it thereby makes goods artificially dear; and this artificial dearness of goods impairs, and may even destroy foreign trade; and thus it *re-acts upon wages, pulls them down, and deprives workmen altogether of their employment.*[34]

A commitment to the belief in the causal link between free trade and high wages overrode the League's economic heterodoxy. A result was a certain inconsistency as to how soon could high wages be expected once the Corn Laws were repealed. The Revd Baptist Wriothesley Noel (1798–1873), then an evangelical minister of St John's Chapel, Bedford Row, London, argued in a popular pamphlet, published in 1839, and reissued in an abridged form by the League, that

> The first momentary effect . . . of the reduction of the duty would be to lower wages; because workmen, finding that they could live for less than before, would rather work for less than not work at all. Wages, being reduced, the manufacturer could finish his goods at a less cost, and therefore could afford to sell them at a less price. The competition among manufacturers, and their desire to effect large sales, completely secure that they shall sell at the lowest price which will return them a fair profit [will lower] prices [and] would enable them to compete with foreign manufacturers, and to find markets from which they are now excluded by the cost of production, or, in other words, by the price of corn.
>
> By these means larger numbers of workmen may be employed, and those who see their children starving would have the happiness of seeing them fed . . . wages would not fall as far as prices . . . an abundance of employment making labourers scarce, produces a competition among masters to obtain them. Masters are obliged to bid above each other, and wages rise. The extension of our commerce, therefore, by giving more employment, would raise wages.[35]

In a period of high unemployment, short-term low wages and an immediate increase in employment were probably regarded as an acceptable and even desirable consequence of repeal, especially since the long-term result would be high wages.

One of the most detailed statements issued by the repealers on the import-ance of consumption, as opposed to the argument which blamed over-production for the country's economic distress, was William Rathbone Greg's *Not Over Production but Deficient Consumption, The source of our suffering.* W.R. Greg (1809–81), younger brother of R.H. Greg, stated that during the period 1824–38 the home market had absorbed 40–50 per cent, or an annual average of 44 per cent, of the cotton industry's output. In the following three years home consumption had dropped to 36 per cent, and in 1841 alone to 28 per cent, despite a continuous increase in the size of the population. The simultaneous increase in exports, cited by the League's critics as proof of the industry's prosperity under protection, was simply dumping forced by the under-consumption at home.[36] Under-consumption was the result of the increase in the price of food since 1835, unemployment, and lower industrial wages compared with only a slight increase in farming wages. 'The evil has been, not that manufactures have increased too fast, but that they have not increased fast enough. . . . *Limitation of production means and implies limitation of employment.*'[37]

W.R. Greg rejected emigration as impractical, considering the scale of the problem. Full employment, then, could be secured for a growing population only by '*a regular and continued augmentation in our manufacturing industry.*'[38] The home market was important, but it was insufficient to bring about an economic revival, nor could it, on its own, sustain continuous growth. Hence to '*encourage the consumption of all nations, should . . . be the great aim of our policy; – to remove all artificial stimuli to production on the part of our Competitors, should be another, but a very secondary object.*'[39] This could be accomplished through free trade, despite England's higher wages, by building on its one clear advantage, the capacity to increase production rapidly. Finally,

> by reducing the price of necessaries of life in England, (and still more by preventing those extreme fluctuations which have been so ruinous to all) enable the mass of our citizens again to become extensive purchasers of articles of clothing, and thus restore the home demand to its natural and healthy state, and give us a right to anticipate its steady annual increase.[40]

In an article published in the *Westminster Review* on the 1842 parliamentary debate on the Corn Laws, Greg added to his economic analysis a social and political dimension.

> In all aristocratic nations the inequality of ranks presses heavily upon the poor. Almost by law of necessity, the privilege of one man entails the burden of another; the exemption of one class becomes the

burden of the class below. . . . There is nothing repugnant to the feelings of human nature in the circumstance that one man should be rich and great, and his neighbour poor and low; and consequently this of itself involves no peril to the stability of the existing order of society. But a country in which the wealthy and the powerful show no sympathy and offer no assistance to their suffering fellow-citizens . . . in which the aristocracy seek to multiply the burdens of the class below them, in order to multiply the exemptions of their own, – assuredly such a country presents neither a safe nor a seemly state of things, and it behooves every one who lives in it to 'set his home in order' and prepare for the coming change.[41]

A similar note was sounded by Richard Cobden in the parliamentary debate that Greg wrote about, when, speaking on behalf of the manufacturers and the workers, he warned the House: 'If you are not prepared to ameliorate the condition of the people, beware of your own position – nay, you must take care that even this House may not fall under the heap of obloquy which the injustice you are perpetrating will thrust upon you.'[42] In the same speech Cobden employed the high wages theory in order to underline the unity of interests between the manufacturers and their workers.

Have low wages ever proved the prosperity of our manufactures? In every period when wages have dropped, it has been found that the manufacturing interest dropped also; and I hope the manufacturers will have credit for taking a rather more enlightened view of their interest than to conclude that the impoverishment of the multitude, who are the great consumers of all that they produce, could ever tend to promote the prosperity of our manufacturers.[43]

High wages as an inevitable result of free trade formed one of the main unifying themes of the League's rhetoric. The premises were not always identical, indeed much of the argument had been adopted from the Whig free traders, whose style and point of departure were very different from the League's, but the conclusion was always the same. Nor could it be otherwise in a movement that believed its case to be universal and whose outlook was essentially optimistic. The prospect of full employment, high real wages, and high consumption were important arguments in the League's efforts to disprove its critics' accusations that its members were solely motivated by narrow self-interest at the expense of the rest of society. Instead, the League wished to convince the public that its cause was not only the most practical but also the most moral. It represented the real interests of the nation if not the whole of humanity.

Finally the Anti-Corn Law League was largely instrumental in introducing the economic perspective into popular national politics. The development of popular economics as in the case of free trade and high wages suggests the possibility and utility of a different approach to the study of the history of economic thought, which hitherto has been largely confined to the study of successive classical theoretical texts. As the study of the League and high wages demonstrates, popular theory was influential in shaping politics and policies. It clearly was not a simplified version of formal theory but constituted an elastic approach to the explanation of economic problems often both inconsistent and innovative. Its influence on the evolution of formal theory is yet to be explored.

Notes

1 *The Speech of W.W. Sleigh, Esq., M.D. Delivered on his nomination for the representation of the borough of Hastings and St. Leonard's, March 28th, 1844, exposing the sophisticated arguments of the Anti Corn Law League*, London: John Oliver, 1844. Sleigh withdrew in favour of Musgrave Brisco, who was elected as the Conservative candidate, defeating the League's candidate R.R.R. Moore.

2 John Moseley, *An Inquiry into the probable results consequent to a Repeal of the Corn Laws with Observations on the inconsistent statements made by the manufacturers, and with arithmetical illustrations of the injury to the tenants and the labourers by annulling that law*, 2nd edn, London: Ridgway, 1840 (1st edn 1838), p. 16. The preface of the second edition is signed Glemham House, near Saxmundham.

3 T.S. Ashton, *Economic and Social Investigation in Manchester, 1833–1933. A Centenary History of the Manchester Statistical Society* (1934), Fairfield, NJ: Augustus M. Kelley, 1977, pp. 3–4.

4 Ibid., p. 4.

5 Ibid., p. 11.

6 James Phillips Kay-Shuttleworth, *The Moral and Physical Condition of the Working Classes*, 2nd edn (1832), New York: Augustus M. Kelley, 1970, pp. 111–12.

7 Ibid., pp. 8, 9.

8 Ibid., p. 10.

9 Ibid., p. 12.

10 Ibid., p. 57.

11 Ibid., p. 26.

12 Ibid., p. 42.

13 Ibid., p. 96.

14 Ibid., p. 91.

15 Ibid., p. 88.

16 Sir James Graham, Bart, MP, *Corn and Currency; in an address to the Land Owners*, London: Ridgway, 1826.

17 On the government's position see Boyd Hilton, *Corn, Cash, Commerce*, Oxford: Oxford University Press, 1977.

18 'A Cumberland Landowner' [John Rooke], *Free Trade in Corn: the real interest of the landlord, and the true policy of the state*, London: Ridgway, 1828, pp. 19–20.

19 According to John Wade's *Black Book* (1832) Fitzwilliam controlled three boroughs and five MPs.

20 Earl Fitzwilliam, *First, Second, and Third Addresses to the Landowners of England on the Corn Laws*, London: Ridgway, 1839, p. 18.

21 Ibid., pp. 36–7.

22 Ibid., pp. 57–8.
23 Earl Fitzwilliam, *A Letter to the Bishop of Peterborough and The Clergy of England on the Corn Laws*, London: Ridgway, 1840, pp. 6–7.
24 Ibid., p. 10.
25 Fitzwilliam, *First, Second, and Third Addresses*, p. 59.
26 David Salomons, Esq., *Reflections on the Operation of the Present Scale of Duty for regulating the importation of foreign corn*, London: Pelham Richardson, 1839, pp. 5–6.
27 Robert Hyde Greg, *Corn Laws: Speech in the House of Commons, Friday 3 April, 1840*, printed for private circulation only, London: Ridgway, p. 3.
28 Manchester Central Library, J.B. Smith papers, Greg to Smith, 13 February 1840.
29 *The Corn Laws. An authentic report of the late important discussions in the Manchester Chamber of Commerce, on the destructive effects of the Corn Laws upon the trade and manufactures of the country*, London: Ridgway, 1839, p. 56.
30 'Anglus', *Artisans, Farmers, and Labourers*, London: Ridgway, 1839, p. 25.
31 *The Corn Laws Condemned on account of their Injustice and Immoral Tendency, by upwards of Five Hundred Ministers of different denominations, Resident in Scotland*, 2nd edn, Edinburgh: Adam and Charles Black, 1842, p. 89.
32 'Anglus', p. 5.
33 'A Manufacturer', *Reciprocity*, Leeds: Baines & Newsome, [n.d.], p. v.
34 Edward Baines, Jr., *Reasons in Favour of Free Trade in Corn, and against a Fixed Duty. In Three Letters to the Right Honourable Lord John Russell (From the Leeds Mercury)*, Leeds: Edward Baines, [1843].
35 Baptist W. Noel, *A Plea for the Poor showing how the proposed repeal of the existing Corn Laws will affect the interests of the Working Classes*, London: James Nisbet, 1841, pp. 8–9.
36 W.R. Greg, *Not Over Production but Deficient Consumption: The Source of our Suffering*, London: Henry Hooper, 1842, p. 4n.
37 Ibid., p. 18.
38 Ibid., p. 20.
39 Ibid., p. 27.
40 Ibid., p. 27.
41 W.R. Greg, 'Corn Law Debate', *Westminster Review*, 37, 2, 1842, p. 367.
42 In J. Bright and J.E.T. Rogers (eds) *Speeches on Questions of Public Policy by Richard Cobden MP*, London: Macmillan, 1878, p. 14.
43 Ibid., p. 10.

2

GLADSTONE, PEEL AND THE CORN LAWS

John Maloney

Had Peel's government fallen a year earlier than it did, it would be remembered as a great free-trading government which held back, cautiously, on the Corn Laws. Furthermore, both Peel and Gladstone would have justified this. To both, corn was an untypical case when it came to weighing up the arguments for and against protection, and, to both, the special considerations regarding corn fell entirely into the protectionist scale of the balance. To Gladstone, nothing could be more important than maintaining a supply of corn uninterruptable by war, trade war or blockade – unless it was avoiding the disruption, distress and unemployment that would result from any sudden alteration in corn duties. Meanwhile Peel (though never Gladstone) subscribed with enthusiasm to the claim that landlords bore unique burdens and thus deserved a unique privilege.

However, in his first months in office, after his appointment in 1841 as Vice-President of the Board of Trade in Peel's incoming government, Gladstone's most forceful defence of the Corn Laws was the negative one of denying their part in causing the deepening depression of manufacturing. The Corn Laws, he wrote, had not depressed manufacturing by provoking higher foreign tariffs: tariffs had not shown an upward trend for some time. They had not prevented foreign countries buying British manufactures: America had been paying even higher corn duties in 1834–6 yet had taken British goods an 'enormous' extent. They had not prevented the home customer from buying: for 'the home market is not considered to have been in a state of peculiar deadness.' Finally, they had not damaged competitiveness by raising workers' wages in line with the price of corn: 'no one pretends that the wages of the operatives have been raised.'[1]

No one *was* pretending, in late 1841, that wages were rising at that moment: but plenty of protectionists were claiming that in general wages were sensitive to the price of corn, so that workers would gain nothing from repeal. Gladstone, however, had by now rejected this claim: 'Wages . . . do not vary much with the price of necessaries.'[2]

But if Gladstone's private notes on the corn question were common-place and sometimes hesitant, the same cannot be said of the long and remarkable memorandum which he first sent to Peel on 9 October 1841. (He sent it again, with some changes, after Peel lost it, so it cannot be said exactly which of its conclusions Gladstone had already reached by 9 October.)

The parties involved in the Corn Law question, Gladstone told Peel, were 'in descending order of importance'

1   Consumer
2   Grower
3   Manufacturer
4   Corn merchant
5   Foreign grower.[3]

The consumer, then, had 'a paramount claim to a price as low as can be afforded without detriment to national interests.' In particular, he might reasonably expect not to have to pay the prices of 1838–40 (average 67s. 2d.), at any rate when cheaper corn was available for import: while 'above 70s the price is as extravagant and oppressive to the consumer as a price below 50s (without great plenty) must be to the grower.' Gladstone, in this first as in later attempts at a reformed sliding scale, stuck with the existing 73s. as the price at which duty should fall to a nominal 1s.[4]

But it was not even in the consumer's interest, Gladstone continued, that the price should be too low. The 'oppressive' region below 50s. would oppress the consumer too, so far as farmers gave up planting corn in favour of something else. A steady domestic supply was in the interest of 'the nation at large'. Indeed any scale of duties should support a price floor adequate 'not just to keep the current acreage under corn but also to stimulate [the grower] to increase and cheapen the production.'[5] On this basis Gladstone chose 50s. as the price at which 'the consumer has no right to complain if the duty be such as practically to prohibit importation',[6] and proposed 52s. as the point where duty should reach its maximum of 30s.[7]

Both endpoints of the sliding scale thus established, it remained to ask only if it should have a constant slide. Not for an instant did Gladstone contemplate such crudity. From the start, it was plain to him that a cunning variation of the gradient was at least as good a policy weapon as having a sliding scale in the first place. Why?

Gladstone's analysis here is complex and sophisticated, and we approach it indirectly, indeed anachronistically, by looking first at the most basic arguments for a steeply or a gently graduated duty.

Figure 2.1 refers to imported corn alone, so that (say) a bad harvest at home will shift the demand curve to the right. Let SS represent the supply curve when duty is gently inverse to selling price and S'S' when it is strongly

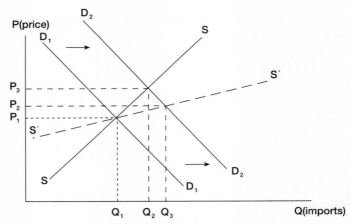

Figure 2.1 Effect of a bad harvest on the price of corn

inverse. In the second case price rises only to P_2 but quantity imported goes up to Q_3.

So a steeper slide means a steadier price but a more variable quantity imported.[8] Gladstone never stated either part of this proposition directly. The nearest he came to putting the point about quantities occurs in a parliamentary speech of 13 February 1842, and even here he is conceding the superiority (in this context) of a flat over a sliding scale, not of a gradual slide over a steeper one.[9] In the memorandum of 9 October 1841 he argues that too steeply graduated a duty will reduce, rather than destabilize, the amount of corn supplied. A typical American shipment, Gladstone pointed out, took about eight weeks to arrive – more than long enough for price, and hence duty payable, to turn out very different from what the supplier had expected. Too violent a storm in the tariffs, as the trading vessel traversed the high seas, and the trader might never put out again, permanently lowering the potential supply of imported wheat.[10]

On prices, Gladstone's starting point is that a steep slide in duty between 52s. and 65s. is necessary, not in order to stabilize prices, but as a consequence of his prior conclusion that virtually complete protection is desirable at 52s. and virtually free trade at 65s.[11] While he does indeed want to hold the price of corn within these limits, his explicit weapon for doing so is not the steep slide between them, but rather a couple of 'rests' (i.e. zero slides) either side of them. And the rationale for doing this is all to do with speculators.

In Gladstone's analysis speculators came in two distinct varieties. There was the 'warehouser of foreign corn' whose speculation consisted of holding corn back when cheap and releasing it when dear. This figure was assumed to import, pay duty, warehouse the corn and only then commence any speculation as he decided when and when not to sell. The relevant price in his case, therefore, was the full price paid by the consumer, and he would of course help to stabilize this price.

The warehouser's less admirable counterpart, and Gladstone's second type of speculator, was the 'importer for money, who has no regular course of operations succeeding one another.'[12] This figure differed from the warehouser in two critical respects: first in contrast to the warehouser's decision to release or not to release corn he had already brought in, type 2's characteristic speculative decision was whether or not to import corn in the first place. His interest, therefore, was in the selling price net of duty. Second, the type 2 speculator, Gladstone believed, was more likely to hold his corn back as price rose, in the hope that it would rise still further. The more steeply the duty fell as price rose, the stronger the incentive to act on these extrapolative expectations and postpone the import of corn, thus exacerbating any rise in price. This was why Gladstone proposed a rest from 65s. to 70s.[13] For as soon as the 65s. rubicon was crossed, type 2 speculators would get no more encouragement in the shape of a falling duty. This, presumably, would make them more likely to take their profits as the price touched 65s. and less likely in the first place to hold corn back in the hope of a profit.

Let us recapitulate. A secure supply of imported corn requires a gradual descent of duty as price rises. The imperative (to Gladstone) of complete protection at 52s. and no protection at 65s. required a steep slide between these limits. A steeply sliding scale is bad for price stability so far as speculators have extrapolative expectations, but the bad effect can be weakened by putting a 'rest' at the top of the range within which you wish to stabilize price.

G1 in Figure 2.2 is the actual scale Gladstone proposed in October 1841. The new scale thus meant a fall in the average level of duty as well as a carefully thought out reworking of the marginal rates. But, said Gladstone, some of the reduction was illusory. For, at the same time, he was proposing a new measure of corn prices which would bring the estimated price down. Currently, Gladstone said, official prices were an overestimate, so that less duty was being paid than the existing scale had intended.

The reason for the inaccuracy was simple – jobbers and their customers were conspiring to record fictitious sales at an exaggerated price, to push up the average recorded price and thus bring down the duty payable. 'There is no limit to the opportunity at present offered of effecting by conspiracy almost any number of sales.'[14] Gladstone suggested excluding the jobbers by taking the averages on the basis of 'first hand sales alone' (official forms should in future specify whether the seller was the actual grower). While Gladstone was still reaching this conclusion, Peel wrote to him asking how, in any case, the alleged frauds could be effective unless they were organized on a national scale.

31

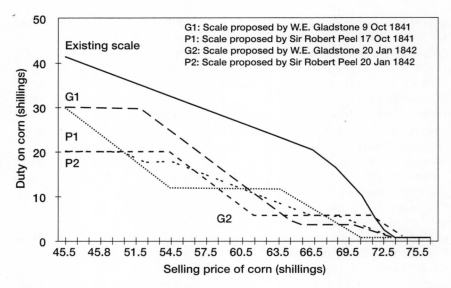

Figure 2.2 How much to cut the corn duty?

There surely must be concert – and most extensive concert – to induce individuals to practise frauds. The unconnected frauds of a single market – however extensive – could exercise, I apprehend, no practical influence on the aggregate average.[15]

Gladstone replied:

sympathy, similarity of objects, and the facility with which the signs of these processes are discernible, render it very easy for parties to concur in promoting the fictitious movement of prices even without express covenant or communication between them and their leaders.[16]

In the meantime other ministers had been coming forward with their own sliding scales. Lord Ripon, Gladstone's chief at the Board of Trade, had proposed a scale without rests, prompting Peel's first sortie into the field (17 October 1841), notable for the long rest proposed at 56s. to 64s., exactly the range which Gladstone thought should have the sharpest slide.[17] By December Ripon had caught up with Peel, or would have, if Peel had not meanwhile caught up with Gladstone. His first memorandum to the full Cabinet criticized the existing Corn Law for encouraging rapid price fluctuations, and a second one (January 1842) sought to tame them by inserting a rest in much the same place as Gladstone had put it.

The circulation of, argument over, amendment to, and analytical justification of various people's various tariff scales is a complicated story. As individuals' attitudes changed, hardened or swung back again, their rankings on the free trade ladder were equally fickle. Gladstone, writing in November to R.A. Christopher (a Lincolnshire MP whose expertise on the Corn Law was much respected), sounds the more protectionist of the two – and more protectionist than his memorandum to Peel of the previous month.[18] But by the following March Christopher was trying to amend, in a protectionist direction, the government Bill which had nearly made Gladstone resign as not going far enough. Sir James Graham, the Home Secretary, had been the free-trading front-runner in the government in the autumn. Yet by February the baton had passed to Gladstone.

But all this is much less important than the two key questions: was Gladstone consistently less protectionist than Peel? If so, does he deserve the credit – which some gave him but which he consistently refused – for any part of Peel's free-trading education?

Any initial differences between Peel and Gladstone seem to have concerned not what to do but how much to say. As early as 17 September 1841 Gladstone was urging Peel to give corn merchants a public assurance that 'action to avoid all unnatural action on prices' be taken.[19] Peel, however, responded that there was no point in saying this without going into detail, and that to do this 'several months before [any proposals] were to be formally submitted for the consideration of Parliament' was 'greatly injurious of the dispassionate discussion of them.'[20] Gash (1972, p. 308) also points out that Peel showed more concern than any of his colleagues with the strategic side of Corn Law reform, as when he asked Ripon about the chances of using it to get better terms from Russia for the export of manufactures.

It was not until late January 1842 that any differences between Gladstone and Peel crystallized into a clear indication of who was the more enthusiastic free trader. On 20 January Peel read his latest paper on the Corn Laws to Gladstone. Their discussion produced broad agreement on the aims of any new law. When Peel called 56s. 'a remunerative price to the British grower', Gladstone agreed; when Gladstone proposed the objective that not more than 1 million quarters be imported at 40s. and not more than 2 million at 45s., Peel agreed.[21] The conflict to come was mostly over means, not ends. The following day Peel, in the light of his discussions, suggested scale P2 (Figure 2.2), Gladstone retaliating with G2.

Actually G2's duties are, on average, only marginally lower than P2's: the difference is 1s. 6d. if differentials at all prices from 50s. to 73s. are averaged on an unweighted basis. Indeed at the near-extremes (i.e. just above 50s. and just below 73s.) Peel was actually proposing lower duties than Gladstone. But in the middle of the range it was a very different story. Gladstone's scale was put forward with the express intention of eliminating effective protection at 60s. and above. This was going too far for Peel.

Peel's proposed scale was equally unacceptable to Gladstone. The duty fell too slowly over the crucial 55s. to 60s. range, and the resulting 12s. duty at

61s. was 'a measure of relief considerably short of what the country has a claim to receive.'[22] The difference, as Gladstone indicated he realized, was between a scale (G2) which did the minimum necessary to give the farmer what both Peel and Gladstone considered to be fair remuneration, and a scale (P2) that threw him a modest additional cushion while Peel, in Gladstone's words, 'felt the pulse of the agricultural folks.'[23] Peel's superior perception of the political realities – and, in particular, of the importance of landed Toryism compared with the free trade movement and its recent semi-converts – were to be Gladstone's grounds, two weeks later, for withdrawing his resignation and apologizing to Peel.

But this is to run on ahead. On 22 January Peel put his proposals to the Cabinet: on 2 February Ripon told Gladstone that the Cabinet had accepted it: 'I said in a marked manner "I am very sorry for it" – believing that it would be virtual prohibition up to 65s or 66s and often beyond.'[24]

In a memorandum fired off to Peel the same day, Gladstone argued that, since 1832, the minimum price at which any substantial amount of corn had come in had normally been around 70s. when prices were falling and 73s. when they were rising. The Corn Laws had been 'equivalent to a *prohibition* up to 70s.'[25] Three days later he told Peel he was considering resignation. Peel said this would threaten the government's existence, and that he had thought Gladstone had assented to the Cabinet proposals. Gladstone said he had not been asked and had not thought his assent was needed. But since then his apprehensions had grown stronger, and were centred on the issue of slides and rests. Instead of deterring speculators with a long rest immediately above the desired price range, Peel was proposing a 'continuous or nearly continuous descent in the duty.'[26]

Next day Gladstone wrote to Peel, withdrawing any threat of resignation, and promising not to further publicize his doubts about Peel's proposal. The measure was, he said, 'a step in the right direction, and one to be gained in concurrence with the feelings of the agricultural body, which I believe to be an essential element in the success of any such plan at the present time.'[27] Peel's note of reply further stresses the need to propose tariff cuts which could actually be carried through Parliament. On 25 February he enlarged on the point, telling Gladstone and Ripon (in Gladstone's paraphrase):

Among ourselves, in this room I have no hesitation in saying, that if I had not had to look to other than abstract considerations I would have proposed a lower protection. But it would have done no good to push the matter so far as to drive Knatchbull out of the Cabinet after the Duke of Buckingham; nor could I pass a measure with greater reductions through the House of Lords.[28]

'I poor fool,' commented Gladstone, 'had looked at nothing, and thought there was nothing to look at, but the figures.'[29]

It was more a matter, apparently, of Peel making Gladstone into a politician than of Gladstone making Peel a free trader. On the basis of the story
above, it is hard to find daylight between Peel and Gladstone which is not
adequately explained by the prime minister's more developed sense of who
had to be carried along and how this had to be done. The words 'more
developed sense' are used advisedly. Gladstone appears no less concerned
about getting the Bill through the Lords once the political realities had been
stated explicitly by Peel. Yet this makes Gladstone's resignation threat –
ostensibly over the length of the rest in a new sliding scale – more, not less,
bizarre. Is it easy to believe that Gladstone, after nine-and-a-half years in
Parliament, and the person at the Board of Trade most closely concerned
with drawing up a set of parallel tariff reductions, never gave a moment's
thought to what was politically feasible until his own threat forced a statement of the situation out of Peel?[30]

Whatever the answer to this last question, it is clear that Gladstone was
inclined to play down any supposed influence he had had on Peel. Writing to
his father in 1849, he denied that he had 'made Peel a free trader', saying
however that 'if there was any influence at all on Peel's mind proceeding
from me between 1841 and 1845, I have no doubt that it may have tended
on the whole towards Free Trade.' However, Gladstone characteristically concluded, 'it is not easy to discuss . . . any influence of mine over a mind so
immeasurably superior, without something of egotism and vanity.'[31]

Gladstone here is speaking of the entire thrust of trade policy over the
whole of Peel's government: to apply his words unthinkingly to a few
months in the life of a single (and, as we have argued, largely untypical)
commercial issue would be dangerous. All the same, it is notable that, as
both men revised their duty scales in the light of discussions with each other
and the rest of the Cabinet, Peel came closer to Gladstone's position than
Gladstone did to Peel's. P2 is more like either G1 or G2 than it is like P1. As
for the modest finale of Gladstone's 1849 letter, the discussion of 1841–2
displays, on both sides, a level of argument and a depth of economic analysis
that is a revelation to the modern reader. Most of the analytical issues appear
to have been first advanced by Gladstone though, in the case of the proposed
'rests' at least, it is Peel who eventually produces the subtler disquisition.[32]

The months of high theory were over. The debate shifted to the parliamentary stage: Peel found Gladstone a role which would both harness his
enthusiasm and contain any airing, however implicit, of his disappointment:

> Will you have the goodness to follow Lord John Russell in the debate
> tomorrow night?
>   The question ought to be limited as far as possible, to the com-
> parative merits of a fixed duty, abstractedly, and of a scale of
> duty varying inversely with price, and though other speakers will

probably deviate from this line of discussion, Lord John will probably adhere to it.

I shall be much obliged to you if you will undertake at the outset
of the debate to state the general argument in favour of the principle
of a variable duty as applied to grain.[33]

A fixed duty was more Russell's personal preference than in any way the
official policy of the Whig party which he led in the Commons. To
Gladstone it was an attractive and not particularly difficult target. To the
government's delight, Russell had not actually propounded a duty that was
literally invariable. By a 'fixed duty' he meant 6s. until the price of corn
reached 73s. and thereafter (as in the government's proposal, Gladstone's
personal scale and for that matter the existing law) a nominal duty of 1s.
Russell had little choice but to dilute the fixed duty principle in this way.
He knew, and all those on whose votes he relied knew, that there was no
possibility of a future Parliament standing by a 6s. duty while the price of
corn climbed into the mid-seventies and above.

Gladstone seized on Russell's concession. The sudden drop at 73s. stood
condemned by the (by now, and largely thanks to Gladstone) standard arguments against too sharply graduated a duty. Did too steep a slide encourage
speculators to hold out and force up the price? Then what would be the
result of promising them a precipice, so long as they pushed the price all the
way to 73s? Were American ships staying at home rather than staking their
cargoes on the uncertainties of eight weeks in the life of a sliding tariff? How
much more cautious they would be – and at just the price range when their
supplies were needed most – when a penny fall in the price of corn might
trigger off a five-shilling rise in duty.[34]

Gladstone had the best of the argument though, read in cold print, his
speech seems scarcely impressive enough to deserve some of the encomia of
his parliamentary colleagues.[35] Within the context of the basic positions they
had chosen, Russell's command of economic analysis comes across as in no
way inferior to Gladstone's, whose victory on points can be attributed to having a more defensible case to propound in the first place. The one part of the
argument Russell undoubtedly did win concerned the claim, still upheld by
Gladstone, that too low a duty would jeopardize a secure supply of corn. This
was nonsense, said Russell. In the first place, the lower the duty, the more
varied the sources of import, and the less likely that all would be blocked at
once. Second, how ever high the duty, it was impossible to guarantee an
adequate supply of corn on all occasions and in all circumstances. High
protective duties, in short, were neither necessary nor sufficient for a secure
supply. It may be significant that, after hearing this speech, Gladstone never
made much of the security argument again.

We can, in fact, trace Gladstone's further progress towards free trade by asking what happened to the various protectionist arguments he had used up to February 1842. Though little more was heard of the need for protection to secure the supply of corn, Gladstone continued to dissociate the Corn Laws from the industrial depression. In March 1842 he replied to the contention that repeal would stop competitors undercutting Britain by declaring, buoyantly, that Britain was already less undercut than undercutting.[36] So far as exporters were in difficulty, he later told Peel and Ripon, the culprit was not the corn duty but the punitive tariffs against manufactures imposed by almost every other country in the world.[37] In 'The Course of Commercial Policy at Home and Abroad', his (anonymous) article in the *Foreign and Colonial Quarterly Review* (January 1843) he listed the causes of distress as (1) overproduction (2) over-extension of credit by joint-stock banks (3) displacement of labour by machinery (4) absorption of capital in inactive and now useless loans abroad (5) four bad harvests in a row (6) increased taxation and public spending (7) obstruction of free trade by foreign countries (8) loss of trade with China.

In his private notebook Gladstone essayed an altogether more analytical approach to the relation between the Corn Laws and industrial distress, using a lengthy arithmetical example to argue that a manufacturing sector facing hostile foreign tariffs might actually have its troubles mitigated by agricultural protection at home. If, for example, Russia placed a prohibitive tariff on British industry, then, even if Russian corn were somewhat cheaper to produce than British, it might be better for everyone in Britain to keep the Russian corn out. Otherwise the prognosis was a drain of gold which 'diminishes employment, perhaps creates a panic at home . . . where is the advantage?' Gladstone, then, far from coming round in private to a free-trade position which caution or loyalty impelled him to play down in public, used his notebook for more mercantilist sentiments than he had yet expressed in Parliament.

Even on this occasion, however, Gladstone was not so mercantilist as to think the effects of the drain of gold would last for ever: and, as the 1841–6 Parliament progressed, he was increasingly driven back to stress the temporary disruptive effects of any repeal or further abatement of the Corn Laws. This, however, he did whole-heartedly, from the day he joined the Board of Trade to the day he resigned from it. It also seems to be the facet of the Corn Law question where he found the authority of political economy most useful. Thus, in March 1842, he was invoking Ricardian rent theory to warn of the consequences of sudden change:

> Is it possible any man can doubt that a repeal of the Corn Laws would at once displace a vast mass of agricultural labour? . . . the most approved authorities in political economy have defined rent as the surplus produce the land yields after the cost of cultivation and maintenance of the cultivator . . . and . . . taught . . . that the lowest class yields no rent . . . it follows that if you diminish prices, so as to

limit production, that the effect must be to throw the poorer soils out of cultivation. This might diminish rents, but in the present extent of cultivation, it is clear that if you reduce rents, it must be by throwing certain lands out of cultivation, and you must, therefore, at the same time, throw out of employment a great body of labourers.[39]

On 13 June 1843 he repeated the point in almost identical terms.[40]

By 1844 the case for corn protection, in Gladstone's hands, had become exclusively conservative. Nothing could be more distinct, he told Parliament in March, than the question of whether a new community with a blank sheet of paper should write protection on it, and the question of whether this Parliament 'composed of practical men [should] adopt, in a country where they found a system of protection established, a sudden disruption of the relations between great masses of the people which had grown up under that system.' Abolitionists had said repeal would have the 'further benefit' of forcing farmers into cheaper modes of cultivation. That was quite likely, said Gladstone, but only by driving existing farmers off the land in favour of newcomers with enough capital to bring in a system of 'wholesale management' needing fewer workers. Unemployment would also be created so far as farmers shifted out of corn into the less labour-intensive business of raising livestock.[41]

Gladstone of course was conceding – and meaning to concede – ground to the repealers when he withdrew his once-versatile protectionist case into the fortress of pure conservatism. The retreat caused concern to many on the government side (the last thing Tory protectionists wanted was for protection to rest on nothing but Toryism), a concern which first surfaced after a notorious speech Gladstone made in February 1843. We call the speech notorious because even Gladstone, in fact especially Gladstone, was quick to condemn it as unwise, muddled and thoroughly deserving of the 'gestures' by which Peel 'tried to indicate to his younger colleague that he was getting on dangerous ground.'[42] In fact it was none of these things.

Gladstone had indeed started by arguing that you could not uphold the Corn Laws on abstract principles: but only as a preamble to a broadside against allowing any abstract principles to determine Parliamentary decisions: 'Mr Burke said, that the statesman who refused to take circumstances into his view and consideration is not merely in error, he is mad – stark mad – metaphysically mad.'[43]

Gladstone went on to expound the main point of his recent jottings on whether protection should be removed when manufacturing faced prohibitive foreign tariffs. The warning was again sounded that a drain of bullion would produce severe and long-lasting hardship, notwithstanding

arguments in the storehouses of political economy about the distribution of precious metals and a course of circumstances tending to neutralise this derangement of the terms of exchange.[44]

He then contended that repeal would destroy more jobs in agriculture than it would create (via increased foreign demand) in industry. Gladstone ended by predicting that cuts in the duty on corn would extract no matching concessions from other countries:

> In the month of July [1842] the new tariff became law in this country; and it was on the last day of the same month, I believe, that America passed its tariff, increasing the duties on the importation of all articles of British produce.[45]

It is hard to see why Gladstone came to regard this workmanlike protectionist speech as either rash or confused, and unless Peel's reproving gestures came in the first few minutes — dictating perhaps the contents of the rest of the speech — they are equally surprising. A close reading does not uphold the picture of a young hothead leaning so far into the arms of abolitionism that he had to be saved by a timely prime ministerial tug on his coat. Such an image would, in fact, be highly inconsistent with the rest of Peel's relations with Gladstone between 1842 and 1845. If, in the months before the 1842 tariff, Gladstone and Peel were separated largely by Peel's finer sense of what the House of Lords would tolerate, the post-1842 years do not seem to possess even this distinction. Peel's own public sentiments, like Gladstone's, dwindled rapidly into a defence of protection largely on the grounds of the hardship attendant on its sudden death.

Which of the arguments against the Corn Laws did Gladstone come to concede? He made nothing of the principle of comparative advantage, as we have seen, and there are few references even to absolute advantage. Nevertheless, Gladstone's article in the *Foreign and Colonial Quarterly Review* unequivocally supports 'those who advocate the extension of the foreign market' in order to 'buy from other nations that which Providence has enabled them to give you on better terms than you can give it yourselves.'[46] Gladstone then proclaims that freer trade is likely to bring gains by forcing newly exposed industries to be more efficient: he even ties this up with the absolute advantage argument by suggesting that, if and only if subjected to an adequate competitive stimulus, British agriculture could become as productive as any in the world.[47]

The most 'technical' of Gladstone's free-trading arguments comes in a private note entitled 'Cattle', and seeks to show that consumers would gain more than producers would lose if duties on imported meat were reduced. The consumer's gain, says Gladstone, can simply be measured by the initial fall in price. The producer's loss, by contrast, is the initial fall in price minus the effects of the resulting 'tendency to increase consumption which of course will check the fall' and 'the general increase in trade and employment from these measures [which] will also increase demand.'[48] Clearly there is a lot wrong here by the standards of modern economic theory, but to characterize

Gladstone as a failed Paul Samuelson would be something a great deal worse than merely anachronistic.

We have seen Gladstone invoking Ricardo's theory of rent. But in general he made less use of classical political economy than any other major contributor to the debates on the Corn Laws. In a single speech (14 February 1842) Lord John Russell had quoted Smith on the economic convulsions inevitable if high duties and prohibitions were taken away at once; cited Ricardo's statement that even if the burden of corn tax was generally borne, that did not justify taxing corn; and disputed, as unfeasible, the principle that 'you ought to make this country independent of foreign nations' even though 'it is a principle which has indeed been sanctioned by one great writer, I mean Mr Malthus.' He ended by claiming the unanimous authority of Malthus, Ricardo and McCulloch for a fixed duty on corn.[49] Peel's favourite authority was Adam Smith, whom he too used to counsel caution on sudden changes in the Corn Law,[50] as well as to put down a backbencher who had argued that the existence of tithes did not of itself entitle the landed interest to protection:

> The hon. Gentleman may be a very great authority on matters of political economy but I must observe that there are others, nearly equal to him perhaps, who have entertained a very different opinion on this question. . . . They wrote, perhaps, in times comparatively barbarous, and their names, perhaps, may not be as eminent as that of the hon. Member: but Adam Smith, for one, expressly declares that he regards tithes as constituting a burden on the land.[51]

Sir James Graham, the Home Secretary, held Smith to have declared labour to be most productively employed in agriculture, and if Smith's opinions were now antiquated ('Mr Wallace: "They are"'), a brand new pamphlet by Col. Torrens said the same thing, not to mention

> that great apostle of free trade – the Coryphoeus of modern philosophers – a gentleman who enjoys a European reputation and has lately been admitted a member of the French Institute. Will the House permit me just to read what Mr McCulloch says, on the very point to which I am referring, in the last edition of his work of political economy? (Mr M. Gibson: 'Take the first edition'.)[52]

In a debate initiated by J.L. Ricardo (nephew of David) there was hardly a major speaker who failed to sign up as a standard-bearer for one or more of the great. Ricardo himself quoted Say, Russell chose Smith, Peel cited Ricardo and Torrens, and Disraeli – as befitted the future leader of the protectionist rump of the Tory party – invoked Friedrich List.[53]

Gladstone's speech had cited none of these authorities. Instead he preferred to consider the views of Mr Deacon Hume, one of his civil servants at the Board of Trade. Even more revealing had been his reply to Russell during the first reading of the 1842 Corn Bill. Russell, said Gladstone, had conceded that Malthus favoured the principle of independence from foreign supply. 'He [Gladstone] was surprised that the noble Lord, when referring to authorities, did not bear in mind a far higher name, or that, if he recollected, he did not quote the sanction of Mr Huskisson.'[54]

The picture is becoming clear. Until his unwanted appointment to the Board of Trade, Gladstone read extensively on almost every subject except political economy. Such reading as he felt he had to do was largely confined to the pamphlets of the day. In sharp contrast to the case of his reading in philosophy and theology, he declined to spend time taking notes on what he read. On joining the Board, Gladstone stepped up his economic studies, reading two successive editions of McCulloch, James Mill's *Principles of Political Economy*, Tooke's *History of Prices* and pamphlets by Torrens, and at least consulting 'Adam Smith on corn' on the day of a parliamentary speech on the subject.[55] But, the two references to Ricardian theory aside, there is no case of Gladstone citing any of the specific doctrines of the classical economists in Parliament.

Even the type of lesson which Gladstone thought politicians could learn from political economy was characteristic. Peel's habit was to stress how often political economy was true in theory but dangerous as a precipitate counsel for policy.[56] Cobden would berate the Commons for clinging to outdated and overthrown dogmas, such as the proposition 'laid down mathematically in 1815 by one M.P. ' (presumably Ricardo) that the price of food regulated the price of labour:

> What has surprised me more than anything is, to find that in this House, where lecturers are, of all men, so much decried, there exists on the other side such an ignorance on this subject ['Oh, oh'] that I never saw equalled in any body of working men in the North of England ['Oh, oh'].[57]

Gladstone's view was different from either of these, and comes over most clearly in a speech he made in March 1844. Challenging the claim that the Corn Laws were harmful to tenant farmers and agricultural labourers, he categorized such issues as

> difficult questions of political economy [which] could not be investigated on a statement of facts. They were as pure propositions in political economy as any other in Adam Smith, McCulloch and Ricardo. The questions how the interests of different classes were affected by protective laws – in what proportion the benefit accrued to each – what were the different modes and channels through which

each received its share were the most important, interesting and difficult questions: but he contended they were not questions on which they with advantage could put men into the witness-box and question them as to facts. If there was any ground for the distinction between questions of fact and of opinion, these were questions of opinion and not of fact. Instead of being fit for the consideration of a Select Committee, they were the very last that should be referred to such a tribunal . . . on account, then, of the complicated and unsuitable nature of the subjects which must be investigated, he was opposed to the Motion for a Committee [*Laughter*].[58]

It would doubtless be going too far to recruit Gladstone, on the strength of this passage, as the first Austrian economist. But the alleged inability of classical economics and the world to cast any light on one another, however elevating it may be to the former, not only leaves it with little to do but also explains Gladstone's lack of interest in it.

Yet, for all the idiosyncrasy of Gladstone's excursion into methodology, his practical attitude to political economy differed little from Peel's. Neither used the authority of the classical economists with any notable skill. Peel's quotations from Smith and Ricardo, though reasonably apt, are more cultural garnish than a source of added value. Gladstone's invocation of Ricardo's rent theory adds nothing to his defence of protection – the proposition that repeal would reduce agricultural employment hardly requires discussion of no rent margins and the direction of causality between rents and prices. And both Peel and Gladstone were more impressive at working out their own ideas than at discussing those of greater economists.

This chapter has so far concentrated on the Corn Laws as the free trade issue that yields by far the most about Gladstone's, and his contemporaries', knowledge of, use of, ability to construct and attitude to political economy. Yet, as we said at the start, in many ways the Corn Laws are a bad guide to the free trade issue at large. Right from the beginning Gladstone was singling out corn as special, and entitled to protection for reasons peculiar to itself.[59] Neither the 'secure supply' argument nor the 'compensation for agricultural burdens' argument applied to any other commodity in quite the way they applied to corn. An exceptional state of distress was expected from sudden repeal of the Corn Laws. Whereas other goods carried fixed duties, corn's sliding scale was considered – by Gladstone if not by some of the Whigs – sacred and immutable.

By contrast Gladstone's anonymous article 'The Course of Commercial Policy at Home and Abroad' (1843) gave few explicit reasons why corn should have special treatment. Instead Gladstone applied to the general question of freer trade various arguments he had ostentatiously failed – and was still failing – to apply to corn. It gave the recent tariff reductions on a variety of goods the rationale that they had cut the price of raw materials and thus bolstered industry against stiffening competition. This argument could have been extended to corn only by conceding the diehard protectionists' point that wages would fall along with corn prices. The article was also notably self-confident that, in general, increased imports would be matched by increased exports as trading partners spent their new earnings: precisely the point Gladstone had scoffed at when Russell had made it in reference to corn. The inconsistency was seized on the following month when the Commons debated the 'National Distress'. Lord Howick exhibited Gladstone's claim that the import of 80,000 head of cattle would 'produce an export trade in return of an equal amount', and inquired why the same reasoning did not apply to corn.[60] Gladstone having spoken, and defended the Corn Laws as justified by hostile foreign tariffs against manufacturing, an MP named Stewart asked him if 'he had seen an article which had appeared in the *Foreign and Colonial Review*', which was 'in many respects, so like the speech delivered by the right hon. Gentleman the other evening, that he could not help recommending him to peruse it', but which on the subject of tariffs as a whole, contradicted the position Gladstone had just taken specifically on corn.[61]

This sounds like a direct hit, but was not. All the passage quoted by Stewart says is that 'England, with courage and consistency, will succeed and that ere long, in imparting to other nations much of the tone of her own legislation.'[62] But Gladstone at this time was riding two protectionist horses – the static one, consisting of the argument that if hostile tariffs were taken as given, there was an economic case for retaining one's own; and the strategic one, the claim that the best way to beat down your rivals' tariffs was to make your own concessions conditional on theirs. Even if we stretch a massive point and interpret the words Stewart quoted as meaning that specific tariff cuts would probably lead fairly quickly to reciprocal action, we have at most dislodged Gladstone from his strategic horse. The static argument – the one actually used in Gladstone's speech on this occasion – is left untouched.

All the same, Stewart's remarks were prescient so far as they focused on the source of Gladstone's further progress towards free trade. Essentially what happened over the next two years was that the static argument faded away while the strategic one was killed by events. Replying to J.L. Ricardo's motion of April 1843 (which opposed postponing any tariff remissions in order to make them conditional on reciprocation) Gladstone argued that not only conditionality but also actual retaliation could sometimes be desirable. It had worked very recently against Naples, which had then removed the offending duties on British manufactures. Retaliation (or refusal to cut tariffs) hit at vested interests, who were always the prime movers behind commercial policy, the benefits and costs to others being spread too thinly for them to make much effort.[63] But when Ricardo reintroduced his motion – and in stronger form than before – a year later, the response was a specimen of fudging Gladstonian verbiage so fine that it deserves quotation at some length. After admitting that all the recent commercial negotiations instanced by Ricardo had failed, and calling up, as a success, only a treaty with France of 1787, he went on:

> If hon. Gentlemen were to put the question, whether he would admit that it was more probable that favourable negotiations would be formed between this and foreign countries within a certain space of time, or whether it were more probable that they would not – he would reply, that he did not deem it necessary at present to answer the question. He did not object to hon. Gentlemen raising the question, he did not object to a strong statement of the disadvantages and difficulties of commercial negotiations, but he would, in the first place, say that there had been treaties of this sort which had been very advantageous; and, in the second place, that even if there had not, it was possible that at some future time there might.[64]

And by the end of the year (1844) Gladstone and Peel were admitting to each other that all the major bilateral commercial negotiations they had tried over the last three-and-a-quarter years had failed, and that the only response left to 'the protection or prohibition mania which appears to be raging in foreign countries' was further cuts in tariffs on raw materials to give British industry a renewed competitive edge.[65]

These were carried through, but only after Gladstone had left office on a matter about as unconnected with trade as it would be possible to imagine. Late in 1844 the Cabinet, in pursuit of a policy of religious conciliation in Ireland, decided to increase the grant made to the Roman Catholic seminary at Maynooth. Gladstone actually agreed with the decision. But seven years earlier he had published *The State in its Relations with the Church*, in which he had objected to giving Catholic colleges any money at all, and prophesied dire consequences from the kind of tolerance such grants embodied. He had long since dropped this view: but he had never publicly repudiated it. Therefore his integrity – or rather his reputation for integrity – bade him resign.

Gladstone rejoined the government the following December (1845), taking over the Colonial Secretaryship from Lord Stanley, the only member of the Cabinet to resign over Peel's intention to repeal the Corn Laws altogether. By accepting office Gladstone automatically vacated his seat at Newark: by accepting repeal he automatically lost his patron for the seat, the Duke of Newcastle. In his new post he had little to do with repeal itself, and, out of Parliament, little occasion to pronounce on the subject: his silence prompting a group of Liverpool merchants, considering sinking their party differences to adopt him as a candidate, to solicit 'a declaration of your sentiments upon the great question of free trade, which your present position precludes you from giving in Parliament.'[66]

Gladstone's sentiments were more clear-cut than at any time since 1841. Writing to his father three years later, he summed them up thus:

> I myself had invariably, during Peel's government, spoken of protection not as a thing good in principle, but to be dealt with as tenderly and cautiously as might be according to circumstances, always moving in the direction of free trade. It *then* appeared to me that the case was materially altered by events; it was no longer open to me to pursue that cautious course.[67]

The only discordant note between Gladstone and Peel came when the prime minister, defeated on a separate issue a few hours after the Corn Bill had successfully completed its passage through Parliament, indulged in a valedictory eulogium of Cobden as one of the main architects of repeal. Gladstone's conversion had in no way diminished his dislike of the Anti-Corn Law League and its politics. Now he used his diary to castigate Peel's praise of a man most distinguished for his 'incessant . . . imputation of bad and vile motives to honourable men.'[68] 'Mr Cobden,' said a memorandum Gladstone wrote two weeks later, 'has throughout argued the corn question on the principle of holding up the landlords to the people, as plunderers and knaves for maintaining the corn law to save their rents, and as fools because it was not necessary for that purpose.'[69] Forty-eight years later Gladstone pronounced it 'futile to compare any other man with him as the father of our system of Free Trade.'[70]

References

Gladstone Papers, British Library (*GP* in the notes).
Peel Papers, British Library.
Gladstone Diaries (*GD* in the notes): vol. 2 , ed. M.R.D. Foot, Oxford, Clarendon 1968; vol. 3 , ed. M.R.D. Foot and H.C.G. Matthew, Oxford, Clarendon, 1973.
N. Gash, *The Life of Sir Robert Peel after 1830,* Harlow, Longman, 1972.
W.E. Gladstone, 'The Course of Commercial Policy at Home and Abroad', *Foreign and Colonial Quarterly Review*, 1843, vol. 3, p. 230.
P. Magnus, *Gladstone*, London, Murray, 1954.
J. Morley, *The Life of Gladstone*, London, Macmillan, 1905, 2 vols.

Notes

1 'Note on the Corn Laws' (n.d., 1841), *GP*, Add MS 44729, f. 154.
2 memo. 'Provision Laws' (n.d., 1841), *GP*, Add MS 44729, f. 166.
3 memo. 'Corn' (9 October 1841) 'rewritten for Sir R. Peel with modifications', *GP*, Add MS 44729, f. 177.
4 Ibid., ff. 177–8.
5 Ibid., f. 178.

6 Ibid., f. 179.

7 Ibid., f. 186.

8 Such stability was desirable : so far as foreign suppliers used their earnings to buy British goods, anything which steadied imports steadied employment. So far as they did not, a steadier import bill meant less 'derangement of the currency'. In this way 'the foreign grower' found his way onto Gladstone's list of those who should be studied.

9 *Hansard*, 60 (14 February 1842) col. 379.

10 memo. 'Corn' (9 October 1841), *GP*, Add MS 44729, f. 195.

11 Ibid., f. 190.

12 Ibid., f. 181.

13 Ibid., f. 190.

14 Ibid., f. 196.

15 Peel to Gladstone, 13 November 1841, *GP*, Add MS 44275, f. 94.

16 Gladstone to Peel, 16 November 1841, *GP*, Add MS 44527 f. 50.

17 Peel Papers, British Library, Add MS 40464 ff. 27, 37.

18 Gladstone to Christopher, 10 November 1841, *GP*, Add MS 44527, f. 49.

19 Peel Papers, British Library, Add MS 40469, ff. 11–14.

20 Ibid., f. 15.

21 memo. (21 January 1842), *GP*, Add MS 44819, f. 74.

22 Ibid., f. 75.

23 Ibid., f. 75.

24 memo. (2 February 1842), *GP*, Add MS 44819, f. 77.

25 Gladstone to Peel, 2 February 1842, *GP*, Add MS 44730, f. 38 (Gladstone's underlining).

26 memo. (5 February 1842), *GP*, Add. MS 44819, f. 77.

27 Gladstone to Peel, 6 February 1842, *GP*, Add MS 44275, f. 105.

28 memo. (26 February 1842), *GP*, Add MS 44819, f. 79.

29 P. Magnus, *Gladstone*, London, Murray, 1954, p. 56.

30 Yet Gladstone was still sticking to this line fifty years later: 'I was absolutely without comprehension of the political situation and acted like a schoolboy, which indeed I still was to some extent' ('Autobiographical Fragment', 16 July 1892, *GP*, Add MS 44790, f. 48).

31 Gladstone to Sir John Gladstone, 30 June 1849, quoted in J. Morley, *The Life of Gladstone,* London, Macmillan, 1905, vol. 1, p. 284.

32 See the memorandum (n.d.), Peel Papers, British Library, Add MS 40469, ff. 134–7.

33 Peel to Gladstone, 13 February 1842, *GP*, Add MS 44275, f. 110.

34 *Hansard*, 60 (14 February 1842) cols 367–84 *passim.*

35 But he always sounded best in person: 'Marvellously effective as it was, Gladstone's oratory was never quite of the highest or most enduring quality . . . deprived of the magic of his delivery and of his gestures, the printed texts of his speeches lack prophetic inspiration and poetic power' etc., Magnus, op. cit., p. 49.

36 *Hansard*, 61 (9 March 1842) col. 373.

37 memo. (n.d., 1843) to Peel and Ripon, 'Prospective Commercial Policy', *GP*, Add MS 44732, f. 100.

38 memo., n.d. (someone has written 'probably 1843'), *GP*, Add MS 44733, ff. 143–4.

39 *Hansard*, 61 (9 March 1842) col. 374. There was no question of Gladstone evening things up by using Ricardo's theory of comparative advantage to support free

trade. He never mentioned it, even in his private notebooks. Had he heard of it? Though he never read anything by Ricardo, it seems inconceivable that he had not. Most probably he thought it a complicated irrelevance in the context of the Corn Law question – as it was. No one disputed that Britain had absolute advantage in manufacturing and absolute disadvantage in corn. If Gladstone and his contemporaries saw Ricardian refinement as superfluous, that makes them good economists not bad ones.

40 *Hansard*, 69 (13 June 1843) col. 1475.
41 *Hansard*, 73 (12 March 1844) cols 900–4.
42 N. Gash, *The Life of Sir Robert Peel after 1830*, Harlow, Longman, 1972, p. 370.
43 *Hansard*, 67 (13 February 1843) col. 499.
44 Ibid., col. 502.
45 Ibid., col. 506.
46 W.E. Gladstone, 'The Course of Commercial Policy at Home and Abroad', *Foreign and Colonial Quarterly Review,* 1843, vol. 3, p. 230.
47 Ibid., pp. 242.
48 memo. 'Cattle' (n.d.) *GP*, Add MS 44730, ff. 146–7.
49 *Hansard*, 60 (14 February 1842), cols 336, 337, 338, 350.
50 *Hansard*, 67 (17 February 1843), col. 849.
51 *Hansard*, 61 (14 March 1842), col. 552.
52 *Hansard*, 67 (16 February 1843) cols 689–91.
53 In a grotesque epilogue, J.L. Ricardo appeared to accuse Peel not just of chasing advance copies of new pamphlets so as to steal a debating advantage, but even of removing relevant items from the Commons library to give himself a monopoly of august advice: 'He must also observe that [Torrens' latest] pamphlet, though advertised yesterday, was not published till that evening, and it was curious that when he went to the library to look for the book, written by a near relative of his own, which had also been referred to by the right hon. Gentleman, that was absent too.' *Hansard*, 68 (25 April 1843) col. 970.
54 *Hansard*, 60 (14 February 1842), col. 360.
55 *GD*, vol. 3, pp. 154, 170, 194, 220, 257, 278, 279.
56 See e.g. *Hansard*, 75 (26 June 1844) col. 1527.
57 *Hansard*, 60 (24 February 1842) cols 1043–5.
58 *Hansard*, 71 (12 March 1844) cols 905–6.
59 e.g. 'Fragment on Corn Protection' (Sept.–Oct. 1841), *GP*, Add MS 44729, f. 144.
60 *Hansard*, 66 (13 February 1843), col. 471.
61 *Hansard*, 66 (16 February 1843), col. 247.
62 Ibid., col. 247.
63 *Hansard*, 68 (25 April 1843) col. 915.
64 *Hansard*, 73 (19 March 1844) col. 1284.
65 Gladstone to Peel, 2 January 1845, *GP*, Add MS 44528, ff. 1–2.
66 *GP*, Add MS 44363, f. 156.
67 Gladstone to Sir John Gladstone, 30 June 1849, quoted in Morley, op. cit., vol. 1, p. 284.
68 30 June 1846. *GD*, vol. 3, p. 547.
69 memo., 12 July 1846, quoted in Morley, op. cit., vol. 1, p. 292.
70 memo: 'Protectionism and Free Trade', 12 July 1894, *GP*, Add MS 44790. ff. 120–30.

3

COMMENTS ON KADISH AND MALONEY

Norman McCord

In Chapter 1 Alon Kadish has provided us with an admirable summary of the economic arguments used by the Anti-Corn Law League, as well as something more in the nature of a general introduction to this area of our discussions at the conference. I have only one or two minor glosses to add. The Cumbrian landowner Sir James Graham, mentioned as 'owner of a large debt-ridden estate in Cumberland', believed in the concept of high farming as the best safeguard of the agricultural interest. He borrowed large sums to improve the family estates, but found the income-generating returns so disappointing that on at least one occasion he considered selling up and abandoning the programme.

The statement that 'Fitzwilliam and the other Whig free traders were primarily concerned with devising a strategy that would ensure the survival of their class' reminded me of the earlier mention of the attacks on the League as consisting of 'manufacturers who sought to repeal the Corn Laws in order to reduce wages.' No doubt both accusations of selfish interests contain substantial elements of truth, but we should also remember that such unavoidable compressions must also include substantial elements of over-simplification. It would have been interesting to know what the League's 'tame' farmers who joined in the attacks on the Corn Laws thought of Peel's legislation providing for government-backed cheap loans for land improvement, including drainage schemes.

One point which struck me on reading John Maloney's fascinating Chapter 2 was the relatively sophisticated nature of the detailed discussions about the possible effects of different scales of corn duties. This reminded me of a thought I have entertained ever since I took the trouble some years ago to read the Corn Laws of 1815, 1828 and 1842. It struck me then that they provide an interesting example of another 'pattern of government growth', on the lines of Oliver MacDonagh's classic, *A Pattern of Government Growth, 1800–60: The Passenger Acts and their Enforcement* (London, 1961), on the development of regulation of the emigrant traffic. These successive Corn

Laws provide good evidence for growing sophistication and expertise in a variety of ways, including the provisions for the taking of the price averages.

Maloney's remarks about Gladstone's disdain of the League will not surprise anyone acquainted with the murkier aspects of the League's electoral activities, including the celebrated Walsall by-election in which Gladstone and his brother were closely involved. The mention of speculation in the corn trade reminded me of a number of north German immigrants involved in the Baltic corn trade to Tyneside, who in a short time contrived to amass the substantial sums which enabled them to emerge as major figures in the Tyneside chemical industry and the Teesside iron industry.

4

PEEL, ROTTEN POTATOES AND PROVIDENCE

The repeal of the Corn Laws and the Irish Famine

Christine Kinealy

The repeal of the Corn Laws in 1846 has tended to be linked inextricably with the onset of the potato famine in Ireland in 1845. This connection was made by contemporaries including the Duke of Wellington, who, in a memorable (if inaccurate) retort, declared 'Rotten potatoes have done it all. They put Peel in his damned fright.'[1] Yet, the connection between the ending of protection and the failure of the Irish potato crop is complex. The repeal of the Corn Laws, so far as Ireland was concerned, had more to do with the desire to bring about long-term agricultural and social restructuring, than with the short-term need to alleviate the food shortages. In this context, the traditional notion that the need for famine relief in Ireland was a trigger for repeal may be seen as a convenient political myth. In reality, the attempt to link repeal to the need for famine relief was an example of political opportunism and administrative pragmatism rather than a practical proposal intended to alleviate suffering in Ireland.

Few scholars of Corn Law history have addressed the relationship between Ireland and Britain at that time or have examined in detail the nature of the food crisis whose existence is thought to have contributed to the case for the repeal of the Corn Laws. This has been an unfortunate omission. The Corn Law legislation had come to symbolise an economic dinosaur. However, the coincidence of the Irish food shortages and of the pinnacle of pressure for the repeal of the Corn Laws provided both the motivation and trigger for the generation of the myth mentioned earlier. The potato blight allowed the resultant political discourse to be expressed in humanitarian rather than pragmatic terms. Paradoxically, however, Ireland benefited little from the subsequent repeal of the Corn Laws. The loss of 1 million people through excess mortality and a further 1 million through emigration in the six years of famine was a clear demonstration that the suffering of Ireland was not a priority of successive British governments.

As a result of the Act of Union of 1800, Ireland had become an integral part of the United Kingdom. Consequently, Ireland lost its own parliament in Dublin. Subsequently, all legislation and political power emanated from London. Although Ireland had parliamentary representation in Westminister (100 MPs, which was raised to 105 in 1832) Irish MPs were always in a minority. Moreover, with few exceptions, the Irish MPs tended to follow traditional party divisions rather than represent an exclusively 'Irish' interest. Even Daniel O'Connell and his Repeal (of the Union) Association in the 1830s allied with the Whig party on many political issues. The inducement to abolish the Irish parliament was two-fold: economic prosperity and Catholic Emancipation were promised. The first incentive was elusive, however, and the second proved to be a political impossibility in the short term. Therefore, the Union with Britain disappointed the majority of the Irish population from the outset.

In the early nineteenth century, the Irish economy was overwhelmingly agricultural. The non-agricultural sector, however, was large. In the 1821 Census, it was claimed that three-fifths of the population was employed in 'trades, manufactures or handicrafts'. Twenty years later, there was more regional specialisation, which meant that the industrial sector had become centred around Dublin and Belfast. Parts of the west of Ireland had undergone a process of de-industrialisation after 1815, due largely to a contraction in the cottage linen industry. Economic expansion had been most evident in the north-east of the country largely, but not exclusively, based on a highly efficient and commercialised linen industry, which had benefited from the constitutional and commercial linkage with Britain.

Ireland's image as an underdeveloped agricultural country was due substantially to its high dependence on a single crop – the potato. Within Ireland, potatoes were grown extensively. By 1841, approximately two-thirds of Ireland's population of almost 8.5 million persons depended on potatoes as their staple food. However, it was not only humans who ate potatoes; they were also used to feed farm animals, poultry and horses. Approximately one-third of the potato crop was consumed in this way. Thus when the crop was poor, it was animals rather than humans who bore the initial brunt of the shortages.

Potatoes were believed to have been brought to Ireland by Sir Walter Raleigh in the middle of the sixteenth century. Initially they were consumed as a vegetable of the gentry but by the seventeenth century, potatoes were used to supplement the traditional diet of oats and dairy foods. The reliability and high yields of this crop led to increased dependence on the potato and a corresponding decrease in the oat-growing zone. Increasingly, oats were grown and consumed in the north of the country, while potatoes became the staple diet of the poor elsewhere. Although oats continued to be grown, they were rarely consumed (except in the so-called 'hungry months' of June, July and August) but were used as a cash crop. As the bread-hungry population of Britain expanded, corn became an important export commodity.

The dependence on potatoes was facilitated by unusually high crop yields. All agricultural produce in Ireland, in fact, outperformed that of other European countries (it was twice that of France for example). Although the ridges in which potatoes were grown were pejoratively known as 'lazy beds' they were an efficient means of production. The high yields were facilitated by the intensive manual preparation of the land, especially the extensive use of manure. The lack of mechanisation of Irish agriculture, however, led to it being judged as backward.[2]

Potatoes were also extremely nutritious and while the Irish peasants had few material possessions or capital, they were acknowledged to be healthy, tall and fertile. The economist, Adam Smith, had noted that

> The chairmen, porters, and coalheavers in London, and those unfortunate women who live by prostitution, the strongest men and the most beautiful women perhaps in the British dominions, are said to be, the greater part of them, from the lowest rank of people in Ireland, who are generally fed with this root. No food can afford a more decisive proof of its nourishing quality, or its being particularly suitable to the health of the human constitution.[3]

Despite their nutritional value, potatoes were looked upon as being an inferior foodstuff, largely because they had little commercial value. It was widely accepted that the ending of the dependence on this crop would be of moral and social benefit to Ireland and thus England. This belief became particularly apparent in the wake of the first appearance of potato blight in 1845. Sir Robert Peel, in a debate on the Corn Laws, informed the Commons, 'I wish it were possible to take advantage of this calamity for introducing among the people of Ireland the taste for a better and more certain provision for their support than that which they have hitherto cultivated.'[4] Randolph Routh, the government's chief relief administrator in Ireland, put this even more plainly when he stated

> The little industry called for to rear the potato, and its prolific growth, leave the people to indolence and all kinds of vice, which habitual labour and a higher order of food would prevent. I think it very probable that we may derive much advantage from this present calamity.[5]

Although potatoes played such an important role within the economy, Irish agriculture was not monolithic – potatoes accounting for only one-fifth of all agricultural output. Grain – especially oats and wheat – was grown extensively throughout Ireland. However, wheat, which was grown mostly in the south-east of the country, was purely a commercial crop, while oats, with the exception of Ulster, was grown largely for sale and export. Like the linen industry, the expansion of the grain trade was also based on trading links with Britain. By 1841, oats were the biggest single Irish export, and overall, Ireland was exporting enough corn to England to feed 2 million people, leading Ireland to be described as the 'bread basket' or 'granary' of the United Kingdom. The impact of the loss of this supply was an important consideration in any debate on the removal of protective legislation.

While oats had been a traditional part of the Irish diet, the growth of wheat was a relatively new area of production within Ireland. This grain was not suited to the Irish climate, nor was it consumed within the country. The reasons for its widespread cultivation therefore lay outside the immediate needs and experiences of the Irish economy. These reasons were various. The expansion of corn production in Ireland in the eighteenth century was due partly due to legislative restrictions combined with developments within the British economy. In the second half of the century, a series of acts was passed by the Irish parliament to encourage tillage, including the provision of transport subsidies on internal grain. Moreover, a number of agrarian experts warned that the growth of grain was inappropriate for Ireland's landscape and climatic conditions, while Irish ministers viewed grain as giving Ireland strength in Anglo-Irish trading. By the time of the Act of Union, grain dominated the Dublin markets, much of it going en route to England. Between 1792 and 1819, all food exports from Ireland to Britain increased dramatically but the largest growth was in the wheat trade, which grew twenty-fold.[6]

The Napoleonic Wars had increased the demand for Irish grain within Britain and the high profits increased the attractiveness of this market for Irish farmers. Following the ending of the wars, legislative intervention in the shape of the 1815 Corn Laws provided a vital layer of protection for Irish corn. The export of corn was also facilitated by the introduction of steam shipping on cross-channel routes. Significantly, in the early decades of the nineteenth century, wheat output increased by approximately 20 per cent. This was due to an increase in crop yield rather than an increase in crop acreage. As a consequence, in the 1790s, Ireland supplied Britain with only 16.5 per cent of its corn imports. This had risen to 57 per cent in 1810; while by 1830, Irish corn exports accounted for 80 per cent of British imports.[7] In addition to the protective legislation and developments in transport, the growth in corn production had been made possible in Ireland as a consequence of the low costs of Irish labour and, an offshoot of this, the practice of intensive manuring. Significantly also, the spread of potato culti-vation allowed Ireland to sustain its fast growing population on poor-quality and marginal soil.

The growth of potatoes underpinned the productivity of the whole agricultural sector. The potato economy provided farmers with a cheap, well-fed workforce who had few material aspirations. Surplus potatoes were used to feed pigs, which, in turn, could be sold to pay the rent. In the interim period, however, the pigs were a rich source of high-class manure, which was recycled onto the growing potatoes. The traditional dung-heap outside the cottage, therefore, was a symbol of economic probity rather than low living standards.[8] This system allowed massive exports of grain from Ireland while the majority of the population survived on potatoes. However, it tied the people to the land and encouraged subdivision of estates.

The appearance of a mysterious new blight on the potato crop in 1845 was not confined to Ireland. The disease first appeared in Belgium and from there spread to parts of France, Germany, the Netherlands and Sweden. By late summer, it was reported in the south of England, the lowlands of Scotland and, in late August, the east of Ireland. Within Europe, however, Ireland was unique in having such a high dependence on this single crop. Although blight was first noticed at the end of August, it was not until general digging took place in September that the people started to panic. Concern deepened when it was found that potatoes which had been removed from the ground, apparently healthy, rotted in storage. The British government, led by Sir Robert Peel, responded calmly to what appeared to be a widespread but not unusual crop failure. As Peel was aware, the impact of the shortages would not be felt until the following spring and summer, which gave him time to devise and implement a package of suitable relief measures. In October, he appointed a Scientific Commission in order that the government would have an accurate and objective account of the extent of the potato crop lost. He justified this on the grounds that 'there is such a tendency to exaggeration and inaccuracy in Irish reports that delay in acting upon them is always desirable.'[9] Only when Peel had received an initial report from the 'men of science' was a package of relief measures put into place.

From the outset, Peel viewed the appearance of blight in Ireland as an opportunity to shape policy formulation within the United Kingdom and to reopen the debate surrounding the duties on corn imports. This agenda was made clear in a letter to the Lord Lieutenant of Ireland dated 15 October 1845 in which Peel stated that the only solution to the food shortages was 'the removal of all impediments to the import of all kinds of human food — that is, the total and absolute repeal for ever of all duties on all articles of substance.'[10] The early commitment to permanent repeal was made a month before the Scientific Commissioners submitted their final report to Peel.[11]

The British government's response to the blight was shaped by a number of complex, and at times conflicting, beliefs, expectations and experiences. Within Ireland, there was a widespread acceptance that the blight was sent by God as a punishment for some imagined misdemeanour. Within England, a number of evangelicals interpreted the blight as a warning to the English population of their own vulnerability before God.[12] These providentialist interpretations dovetailed with the viewpoint of a number of influential politicians and civil servants, notably Sir James Graham, the Home Secretary, and Charles Trevelyan, Permanent Secretary at the Treasury.[13] They viewed the blight as a punishment from God, inflicted on a lazy and improvident people, and they believed that atonement was the only antidote to the mysterious fungus. For Peel, the appearance of blight presented a unique and valuable opportunity to bring about two more terrestrial aspirations – the completion of a free-trade programme within the United Kingdom, and the modernisation of Irish agriculture. Within both visions, the need for Irish people to end their dependence on the potato was a key component.

Peel's association with Ireland was long-standing and bitter-sweet. In 1809, on the recommendation of the Duke of Wellington, Peel had become the Member of Parliament for the Irish seat of Cashel, County Tipperary. Three years later, at the age of only 25, Peel was appointed Chief Secretary for Ireland. He held this position for six years (making him the longest serving Chief Secretary in the nineteenth century), finally retiring in 1818 on the grounds of exhaustion. After he left Ireland in 1818, he never returned to the country. During his stay in Ireland, Peel, known for his Ultra-Protestant views, antagonised the young nationalist, Daniel O'Connell, who gave him the sobriquet 'Orange Peel'.

In 1822, Peel's appointment as Home Secretary again brought him into contact with Ireland. During these years, Peel gained valuable experience in dealing with food shortages in Ireland, as the years 1816–17 and 1822 were periods of food shortages and potential famine within Ireland. In 1816, Peel arranged for oats to be imported into the distressed districts within Ireland and sold at low prices, and grants to establish public works were made to local relief committees. In 1822, a similar pattern of relief, which combined short-term assistance with long-term benefits, was followed and it again proved to be successful.[14] Consequently, in 1845, Peel already had considerable first-hand experience in dealing with food shortages and hunger within Ireland. These earlier periods of scarcity demonstrated that crop failure did not have to result in mass mortality.

Peel's subsequent career often brought him into association with Irish issues in a public and controversial way, notably on the question of Catholic Emancipation in 1829, the grant to Maynooth College in 1845, and the repeal of the Corn Laws in 1846. On each of these occasions, Peel's actions caused a rift within the Conservative party and lost him much personal support. Hence, by 1845, despite having won the 1841 election with a large majority, within his own party Peel was vulnerable. Ironically, Peel's final parliamentary defeat in 1846 was caused by an Irish issue – the introduction of a Coercion Bill which was heavily defeated as an act of political revenge by his own party.

By the mid-1840s, Peel had become disillusioned with the Protestant Ascendancy within Ireland, whom he blamed for many of Ireland's economic and social ills. He felt that a restructuring of Irish society was necessary – from potato growers to large landlords. Peel favoured a system of 'high farming' which would be possible only if the small plots of land used for growing potatoes were consolidated and landlords adopted new agricultural methods and invested capital in their properties. Peel's initial approach was cautious, thorough and gradualist. In 1843, for example, he appointed a Commission under Lord Devon to inquire into the system of landholding in Ireland and to suggest changes. The Commission, however, from the outset appeared to believe that the solution lay in an 'anglicisation' of Irish agriculture. The report of the Devon Committee at the beginning of 1845 was overshadowed by the appearance of the potato blight. For Peel and his Whig successors, the blight and the resultant famine provided an opportunity to bring about more radical and rapid changes than would otherwise have been possible.[15] The repeal of the Corn Laws was an important part of these changes.

When blight appeared in Ireland in 1845, the relief measures introduced by the British government were traditional and similar to those adopted in earlier years of shortages. At this stage, the blight was regarded as a temporary calamity and short-term palliatives were applied. Local relief committees were established which could provide either employment or food to the population, and the government secretly purchased £100,000 of Indian corn from America. Indian corn (or maize) was chosen because it was the cheapest grain available. It had been imported in previous periods of scarcity but Peel was hopeful that it might become a permanent item in the Irish diet. Despite it being difficult to cook, hard to digest and nutritionally unimpressive, Indian corn was regarded as an ideal food for Irish peasants and replacement for the potato diet. The change from a potato to a grain diet was seen as an important aspect in the regeneration of Irish society and ministers were anxious that its presence should be made permanent. *The Times* newspaper, which had frequently attacked the 'potato people' of Ireland, predicted that if potatoes were replaced by a 'higher order of food' such as grain by the Irish poor 'it would go a great way to improve their social and therefore their political habits.'[16] Government officials, including Randolph Routh and Charles Trevelyan, experimented with the corn in an effort to make it more palatable by making it into 'suppawn' or porridge, 'mush' or 'samp'.[17] During the Corn Law debate in Parliament, Peel admitted that 'I wish it were possible to take advantage of this calamity for introducing among the people of Ireland the taste for a better and more certain provision for their support than that which they have heretofore cultivated.'[18]

While the importation of Indian corn was generally successful, it did not replace the potato as the staple food of the Irish. Unlike potatoes, corn had to be carefully processed before it could be consumed. Also, the quantities available to the destitute (initially one pound of corn a day per adult, although this fluctuated as the famine progressed) was far below the amount of potatoes consumed before the famine (an adult male would have eaten on average fourteen pounds of potatoes each day for nine months of the year). In terms of bulk, taste and nutrition, the Irish peasants found Indian corn to be far inferior to their traditional potato diet. The determination to return to the potato diet was indicated by the fact that despite the shortages in 1845, in the spring of 1846, approximately 80 per cent of the usual potato acreage was planted.[19]

The purchase of Indian corn in 1845 was never intended to fill the deficit created by the potato blight, but instead to regulate the price and supply of food within Ireland and to stimulate private imports. Although there were many calls for immediate short-term measures such as the opening of the ports and a ban on distillation, these short-term measures were rejected in favour of a more permanent solution.

In view of the estimates of the crop losses by the Scientific Commissioners (upwards of 50 per cent) the relief provision was not very generous. However, by the end of 1845, contrary to expectations, the potato disease appeared to have plateaued and crop losses were less than had been predicted. Also, with few exceptions, the blight was most virulent in the east of the country, where the economy was more diverse.[20] This meant that the relief was more extensive than it would otherwise have been. As a consequence, Peel's relief measures were effective. This was evidenced by the absence of excess mortality in the wake of the 1845 potato failure, leading even traditionally antagonist newspapers such as *The Freeman's Journal* to congratulate Peel on his handling of the crisis. There was no famine in Ireland in 1845.

In the winter of 1845–6, when the repeal of the Corn Laws had been first debated, there was no perception that the potato blight would reappear and transform the temporary failure into the most demographically lethal famine in modern Europe. When repeal was finally achieved in June 1846, both members of Peel's government and relief officials within Ireland were congratulating themselves on their handling of the temporary crisis, unaware that the blight had not yet run its course Yet, in 1846 the potato blight appeared in Ireland in a far more virulent form than it had in the previous year. For a potato crop to fail in two successive years was highly unprecedented and took many people – politicians and potato growers alike – by surprise.

The piecemeal and gradual way in which the Corn Laws were dismantled made it unlikely that they could have brought immediate benefit to a country undergoing famine. In November 1845, Peel had been discussing the possibility of an immediate suspension of duties on corn which would be integrated into a more permanent measure. Two months later, however, he was suggesting that the dismantling should be gradual, that is, spread over three years until February 1849, when a uniform rate of one shillings a quarter was to be charged on all grain. Indian corn, however, was immediately to be exempt from the new sliding scale and was to be subject to lower duties instantly.[21] Within this framework, the repeal of the Corn Laws could not be viewed as a remedy for famine. Moreover, even if the repeal of the Corn Laws had been immediate and total, it could not have resulted in an immediate transfer of food supplies to Ireland. This was especially true between 1845 and 1847, when potato failure and bad corn harvests throughout Europe had pushed grain prices up. In addition, the continuation of the Navigation Acts, which hampered the movement of goods, acted as an impediment to free trade.

By the beginning of 1846, the repeal of the Corn Laws was being presented increasingly as an integral part of a package of tariff reform. Long-term economic benefits rather than short-term relief became the corner-stone of the debate. Moreover, the so-called 'Condition of England' question rather than the relief of Ireland became the rationale for such an action. The public debates, however, continued to refer to the distress in Ireland as the trigger for making such action necessary and Peel was frequently criticised for having done so. The Irish radical nationalist, Sir William Smith O'Brien, was critical of the limited relief provided by the government and criticised Peel personally for having 'deemed it necessary to combine the relief of just distress with the repeal of the corn-laws.'[22] Within Ireland also, there was a belief that the real needs of the Irish destitute had been overshadowed and obfuscated by 'Peel's gigantic scheme of commercial policy'.[23]

In England, Lord George Bentinck, the leader of the protectionist Tories, frequently accused Peel of having used the Irish potato famine as a ploy for introducing reforms which he desired anyway. There is little doubt that Peel had become an intellectual convert to free trade in the 1820s and the tariff reforms of 1829 and 1842 were an indication of the path that he was taking.[24] By the 1840s, however, trade reform had become a prerequisite to changes in both the condition of Ireland and the condition of England – although for very different reasons. In both countries he insisted that the first step towards social improvement was 'an abundance of food'.[25] In Ireland, however, potatoes, in spite of their abundance, were to be replaced with cheap corn.

Despite this aspiration, Peel and his contemporaries were aware that the repeal of the Corn Laws could bring little immediate economic benefit to Ireland. Peel himself, in his many public speeches, displayed an ambivalence as to how the repeal of the Corn Laws would, in fact, benefit Ireland. Although the distress in Ireland had become less central to the debate, Peel occasionally and perhaps cynically referred to the Irish Famine. In an unusually emotive speech defending the need for repeal, Peel chastised his colleagues for their lack of action regarding the blight in Ireland, demanding from them 'are you to sit in cabinet, and consider and calculate how much diarrhoea, and bloody flux, and dysentery a people can bear before it becomes necessary for you to provide them with food?'[26] Two months later, however, he appeared to contradict this when he stated

Sir, I do not rest my support of this bill upon the temporary ground of scarcity in Ireland. . . . Now all of you admit that the real question at issue is the improvement of the social and moral condition of the masses of the population; we wish to elevate in the gradation of society that great class which gains its support by manual labour – that is agreed on by all hands.[27]

However, if the potato blight in Ireland provided a convenient trigger for a reopening of the Corn Law debate, in both the short and the long term it was unlikely that Ireland would be the beneficiary. Peel appeared unequivocal on this matter when he stated that 'If there be a part of the United Kingdom which is to suffer by the withdrawal of protection . . . it was Ireland' and he went on to explain that this was because 'Ireland had not, as England had, the means of finding employment for her agricultural population in her manufacturing districts.'[28] This sentiment was echoed by a number of contemporaries within Ireland who argued that the blight had destroyed potato production and the repeal of the Corn Laws would ruin corn production. By 1849, this appeared to be the case as the price of Irish corn had fallen dramatically, resulting in massive imports. Charles Wood, the Chancellor of the Exchequer, estimated that out of the 105 Irish MPs, 90 were protectionists.[29] John Young MP also warned that nobody in Ireland now supported free trade and added 'What can we say to tired or desperately struggling men?'[30]

In the long term, grain acreage dropped dramatically. The second half of the nineteenth century witnessed a shift from tillage to livestock, and while cattle numbers rose by one-third, the acreage under potatoes and grain fell by a half.[31] In the 1840s, wheat, oats and potatoes together had accounted for approximately half of total agricultural output. By 1910, they had been overtaken in importance by the humble farmyard hen and duck. The livestock trade was one of the great success stories of Irish agriculture in the late nineteenth century.[32]

In the short term, however, did the repeal of the Corn Laws alleviate the impact of the potato blight in Ireland? Throughout the famine, corn continued to be exported from Ireland, a fact which has figured as a major issue in nationalist historiography of the famine. Following the fall of Peel's government, the Whig party led by Lord John Russell came to power. It was to remain in power for the remainder of the famine. The situation facing Russell's government was far more serious than a year earlier. The second appearance of blight was extensive, especially in the west of Ireland, where a high portion of people depended on this vegetable. The resulting scale of distress and food shortages facing Russell greatly exceeded the crisis that had faced Peel in the previous year. A number of significant changes were made in the provision of relief, especially in regard to the importation of food. The Whig government, in an effort to appease Irish corn merchants, promised that they would not again intervene in the market place in the manner that Peel's government had done, but would leave the import of food into Ireland to market forces. Instead, in the second and more critical year of food shortages, the main form of relief provision was the public works.[33]

Although, as Table 4.1 shows, by 1847, imports of grain (usually low-quality Indian corn) were exceeding exports of corn (including high-quality wheat), this had little to do with the ending of protection. Furthermore, most of the exports had left Ireland at the beginning of the winter of 1846–7, while food imports did not begin to arrive until the spring of 1847. Food prices in the months following the harvest were abnormally high and out of reach of the people employed on the public works. Thus, in the winter of 1846–7, there was a 'starvation gap' in Ireland between the need for food and access to it. As a consequence, mortality in these months rose sharply and has been estimated as being in excess of 400,000 people.[34] Other social indicators of extreme distress were also evident, notably high levels of disease, emigration and evictions, and low marriage and birth rates.

The inadequacy of the relief measures introduced by the Whig party resulted in a major change of policy at the beginning of 1847. Public works were disbanded and replaced in the short term with soup kitchens, and in the long term with an expansion of the workhouse system. Significantly also, in January 1847, Russell was forced to amend the Corn Law legislation which had been passed only a few months earlier. Consequently, a Bill was passed which suspended duties on foreign corn, and the cumbersome Navigation Laws were relaxed. This Bill was meant to be effective only until 1 September 1847, but ongoing famine in Ireland resulted in it being extended until 1 March 1848.

Increasingly, members of the Whig government, as Peel had done, viewed the famine as an opportunity to end the dependence of the Irish people on the so-called 'lazy crop' – the potato. The widespread acceptance that the

Table 4.1 Irish grain trade, 1839–48

Year	Net grain flow outward (thousands of tons)
1839	+293
1840	+294
1841	+377
1842	+313
1843	+465
1844	+394
1845	+485
1846	+87
1847	−743
1848	−125

Source: Based on calculations by Austin Bourke, *The Visitation of God?*

blight was a 'visitation of God', sent as a warning to a lazy and feckless people to change their ways, added strength to the government's desire to modernise Irish agriculture, which had been a goal of Peel's government prior to 1845. Repeal of the Corn Laws would be an important step towards agricultural restructuring as it was hoped that a consequence of ending protection would be that low-quality grain such as Indian corn, rather than potatoes, would become the staple food of the Irish people. While potato production did decrease, this was largely due to the fact that many of the people who had died or emigrated during the famine (in total over 2 million people) were drawn from the potato-growing section of the population. Those who survived or remained in Ireland, however, remained loyal to a potato-based diet although as the standard of living rose, diets inevitably became more varied.[35]

Peel had repeatedly made the point that the repeal of the Corn Laws should be viewed as a measure to bring about permanent changes rather than short-term benefits. In regard to Ireland, Peel believed that this would result in the substitution of potatoes for wheat. Conversely, he argued that if repeal did not come, within England 'potatoes would be substituted for wheaten bread'. The aspiration to end the dependence of poor Irish people on potatoes was also outlined by Sir Charles Trevelyan, Permanent Secretary at the Treasury and commander-in-chief of famine relief, who described the policies of the government as having the intention of bringing about 'the change from an idle, barbarous, isolated potato cultivation, to corn cultivation, which enforces industry, and binds together employer and employed in mutually beneficial relations.'[36]

Within the context of the desire for the economic and agricultural regeneration of Ireland, the repeal of the Corn Laws provided a tool to facilitate this long-term social revolution, rather than a mechanism for alleviating short-term famine distress. Potato blight and Providence provided Peel with a political and spiritual rationale, and an opportunity to end protection, but the repeal of the Corn Laws did little, in turn, to alleviate the impact of the famine in Ireland.

Notes

1 Quoted in R.J. Cootes, *Britain since 1700*, (Harlow, 1968) p. 165.
2 P.M. Austin Bourke, *The Visitation of God? The Potato and the Great Irish Famine* (Dublin, 1993) pp. 62–5.
3 Adam Smith, 'The Wealth of Nations' Book 1, quoted in Peter Mathias, *The First Industrial Nation: An Economic History of Britain 1700–1914*, 2nd edn (London, 1983) p. 174.
4 *Hansard*, 83, 27 January 1846, p. 261.
5 Randolph Routh to Charles Trevelyan, 1 April 1846, *Correspondence Explanatory of the Measures Adopted by Her Majesty's Government for the relief of distress arising from the failure of the potato crop in Ireland*, 1846 [736] xxxvii, p. 139.

6 Roy Foster, *Modern Ireland*, pp. 200–1. Foster's Corn Law, passed in 1784, was an attempt to protect Irish corn from English demands in times of shortages. In 1797 due to an economic crisis, transport subsidies on internal grain trade were ended.

7 Cormac O Grada, *A New Economic History of Ireland* (Oxford, 1984) p. 120.

8 The Halls, *Ireland, its Scenery, Character etc.* (London, 1841) Book 1, provide an Excellent (and sympathetic) insight into rural life in Ireland on the eve of the famine.

9 Peel to Sir James Graham, 13 October 1845, Sir Robert Peel, *Memoirs*, vol. ii (London, 1857) p. 113.

10 Peel to Lord Heytesbury, 15 October 1845, *Memoirs*, p. 121.

11 *Copy of the report of Dr Playfair and Mr Lindley on the present state of the Irish Potato Crop and the prospect of the approaching scarcity*, PP 1846 [28] xxxvii.

12 For example see H. McNeile, *The Famine a Rod of God: Its Provoking Cause, its Merciful Design* (Liverpool, 1847). Canon McNeile was a vociferous opponent of the grant to Maynooth – 'a college for instruction in bowing down to images', *The Times*, 29 April 1845.

13 For more on the links between providentialism and political ideology during this period see Boyd Hilton, *The Age of Atonement: The Influence of Evangelicalism on Social and Economic Thought*, (Oxford, 1988).

14 Eric J. Evans, *Sir Robert Peel: Statesmanship, Power and Party* (London, 1991) pp. 4–10; Boyd Hilton, 'Peel: a reappraisal', *Historical Journal*, xxii, 1979.

15 Christine Kinealy, *This Great Calamity* (Dublin, 1994), Chapter 9.

16 *The Times*, 10 October 1845.

17 Memorandum on Indian Corn sent by Routh to Trevelyan, 31 July 1846, *Correspondence Explanatory*, p. 226.

18 *Hansard*, 83, 27 January 1846, p. 261.

19 Austin Bourke, *Visitation of God?* pp. 100–10.

20 For more on the mechanisms of relief throughout the famine see Christine Kinealy, *This Great Calamity: The Irish Famine 1845–52* (Gill and Macmillan, Dublin, 1994), Chapters 2–5.

21 *Hansard*, 83, 27 January 1847, pp. 260–4.

22 Speech by O'Brien in House of Commons, 17 April 1846.

23 *The Belfast Vindicator*, 4 February 1846.

24 Boyd Hilton, *Corn, Cash, Commerce: the Economic Policies of the Tory Governments of 1815–30* (Oxford, 1977).

25 Robert Peel, *Speeches*, IV, p. 650 (27 March 1846).

26 Robert Peel, *Speeches*, IV, p. 639 (27 March 1846).

27 Robert Peel, *Speeches*, IV, pp. 689–91 (15 May 1846).

28 Stated during debate in House of Commons on Corn Laws, 5 May 1846, pp. 122–8.

29 Charles Wood to Peel, 15 December 1849, in Parker, *Peel*, p. 526.

30 Ibid., John Young MP to Peel, 4 December 1849, p. 525.

31 O Grada, *New History*, pp. 258–60.

32 Cormac O Grada, *Ireland Before and After the Famine: Explorations in Economic History, 1800–1925* (Manchester, 1988) pp. 128–30.

33 Kinealy, *This Great Calamity*, Chapter 3.

34 Throughout the course of the famine, the government did not keep a record of mortality but this figure was the unofficial estimate of the Irish constabulary.

35 Even today, Ireland has the highest per capita consumption of potatoes within Europe.

36 C.E. Trevelyan, 'The Irish Crisis', *The Edinburgh Review*, January 1848.

5

INTERESTS, IDEOLOGY AND POLITICS

Agricultural trade policy in nineteenth-century Britain and Germany

Cheryl Schonhardt-Bailey

Few would disagree that economic interests are central to explaining political outcomes. Yet several authors have started to identify the limitations of theories that rely solely on economic interests to explain political behaviour, and the pendulum seems to be swinging towards a more 'political' bent to political economy. Some authors emphasize the political process of policy making, while others integrate ideas and ideologies into models of decision making.[1] In this chapter I build on the new 'ideas and ideology' literature. I develop hypotheses for how variations in the means by which ideology and interests are channelled through political organizations (parties, groups) can affect trade policy outcomes. The logic of the hypotheses derives from party theory, and is complemented by insights from the electoral and legislative voting literatures. These hypotheses are applied to Britain and Germany in the nineteenth century.

Defining ideology

One fairly common misunderstanding of ideology is that it suggests some form of non-rationality, that is, some 'residual or random component of conscious human decision making.'[2] Hinich and Munger, who rightly object to this characterization of ideology, note that Marx's definition of ideology as false consciousness is chiefly responsible for giving ideology a bad name.[3] Indeed, so distasteful is the word 'ideology' that the international relations literature avoids it altogether, and instead speaks of 'ideas'.[4] This chapter will adhere unabashedly to the term ideology, but will aim to explore in detail the related concepts of ideas, partisanship and political doctrines.

Work by Hinich and Munger and by Goldstein offers a strong foundation for a functional definition of ideology. Hinich and Munger build a theory of elections based on ideology, while Goldstein explains inconsistencies in American trade law by envisaging policy as a patchwork quilt of new and old policy ideas. The authors agree that, informally, ideology may be defined as a collection of ideas. Yet their formal definitions differ markedly. Simply put, for Hinich and Munger ideology helps to explain the choices that voters make in elections, while for Goldstein ideology explains the policy choices that politicians make. Taken together the volumes identify three distinct functions of ideology: (1) ideology acting as some form of 'road map' for both voters and policy makers; (2) ideological 'images' on which voters, politicians and parties rely to distinguish one political party from another; and (3) ideology encased in institutions, within which it then affects the evolution of public policy. In this chapter, functions (1) and (2) are most relevant.

Turning to the second function, Hinich and Munger are not the first authors to find that parties provide 'images' or shorthand understandings for candidates' ideologies, but their work makes explicit that such images provide cues to voters about the policies that candidates are likely to adopt once in office:

> [The] investment in ideology as an asset, or brand name, suggests that ideological reputations can be thought of as cues. The cues serve as signals to voters about how certain types of outcomes are related to the choices that they and others make. . . . ideology provides voters with some means of comparing candidates and parties.[5]

The authors maintain that political parties – particularly new parties – cannot be successful without a 'coherent and understandable ideology.'[6] Indeed, parties do not organize themselves around policy positions, but rather around ideologies: 'Platforms are more than a point in an n-dimensional space; they become abstract, even ethical statements of what is good, and why.'[7] Policy positions of parties (and politicians) are constrained by their ideological reputations; too much movement diminishes the credibility of the party image.

Because much of the current political economy literature ignores ideology, it misses why political parties are not simply representatives of economic interests. Political parties must compete for the votes of individuals, who are not only concerned with their own (and their community's) economic well-being, but who must also gauge the reliability of candidates to deliver on their promises. The most viable way to gauge this reliability is by considering the ideological reputation of the candidate, and the simplest way to measure reputation is his party label. Thus, for Hinich and Munger, voters use the ideological positions of candidates 'as a cue, a predictor of the positions of the candidate once he takes office, based on *the particular correspondence or mapping* between ideology and policy' (emphasis added).[8] Goldstein too

sees ideology as serving the 'road map' function, but for her ideology constitutes the causal ideas which help politicians to select from a number of
possible policy options. Both volumes agree that ideology serves the road
map function precisely because of uncertainty, although it is policy makers
who experience this uncertainty in Goldstein's view, and voters who
experience this uncertainty in Hinich and Munger's view.

Functionally, then, ideology provides political actors with a means of dealing with uncertainty about what causes what or about which policies candidates will actually pursue once in office (road map function) and provides
parties with a tool to compete for voters' support (party image function). Our
next step is to explore the relational aspects of ideology. That is, what is the
nature of the relationships between (a) ideology and economic interests, and
(b) ideology, political parties and interest groups?

Ideology and economic interests, political parties and groups

Ideology and economic interests

Authors who stress the importance of ideology do not argue that ideology
replaces economic interests, but rather that ideology *intervenes* between economic interests and political outcomes (Figure 5.1, Arrow A). It is the nature
of this intervention that distinguishes these authors. For Goldstein, an array
of possible policy options exist from which policy makers select. Politicians,
seeking to maximize their own, their constituencies', and the nation's interests, rely on the road map function of ideology to guide their selection.
Politicians select convenient ideologies, with convenience defined as that
which serves their 'larger interests'.

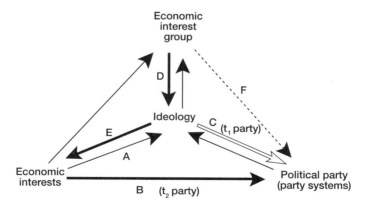

Figure 5.1 A model of ideology, interests and parties

Hinich and Munger make essentially the same point, but expose more starkly the legitimizing role that ideology can play:

> Ideologies . . . serve to legitimize what a group wants to do anyway, be it to maintain or overturn the status quo. The argument 'because it would be in our interest' is not sufficient to persuade the listener, so the terms of debate must derive from the ideological cleavage that organizes political discourse. . . . Political arguments will virtually always be made in terms of ideologies with contradictory implications for how the dispute should, in a normative sense, be resolved, not in terms of the self-interest of the disputants. . . . It may often occur that an ideology is popularized or adopted by a party or coalition, not because they are persuaded by the ideas advanced, but because of the interests advantaged.[9]

Clearly, the authors agree that ideology may serve as a fig-leaf for interests – yet ideology is not solely epiphenomenal. Once ideology is formed around interests, it may become self-sustaining, and thereby have its own independent effect. The independent effect of ideology may be felt through institutions (as Goldstein argues) or through the electoral process (as Hinich and Munger argue). I agree that ideology is not simply epiphenomenal, but will attempt to explore its 'independence' in terms of a causal model which includes interest groups and political parties.

Ideology, political parties and interest groups

Political parties reflect (or even represent) economic interests,[10] but party platforms must also exhibit some underlying ideological framework – i.e., parties contain both interests and ideology. At the same time, some economic interest groups *will also* contain an ideological element. To understand the relationship between ideology and party, one must explore both the balance between ideology and interests within parties, *and* the extent to which parties (as opposed to interest groups) dominate the ideological debate. I make two assertions, both of which have policy consequences. First, the balance between ideology and interests varies between parties (Arrows B and C). Second, while political parties may gain competitive advantage from ideology, so too can interest groups tap into ideological precepts to achieve political objectives (Arrow D).

Ideology and interests in parties

Sorting out the ideological and interests components of parties has long challenged party theorists. In the 1960s, the ideological age of fascism and communism was said to have come to an end.[11] Ideological cleavages, particularly those between and among political parties, were being replaced by interest group competition. The reason for this shift was that liberal democracy and the welfare state had solved many of the great struggles.[12] Having gained numerous concessions, the left had become 'domesticated' within the established political system,[13] and the policy debate shifted to specific details of policies where interest groups, rather than parties, were the main players. Political parties too were said to be undergoing a transformation. Whereas Duverger had emphasized the importance of leftist ideology in mass parties,[14] Kirchheimer argued that parties (and voters) were losing their 'ideological baggage', thereby giving rise to 'catch-all peoples' parties' which recruited voters from the whole population and formed close links with interest groups.[15]

Since the early 1980s, the end of ideology thesis appears to have lost its appeal among party theorists. At least two reasons might be given for this: its view of ideology was too narrowly focused on socialist ideology, and it failed to recognize that interests and ideology are often inextricably joined. Party systems may exhibit several ideological dimensions (not just socialism versus capitalism) – even as many as the seven identified by Lijphart.[16] For Lijphart, urban/rural is one of the major ideological dimensions in party systems. In this dimension (as we shall see), the inextricability of interests and ideology is particularly acute; indeed, the ideological debate over urban versus rural lifestyles can hardly avoid coinciding with conflicts of economic interests.[17]

Thus, party theory has more recently acknowledged that ideology and interests can *both* find expression within parties. This raises the question of whether the ideology/interests mix *varies* between parties, and from party system to party system – and if so, why? For Duverger, leftist ideology coincided with newer political parties that had originated outside the electoral and parliamentary framework. The extension of the popular suffrage gave rise to leftist parties, which evolved into 'mass parties'. In contrast, 'cadre' parties were older parties which had originated from the union of parliamentary groups and electoral committees, and were supported by a few influential individuals.[18] Because their origins dictated a top-down organizational structure, the newer leftist parties were *more ideologically coherent, more cohesive and centralized* than were the cadre parties.[19]

Duverger maintained that internally created parties constituted the greater number of political parties up to 1900, but after that time most parties were created outside parliament.[20] Yet, because he linked party age with party origin, he did not develop the independent effect of party age on party ideology. According to Hinich and Munger, ideology is much stronger in new parties than in old parties since new parties must define their party 'image' while old parties may to some extent rest on their laurels:

> When parties are first established, and (if successful) are growing, they must appeal to the beliefs and interests of prospective members

through an ideology. Once the party is established, the link to a specific ideology may grow more tenuous, and the party becomes a brokering agent among factions in the legislature.[21]

For these authors, 'a coherent and understandable ideology' is the key to political success, and without one new parties face 'a substantial barrier to entry'.[22]

So far, it may be seen that ideology *between parties* varies according both to party origin and to party age. Ideology may also vary by type of party system. Sartori has developed a typology of party systems that combines the number of relevant parties and a measure of 'ideological distance' based on the overall spread of the ideological spectrum within the polity, and the intensity of ideological competition.[23] He distinguishes four types of competitive party systems: the two-party system; systems of moderate, and polarized, pluralism; and a predominant-party system. Systems of polarized pluralism are defined as having (1) anti-system parties; (2) two oppositions to the government which are mutually exclusive (and therefore cannot join forces); (3) a centre that faces both a left and a right (and because the centre is occupied, this discourages movement towards the centre and encourages polarization of political opinion); (4) a large ideological space, where parties 'disagree not only on policies but also, and more importantly, on principles and fundamentals'; (5) extreme parties that 'are not destined to govern', limiting governing coalitions to centre-left or centre-right parties only; and (6) a pattern of parties that overpromise and then cannot deliver on these promises. Systems of polarized pluralism therefore exhibit far greater ideological conflict than do two-party and predominant-party systems, and still greater ideological conflict than systems of moderate pluralism. The point is that ideology can vary considerably across types of party systems, as well as among parties themselves. The ideology/interests balance is essentially twofold – one balance is internal to each party, and another reflects the whole of the party system.

Turning to the policy relevance of variations in the ideology/interests balances, I argue that the more ideological the parties in a polity are, the narrower the policy space will be. In general, others have agreed that ideologies constrain the political debate and the menu of choices available to politicians and parties. Hinich and Munger maintain that election campaigns limit the sorts of policies available to policy makers, since they cannot move from one position to another without damaging their credibility in future elections. Because the purpose of election campaigns is to convince voters that candidates are so committed to their position that they will pursue it once in office, ideological reputation is extremely important. Party affiliation informs voters of this ideological reputation. Once in office, the need to maintain credibility can also make compromise with proponents of opposing ideologies difficult, if not impossible. As Hinich and Munger explain, '[changing] position in the policy space requires changing position along the ideological dimension – saying, in effect, "I no longer believe what I once asserted and tried hard to persuade you was moral and good".'[24] If we assume that positions on the policy space correspond to positions on the ideological dimension, what then determines the spread of the ideological spectrum? If the polity resembles Sartori's polarized pluralism, the ideological distance will be high, but if it resembles a two-party system, the ideological distance will be low. Clearly, policy compromise is easier (i.e., has less damaging electoral repercussions) within a narrow ideological band that encourages gravitation towards the centre, and more difficult when the ideological spread is wide and encourages polarization towards the extremes. In other words, *policy compromise will be more constrained in a party system of polarized pluralism than in a two-party system* (Hypothesis 1a).

Party theory suggests a second way in which policy compromise is constrained. Duverger and his followers make clear that ideology is stronger in new parties than in old parties, since new parties must define and publicize their party 'image', while old parties enjoy an 'image' advantage (having already established their reputation). Thus as parties evolve, they become less wedded to ideology and more concerned with brokering the interests of members. Of course, this progression is ill-defined: I leave unspecified (as do others) what constitutes 'new' and 'old'; and I do not specify the function for the transformation from ideology to interests. I simply suggest that *polities with new parties will be more constrained in making policy compromises than polities with only old parties* (Hypothesis 1b).

Interest groups and ideology

Parties and interest groups both recruit members and aim to influence the direction of government policy. The difference between the two organizations is said to hinge on the unique functions of political parties, which include mobilizing the citizenry and formulating public policy.[25] Political parties have a third function – aggregating diverse interests – whereas interest groups articulate specific interests. Aggregation, unlike articulation, is likely to call into play ideology as the tie that binds. However, the distinction between parties as aggregators and interest groups as articulators is not ironclad. Broad interest groups can (with the assistance of ideology) aggregate interests better than political parties, 'and some parties rival interest groups in articulation. The narrower the social basis of a party's support, the more likely they are to articulate interests.'[26] Consequently, one should expect parties to differ in the extent to which they articulate interests. A fourth function of parties – recruiting leaders for public office – is said to be *the key feature* that separates them from interest groups: 'To qualify as a party, an organization must have as *one* of its goals that of placing its avowed representatives in government positions. . . . If an interest groups [*sic*] openly runs its own candidates, it becomes a party.'[27]

Hinich and Munger further distinguish parties from interest groups by arguing that parties are proponents of ideologies while interest groups are not:

> Pressure groups focus on only a few, or even a single, issue. There need be no overarching set of ethical norms or ideas; pressure groups want what they want because they want it. Party ideologies represent a recounting of the shared ideas of a coalition of interests, but pressure groups focus on an interest or idea that may have no relation to any other policy.[28]

The first and second functions of parties that distinguish them from interest groups (mobilizing the citizenry and formulating public policy) are unproblematic. However, an analysis of the third function (aggregating diverse interests) reveals an underlying fault in Hinich and Munger's claim that interest groups are non-ideological. As noted above, in some circumstances broad interest groups can utilize ideology in order to aggregate a number of diverse interests under their umbrella. Interest groups that have the ability to tap into ideologies have the ability to acquire supporters who do not share the particular interests of their members. Thus, not all interest groups are limited to focusing on one idea. To repeat, some interest groups *do* tap into ideologies (as collection of ideas), and when they do, they improve their chances of obtaining their political objectives (Arrow D). In the final section of this chapter, I shall illustrate this strategy, which I call 'nationalizing the interest'. Nationalizing the interest means that parochial interests are given the illusion (which may or may not be based in fact) that their political objective is (or should be) shared by the larger citizenry (or by a particular social or economic class). In the earlier discussion of ideology and interests, it was seen that however well groups pursue the interests of their members, they will not gain the support of the general public without some recourse to ideology. Ideology persuades the general public to support or to become indifferent to the groups' policy preferences; that is, it makes the policy goal palatable to non-members of the group. Ideology may appeal either to individuals' own values or to their own economic interests, or some mixture of the two. Moreover, *even the economic interests of individuals can be shaped by ideological persuasion*, particularly in so far as changes in policy (e.g., economic policy reform) make it difficult for individuals to calculate what their interests actually are (Arrow E). Bates and Krueger emphasize the importance of ideology in shaping individuals' interests:

> A result of this uncertainty [in economic policy reforms] is that people can be persuaded as to where their economic interests lie;

wide scope is thus left for rhetoric and persuasion. In such situations, advocates of particular economic theories or of ideological conceptions of how economies work can acquire influence. . . . Under conditions of uncertainty, people's beliefs of where their economic interests lie can be created and organized by political activists; rather than shaping events, notions of self-interest are instead themselves shaped and formed. In pursuing their economic interests, people act in response to ideology.[29]

Consider, for example, contemporary farmers groups that seek to obtain or retain trade protection. Appeals to the public are phrased in terms of the broader societal welfare: 'self-sufficiency in agriculture is necessary for the nation's security';[30] 'the family farm must be protected in order to preserve traditional rural values' and/or 'the countryside'; and 'agriculture must be protected as an environmentally friendly "green" industry.'[31] This strategy is precisely the same as that used by parties that seek to enlarge their membership.

Two other elements underpin the ideological capacity of interest groups – good leadership and organization – but space prohibits their discussion here.

Finally, the key function that most party theorists agree separates parties from interest groups is that the former run their own candidates for public office, while the latter do not. While this rule holds in general, it may become blurred somewhat where interest groups embark upon quasi-electoral activities (Arrow F).

The model

The discussion in the previous section is summarized graphically in Figure 5.1. At this stage in developing the model, I do not indicate signs for each of the arrows. To do so would demand a more precise theoretical framework than the one offered in this paper. It should also be noted that because the model is non-recursive (i.e., bidirectional causality is hypothesized between ideology and economic interests, interest groups, and political parties), any attempt to estimate it properly would be complex. The model is therefore suggestive and informal. Arrows A through F have been discussed in the previous section. Arrow A refers to ideology as an intervening variable between economic interests and political outcomes (where political outcomes can refer to political organizations or to public policy: see pp. 65–66). Arrows B and C reflect the contribution of economic interests and ideology respectively to parties and party systems. As noted earlier, the effects of interest and ideology can vary both from party to party and by type of party system. New parties tend to be more ideological than old parties. Hence, Arrow C is accompanied by a 't_1 party' to indicate a within-party balance that favours ideology, while Arrow B is accompanied by a 't_2 party' to indicate a within-party balance that favours interests (see pp. 66–69). Hypotheses 1a and 1b refer to Arrow C. Arrow D captures the ability of *some* interest groups to tap into an idea or ideology which allows them to 'nationalize the interest' of the group. In times of uncertainty – particularly surrounding economic policy reform – interest groups (and, though less likely, political parties) may even use ideology to shape the economic interests of individuals. This possibility is given as Arrow E (see pp. 67–71). Arrow F refers to a small number of instances in which interest group activity can affect political parties directly or may help to shape the rules of the electoral system. This can give these groups an advantage beyond the strength of interests or ideology. However, because this is certainly not the norm, Arrow F is represented with a broken line. Unmarked arrows are posited for the effect of ideology on groups, the effect of parties on ideology, and the effect of interests on interest groups. Exploration of these effects lies beyond the scope of this paper. The unmarked causal arrows are included for heuristic value only.

Taken as a group, Arrows B, D and E hint at a second hypothesis. *When any of these conditions hold, economic interests will be more successful in obtaining their political objective(s): (1) interest groups 'nationalize the interest', (2) ideology shapes and forms notions of self-interest, or (3) political parties represent economic interests over ideology* (Hypothesis 2). That is, when the thick solid arrows dominate the model, economic interests will, *ceteris paribus*, more likely achieve their desired policy goal.

Case studies (in brief)

If political economy has a folklore, a set of historic 'tales' with which virtually all readers are expected to be familiar, then Britain's repeal of the Corn Laws in 1846 and Germany's 'marriage of iron and rye' (from 1879 to the First World War) are central to its folklore. It is in the telling of the tales, however, that political economists reveal their theoretical leanings. Political economists ('internationalists') who emphasize the constraints and opportunities afforded by the international economic structure attribute Britain's unilateral trade liberalization to its 'hegemony' and/or its early industrialization.[32] For the internationalists, Britain is a unique case, comparable only to the single other post-industrial hegemon – the USA after the Second World War. For other political economists ('comparativists'), Germany is an equally important anomaly.[33] The prevailing historiography maintains that the coalition of high tariffs for agriculture and industry helped to preserve traditional authoritarian values, to perpetuate political backwardness of the bourgeoisie, and eventually to give rise to fascism. Thus, for the internationalists, Britain's dominant position in the international economic structure gave rise to unilateral liberalization, whereas for the comparativists, Germany's tradition of authoritarianism, coupled with a politically weak, underdeveloped industrial class, paved the way for a coalition of reactionary interests, intent on protecting their economic interests with high tariffs. Much is given to *contrasting* Britain with Germany, or each country with other country cases (e.g., hegemons with small/medium states, authoritarian with democratic regimes). Not much is given to *comparing* Britain with Germany in order to locate similar patterns and processes. Below I seek to *compare* and *contrast* the British and German cases, giving special attention to what both internationalists and recent comparative political economists have virtually ignored – the effect of ideology on interests and political organizations.

The repeal of the Corn Laws

Apart from the internationalists, other authors have examined the role of political parties,[34] interests and interest groups,[35] and liberal economic ideology[36] in the repeal of the Corn Laws. However, none of these works models explicitly the links between interests, parties *and* ideology. What follows is a cursory overview of how Hypothesis 2 applies to the British case. (Discussion of Hypotheses 1a and 1b will follow the German case.)[37]

According to party theorists, the Conservative and Liberal parties of the 1830s/1840s were *cadre* parties, or groupings of notables, and the real impetus for *modern* parties arose with the extension of the suffrage in 1867 and 1884. Thus, in 1846, the parties were internally created and faced no new (mass) parties in what approximated a two-party system. Both exhibited weak organization and cohesiveness, and neither had a coherent ideological grounding.[38]

The Anti-Corn Law League was formed in 1838 by the Manchester textile manufacturers to push for the repeal of protection for British agriculture. Historians refer to the League as 'the most impressive of nineteenth-century pressure groups, which exercised a distinct influence on the repeal of the Corn Laws.'[39] Its centralized administration and 'formidable propaganda apparatus' has earned it the name, the 'league machine'.[40] A key feature of the League's operational strategy was its nationwide propaganda and electoral registration campaign.[41] After electoral losses in 1841–2, the League focused on returning a pro-free trade majority in the anticipated general parliamentary election of 1848. Its strategy included manipulating the voter registers, by adding as many free traders and deleting as many protectionists as possible (through objections at the annual revisions of the registers). The League exploited a loophole in the 1832 Electoral Reform Act, the forty-shilling county property qualification, to create several thousand new free-trade voters in county constituencies with large urban electorates, constituencies whose representation was increased by the Reform Act. While the 40s. qualification had existed since 1430, the increase in county seats from 188 to 253 (from 29 per cent to 38 per cent of total seats) magnified the importance of this overlooked 'loophole' in the 1832 Act.

Across the country the League combined its voter registration campaign with a massive propaganda effort. As League agents distributed propaganda tracts to every elector in 24 county divisions and 187 boroughs, these agents submitted to League headquarters extensive reports on the electorate in their districts. These reports provided a comprehensive picture of the electoral scene throughout England, thereby allowing the League much greater knowledge of, and control over, electoral districts than either the Conservatives or Liberals possessed 'with their more limited and local organization'.[42] This provided the League with an extensive database from which it could inflict political pressure on MPs seeking re-election.

This brief description of the activities of the League goes some way to meeting conditions (1) and (2) of Hypothesis 2. The explicit strategy of the League was not limited to 'nationalizing the interest' by creating a national network of free trade interests (condition (1)). It also sought to articulate a well-defined liberal ideology (the 'Manchester School') through publishing pamphlets and an extensive national lecture series. It is difficult to provide unambiguous evidence of the League having actually *shaped* notions of self-interest among the general public through its free-trade propaganda campaign. It is equally difficult to distinguish between the political and the ideological effects of the League's activities on MPs. What is *not* difficult to see is that the League (1) dominated the ideological vacuum left by the political parties, persuading doubters either through appeals to their interests or ideological argument, and (2) recognized the potential of the 1832 Reform Act in a way that was beyond the organizational capacity of either party. Moreover, the League even aimed to run its own candidates for office, although in the end, repeal pre-empted the general election. The distinction between the League and the parties is therefore blurred by its electoral activities, which illustrates the atypical bridge that can occur between interest group and party (Arrow F).

The marriage of iron and rye

Germany's 'marriage of iron and rye' refers to a series of trade policies that occurred over several decades (from 1879 through approximately the First World War). The 'marriage' was a coalition of diverse interests, in which heavy industry and the large agricultural estate owners of east Elbian Prussia (the Junkers) coalesced around a tariff policy for both industrial and agricultural imports.

Overview

In the early 1870s rapid advances in transportation coupled with increased competition in world grain markets meant that German Junkers, who were formerly net exporters of grain, became import-competing producers.[43] At about the same time, the Great Depression squeezed the profitability of industrial firms.[44] Because many of these firms were newly created, or had expanded during the previous boom years, the problem of excess capacity in the domestic market was severe – and made worse with the integration into the Zollverein of the Alsace-Lorraine iron, steel and cotton-spinning industries. Reductions in iron and steel tariffs (1873) and the complete abolition of the pig iron tariff in 1877 helped to mobilize heavy industry against Germany's free-trade orientation. Grain producers and heavy industrialists, heretofore suspicious adversaries, converged upon a common interest in protection. The tariff of 1879 enacted this policy shift into legislation.

In the 1880s agricultural tariffs were raised twice, while industrial tariffs remained virtually constant. By the early 1890s, real and potential retaliation from Germany's trading partners convinced German industry of the need to regain (and expand) export markets. Between 1891 and 1894, Chancellor Bismarck's successor, Caprivi, negotiated numerous foreign trade agreements that exchanged lower German tariffs on agriculture for reductions in foreign tariffs on German industrial goods. As Caprivi's treaties approached their expiration, Chancellor Bülow introduced the 'general tariff' in 1902, thereby signalling a resumption of high agricultural tariffs.[45]

Discussion

Most historians of Imperial Germany accept that the 1879 tariff marked a watershed in Imperial German politics. Political party ideology, it is argued, gave way to pressure group politics. Elsewhere I test this proposition and find partial support for the ideology-to-interests thesis.[46] For the period 1879 to 1902, roll-call votes in the Reichstag reveal that ideology mattered more for the leftist parties – the Social Democrats and Left Liberals – than for the Conservatives, the National Liberals, or the Centre. Yet this interpretation oversimplifies ideology within each party, and particularly within the Conservatives.

Conservativism underwent a distinct ebb and flow in balancing ideology and interests. Whereas 'old' German conservatism was ideological in orientation, new conservatism (organized in 1876 as the *Deutsch-Konservative Partei*) represented the economic interests of the land-owning aristocracy.[47] By the early 1890s, under threat from the Caprivi trade reforms, militant Prussian landowners created an interest group, the *Bund der Landwirte*. Rather than competing with the Conservative Party, the *Bund* strengthened it by broadening the electoral support base for conservatism, particularly among the smaller proprietors and lower middle classes. The *Bund* appealed to smaller farmers with a new ideology of *völkish* nationalism, thereby enveloping the protectionist interests of the Prussian landowners into a more national conservative movement.

The *Bund* undoubtedly engaged in a strategy of 'nationalizing the interest' of agricultural protection, particularly among the peasant farmers. Historians disagree on how far conservative ideology *shaped* the interests of the peasant farmers, and notably whether the Junkers benefited from agricultural protection (through the perpetuation of feudalism) at the expense of the peasant farmers, or whether the latter, as producers primarily of livestock (and therefore consumers of grain for feed), obtained some benefit as well.[48] The traditional interpretation, focusing on Junker benefits, cannot explain why peasant farmers generally supported agricultural protection, except to lament that they were duped into regarding the large landowners as spokesmen for the whole of agriculture.[49] Various studies have given more credit to the rationality of peasant farmers, arguing that they gained from restrictions on the import of livestock, and from grain tariffs themselves.[50]

The three conditions of Hypothesis 2 are, on the whole, supported by the German case. The *Bund* clearly sought to nationalize the interest of German agriculture, and may even have succeeded in shaping the economic interests of the peasant farmers. The third condition – that parties represent economic interests over ideology – can be said to apply fairly well to the Conservatives, less well to the Centre,[51] and only marginally to the liberals and leftist parties.[52]

Central to Hypotheses 1a and 1b is whether a party system exhibits low or high ideology. Recall that systems of polarized pluralism (e.g., Germany) will exhibit high ideology, while a two-party system (e.g., Britain) is much less ideological. While Sartori and other party theorists have debated how closely the British system of the 1840s fits the two-party type, and have differed on whether Germany of the late nineteenth century more closely resembles a system of moderate as opposed to polarized pluralism, sufficient agreement exists among historians to warrant these categorizations. For Britain, while repeal of the Corn Laws had a disastrous effect on the Conservative party (and, indeed, on Peel himself), Peel was nevertheless able to enact the legislation. One reason why the 'Peelites' were able to moderate their views on protection was that, within a two-party system, gravitation towards the centre was a natural tendency. Contrast this with the German case, where the centre was already occupied by the Catholic Centre party, and anti-system factions in both the SPD (Social Democratic party) and the new Conservatism of the 1890s exacerbated tensions between the right and left thereby creating an even larger ideological space. Caprivi's limited attempt at compromise served only to widen the distance between left and right. Sustainable policy compromise on freer trade was simply not possible in this political environment.

While Hypothesis 1a refers to party systems, Hypothesis 1b highlights certain types of parties within a system. To reiterate, new parties are more ideological than old parties because they must define their party 'image' to the electorate. A clear, well-articulated ideology is essential for a party's 'image', and only after this has been established over time does a party have the 'luxury' of serving as a brokering agent between various interests. But, Britain had no new parties while Germany did. The British Conservative and Liberal parties did not face the same ideological challenge as did the German Conservative party. Neither British party was forced to refine and strengthen the ideology underpinning its 'image' and therefore neither was forced to move away from the centre of the ideological spectrum. While the League dominated the ideological debate, it did so as a pressure group with one policy goal in mind. And once that goal – repeal – was obtained, the League disbanded. The SPD in Germany offered an ideological challenge of a different magnitude – one that extended across virtually all of the government's social and economic policies. Free trade was but one of many policies pursued by the SPD. As a new party, the SPD sought to define its party image by emphasizing the ideological contrast (and conflict) with the Conservatives (and its coalitional partners). The Anti-Socialist Legislation of 1878–90 temporarily constrained this conflict but, with the expiration of this legislation, the conflict deepened and broadened. Polarization could hardly be avoided under these conditions, once again making policy compromise unattainable.

Conclusion

This chapter has two essential points: (1) the more weight that is given to ideology within parties and party systems, the more difficult policy compromise will be between parties; and (2) the more embedded interests are within parties and ideology within (an) interest group(s), the greater the likelihood that economic interests – whether protectionist or free-trade – will be successful in their policy objective. This is not to diminish the importance of other factors that condition policy compromise between parties. Also, the success or failure of interest groups does not hinge on ideology alone. Certainly, leadership and organization matter; elsewhere I show that industry and export sector concentration, and the weakness of opposing interests, contribute to success.[53] Ideology should be seen not as a residual category for that which cannot be accounted for by interests, but rather as a 'turbo thruster' that creates political momentum and leverage that is not possible through interests alone.

If ideology provides political actors with extra leverage, it is critical to know which set of actors controls the dominant ideology (or ideologies) – political parties or interest groups. In Britain, the two political parties were only weakly ideological, thereby making the Peelites' compromise (and the Conservative party's disintegration) easier. On the other hand, the League embraced a clear and well-defined ideological message, which could only increase its chances of success. Arguably, the League so mastered the ideological debate that it was able to use liberal free-trade ideology to shape the interests of the electorate and politicians alike.

In Germany, socialism, Bismarck's Kulturkampf, and a reactionary landed aristocracy provided the ideological intensity conducive to polarized pluralism. In this climate of high ideology, policy compromise was inevitably difficult. This is not to say that interests were unimportant, since they were certainly deeply embedded in the older Conservative party. Here, it is useful to bear in mind the distinction between the old, less ideological parties (Conservatives, National Liberals) and the new, highly ideological parties (especially the SPD). The interesting question is, how did old parties meet the ideological challenge of newer parties? While the Anti-Socialist Legislation restricted the activities of the SPD, the socialist ideological challenge was contained. However, with the expiration of this legislation, the Conservatives were confronted with a growing ideological (and electoral) challenge from the left. The Junkers, meanwhile, faced the immediate economic setback of lessened trade protection. The challenge to the Conservatives was, therefore, both ideological and economic – and the Conservative party was ill-equipped to meet either challenge. It was the *Bund* that provided the ideological cohesion, the leadership and the organization to shift the ideology/interests balance within the Conservative party towards a new, more nationalistic ideology, thereby giving conservatism a broader base of support, and to re-enact high tariffs for agriculture. In sum, the German case reveals that the ideology/interests balance varied from party to party, as well as within the Conservative party over time. Thus, to ascertain whether interests were more or less embedded in parties requires careful dissection. What is far from ambiguous is that ideology was firmly embedded in the *Bund*, giving this pressure group considerable leverage in regaining high tariffs for German agriculture.

Notes

1 In political economy: Judith Goldstein, *Ideas, Interests, and American Trade Policy* (Ithaca, NY: Cornell University Press, 1993); Ngaire Woods, 'Economic Ideas and International Relations: Beyond Rational Neglect', *International Studies Quarterly* 39, 2 (June 1995): 161–80; Christopher Hood, *Explaining Economic Policy Reversals* (Buckingham: Open University Press, 1994); Peter A. Hall (ed.) *The Political Power of Economic Ideas: Keynesianism across Nations* (Princeton, NJ: Princeton University Press, 1989); Kathryn Sikkink, *Ideas and Institutions: Developmentalism in Brazil and Argentina* (Ithaca, NY: Cornell University Press, 1991); John Kurt Jacobsen, 'Much Ado About Ideas: The Cognitive Factor in Economic Policy,' *World Politics* 47, 2 (January 1995): 283–310.

The revival of ideology also extends to the foreign policy, electoral choice, and legislative voting literatures: Judith Goldstein and Robert O. Keohane (eds) *Ideas and Foreign Policy: Beliefs, Institutions, and Political Change* (Ithaca, NY: Cornell University Press, 1993); Melvin J. Hinich and Michael C. Munger, *Ideology and the Theory of Political Choice* (Ann Arbor: University of Michigan Press, 1994); James M. McCormick and Michael Black, 'Ideology and Senate Voting On the Panama Canal Treaties', *Legislative Studies Quarterly* VIII, 1 (February 1983): 45–63; Lawrence Silverman, 'The Ideological Mediation of Party-political Responses

INTERESTS, IDEOLOGY AND POLITICS

to Social Change', *European Journal of Political Research* 13 (1985): 69–93; Kevin

B. Grier (ed.) *Public Choice: Empirical Studies of Ideology and Representation in American Politics (Special Issue)* 76, 1–2 (June 1993).

2 Hinich and Munger, op. cit., p. 236.
3 Ibid.
4 Woods, op. cit., 163.
5 Hinich and Munger, op. cit., pp. 99–100.
6 Ibid., p. 61.
7 Ibid., p. 3.
8 Ibid., pp. 101–2.
9 Hinich and Munger, op. cit., pp. 192, 63.
10 Giovanni Sartori, 'The Sociology of Parties: A Critical Review', [1968] reprinted in Peter Mair (ed.) *The West European Party System* (Oxford: Oxford University Press, 1990).
11 Daniel Bell, *The End of Ideology* (New York: Free Press, 1960); Chaim I. Waxman (ed.) *The End of Ideology Debate* (New York: Funk and Wagnalls, 1968).
12 See Peter Mair (ed.) 'Introduction', *The West European Party System* (Oxford: Oxford University Press, 1990).
13 Seymour Martin Lipset and Stein Rokkan, 'Cleavage Structures, Party Systems, and Voter Alignments', [1967] reprinted in Mair, op. cit., p. 110.
14 Maurice Duverger, *Political Parties: Their Organization and Activity in the Modern State*, 2nd edn (London: Methuen, 1961).
15 Otto Kirchheimer, 'The Catch-All Party' [1966] reprinted in Mair, op. cit., pp. 50–60.
16 Arend Lijphart, 'Dimensions of Ideology in European Party Systems' in Mair, op. cit., pp. 253–65.
17 Ibid., p. 262.
18 Duverger, op. cit., p. 63.
19 Joseph LaPalombara and Myron Weiner, 'The Origin of Political Parties' in Mair, op. cit., pp. 25–30.
20 Duverger, op. cit., p. xxxvi. He notes the exception, however, of countries new to democracy, where internally created parties would still be the rule.
21 Hinich and Munger, op. cit., p. 83.
22 Ibid. The authors qualify this point by noting that 'the party may . . . come into existence with only the simplest of doctrinal commitments, and then its ideology [evolves] into a more complete set of ideas', pp. 85–6.
23 Giovanni Sartori, 'A Typology of Party Systems' in Mair, op. cit., pp. 332–4.
24 Hinich and Munger, op. cit., p. 75.
25 Peter Mair, op. cit.; Anthony King, 'Political Parties in Western Democracies: Some Sceptical Reflections', *Polity* 2, 2 (1969): 111–41.
26 Kenneth Janda, 'Comparative Political Parties: Research and Theory', in Ada W. Finifter (ed.) *Political Science: The State of the Discipline II* (Washington, DC: American Political Science Association, 1993), p. 170 (paraphrasing Richard Jankowski).
27 Ibid., p. 166.
28 Hinich and Munger, op. cit., p. 92.
29 Robert H. Bates and Anne O. Krueger, 'Generalizations Arising from the Country Studies', in Robert H. Bates and Anne O. Krueger (eds) *Political and Economic Interactions in Economic Policy Reform: Evidence from Eight Countries* (Oxford: Basil Blackwell, 1993), p. 456.
30 L. Alan Winters, 'Digging for Victory: Agricultural Policy and National Security', *The World Economy* 13, 2 (June 1990): 170–90; Fred J. Ruppel and Earl D.

79

Kellogg (eds) *National and Regional Self-Sufficiency Goals* (London: Lynne Rienner, 1991).

31 Kym Anderson, 'Agricultural Trade Liberalization and the Environment: A Global Perspective', *The World Economy* 15, 1 (January 1992): 153–72.

32 Cheryl Schonhardt-Bailey, 'Introduction', *The Rise of Free Trade* (in four volumes) (London: Routledge, 1997), and articles in vol. 4.

33 Alexander Gerschenkron, *Bread and Democracy in Germany* (Berkeley: University of California Press, 1943); Alexander Gerschenkron, *Economic Backwardness in Historical Perspective* (Cambridge, MA: Harvard University Press, 1962); Ronald Rogowski, *Commerce and Coalitions: How Trade Affects Domestic Alignments* (Princeton, NJ: Princeton University Press, 1989).

34 W.O. Aydelotte, 'The Disintegration of the Conservative Party in the 1840s: A Study of Political Attitudes', in W.O. Aydelotte, A.G. Bogue and R. Fogel (eds) *The Dimension of Quantitative Research in History* (Princeton, NJ: Princeton University Press, 1972); Daniel Verdier, 'Between Party and Faction: The Politics Behind the Repeal of the Corn Laws', in Schonhardt-Bailey, op. cit.

35 See articles in Schonhardt-Bailey, op. cit., vol. 4, section I. a. 'In Whose Interests?'.

36 See articles in Schonhardt-Bailey, op. cit., vol. 4, section I. b. 'Ideology, Individual Leadership, and the State'.

37 For further details, see Cheryl Schonhardt-Bailey, *The Strategic Use of Ideas: Nationalizing the Interest in the Nineteenth Century* (forthcoming).

38 Ian Newbould, 'Whiggery and the Growth of Party 1830–1841: Organization and the Challenge of Reform', *Parliamentary History* 4 (1985): 137–56; Norman Gash, 'The Organization of the Conservative Party, 1832–1846, Part 1: The Parliamentary Organization', *Parliamentary History* 1 (1982): 137–59.

39 Anthony Howe, *The Cotton Masters, 1830–1860* (Oxford: Oxford University Press, 1984).

40 Norman McCord, *The Anti-Corn Law League, 1838–1846* (London: George Allen & Unwin, 1958), p. 187.

41 Cheryl Schonhardt-Bailey, 'A Model of Trade Policy Liberalization: Looking Inside the British "Hegemon" of the Nineteenth Century', Ph.D. diss., University of California, Los Angeles (1991), chapters 1 and 5.

42 McCord, op. cit., pp. 147–50.

43 Ivo Nikolai Lambi, *Free Trade and Protection in Germany 1868–1879* (Wiesbaden: Franz Steiner Verlag GMBH, 1963).

44 David Blackbourn, 'The Discrete Charm of the Bourgeoisie: Reappraising German History in the Nineteenth Century', in David Blackbourn and Geoff Eley (eds) *The Peculiarities of German History* (Oxford: Oxford University Press, 1984); Martin Kitchen, *The Political Economy of Germany 1815–1914* (London: Croom Helm, 1978); Hans Rosenberg, *Grosse Depression und Bismarchzeit* (Berlin, 1967).

45 Percy Ashley, *Modern Tariff History: Germany–United States–France* (London: John Murray, 1920), p. 86.

46 'Parties and Interests in the "Marriage of Iron and Rye"', *British Journal of Political Science* (April 1998).

47 Robert M. Berdahl, 'Conservative Politics and Aristocratic Landholders in Bismarckian Germany', *Journal of Modern History* 44 (1972): 20; Hans-Jurgen Puhle, 'Conservatism in Modern German History', *Journal of Contemporary History* 13 (1978): 698.

48 Gerschenkron, *Bread* op. cit., and *Economic* op. cit.; Barrington Moore, *Social Origins of Dictatorship and Democracy* (Boston, MA: Beacon Press, 1966).

49 For a more nuanced interpretation see David Abraham, *The Collapse of the Weimar*

Republic: Political Economy and Crisis (Princeton, NJ: Princeton University Press, 1981), p. 65; Hans-Jurgen Puhle, 'Lords and Peasants in the Kaiserreich', in Robert G. Moeller (ed.) *Peasants and Lords in Modern Germany: Recent Studies in Agricultural History* (Winchester: Allen & Unwin, 1986), p. 99.

50 James C. Hunt, 'Peasants, Grain Tariffs, and Meat Quotas: Imperial German Protectionism Reexamined', *Central European History* 7 (1974): 311–31; Robert G. Moeller, 'Peasants and Tariffs in the *Kaiserreich*: How Backward were the *Bauern?*', *Agricultural History* 55 (1981): 370–84; Steven B. Webb, 'Agricultural Protection in Wilhelminian Germany: Forging an Empire with Pork and Rye', *Journal of Economic History* XLII (1982): 309–26.

51 The Centre was a Catholic party, but since farmers were overrepresented in the Catholic population, the party tended to favour the interests of agriculture. Gerhard A. Ritter, 'The Social Bases of the German Political Parties, 1867–1920', in Karl Rohe (ed.) *Elections, Parties and Political Traditions: Social Foundations of German Parties and Party Systems, 1867–1987* (Oxford: Berg, 1990), p. 35.

52 The National Liberal party, which was permanently weakened in the late 1870s after losing its position as the 'government party', split on the question of tariffs as a result of the internal divide between light and heavy industries (Lambi, *Free Trade*, op. cit., pp. 209–11). Its leaders subsequently refused to include tariff policy as a party matter. Many authors have noted that the National Liberals (and to some extent all liberal parties) lacked both a distinctive social profile and a regional identity: Dieter Langewiesche, 'German Liberalism in the Second Empire, 1871–1914', in Konrad H. Jarausch and Larry Eugene Jones (eds) *In Search of a Liberal Germany* (Oxford: Berg, 1990); Ritter, op. cit.; James J. Sheehan, *German Liberalism in the Nineteenth Century* (Chicago: University of Chicago Press, 1978), pp. 160–241. This coincided with the National Liberals' claim to speak for the nation rather than for any particular group, but it also meant that the liberals were unable to consolidate any electoral strongholds (in contrast to, say, the Centre party, which controlled the Catholic rural districts, and the Conservatives, who held the agricultural regions east of the Elbe). Socio-economic and regional diversity thereby weakened the political party 'focus' of liberalism: Frank B. Tipton, *Regional Variations in the Economic Development of Germany During the Nineteenth Century* (Middletown, CT: Wesleyan University Press, 1976), p. 141.

53 Schonhardt-Bailey, *Rise*, op. cit., vol. 4.

6

COMMENTS ON KINEALY AND SCHONHARDT-BAILEY

Boyd Hilton

Dr Schonhardt-Bailey has constructed an interesting model relating pressure groups to political parties and ideologies in two important cases: the culmination of Britain's gradual movement towards free trade in 1846 and Germany's switch to protection in 1879. However, this necessarily brief comment will be confined to the point of overlap between her chapter and that of Dr Kinealy, i.e. the long-vexed question as to which was the dominant motive behind the decision to repeal the British Corn Laws in 1846: pressure from material interests, ideological conviction, executive pragmatism, or political manoeuvre.

Schonhardt-Bailey argues for a combination of pressure and conviction. In her view the vital contribution was that of the Anti-Corn Law League, which was all the more powerful because the Liberals and Conservatives were merely *'cadre* parties, or groupings of notables', rather than mass parties. As she points out, recent decades had seen a dramatic hardening of two-party loyalties, within national and local electorates as well as among MPs, and the resulting sense of partisan rivalry between groups which were themselves divided created a situation which (to paraphrase E.P. Thompson) might be described as 'a party system without party'. This was a situation in which the Anti-Corn Law League could thrive as a determined single-issue pressure group.

Schonhardt-Bailey is right to emphasize the League's success in registering 40s. borough freeholders in county seats, although Cresap Moore, John Prest, John Cannon, Michael Brock, and others would dispute her view that the borough freeholder 'loophole' has been 'overlooked' by previous historians. She is also right to point out that repeal 'pre-empted' a general election and that the League was 'disbanded' once its goal had been achieved, single-issue groups being always vulnerable to success. However, she might also have considered the possibility that these facts make a case for seeing repeal as a political manoeuvre. According to Prest, for example, Peel was afraid that the League's electoral tactics would benefit the Liberals at the polls, and so decided to get rid of the League before the next election, the only sure way to get rid of it being to give it what it wanted (John Prest, *Politics in the Age of*

Cobden, London, Macmillan, 1977, pp. 72–134). If so, 1846 mirrors 1829, when Peel was so alarmed by the Catholic Association's ability to establish a rival system of executive authority in Ireland that he resolved to get rid of it, partly by official proscription but mainly again by giving it what it wanted – i.e. emancipation.

More generally, Schonhardt-Bailey claims that, thanks to its well-honed and well-publicized ideology, the League 'dominated the ideological vacuum left by the political parties.' Other historians have argued that, far from there having been a vacuum there was a very real ideological division, but that it existed inside the two coalition parties rather than between them (Peter Mandler, *Aristocratic Government in the Age of Reform: Whigs and Liberals*, Oxford, Clarendon Press, 1990, *passim*; Boyd Hilton, *The Age of Atonement*, Oxford, Clarendon Press, 1988, pp. 203–51). Broadly this division pitted a social market, non-interventionist, individualist, and mechanical view of society against a more paternalist, interventionist, and organic view of society.

Schonhardt-Bailey might also have taken into account the possibility that Peel was motivated by a different ideology from that of the League. It can certainly be argued that repeal was a continuation of previous social-market policy positions adopted by him – for example, the return to gold (1819), withholding short-term relief to businesses (1826), his support for the new Poor Law (1834), the switch from indirect to direct taxation (1842), and the Bank of England charter (1844) – in other words, that Peel's essential market economy instincts survived from the 1820s rather than that they resulted from a conversion during the 1840s. This is important because, if Peel was converted to free-market economics in the 1840s, then – in so far as he was motivated by an ideology of free trade at all – it was likely to be that version of the ideology which the League promoted and which was conventional wisdom in the 1840s: i.e. an expansionist optimism which envisaged a high-wage economy and a growth in the size of the national cake, any short-term sufferings caused by the policy being alleviated in the long run by the diffusion of economic benefits downwards. As Lord Blake put it, in a comparison of Peel and Thatcher,

> Peel believed in an enterprise culture. He thought that if the barriers on trade were removed the increased wealth of the commercial and business classes would have a 'trickle-down effect' and benefit all classes. The role of the state should be minimised. His free trade policies laid the foundations of the prosperity which made Britain the workshop of the world.
>
> (*The Times*, 30 November 1990).

No doubt the League and many of the MPs who voted for repeal in 1846 were motivated by such views, but hardly Peel. He wished to retain Britain's place as the *warehouse* and *money market* of the world, and he also saw the need to sustain in employment those manufacturing operatives who were already in being, but he hardly sought deliberately to advance manufacturing progress or to make Britain even more of an industrial workshop. 'We have been working too fast, building too fast, importing too fast', he wrote in 1826, but, given that by 1842 'our lot is cast and we cannot recede', the country could not now 'with safety retrograde in manufactures'. His fiscal policy was therefore directed towards making Britain, not the high-wage economy of the Cobdenites, but 'a cheap place for living'. This hardly amounted to a policy for economic growth, and the tight fiduciary limits to note issue which were imposed by the Bank Charter Act of 1844 were intended to be highly restrictive. If that Act had also succeeded (as Peel intended) in restricting the money supply as well as the supply of banknotes, then there could have been no mid-Victorian boom, which is why the Act was opposed by Cobden, who typically called for the removal of all restrictions on banking.

Norman Gash has argued that to depict Peel as a supporter of a static economy 'seems to defy common sense'. Well, it certainly defies that twentieth-century common sense in which Gash is steeped, and it also defied the Cobdenite common sense of the 1840s. This is why it is important to realize (as Kinealy does) that Peel's free-market instincts dated from the Huskissonite tradition of the 1820s. It follows that – in so far as he was motivated by ideology at all – it was by an earlier version of free-market economics in which a deep Malthusian pessimism as to the finite limits of the Earth's natural resources ruled out any visions of economic growth. For Peel, free-market or social-market economics was all about creating, not a growth-oriented or simple opportunity society but a *just* society, in which personal merit would be naturally rewarded, in which 'industry, sobriety, honesty, and intelligence' would cause the poor to rise, while 'idleness, profligacy, and vice' would cause the rich to fall. In such a society of snakes and ladders, when human beings encountered economic distress ('sufferings as difficult to remedy as they are deserved'), they could at least console themselves with the thought that such sufferings were natural, part of the 'dispensations of providence'.

Providence plays a leading role in Kinealy's account of British responses to the Irish famine. This is certainly a correct emphasis, though it is important to distinguish between those like Trevelyan (who believed that the famine was directed at the Irish for being too feckless) and those like Gladstone (who believed that it was directed at the English for being too materially successful). In other words, between those who saw the famine as a punishment and those who saw it as a warning of future judgment. For Gladstone, the 'calamity legibly divine' pointed directly to repeal of the Corn Laws, if only as an act of atonement by a hitherto selfish aristocracy, but for Peel – more of a believer in the 'secondary causes' of providence – the connection between famine and repeal was much more complex.

Kinealy lends her authority to what is now a well-established consensus that the famine was no more than an occasion for repeal and was certainly not intended as a cure. Apart from anything else, as she acutely points out, 'there was no famine in Ireland in 1845.' The potato blight provided Peel with an emotional pretext for overturning his implicit commitment to agricultural protection at the previous general election, but Corn Law repeal could not do anything to help the starving Irish, and ministers knew it. If Peel had wished to help Ireland in the immediate term he would have suspended the operation of the market by interdicting exports of corn from that country. (Indeed, it is interesting to speculate that he might possibly have done just that if he, and not the Whigs, had been in office in 1847–8.)

However, Kinealy's explanation of Peel's motives are based not so much on ideology (providential or otherwise) as on executive pragmatism. Peel's long-term project (towards which repeal was a first step) was to wean Ireland off the potato and to make the landlord–tenant structure of wheat farming more efficient. The latter was widely regarded as the glory of English agriculture, and as so much finer than the serf or peasant-based agriculture of most of Europe, being economically efficient while at the same time creating political and social responsibility and deference.

This argument – an extension to Ireland of D.C. Moore's thesis that repeal was intended to promote 'high farming' – seems all the more compelling when seen in relation to Peel's previous act of political apostasy, Catholic Emancipation in 1829. This was no mere concession to agitators but was part of a package (possibly inspired by Pitt's policies) designed to make Ireland safe for political economy and thus a fully integrated part of the United Kingdom. The 40s. freeholders had to be disfranchised, not so much because they had voted for O'Connell as because they were priest-ridden Catholics (and therefore, in Peel's view, inimical to capitalism). A regime of 'policing and punishment' was to be imposed immediately (and at the expense of Ireland's own ratepayers), while schemes of poor relief and education were to be postponed. Only by such means could Ireland be successfully integrated into the benefits of British rule.

The Encumbered Estates Act of 1849, the disestablishment of the Irish Church, and the Irish Land Acts of 1870 and 1881 can be seen in part as attempts to keep capitalized arable farming alive in Ireland and to preserve (by modifying) the landlord–tenant relationship. It was only after British politicians had realized that the attempt would never succeed that they decided – either, like Gladstone, to exclude Ireland from the United Kingdom's political economy by means of home rule – or, like Salisbury, to abandon political economy in Ireland in favour of public works, land purchase, and trying to 'kill home rule by kindness'. If, therefore, the German 'marriage of iron and rye' in 1879 ended the prospect – which 1846 had inaugurated – of an era of international free trade, so 1886 marked the end of Peel's project for the economic anglicization of Ireland.

7

MERCHANT CITY

The Manchester business community, the
trade cycle and commercial policy, *c*.1820–
1846

Roger Lloyd-Jones

In 1843 W.J. Fox, a London free trader and Unitarian churchman, wrote
somewhat despairingly: 'The League office is becoming perfectly horrible
since the main body of the Goths and the Vandals came down from Manchester: it is worse than living in a factory.'[1] Manchester men may have been
despised by their 'sophisticated' London friends and hated by their enemies;
but they were also feared and by the 1830s and 1840s certainly could not be
ignored.[2]

The story of how Manchester became so important is, of course, well
documented.[3] But why did it raise such hostility and what role did its manufacturers and merchants play in the long process which led to the adoption of
free trade? The first section of this chapter will provide a brief sketch of
Manchester at the beginning of the nineteenth century and trace its rapid
rise as 'Cottonopolis'. The second section explores the Manchester business
community's role in shaping and developing a commercial strategy that was to
take on a national significance. The concluding section examines the crisis of
1837–42, its impact at national level and on Manchester, and the growing
demand for the repeal of the Corn Laws.

Manchester became the commercial and industrial capital of the first
industrial revolution . As Eric Hobsbawm has claimed:

> It was not Birmingham, a city which produced a great deal more in
> 1780, but essentially in the old ways, which made contemporaries
> speak of an industrial revolution, but Manchester, a city which
> produced more in a more obvious revolutionary manner.[4]

Manchester, that is, was both an entrepôt for all kinds of cotton goods and a
factory centre concentrating on the spinning and subsequently the weaving

of a wide variety of cotton yarns and cloths.[5] Certainly the city became synonymous with technological innovation, a large and volatile industrial workforce and an enterprising and brash commercial and entrepreneurial class. Not surprisingly Manchester was a focal point of interest to contemporaries and attracted a flow of visitors, both British and foreign, who were not slow in making public their observations and opinions.

Different impressions over the status and size of the towns spilled over into differing observations concerning the behaviour and manners of Manchester's inhabitants. The Archduke of Austria visiting Manchester in 1806 warmed to the Mancunians: 'Wheresoever we went in Manchester we [are] astonished by the decorum and politeness of the people.'[6] Richard Holden, a Rotherham attorney, visiting Manchester in May 1808 clearly met quite a different set of Mancunians from the Archduke. He recorded in his diary:

> A degree of insolence and brutality in the lower orders more than usually met with, but such as might be expected in a Town where none are so far elevated above them as to command respect nor any inclined to espouse the side of good manners, . . . a few of the manufacturers we are told attend to the principles and morals of those they employ but these are rare examples.[7]

Holden's view is jaundiced; he no doubt sensed that Rotherham could never aspire to the modernity of Manchester, but none the less his observations may signal something about the nature and structure of the city's business community. His comment that 'none are so elevated above them' (the lower orders) suggests a local business system characterised by small-scale activity and we should not assume that Manchester was a citadel dominated by wealthy and powerful merchants and cotton lords. To deny the existence of the latter would of course be foolish, but Manchester's business system was variegated, dynamic and open, as indeed the young Richard Cobden himself observed. Cobden, with two friends, arrived in Manchester in 1828, determined to 'make an arrangement with some large firm of calico printers for selling goods on commission.'[8] Recalling his first connection with the Manchester cotton trade in later life, Cobden wrote:

> We introduced ourselves to Fort Brothers and Co, a rich house and we told our tale, honestly concealing nothing. In less than two years from 1830 we owed them forty thousand pounds for goods which they had sent to us in Watling Street, upon no other security than our characters and knowledge of our business. I frequently talked with them in later times upon the great confidence they showed in men who avowed that they were not possessed of £200 each. Their answer was that they would always prefer to trust young men with connections and with a knowledge of their trade, if they knew them

to possess character and ability, to those of who started with capital without these advantages, and that they had acted on this principle successfully in all part of the World.[9]

We might, of course, legitimately ask whether Cobden's observations were mere exaggeration, the rags to riches story of a subsequently successful man of the world? John Owens, partner in the cotton manufacturing and dealing firm of Owen Owens, was by the 1830s a rich Manchester merchant, who, Clapp informs us, 'waited in his counting-house for tempting offers from pushing but often penurious young men from Liverpool.'[10]

We can safely assume that Cobden's enterprise was illustrative of the opportunities for the small entrepreneur to set up in business in Manchester in the early decades after Waterloo. But Cobden was also alive to the volatile nature of the cotton trade: 'During the time we have been here' (Manchester), Cobden wrote,

> we have been in a state of suspense, and you would be amused to see us but for one day. Oh, such changes of moods! This moment we are all jocularity and laughter, and the next we are mute as fishes and grave as owls. To do ourselves justice, I must say that our croakings do not generally last more than five minutes.[11]

Cobden captures the paradox of trade in Cottonopolis. Business optimism, which translated into factory construction booms and was supported by mercantile enterprise, was combined with intense anxiety, business crisis and bankruptcy. For example in the trade Cobden entered, calico printing, 60 per cent of firms specialising in this sector failed between 1815 and 1825, yet over the same time period seventy-nine new firms entered the trade.[12] Manchester grew at a phenomenal rate in the first four decades of the nineteenth century but this was by no means a stable unilinear development. The volatility of trade, the distinct possibility of moving rapidly from profit to loss, tested the enterprise of Manchester's business community and made it receptive to those strategies which promised to open up new markets for the vast and increasing volumes of cotton goods that the new mechanised system could produce.

Structure and strategy: Manchester business community 1825–46

In Manchester there was not a clear distinction between manufacturing and merchanting activities. Dealing in cotton goods was frequently combined with various forms of manufacturing. In 1825, for example, in addition to its 82 cotton factories Manchester possessed 267 cotton manufacturing and dealing firms;[13] by 1841 the former had increased to 128 and the latter to 382.[14]

Manufacturing and dealing firms involved themselves in a range of activities; for example, Pigot's Directory of 1825 shows them involved in 21 different forms of combinations in addition to their dealing and manufacturing activities. Adaptability was the golden rule of these firms, as Roland Smith has stated:

> Manufacturers and dealers were partly merchants and partly manufacturers . . . they bought yarn from spinners, paid for them to be woven into cloth, and then marketed the finalised goods themselves in the retail market. There was an immense difference in the size of these undertakings, but they were rarely large and important capitalist concerns, and since most of their capital was not so much in buildings or machinery but in stocks of cloth in the process of production, they could readily transfer their resources from manufacturing to merchanting, or vice versa.[15]

Chapman also points out that 'practically all the big merchants in the North of England in the first half of the 19th Century were in reality merchant-manufacturers.'[16]

Typical of such firms was the previously mentioned Owen Owens, who ran a warehouse in Carpenters Lane, Manchester, in 1825 rated at £30.00d. and by 1845 valued at £100,000.[17] The firm manufactured white shirtings, cambrics and ginghams, and umbrellas, and traded in hat trimmings. They also sold other firms' goods abroad. The firm's historian B.W. Clapp informs us:

> Although the number of spindles installed in American mills increased six fold between 1815 and 1825, production still fell far short of consumption and Owens among many others continued to dispatch the better quality cottons such as printed calicos and cambrics to Philadelphia and New York.[18]

Owens also invested the firm's capital in the Manchester cotton factory system. In 1825 John Owens formed a partnership with Samuel Faulkner, a firm of Manchester fine spinners, who were building a new mill in Ancoats, the main factory district. John Owens was a close personal friend of George Faulkner, one of the partners in the factory firm, and the latter became the first chairman of Owen's College, which ultimately became the University of Manchester.[19] Owens invested altogether nearly £10,000 into the venture and when John Owens withdrew from the partnership in 1844, recovering his original outlay of £10,000, the income earned from the investment amounted to £16,543, a handsome return. As Clapp points out, 'from 1830 to the end of John's connection with the mill it was a source of capital from which the firm's commercial and financial enterprises could draw nourishment'.[20] Manufacturing and merchanting, factory and warehouse, were close-ly interconnected in Manchester, especially from the 1820s, and were sym-bolised by the formation of the Chamber of Commerce, which set out to act both as a forum for business debate and as a vehicle to represent Manchester at both the local and national level.[21]

We now turn to an examination of business strategy in Manchester. In very broad terms business can be said to be concerned with two sets of policies. One set is concerned with the day to day management of business; in particular it seeks to facilitate the conditions for improvements in effi-ciency. The second set deals more with the long-term developments of the trade, with policies and strategies designed to create a business environment conducive to increasing prosperity and growth. While both policies will involve some interaction with the state, it is the second set which is more fully integrated with that flow of communication that links local with national political economy.[22] In pursuing this line of analysis we shall see that while Manchester merchants and manufacturers, from the 1820s, attacked the Corn Laws and advocated free trade and thus generated the appearance of a Manchester strategy, they were by no means consistent in deploying this strategy, were at times divided among themselves, were frequently distracted by other issues, and when economic conditions dictated were quite prepared to go cap-in-hand to government and request state assistance.

In 1828 Robert Hyde Greg and Peter Ewart placed before Manchester's Chamber of Commerce a motion which articulated the business community's support for free trade:

> That we admit, to the full extent, the principles of free trade – we would support no exclusive monopolies either of raw produce or manufacturers – we could sustain no unprofitable trade by bounties or prohibitory duties – we would draw our supplies from the cheapest and best sources.[23]

The Chamber also applauded the activity of government where it had made positive moves towards the deregulation of trade. In February 1825 the Chamber recognised 'the government's sympathy to the removal of restric-tions on trade' and in April of the same year it welcomed the reduction in duties on incoming foreign manufactures and raw products, offering its sup-port to 'the sound and enlightened principles of government on which they are founded'.[24] Not surprisingly Manchester called for further deregulation, including the repeal of the duty on raw cotton and for the 'repeal of the existing Corn Law' and thus allowing for 'free access to the Corn Markets of the world'.[25] However, Manchester's attachment to free-trade principles was not as robust as its critique of the Corn Laws suggested; it specifically excluded from its free-trade world the exportation of machinery. Greg and Ewart ended their 1828 overture to free trade with the following uncompromising statement: 'we would not export the machinery employed in our staple manufactures to enable other manufacturers to undersell us in foreign markets'.[26]

Not all the members of the Manchester Chamber were in favour of restriction. Thomas Sharpe, for example, of the machine makers Sharpe and Roberts, supported free exportation, but the balance of opinion was clearly in favour of restriction. This was a perfectly logical business stance; Lancashire manufacturers had a technological lead over their foreign rivals and that was not to be forfeited simply for a set of principles. Commitment to free trade was contingent, tempered by perceived business needs and the changing business environment in which manufacturers and merchants were expected to conduct their trade. As McCulloch had claimed in his *Principles of Political Economy*, first published in 1825, 'Self-interest is the most powerful spur that can be applied to excite the inventions and sharpen the ingenuity of man.'[27] Agitation against the export of machinery went on throughout the 1830s and, indeed, between the mid-1820s and the formation of the League to 1838 there were a number of issues which exercised the interest of Manchester's business community that displaced a direct focus on free trade. I want to concentrate on three: the response to the panic of 1826, the opposition to factory regulation, and foreign competition and the cyclical pattern of growth in the cotton trade. Matters such as parliamentary and municipal reform and the socio-cultural activities of Manchester's middle class have been dealt with admirably by scholars such as Gatrell, Redford and Seed.[28]

Hertz has argued that Manchester men 'sought no help either from the state or local government.'[29] But in 1826 Manchester business showed few scruples in requesting state assistance. The mid-1820s boom in the cotton trade was followed by panic. The new year of 1826 was not a happy one in Manchester; there were several business failures and confidence drained away. John Owens wrote in February 1826:

> Things here are dreadfully bad . . . and it is with difficulty the best bills can be discounted. Manchester till within the last ten days has been comparatively well off, but now the epidemic seems to have reached us and we believe very great distress prevails for want of money among even houses of known wealth.[30]

The crisis hit all branches of the cotton trade; as Owen went on to declare, 'I cannot adequately express to you the state of alarm, anxiety and distress which is felt by the manufacturing and mercantile community in this district.'[31] Inevitably unemployment rose; the Chamber of Commerce commented on the 'great scarcity of work among the hand weavers' and the fact that weavers would thankfully take on work at almost any rate of wage – 'yet many people cannot obtain it.'[32] The Chamber was more alarmed by what it termed 'the destruction of credit', and by the rapid increase in the accumulated stock of goods and yarn and a lack of sales except those that could be made 'only at ruinous loss'.[33] At its annual general meeting (AGM) in February 1826 the story was one of increased competition, price cutting, falling business confidence and rising distress. Members complained of soaring poor rates as they were forced to partially or fully stop their business activities. The Chamber agreed to send a memorandum to the Lord Commissioner of HM Treasury requesting a temporary issue of Exchequer Bills on loan based on adequate security. The Chamber claimed that its request for 'relief' was 'just and urgent' and the memorandum was signed by such eminent business leaders as John Kennedy, Peter Ewart, Thomas Ashton, Robert Hyde Greg and Thomas Houldsworth. On 6 March the Director announced that the Bank of England had agreed to advance credit to meet Manchester needs. The following day an advertisement was inserted in the Manchester papers:

> The Governor and Director of the Bank of England have authorised the Board of Directors of the Chamber of Commerce, Manchester, to receive applications from persons resident in and connected with the manufacturing district of Manchester for loan of money in sum of £500.00d to £10,000.00d, on deposit of goods or personal security.[34]

The total sum granted was not to exceed £300,000, the advances were granted at 5 per cent per annum, to be repaid four months from the date of the loan, and in the case of non-payment the Bank of England could sell the goods at public sale or private contract.[35] In July 1826 the Directors were still requesting an extension of the loan and further 'hoped that payment in approved bills, not exceeding three months will be accepted under discount – considerable additional accommodation will then be afforded.'[36] Overall eighty-eight applications were made for financial assistance amounting to a claim of £216,440; of these twenty-four were granted on deposit of goods and seventeen on personal security. In total forty-one applications were accepted amounting to £114,040, while nineteen were rejected (£19,000) and twenty-seven were withdrawn (£64,400).[37] The loan was administered in Manchester by a Board of Assistance set up by the Chamber of Commerce. In its report to the Chamber Directors, the Board was somewhat sanguine as to the success of the scheme, but it did acknowledge that some 'parties benefited from a greater accommodation'.[38] The panic of 1826 was an important moment in the political and business history of free trade. It was a political embarrassment for Huskisson, for his fiscal reforms, which had reduced a whole series of duties on imported items, were blamed by the Tory ultras and by elements in the City for the débâcle. During the height of the crisis the Prime Minister, Lord Liverpool, called all Cabinet ministers to London except Huskisson, 'who was so distrusted by the financial world, they thought it best to keep him out of sight.'[39] On the other hand, Boyd Hilton has argued, the government saw the crisis as a necessary 'purge' of a speculative capitalism which required greater self-discipline. A number of government ministers, including Huskisson and George Canning, were influenced by the Scottish cleric and Christian political economist, Thomas Chalmers, who 'seems to have regarded bankruptcy, with its harsh punishment, as a positive check, devised by God, to force businessmen into adopting the preventative or moral check of moderation.'[40] For Manchester businessmen the panic had been a blow to confidence; they bitterly resented the notion of over-trading or speculation, but had been required to seek assistance to ameliorate a state of affairs for which they believed they were not responsible, but for which the government did seem to hold them culpable. While Peel could say of the 1826 crisis 'much good, after some sever suffering, will prevail',[41] what Manchester businessmen faced was the prospect of nursing an industry whose productive capacity had been significantly increased by the mid-1820s boom, through a very difficult business climate. Certainly spare capacity persisted in the Manchester cotton factory system into the 1830s, since reserve capacity was higher in 1834 than it had been in 1825,[42] and the evidence also points to a squeeze on profit margins.[43] Referring to the merchant-manufacturers, Chapman points to 'the high rate of turnover of firms, falling profit margins, unstable banking conditions and increasing costs of overseas selling.'[44] In such a difficult business environment one might have expected a more aggressive pursuit of free-trade policies. Indeed, the Chamber did maintain that 'the stagnation in trade' was 'aggravated by . . . the operation of the Corn Laws' and claimed these same laws acted to retard the return to a more 'healthy state of trade'.[45] But while Manchester businessmen might complain of foreign tariffs curtailing 'the demand for our cotton goods . . . in many of the old markets', in the late 1820s and early 1830s their attention was directed less towards free trade than an issue which embroiled them in a quite different national controversy.

The growing call for factory reform took on the form of an assault on the factory system itself and changed the agenda facing Manchester's business community. Not all businessmen were openly hostile to factory regulation. In February 1832 a deputation of Manchester cotton spinners requested the Chamber to call for a Bill limiting the hours of work of 'children and young persons to . . . 69 hours per week' and to impose the restrictions upon the moving power of mills and factories, 'as the only method of making it effectual'. The Directors declined to act, claiming 'the Chamber does not feel itself competent to give an opinion on the subject and must decline applying to the legislature for that purpose.'[46] In the course of 1832 the position was to change radically, the catalyst being the publication of the Sadler Report. According to Ward the report of the Sadler Committee 'amounted to a massive indictment of industrial conditions' in the factory districts.[47] It attracted a vitriolic attack from the factory masters; every effort was made to discredit the report and attempts were made to compromise witnesses. The hostility shown to the Sadler Committee was indicative of the threat it posed to the factory system and initial attempts to dismiss it as an 'operatives committee' failed to convince. Of the ninety-six witnesses called, sixty were directly involved in the factory system, and of those thirty-eight were 20 years of age or over; there was no question of Sadler packing the evidence with the testimony of children. Further, of the factory witnesses thirteen were employed as overseers or managers of factories. Of more significance twenty-six of the witnesses called to give evidence were in professional occupations, predominantly from the medical profession. Twenty-one medical men were called before Sadler, including Sir Anthony Carlisle, Professor of Anatomy at the Royal Academy and at the Royal College of Surgeons and principal surgeon to the Westminster Hospital; Sir Charles Bell, Professor at the Royal College of Surgeons and surgeon to the Middlesex Hospital; and Sir William Blizard, Lecturer at the Royal College of Surgeons and surgeon to the London Hospital.[48] These leading members of the medical profession severely criticised the factory system. The quality of their medical judgements as to the consequences of factory work on health may or may not have been valid, but the crucial fact was that their elevated position in society and their role as 'experts' carried weight at the bar of contemporary public opinion. Their comments on the factory system were negative, not to say damning. What was required was a robust reply and Manchester was not slow in forthcoming. In July 1833 Poulett Thompson wrote to the Manchester Chamber in his capacity as 'a member of the Borough' inquiring what the Board wished 'him to . . . pursue in discussions of the proposed Bill now before Parliament for the regulation of Factories.' The Chamber replied that the Bill would 'lay the foundation for the ruin of our manufacturing interest.'[49] In March 1833, the employers' spokesman in the House of Commons, Wilson Patterson, MP for North Lancashire, had proposed the establishment of a Commission of Inquiry, which among other things would serve to clear 'the character of the masters from those imputations which seem to be cast upon them by the friends of this measure.'[50] In April the Commission agreed to set up a Parliamentary Commission of Inquiry 'to obtain the most authentic, accurate and complete information within the shortest time.'[51]

The evidence gathered challenged the findings of the Sadler Committee on a number of fronts; in particular the Factory Commissioners claimed that their inquiry showed that factory conditions were improving and where abuses did occur they were mainly confined to the smaller mills.[52] But if legislative regulation was to be thwarted, and, in particular, a Ten Hour Bill scotched, a more robust defence had to be mounted. This took the form of a document published by seventeen Manchester master cotton spinners, including McConnell and Co., T. R. & T. Ogden, Benjamin Sandford, Benjamin Gray, John Kennedy, Robert Scholfield, and Thomas Houldsworth.[53] The thrust of their argument was that the introduction of a Ten Hour Bill would undermine the economics of the cotton trade. They based their critique on three major premises:

1   Reduced hours of work, at the same rate of wages, would increase costs and reduce profits. The Manchester masters argued that reduced hours would lead to a fall in production and this in turn would result in rising costs. This proposition was supported by classical economic theory. Thus Senior declared 'It must never be forgotten, that in manufacturers, with every increase in the quantity produced, the relative expense of production is diminished, and, which is the same thing, that with every diminution of production, the relative expense of production is increased.'[54]

2   If the manufacturers in the short run accepted the existing wage for the reduced hours, in the long run wages, due to falling profits and investments, would be driven down.

3   If wages were reduced in relation to hours worked this would have serious effects for the family economy because of reduced incomes; serious disturbance would probably follow the implementation of the new lower wage structures.

According to the Manchester men all the parties in the factory system would lose by the regulatory reduction in the hours of cotton operatives. As Robert Hyde Greg observed:

> In case of a Ten Hour Bill being passed, the actual migration of English mill owners, machinery and capital will hasten the period, already approaching with certainty, when the markets of Europe and America will be closed and our customers will become our rivals.[55]

The Ten Hour Bill was stopped in its tracks; the 1833 Factory Act limited its legislative remit to children and adolescents and Manchester businessmen continued to extol the virtues of self-regulation. Self-regulation tends to dovetail with deregulation; did, in other words, the momentum towards free trade accelerate after 1833?

As was the norm in the cotton trade contradictory forces were at work. The mid-1830s witnessed a boom in the industry, the consumption of raw cotton increased by 38 per cent 'between 1834 and 1838' and exports of piece goods and yarn rose sharply.[56] But entrepreneurial confidence was tempered by fear of foreign competition, over-production and a squeeze on profit margins. The outstanding feature of the mid-1830s prosperity in the cotton trade was, according to R.C.O. Matthews, 'a rise in demand and in the value of output' which triggered off a substantial investment boom.[57] Table 7.1 shows factory expansion across the main Lancashire cotton towns (plus Stockport) between 1835 and 1838.

Overall growth in the main cotton towns saw the number of factories increase by 56 per cent and steam horsepower generated by 35 per cent. Indeed the latter figure may well be an underestimate; as Matthews has pointed out the 1838 estimate 'took no account of engines in mills currently

Table 7.1 Growth of Lancashire cotton towns (including Stockport) 1835–8

| | No. factories | | Steam horsepower | |
Town	1835	1838	1835	1838
Manchester	122	163	6,205	6,642
Oldham	84	200	2,411	2,932
Bury	82	114	2,173	3,142
Whalley *	79	113	940	1,937
Rochdale	67	95	1,433	1,993
Stockport	64	86	3,526	4,541
Ashton-under-Lyne	51	82	1,617	2,699
Bolton	42	69	1,082	1,683
Preston	25	35	923	1,332
Wigan	25	37	839	1,134
Blackburn	24	44	845	1,692

* Districts of Whalley included Burnley, Accrington, Colne, Padistown, Habersham Ere, Herlington, Ostwaldtwistle, Clitheroe, Marsden, Barrowford, Lower & Higher Booth, Bacup, Deardon-in-Clough.
Source: Compiled from Accounts and Papers, 1836 XLV, pp. 55–79 and 1839 XLII, pp. 16–17.

unoccupied – a category which had been included in the 1835 estimates.' Matthew concludes that if the data had been placed on a comparable basis for the two benchmark dates, the increase in steam horsepower generated 'could scarcely be less than 50 per cent'.[58] But Manchester did not share in this expansion to anywhere near the same extent as the satellite towns. The number of factories did increase by 33.6 per cent but steam horsepower generated rose by only 7 per cent. Manchester's share of total steam horsepower fell from 28.2 per cent in 1835 to 22.4 per cent in 1838. The construction boom of the mid-1830s was more a phenomenon of the Lancashire cotton towns than Manchester itself (indeed the returns show Manchester's factory labour force falling from 37,200 in 1835 to 34,039 in 1838). Certainly debates in the Manchester Chamber during this period do not reflect a confident business class; rather, fear of foreign competition, particularly from Germany and the United States, exercised the minds of Manchester manufacturers and merchants. While the 'pursuit of more or less unqualified prosperity of the Cotton industry was considered to have begun only in 1834',[59] the Manchester Chamber was noting with alarm in June of the same year

> the competition of foreigners and especially of the Americans in the article called 'Domestics' is felt in all markets, whilst the future stability of our cotton trade is threatened by a formidable confederacy amongst many of the Continental powers of Europe.[60]

Perhaps what struck fear in Manchester was less American competition than the threat posed by the newly formed German customs union, the

Zollverein.[61] There are frequent references to the 'union' in the Chamber debates;[62] in 1836 a committee, including Richard Cobden, was appointed by the Chamber to examine cotton cloth produced by the Zollverein. The samples were collected by a 'gentleman who had the confidence of Mr Poulett Thompson' and had been sent to Manchester by the Board of Trade.[63] However government assistance to Manchester was strictly limited to an advisory capacity, as the businessmen quickly discovered. In 1836 the Chamber sent a letter to Lord Palmerston recommending action to be taken against the rise of the Zollverein: 'the Chamber has viewed with concern the formation of this great League, without any successful effort being made to stem its progress towards completion.' They hoped that the influence of the government would have been 'powerful enough to prevent the shutting of that great continental inlet from British manufacturers.'[64] Within a week the Chamber received the following rebuke from the Foreign Office:

> The Chamber of Commerce of Manchester must be aware, that no English government has either the power or the right to prevent independent states from entering into such arrangements. Great Britain would never permit any other country so to interfere with her own commercial arrangements and she is bound to respect in others that freedom of action she asserts for herself.[65]

Dismissed by the state, Manchester would not find any succour either from the political economists. As J.R. McCulloch observed:

> It has been shown, over and over again, that nothing can be more irrational and absurd, than that dread of the progress of others in wealth and civilization, . . . that what is for the advantage of one state is for the advantage of all.[66]

The message was clear; if Manchester was to be consistent in its advocacy of deregulation and wished to meet foreign competition 'on equal terms' it would have to look to its own devices and not call for intervention to suit its own narrow purposes. Manchester's response was shaped, in part, by its trading relationship with the German Customs Union. The Zollverein states had tended to follow a pattern of industrial development contrary to that of Britain. British industrialisation had followed what may be described as upstream development, that is, industry initially focused on such upstream activities as yarn spinning and then subsequently moved downstream to power weaving; the German states concentrated on downstream activities such as cloth manufacture and subsequently moved upstream to yarn production. In its early phase of development, therefore, the German cotton industry was a major purchase of yarns, in particular Manchester yarn. Such was the growth of the trade that an increasing number of 'German houses' were established in Manchester. According to Chapman the number of German firms operating in the town increased from twenty-eight in 1820 to eighty-four in 1840 and he goes on to claim that many but not all of the German houses were 'branches of established concerns in Hamburg, Frankfurt, Leipzig and other commercial cities.'[67] Certainly in the years between the end of the Napoleonic Wars and the repeal of the Corn Laws there was a trend towards exporting a higher proportion of the vast increase in yarn produced. Manchester had a large number of single-process spinning firms; 49 per cent of all firms in the town in 1841 were specialist yarn spinners. Table 7.2 shows the increase in yarn exports.

The increased intensity of competition in the yarn trade is reflected in the falling price of a pound of exported yarns from 29d. (12p) in 1819–21 to 12d. (5p) in 1844–6, a fall of 58.6 per cent. Despite the rapid increase in the volume of yarn exported, Ellison claims that there was a 30 per cent fall in the value of yarn exports between the beginning of the 1830s and the repeal of the Corn Laws in 1846.[68] The 1830s were difficult years for single-process spinners, compounded by fear over the tariff policy of the Zollverein. Thus the growing demand to reform the Corn Laws formed part of a strategy to maintain Manchester's position as a dominant producer and trader in cotton. The Corn Laws, it was argued, not only acted to keep British wage rates higher than the continentals', such disparities weakening the competitive position of Manchester manufacturers, but also the prohibition on continental corn, especially Prussian corn, reduced the capacity of the Zollverein states to purchase Manchester cotton. As Schulze-Gaevernitz, the German historian of Lancashire cotton, put it, the cotton manufacturers of Lancashire fought the Corn Laws in the first instance in the interest of exports.[69] We may well speculate that it was just as much fear as bravado which pushed the Manchester business community into the free-trade camp. Manchester's brashness and highly vocal demand for Corn Law repeal disguised a deep concern over its trading position. Its worries were more than justified as business matters took a distinct turn for the worse from 1837.

Table 7.2 Increase in volume and export of yarn, 1819–21 to 1844–6

	1819–21	*1844–6*	*% Increase*
Yarn production (in thousands of lb.)	106,500	523,300	391.4
Yarn exported	20,880	145,190	595.4
% yarn exported	19.5	27.8	

Source: T. Ellison, *The Cotton Trade of Great Britain*, London, Frank Cass, 1968, p. 59.

Crisis and repeal

Between 1837 and 1842 business suffered a severe depression, experiencing falling profits and wages, and rising unemployment. In the cotton trade by 1841–2 the industry was experiencing a disastrous depression, bankruptcies were widespread, and both employment and production were falling. By the last quarter of 1841, 23.6 per cent of all cotton mills in Lancashire were working short-time or were completely shut down. Not surprisingly, the cotton districts were the centre of the Chartist agitation of 1842, and 'the impact of depression rapidly became a political issue'.[70] The economic crisis requires attention at both the national and local level; for as Henry George Wood, a leading free trader and MP for Sheffield, acknowledged, the Anti-Corn Law League 'came of distress'.[71] An important consequence of the economic downswing was a reduction in government revenue and a growing budget deficit. Between 1838 and 1842 there were five successive years of budget deficits. This acted to undermine the Whig government of Lord Melbourne, and as one colourful critic of the Whigs put it: 'ministers' noses are being rubbed in their own filth, as is done to dogs when they dung a drawing room.'[72] In the summer of 1841 the Whigs were swept aside and Sir Robert Peel and the Tories were elected with a large majority. According to F.E. Hyde, Peel dedicated his administration to creating a stable financing structure based on the principles of sound finance and economy and Levi maintains that the Peel administration was recognised for its 'bold and vigorous commercial and financial policy and its ability to put them into effect.'[73] Peel embarked on a programme of fiscal reforms centred on the introduction of income tax and a reduction of duty on a wide range of manufactured and semi-manufactured goods. The objective was to increase revenue and reduce the budget deficit, but intended or unintended, the consequence of stripping away a whole range of duties was to expose the Corn Laws as the remaining pillar of the protectionist system. As food prices rose this focused greater attention on the landlords as the main beneficiaries of the fiscal system and as the young William Gladstone, Vice-President of the Board of Trade in Peel's government, observed from a Ricardian perspective, 'Corn was not dear because land yielded rent, rather land yielded rent because Corn was dear.'[74] Following the logic of Ricardian theory it seems that the high price of corn and high rents could be checked only by free trade. According to Hyde, Peel accepted Gladstone's assumptions;[75] however, the logical acceptance of an economic proposition is not the same thing as a political commitment to act. Rather we might ask what was Manchester's reaction to Peel's fiscal initiatives and what role did the 'Goths and Vandals' play in the final drama of repeal?

Initially the response of Manchester's business community was negative, but it was were won over by Peel's demonstration that the new tax allowed him to strip away a great deal of irksome duties and still raise revenue.[76] In the more long term we have to set Manchester's response within the overall context of the crisis *c*.1837–42. During this period the Manchester Chamber of Commerce, for example, complained of distressed trade, low profits and prices, increasingly competitive markets and rising unemployment. This is particularly the case from early 1839, when Cobden and the Manchester Anti-Corn Law Association captured the Chamber of Commerce and deposed the incumbent president G.W. Wood, MP for Kendal and a Manchester cotton manufacturer and dealer.[77] Wood had angered the free traders in December 1838 when he had opposed a motion before the Chamber calling for a full and immediate repeal of the Corn Laws. But this skirmish with the free traders was to break out into open war in February 1839 when he made what was considered to be a disastrous intervention in the debate on the Queen's speech in the House of Commons. Wood delivered a remarkably upbeat analysis of the existing economic climate and, while he accepted that 1837 had witnessed great communal distress, he now claimed, 'The House will be glad to hear that this state of things had passed away.'[78] Wood insisted that the economy had made a remarkable recovery and speculated that the cause of the problem had not been 'over-trading' but had been the result of the operations of a 'vicious system of banking'.[79] What incensed the free traders was Wood's failure to make any reference to the Corn Laws and the difficulties faced by the exporters of cotton goods; indeed Wood went out of his way to praise the increase in British export of cotton goods and yarn in 1838. For Manchester men Wood's statistics were too much to stomach but for Sir Robert Peel it was excellent fare. When Peel rose to speak he seized on Wood's assertion that it was the operation of the banking system not the Corn Laws that had triggered the depression of 1837. Peel declared that the House should

> pause before it acceded to any proposition . . . which would materi-ally affect the agricultural interest having received from the Presi-dent of the Chamber of Commerce at Manchester, the account he had given of stable and secure position of the commerce and manufactures of this country.[80]

Peel's evident delight has to be contrasted with the wrath felt in Manchester. The Whigs' chief legal agent, Joseph Parkes, wrote to Cobden that Peel had 'got G.W. Wood's stupid head (for there is nothing in it) under his arm and most unmercifully jabbed him.' Parkes advised Cobden to depose Wood 'from his rank as Chairman of your Chamber' and Cobden acted quickly using the AGM of the Chamber to force Wood's resignation in February 1839.[81] The removal of Wood and other directors sympathetic to his views saw the Chamber and Manchester businessmen taking a more aggressive stance against the Corn Laws and articulating a more forthright exposition of free-trade strategy.

It is possible to identify four interrelated themes which marked the business history of the period up to repeal. First, there was a fear of foreign competition, which in turn was identified as a consequence of the Corn Laws. It was pointed out, for example, that in 1844 the average wage of a British cotton worker was 2.4 times greater than that of a cotton operative in Germany; and as one member informed the Chamber 'the overwhelming tide of competition will never ebb, so long as the cheap food of the foreigners enables them to work at half the money price of labour.'[82] Second, the rise of foreign competition was linked to the problems of creating sufficient demand for Manchester goods abroad, which, it was claimed, was essential for sustaining jobs and supplying 'a profitable field of employment for all capitalists'.[83] The Chamber deployed a simple comparative advantage argument to attack the Corn Laws, which businessmen agreed 'contradicted this natural law'.[84] The Corn Laws were condemned as an artificial device which led to the destruction of British jobs and British capital. Thereby it followed that the only way that the decline in the progress of profits and wages could be checked was 'by the removal of all restrictions on foreign commerce'.[85] Third, to reinforce this proposition, Manchester businessmen blamed the industrial unrest of 1842 on the squeeze of working-class living standards, a direct result they believed of the Corn Laws. The Chamber raised the spectre of hundreds of thousands 'of excited people' who 'roamed the country in disorganised bands, having in their power, for several days many millions of pounds of property.'[86] But the directors were keen to stress that 'no machinery had been wilfully injured or even a thread of yarn broken.'[87] Workers, businessmen claimed, were not rebelling against the industrial system but against a system that kept the price of food artificially high. The effects of the high cost of provisions was undermining the good relation between capital and labour and Manchester businessmen feared that the discontent of their workers might be increasingly directed against themselves, as employers, who were 'their fellow sufferers' and who were 'unable to relieve them'.[88] Finally it was argued that uncertainty over business prosperity and labour unrest had led to 'the virtual suspension of investment'. Manchester warned that 'scarcely any provision is made for the employment of a constantly rising population.' Deploying here Malthusian fears the Chamber claimed that the underlying cause of the problem was the operation of the 'Corn Laws' and 'the problem of Continental markets'.[89]

The connecting thread pulling these theories together was the notion that the common interest of capitalists and workers, their jobs, their prosperity and their future was threatened by the continued operation of the Corn Laws. Further the Laws were condemned because it was alleged that they acted as a divisive agency, creating artificial divisions between the two great industrial classes, their common interests obscured by a system designed to secure the economic and political power of a narrow and privileged elite.[90] Future prosperity and progress, and indeed political stability, required free trade; this was the only means by which the full potential of the industrial system could be realised. By the early 1840s Manchester's strategy dovetailed with Peel's fiscal reforms, themselves a product of the economic crisis, and as the latter exposed the Corn Laws as the central pillar of the protectionist system, it meant that repeal was only a matter of time.

Notes

1 N. McCord, *The Anti Corn Law League, 1838–1846*, London, George Allen & Unwin, 1958, pp. 140–1.
2 A. Briggs, *Victorian Cities*, Harmondsworth, Penguin, 1968, p. 93.
3 See R. Lloyd-Jones and M.J. Lewis, *Manchester and the Age of the Factory: The Business Structure of Cottonopolis in the Industrial Revolution*, London, Croom Helm, 1988.
4 E.J. Hobsbawm, *Industry and Empire*, Harmondsworth, Penguin, 1969, p. 20.
5 Lloyd-Jones and Lewis, *Manchester*, p. 31.
6 W.H. Thompson, *History of Manchester to 1852*, Altrincham, John Sherratt and Son, 1966, p. 268.
7 Ibid., p. 271.
8 J. Morley, *The Life of Richard Cobden*, London, Fisher Unwin, 12th edn, 1905, p. 15.
9 Ibid., pp. 15–16.
10 B.W. Clapp, *John Owens: Manchester Merchant*, Manchester, Manchester University Press, 1965, p. 114.
11 Morley, *Cobden*, p. 17.
12 Lloyd-Jones and Lewis, *Manchester*, pp. 177–8.
13 Ibid., pp. 107, 115.
14 R. Lloyd-Jones and A.A. Le Roux, 'The Size of Firms in the Cotton Industry: Manchester 1815–41', *Economic History Review*, 33, 1 (1980), 75; R. Smith, 'Manchester's changing role in the Lancashire cotton trade, 1820–1830 and its concomitant effects', University of Birmingham, BA thesis, 1950, p. 30.
15 Smith, 'Manchester's role in Lancashire cotton trade', p. 30.
16 S.D. Chapman, *Merchant Enterprise in Britain from the Industrial Revolution to World War 1*, Cambridge, Cambridge University Press, 1992, p. 89.
17 Lloyd-Jones and Lewis, *Manchester*, p. 113; Chapman, *Merchant Enterprise*, p. 90.
18 Clapp, *John Owens*, p. 35.
19 Ibid., p. 44.
20 Ibid., p. 45.
21 Lloyd-Jones and Lewis, *Manchester*, ch. 8; E. Helm, *Chapters in the History of the Manchester Chamber of Commerce*, London, Simpkin, Marshall, 1897, chs VII, VIII.
22 Lloyd-Jones and Lewis, *Manchester*, p. 141.
23 *Proceeding of the Manchester Chamber of Commerce and Manufacturers*, Manchester Central Library, M8/2/1–4 (hereafter *PMCCM*), 8 November 1828.
24 *PMCCM*, 14 February, 13 April 1825.
25 Ibid.
26 *PMCCM*, 14 February 1828.
27 J.R. McCulloch, *The Principles of Political Economy*, New York, Augustus M. Kelley, reprint of Economic Classics, 5th edn, 1864, p. 97.
28 A. Redford *et al.*, *The History of Local Government in Manchester*, vols 1 and 2, London, Longman, Green, 1939; J. Seed, 'Unitarianism, Political Economy and

the Antinomies of Liberal Culture in Manchester', *Social History*, 7, 1, 1982; V.A.C. Gatrell, 'Incorporation and the Pursuit of Liberal Hegemony in Manchester 1790–1839' in D. Frazer (ed.), *Municipal Reform and the Industrial City*, Leicester, Leicester University Press, 1982.

29 G.B. Hertz, *The Manchester Politician, 1750–1912*, London, Sherratt and Hughes, 1912, p. 50.
30 Clapp, *John Owens*, p. 48.
31 Ibid., p. 48.
32 *PMCCM*, 1 February 1826.
33 *PMCCM*, 13 February 1826.
34 Ibid.
35 *PMCCM*, 6 March 1826.
36 *PMCCM*, 26 July 1826.
37 *PMCCM*, 2 May 1827.
38 Ibid.
39 W.D. Jones, *Prosperity Robinson: The Life of Viscount Goderich 1782–1859*, London, Macmillan, 1967, pp. 115–16.
40 A.B. Hilton, *Corn, Cash, Commerce: The Economic Policies of the Tory Governments 1815 to 1830*, Oxford, Oxford University Press, 1977, p. 311.
41 Ibid., p. 313.
42 R. Lloyd-Jones and A.A. Le Roux, 'Factory Utilisation and the Firm: The Manchester Cotton Industry c.1825–1840', *Textile History*, 15, 1, 1984, pp. 121–2.
43 *PMCCM*, 27 April 1833; Lloyd-Jones and Lewis, *Manchester*, pp. 173, 198–9, 204, 206.
44 Chapman, *Merchant Enterprise*, p. 136.
45 *PMCCM*, 8 November 1826.
46 *PMCCM*, 25 February 1832.
47 J.T. Ward, *The Factory Movement 1830–1855*, London, Macmillan, 1962, 61.
48 *Select Committee on the Bill to Regulate the Labour of Children in the Mills and Factories of the United Kingdom*, 1831–2 [Sadler Committee], pp. 571–6, 603–5.
49 *PMCCM*, 9 July 1833.
50 *Hansard*, 16, 14 March 1833, pp. 640–1.
51 PP 1834 *First Report Factory Commission*, XV, 1833 p. 5.
52 See evidence of Commissioner Stuart, who subsequently became a Factory Inspector, *1st Report Factory Commission, 1833*, p. 21.
53 PP 1834, XIX, *Supplementary Report of the Factory Commission*, D2, p. 106.
54 N. Senior, *Letters on the Factory Acts: As it affects the Cotton Manufacture Addressed to the Right Honourable the President of the Board of Trade*, London, B. Fellowes, 1837, p. 22.
55 R.H. Greg, *The Factory Question*, London, James Ridgeway and Sons, 1837, p. 89.
56 B.R. Mitchell and P. Deane, *Abstract of British Historical Statistics*, Cambridge, Cambridge University Press, 1962, pp. 179, 182.
57 R.C.O. Matthews, *A Study in Trade Cycle History: Economic Fluctuations in Great Britain 1833–42*, Cambridge, Cambridge University Press, 1954, p. 134. See also L. Levi, *The History of British Commerce and of the Economic Progress of the British Nation, 1763–1878*, Shannon, Ireland, Irish University Press edition 1971, 1st edition London 1872, pp. 220, 252–3.
58 Matthews, *A Study in Trade Cycle History*, p. 135.
59 Ibid., p. 134.
60 *PMCCM*, 7 June 1834.
61 For a general discussion of the Zollverein and British trade in the 1830s see

L. Brown, *The Board of Trade and the Free Trade Movement 1830–42*, Oxford, Clarendon Press, 1958, ch. 6; also W. Fischer, 'The German Zollverein: A Case Study in Customs Union', *Kyklos*, 1960, pp. 79, 81–2.
62 *PMCCM*, 3 June 1835; 20 January, 8 February, 11 June 1836; 15 February 1837.
63 *PMCCM*, 18 August 1836.
64 *PMCCM*, 20 January 1836.
65 *PMCCM*, 27 January 1836.
66 McCulloch, *Political Economy*, p. 93.
67 S.D. Chapman, *Merchant Enterprise*, pp. 138, 139–40.
68 T. Ellison, *The Cotton Trade of Great Britain*, London, Frank Cass, 1968, p. 60.
69 G. von Schulze-Gaevernitz, *The Cotton Trade in England and on the Continent*, trans. O.S. Hall, London, Simpkin, Marshall, Hamilton, Kent, 1895, p. 58; see also D.A. Farnie, *The English Cotton Industry and the World Market 1815 to 1896*, Oxford, Oxford University Press, 1979, p. 89.
70 R. Lloyd-Jones, 'The First Kondratieff: The Long Wave and the British Industrial Revolution', *Journal of Interdisciplinary History*, 20, 4, 1990, p. 600. Levi also refers to 'evidence of distress from Birmingham, Nottingham, Manchester' i.e. the great provincial centres of industrial England. Levi, *British Commerce*, pp. 22–3.
71 Lloyd-Jones, *The First Kondratieff*, p. 599.
72 J. Parry, *The Rise and Fall of Liberal Government in Victorian Britain*, New Haven, CT, and London, Yale University Press, 1993, p. 142.
73 See F.E. Hyde, *Mr Gladstone at the Board of Trade*, London, Cobden, Sanderson, 1934.
74 Ibid., p. 39.
75 Ibid., p. 44.
76 Ibid., p. 21.
77 For background on G.W. Wood see Lloyd-Jones and Lewis, *Manchester*, pp. 133, fn 8 155; Redford, *Local Government*, p. 305.
78 *Hansard*, 47, 3rd series, 5 February 1839, p. 59.
79 Ibid., p. 59.
80 Ibid., p. 106.
81 McCord, *Anti Corn Law League*, p. 46.
82 Hertz, *Manchester Politician*, p. 39. For further discussion on wages see Kadish, Chapter 1 in this volume.
83 *PMCCM*, 17 February 1839.
84 *PMCCM*, 12 March 1839.
85 *PMCCM*, 13 February 1843.
86 Ibid.
87 Ibid.
88 Ibid.
89 Ibid.
90 It should be noted that a number of years after repeal had been achieved Cobden acknowledged that he 'never made any progress with the Corn Law question when it was stated as a question of class against class', R.D. Edwards, *The Pursuit of Reason, The Economist, 1843–1993*, London, Hamish Hamilton, 1993, p. 9.

8

'EIN STÜCK ENGLANDS'?

A contrast between the free-trade movements in Hamburg and Manchester

John Breuilly

Cobden's conception of free trade

In October 1847 Richard Cobden was coming to the end of a triumphal tour of Europe following the success of the repeal of the Corn Laws in 1846. His last major engagement before sailing for home was a large banquet in Hamburg. At the banquet his principal host, the Hamburg merchant Justus Ruperti, raised the toast: 'To Free Trade, the source of all other freedoms.'[1]

Cobden in his speech replying to this toast expanded on what that toast might mean. He linked the struggle for free trade to other struggles: peace against war, abundance against shortage, fraternity against prejudice, Christianity against barbarism. He further stressed the broad and moral significance of the free-trade movement by denying that it had anything to do with providing employers the opportunity to reduce wages.

Such occasions, of course, stress agreement, not differences. Nevertheless, there does appear to be genuinely strong agreement between Ruperti, who hails free trade as providing the basis for expanding the range of human freedoms, and Cobden, who elaborates on various of these freedoms.[2]

Other contributions to this book consider the vision or ideology associated with Cobden, free trade and the case argued by the Anti-Corn Law League (ACLL). What I want to do here is take Hamburg as an example of superficial agreement on these matters, point to the very different views associated with free trade here compared with those found in the ACLL, suggest some reasons for these differences, and evaluate the significance of such differences. In a final, more speculative section, I want to relate this chapter to the general theme of 'Freedom and Trade' by asking what, if any, were the connections between economic liberalism and other kinds of liberalism in nineteenth-century western Europe.

Cobden understood the expanding role of free trade in two ways. One was geographical: the British example had to be extended to other parts of the world, notably Europe. His diary of his European tour of 1847 is full of critical comments on protectionist sentiments in different European countries, the need to form alliances with those in favour of free trade, and to argue and persuade those in positions of power and influence of the merits of moving towards trade liberalisation.[3] He helped circulate free-trade literature, for example by the French writer Bastiat. In Hamburg he noted with approval that a new journal devoted to free trade was about to appear. (The journal *Deutscher Freihafen* actually began publication the day after the banquet.) There is a sense here in which Britain is seen as showing the way ahead. Partly, of course, this had been part of the case argued by the ACLL: the removal of tariffs on goods Europe wished to export to Britain, in this case corn, would in turn strengthen free-trade elements in Europe as potential exporters would also be potential sterling earners who would wish to purchase British manufactures. Policy and propaganda would work hand in hand.

However, there is also the sense that free trade is both a metaphor for and a cause of further freedoms. It is a metaphor because the image of a free market-place to which all can bring their wares and people can freely choose those which they prefer was extended to the characterisation of non-economic relationships. Cobden had early developed, not without some ironical undertones, a rhetoric built on the principle of depicting the non-economic in terms of the economic. For example, in 1835, when agitating for the establishment of a popular cultural society (this was to be *The Athenaeum*), Cobden declared that:

> It would be a shame that, while they were erecting mills in every direction for the manufacture of cotton, they could not have one manufactory for working up the raw intelligence of the town.[4]

The propaganda of the ACLL turned this rhetorical style into routine prose. The bazaars, for example, organised from 1842, were described as models of human intercourse.[5] Religious liberty, educational reform and freedom of the press were justified in terms of a free traffic in ideas and equipping people with the capacity to engage effectively in that traffic.

The other aspect was a causal argument. The major vehicle here was the notion of interest. Free trade in commerce would deal a blow to aristocratic interests and expand the power of competitive entrepreneurs. By 1843 this had developed into an argument about general economic modernisation, including agriculture as well as manufacturing. The inability to raise punitive tariffs would decrease the power of governments and the dependency upon government of all manner of artificially sustained economic interests. It would also deal a fatal blow to patronage and dependency relationships created with the accumulation of surplus revenue in government hands. The benefits of free trade would be made clear to an increasingly enlightened and powerful public opinion, which in turn would constrain the capacity of governments to pursue alternative, restrictive policies.

Cobden's presentation of Britain as the model and Europe as the potential imitator is perhaps the least fixed of his positions and owes much to the optimism generated by the success of 1846. Less than a decade earlier one finds Cobden favourably comparing Prussia to Britain, above all for its progressive educational system and its efficient administration, which promoted policies of economic liberalism. This was, of course, at a time when repeal of the Corn Laws and free trade were presented as just two of a whole raft of radical-liberal policies, along with educational reform, statistical knowledge, phrenology, currency reform, household suffrage, church disestablishment and much else. That had also been a time of a fairly sharp decline in radical influence although this had helped to shift away the radical centre of gravity from London. Subsequently there had been a battle, even within radical-liberal circles, to establish the centrality of the Corn Laws repeal movement and to develop an appropriate rhetoric and propaganda. With that success and then repeal in 1846 there was a brief moment when this movement appeared to combine principle and power very effectively.

This was apparently confirmed by the reception Cobden received in Europe. British economic policy was, of course, a matter of intense interest to Europeans.[6] Even those who were irritated by the moralism of Cobden's arguments and either rejected them, or at least discerned interest at the bottom of them, tended to assume that Cobden spoke for a powerful body of opinion, one which had altered government policy and, in doing so, destroyed one administration and party and helped bring in another government. This all reinforced the sense that Cobden was bringing a message of general significance to his European hosts.

However, even those who most applauded his arguments, such as the seven hundred members of the Hamburg elite at that banquet in October 1847, did so for reasons that had little to do with Cobden's original case and placed those arguments within a completely different intellectual and political framework. It would be fascinating to use Cobden's European tour as a whole to explore comparisons and connections between liberals in different countries. Here I can focus only on Hamburg.

Hamburg: another kind of free trade

Hamburg as a centre of liberalism

Hamburg was generally regarded as a strongpoint of liberalism within mid-nineteenth-century Germany.[7] Its merchant elite was cosmopolitan, with trading links above all with Britain but also with the Americas, Africa and Asia. Merchants required good networks of communication and information which, once established, also carried ideas and values beyond the purely instrumental needs of trade. There developed a distinct sense of superiority over the more closed, inward-looking worlds of much of Germany: the smaller or more specialised trading houses of inland towns; and the hierarchical societies of monarchical states with their landed aristocracies, bureaucrats and courtiers.[8] Censorship in Hamburg was notoriously lax. Julius Campe, a radical enlightenment thinker and publisher of Heinrich Heine, had operated in the city. Karl Gutzkow, one of the leading members of the radical literary movement *Junge Deutschland*, edited a newspaper, *Telegraph für Deutschland*, from the city.

Hamburg was a republican city-state, one of only four non-monarchical states within the German Confederation. It prided itself on having no officially defined, privileged upper class, a patriciate. Citizenship was in principle open to anyone.

The city-state lived by entrepôt trade. The general pattern was the importation of colonial and British manufactured or semi-manufactured goods (especially cotton) and the export of food and raw materials from a hinterland which extended beyond the German states. Hamburg's position at the mouth of the Elbe and on the western side of the landmass of Schleswig-Holstein that juts north, dividing the North Sea from the Baltic, placed it in an ideal position for land and river-borne trade to and from the south and east and sea-borne trade to and from the west. The expansion of trade since the end of the Napoleonic Wars, in particular between Britain and the continent, with the liberalising by Britain of third-party trade with its colonies, and with the taking up of trading links with the newly independent states of South America, all contributed to a great expansion of this transit trade for Hamburg.

The orientation to Britain was striking. In 1850 about 60 per cent of imports and 40 per cent of exports through Hamburg were of British goods. In 1835 about one-third of the ships in Hamburg's port were flying the British flag. Sons of Hamburg merchants destined to follow the family trade typically spent a portion of their early career working in either an English enterprise or the London branch of a Hamburg merchant house (usually not that of their own family). Ruperti, Cobden's host in 1847, had followed this pattern, subsequently going on to work in South America before returning to join forces with the merchant house run by his father-in-law. It was more important to know English commercial law and practice than that of any German state. Hamburg merchants naturally had fluent English. Many leading Hamburg families, such as that of Richard Parrish, were originally from England. The leading civil engineer who was responsible for Hamburg's modernised sewage and water supply system, William Lindley, was English. He became prominent following the great fire of 1842. So did the English architect of the new Houses of Parliament, Gilbert Scott, who was commissioned to design the replacement for the church of St Nicholas, which was destroyed during that fire. English fashions, English literature, English manners were quickly acquired in Hamburg, which, in good weather, was little more than twenty-four hours sailing distance from London.

Hamburg was also noted for its economic liberalism, although this phrase was only commonly used from the 1860s. In the 1840s terms such as 'Freihändler' (free-trader), 'Manchestertum' or 'Manchester Liberalismus' were more common, though more often used by those hostile to Hamburg and its trading policies than those who supported them.[9] As a centre of entrepôt trade the city-state had always favoured low tariffs. There were major reductions in what tariffs did exist in 1814 and 1830. Hamburg sought, generally successfully, to associate itself with liberalising British trade measures – both concerning tariffs and third-party involvement in the colonial carrying trade. It quickly secured most-favoured-nation agreements with newly independent South American states. Necessary state revenue was raised by excises on consumer goods and raw materials due to be worked up in the city. Indirect taxation was far more significant than direct taxation. Foreign merchants could easily acquire full rights to practise their trade in the city. What tariffs were applied to transit goods were raised through a system of self-declaration and trust. There was no interventionist customs and excise service. Hamburg's own system of government was very 'amateur'.[10] The Senate, the executive branch, was made up largely of merchants who served for life and were replaced by nominations from existing members followed by the drawing of lots between those nominated. A minority of the Senate consisted of professional men, usually lawyers, with more time-consuming responsibilities. There was little in the way of a lower-level state service. There was no state educational system even at elementary level and no university. The bourgeoisie of Hamburg was overwhelmingly an economic bourgeoisie; state officials were virtually non-existent and the major professions – doctors, pastors and lawyers – were subordinate to the economic, in particular the merchant interest. However, sons of leading merchant families often did study law at university and then came back to the city to practise law. Very often this was done in very close connection to the family business or in the few professional positions in the city government.[11]

Hamburg also pressed for further trade liberalisation. Hannover controlled the seaward approach of the Elbe and levied a toll, the Stader Zoll, against which Hamburg ceaselessly campaigned. Hamburg had an interest in developing much better transport links with Lübeck, on the eastern side of the Schleswig-Holstein peninsula, which would have boosted east–west trade. Precisely because of that, however, it was faced with obstruction from the Danish government, which governed Schleswig-Holstein under personal union and wished to preserve as much sea-borne trade as possible through the Sound.

All this should make it clear why Hamburg had a liberal reputation, socially, culturally and politically as well as economically, and why Cobden should feel that he was among friends who thought like him when he was fêted in the city in 1847.

Hamburg as a centre of illiberalism

A closer look at the internal affairs of the city-state suggests that this liberal image is misleading. Hamburg, in institutional terms, operated a dual economic system. With transit trade maximum freedom was the guiding principle. With the domestic economy very different principles applied.

When the French occupied Hamburg between 1806 and 1814, they abolished the guilds. With the second and final removal of the French in 1814, the old constitution of 1712 was restored, including guilds. A general regulation of 1835 preserved the guilds as compulsory corporations with production, pricing and labour recruitment controls over specified occupations. During the revolution of 1848–9 this guild system was criticised and would have been removed under the terms of the new constitution drawn up by the Constituent Assembly (the *Konstituante*). However, the revolution failed and the new constitution (as well as the Basic Rights of the Imperial Constitution of 1849, which included freedom of movement, settlement and occupational choice) never came into existence. The guilds continued to exist until 1865.[12]

There were many other restrictions. Although in principle citizenship was available to all men, in practice it was much more limited. The majority of the inhabitants of Hamburg were people born in the city or of long-term residence and having no status in any other state. The men among these inhabitants were obliged to acquire citizenship if they wished to marry, run a business or acquire real estate. To be eligible they had to be at least 22 years old, Christian and able to pay a citizenship fee. Many who could or would not pay the fee were found, in the 1830s, to be co-habiting with women who were in effect their common-law wives, giving rise to anxiety about illegitimate children.[13] This contributed in 1837 to the construction of a lesser (and cheaper) form of citizenship, that of *Schutzverwandtschaft*, which conferred marriage rights but not the economic rights associated with 'normal' citizenship. Native inhabitants, therefore, were divided into citizens, *Schutzverwandten* and non-citizens. They in turn were distinguished from or divided into further categories.

Within the ranks of the citizenry one must distinguish those with and those without political rights. For a citizen to be entitled to sit in the city-state legislature, the *Bürgerschaft*, it was necessary to own a certain amount of real estate. Poor citizens, or even rich citizens whose wealth was not, at least in part, in the form of real estate, could not sit in the *Bürgerschaft*. The *Bürgerschaft* itself embodied the idea of 'direct democracy'. It was not a representative body but instead consisted of the whole body of the political citizens. In fact only a small minority of these citizens attended meetings, which were also constrained in various ways (lack of pre-circulated agendas, of minutes, or public reporting, etc.) and which had only a limited influence on the executive arm of government.

Some citizens had special economic rights. If one wished to run a large business and to hold a bank account a special *Großbürgerrecht* was required.

There were native inhabitants who could not acquire citizenship because they were not Christian. The significant Jewish population had its own communal organisations within which Jewish men had to acquire equivalent rights to those of citizens in the city-state in order to be able to marry or run a business.[14]

Finally, a great and expanding trading city like Hamburg had a large number of foreigners constantly moving in and out. Some of these acquired a special status, e.g. the *Großbürgerrecht* for merchants, or through diplomatic agreements between their country and Hamburg. At the lower end of the social spectrum, however, there was a large number of people without any rights or status, liable to deportation and in theory supposed to report to various control authorities such as an office for domestic servants, another for foreign workers, or, in the case of skilled craftsmen, to the relevant guild. As part of the method of control of population the city gates were closed each evening and this physical control, the *Torsperre*, continued until 1865.

This *Torsperre* drew attention to another distinction, namely that between the city proper, the suburbs beyond the walls (in particular St Georg and St Pauli) and the rural hinterland which was also part of the city-state. The *Torsperre* cut off the city from the suburbs and hinterland. During this period the suburbs successfully campaigned for a measure of equality, for example in terms of the right to participate in the *Bürgerschaft*.

The system of government introduced yet further restrictions. The *Bürger-schaft* and the *Senat* between them in principle exercised sovereignty within the city-state. The actual work of government was given to deputations, which in turn were divided between the five city parishes, the suburbs and rural areas. Only Lutherans were eligible to serve on the deputations. The Lutheran Church was the state church with special privileges and other Christian denominations, as well as the Jewish communes, practised their faiths only by virtue of Lutheran tolerance and on restricted conditions – for example, in terms of holding any festivals that might have a 'public' character.

All this would have been anathema to Cobden. I doubt that he could even have conceived of the idea that movement into and out of Manchester might be controlled, access to a particular trade restricted, and an elaborate system of legal distinctions be made between the inhabitants of the city. The nearest Manchester came to Hamburg practice concerned the privileges of the Church of England (most of which Cobden opposed in alliance with many Dissenters) and the possibility that a pauper might be returned to his or her parish of origin to receive poor relief. This myriad of restrictions puzzled as well as offended English visitors, even those well acquainted with the city, as when Lindley once confessed to Ruperti that: 'It is curious that in your enlightened Republic there should be such prejudices against Jews.'[15]

Is this a simple contradiction between a liberal and an illiberal aspect of

Hamburg? Or is there some level at which this can be understood as a coherent set of arrangements? How stable were these arrangements and how much consensus did they command within Hamburg? What pressures for change were there upon them? Do these arrangements, and the criticisms and pressures to which they were subjected, suggest that the idea of free trade and associated notions of liberalism took a special form in Hamburg, one that was very distinct from English, or Manchester liberalism, or from attitudes towards the economy and its relations with society as a whole in other parts of Germany? These are the range of questions I now wish to address.

Making sense of the dual economy

Economic interests, arguments and free trade

It was perfectly 'obvious' to most of those concerned with Hamburg that free trade was essential to its very survival as a major trading centre, let alone its prosperity. There was as a consequence little argument for much of the period about the matter, at least within Hamburg. The pattern was rather for self-selected spokesmen for Hamburg to respond to criticisms and threats from outside.

Very barbed criticisms were raised in 1821 in an anonymous pamphlet, *Manuskript aus Süddeutschland,* strongly influenced by arguments advocated by Friedrich List, who was, at this time, the leading figure in a largely south German organisation called the Union of German Merchants.[16] List's vision was of a helpless Germany being flooded with cheap British and colonial goods. Germany needed to respond with protective tariffs designed to provide a shield behind which infant industries could grow. In this way an argument in favour of economic development and industrial growth was linked to a conception of the national interest. The argument had important free-trade elements in so far as it advocated the removal of internal tariff barriers in Germany but it was anti-free trade in its wish to erect external tariffs for industrial promotion rather than revenue purposes.

Hamburg spokesmen made it clear that they supported the first of these positions.[17] However, they rejected the second policy. Subsequent calculations of trade statistics suggest that Germany – a fairly meaningless idea in economic terms – ran a positive balance of trade with Britain from the early 1820s into the 1830s although this probably turned negative in the 1840s. However, without such figures the Hamburg argument was more abstract. The most basic idea was of a 'natural' economy. Thus free-trade pamphlets produced in 1814 and then in response to the *Manuskript aus Süddeutschland* argued that Britain had a natural superiority in cotton and it would be wrong and probably in vain to combat this natural advantage. The purpose of free trade was to allow such natural endowments to develop to their full extent. Hamburg was simply assisting the consumer to buy the best goods at the lowest prices. One pamphlet made a broader liberal point. Hamburg was an 'open society' with its republican constitution and lack of privileged ruling elite and such a society was especially well suited to being an open economy which welcomed the circulation of the goods and people of many different nationalities.

Arguments of this kind started to matter rather more after the establishment of the Zollverein in 1834. From the 1840s there was some pressure on Hamburg to join the Zollverein. Even political liberals from other parts of Germany joined in this pressure. For example, in 1841 the noted south German liberal Welcker visited the city. He was warmly received by leading Hamburg liberals. They agreed with Welcker on all issues bar one: Hamburg and the Zollverein. Hamburg liberals argued that the Zollverein was not liberal enough; until it committed itself against any protective tariffs Hamburg would not join it. Welcker by contrast presented the Zollverein as one of the few practical and liberal ways towards greater national unity and urged Hamburg not to cut itself off from fellow Germans.[18] (The matter is somewhat complicated by the fact that many south German liberals were liberal only in the political sense of being committed to constitutional government, political rights and greater popular participation in government. They often combined this with defence of extensive economic regulation.)[19]

Few voices within Hamburg dissented from the anti-Zollverein line. Until Hannover joined the Zollverein in 1851 pressure to join was not too great as a large part of north German territory still remained outside the Zollverein. However, there were already fears that the Zollverein as a major economic unit could conclude trade and other agreements with non-German states to Hamburg's detriment. The Britain–Zollverein shipping treaty of 1841 treated the Hanse ports as part of the Zollverein. The Zollverein–Belgium trade treaty of 1844 for the first time excluded the Hanse ports from the operation of most-favoured-nation clauses.

Sometimes Hamburg was able to counteract these trends with its own agreements. Thus Hamburg and the other Hanse ports negotiated carrying rights in German and other European goods to Britain and its colonies which disadvantaged other German ports. This, however, only increased resentment elsewhere in Germany and accusations that Hamburg, as well as Bremen and Lübeck, were pursuing their own narrow interests apart from and even against the rest of Germany. This did lead to some debate in Hamburg. Some leading figures, including members of the Senate, argued that there should be more co-ordination of shipping and trading policies between German states. However, in Hamburg, where the shipping interest was quite weak (unlike in Bremen), this argument did not command much support.

In 1848 Hamburg was forced into a more explicit defence of its free trade commitment. By now List's arguments (though List himself was dead, having committed suicide in 1846) were well honed. Hamburg was an agent (witting rather than unwitting) of British economic interests. Britain was

113

flooding Germany with manufactured goods and subordinating Germany to the status of an agrarian and underdeveloped economy. Nationalism and notions of economic development led to a condemnation of Hamburg as both selfish and reactionary. The term cosmopolitan tended to become one of abuse rather than praise. In some cartoons and hostile pen portraits Hamburg was portrayed as a society obsessed with the making of money at the expense of everything else, usually by means of sharp practice.

In response people in Hamburg described protectionism as itself animated by selfish interests and argued for a 'natural' international division of labour which it was foolish to challenge. Trade should drive industry, not the other way around; consumers rather than producers should call the tune in the market-place. Protectionism had been a product of war and inter-state conflict, a clear harking back to the Napoleonic period. (This was an interesting inversion of Cobden's line, which was to stress how protectionism was conducive to war and international conflict.)

There was still little internal debate in Hamburg. In elections to the German National Assembly in April–May 1848 victory went to a slate of a notable liberal and two merchants who would 'speak for Hamburg' as against a more consistently liberal or radical slate. The main newspaper put the issue bluntly:

> Dr Heckscher . . . will fight for the general interests of Hamburg and for the rights of the Hamburg people; Ernst Merck and Edgar Roß will protect Hamburg's interests in relation to proposals for laws concerning trade and shipping.[20]

Anticipating the criticism that this might appear to weigh Hamburg's trade interests above the general interest (and even there, only the general interest of Hamburg, not Germany), the article went on to point out that there would be many fine liberals from other parts of Germany who could deal with those matters. Although it has been argued that the success of this slate demonstrated the manipulative capacities of the well-established merchant interests compared with more popular movements only beginning to take shape in the revolution,[21] there actually appears to have been little deliberate shaping of 'public opinion' and oppositional movements were, in other matters, already quite well organised before 1848. Rather this pattern reflects, on the one hand, the indifference of the merchant elite to popular politics up to 1848, but also the fairly matter-of-fact consensus on free trade, whatever else one might disagree about. Free trade is set aside from other matters. It is not just a question of separating economics from politics, but also of the issue of free trade from all other economic matters as well.

The more theatrical of the two merchant candidates, Ernst Merck (a brother-in law of Justus Ruperti), argued the Hamburg case consistently and effectively as a deputy to the Frankfurt Parliament. He continued to advocate the 'natural economy' argument. For example, he noted the demographic growth of Britain and how this could be expected to continue. This would mean, under free-trade conditions, a continued and rising demand for food products and raw materials from Germany. This, Merck continued, was clearly in Germany's best interests. Furthermore, Germany could find niches in manufactured goods as well, such as high-quality textiles. Some contemporaries also noted the shift to the export of semi-manufactured goods to Britain and could even argue that under free-trade conditions there would take place an industrialisation process in Germany, but one occurring gradually and 'naturally' rather than suddenly and artificially. Protectionism was artificial. It could, if tariffs were sufficiently high, foster industries but these would have little long-term chance of survival, would encourage over-production and attendant economic crises, and would lower living standards by raising price levels.[22]

Any deviations from these arguments within Hamburg appeared to be little more than tactical. Some considered the Zollverein to be actually or potentially so powerful that connections would have to be taken up with it. Others even went so far as to argue that Hamburg would eventually be compelled to join the Zollverein and that it would be better to do this in an early and unforced way which could get the best possible deal for Hamburg than later, under duress and unable to negotiate effectively. A principal condition which was raised by these writers was that Hamburg should preserve a free port. That was the solution eventually adopted when Hamburg did join the Zollverein in 1888 and it was one which was closely associated with the industrialisation of the city.

So there was consensus on free trade, which was seen as clearly in Hamburg's interest. Arguments did not stimulate much internal debate and tended to rationalise and add to positions taken up for simple reasons of self-interest and survival.

The case for Polizei

More difficult to interpret is the support for the retention of the panoply of controls over the city-state population outside the sphere of entrepôt trade.

This aspect of Hamburg policy attracted much criticism. List mocked the argument that free-trade Hamburg was liberal and progressive by pointing to the survival of such absurd practices as the *Torsperre*. One anonymous Hamburg writer in 1848 argued that it was difficult to put the free-trade case with persuasion and conviction given this domestic illiberalism. On the surface this writer was suggesting that the adoption of a more thorough-going liberalism was necessary to sustain the *laissez-faire* line on entrepôt trade.[23] I see it rather as a tactical argument from a more thorough-going liberal to persuade the ruling merchant interest to sweep aside the mass of controls on freedom of movement and occupational choice. Arguments of

115

this kind within Hamburg tended, however, to be political rather than economic. It was less the inefficiency of *Polizei* but the fact that it blocked the way to a more liberal and participatory political system which led to demands for its removal. This was the case that was argued with increasing strength following the crisis associated with the fire of 1842 and which commanded majority support within the *Konstituante* in 1848–9.

To understand the commitment to these controls and the rejection of liberal criticisms we need to juxtapose the idea of *Polizei* with that of the smallness of a city-state.

Hamburg wished to be, indeed had to be, open to the world and its trade. But that was also the cause of many problems and anxieties. The growth of trade after 1815 was associated with a rapid growth in the population of the city. The population doubled from about 100,000 to about 200,000 between 1800 and 1871. Much of this population came from outside the city-state and suburban growth was more rapid than that within the city proper.

This created major problems of control for Hamburg. Above all there was the issue of pauperism. Hamburg was a magnet for masses of unskilled men and women from all over northern Germany and even further afield. The concentration of population into certain quarters, along with difficulties caused by trade cycles, could mean that large numbers of people in the city could quickly become unemployed or, even if employed, earning less than the subsistence costs of themselves and their dependents. Some studies of Hamburg estimate that at certain times, e.g. in 1845–7, over half of the population was in this position.[24] These figures appear surprisingly large and I suspect, although the research has been carried out thoroughly and carefully, that it may neglect the importance of the non-monetary or 'black' part of the economy.

Unlike a small market town Hamburg could not envisage shutting itself off from this influx. Unlike a territorial state (the central governments of which often prevented small towns pursuing such a policy of exclusion) it could not provide individual towns or *Gemeinde* with the power to return paupers to the place of birth. The city-state sought to negotiate a range of bilateral agreements, especially with neighbouring states, concerning the return of unwanted members of those states. However, this was a time-consuming and complex business, especially as there were no agreed procedures for defining state membership (as opposed to the more restricted and privileged category of citizenship as then applied). In any case it could not deal with the problem of illegitimate births – other states could argue that such children were the responsibility of Hamburg, whatever the origins of the parents. I have already touched upon the problem of illegitimate births and common-law marriages as a consequence of restricting access to citizenship. The government could pursue a more relaxed policy but that would create a larger body of citizens with certain rights and claims. Alternatively it could continue with a restrictive policy but that would lead to greater immorality, in terms of the ruling ethos, as well as habituating more people to evasion of the law. (Some of the elite were disturbed by the otherwise respectable and stable nature of many of these common-law marriages, which made it appear that the laws of the state were actually creating immorality.)[25]

Another way forward was greater bureaucratic control in terms of surveillance and control. By the beginning of the 1830s, at a time when pauperism had become associated with popular unrest and political upheaval, the government introduced a twice-yearly census. Ostensibly to obtain information on the number of citizens eligible to serve in Hamburg's *Bürger-Militär*, the city-state's contribution towards the armed forces of the German Confederation, in fact the procedures and instructions for taking the census make it clear that its major purpose was to obtain better information on immigrants – legal and illegal. The problem was that the census took place on particular days known in advance, was conducted by ill-trained officers of the militia who were often not motivated to do a thorough job, and worked by means of interviews with heads of households. It was fairly easy for those without already registered addresses to evade the census, precisely the kind of people who wanted to evade it and whom the census wanted to find out about. Comparison with the first census taken by the North German Confederation in 1867 shows severe undercounting by the Hamburg census, especially among the poorest elements of the population.

Yet the government had no wish to go much further than this. Professional bureaucracies cost money and create vested institutional interests, things which were anathema to the merchant elite with its penchant for low-cost, non-interventionist government discharged mainly by themselves with a little legal support and a few subordinate functionaries. Here the notion of a 'liberal' government appeared to clash with the desire for more knowledge and control.

Another method of control was through the use of corporate institutions. *Polizei* did not mean a uniformed and professional body of men concerned with the maintenance of law and order. Such a body would not be created until after mid-century. It did not mean direct bureaucratic intervention. Rather it meant governmental support for the monitoring efforts of a range of institutions, including various nominally autonomous corporations.

This is most clear in the case of the guilds, especially when one looks at the 1835 regulations that kept the guilds in existence. It is clear that the guilds were not actually autonomous. They each operated under the patronage of a particular senator. Where, as in the case of shipbuilding, a powerful interest had argued for the abolition of guild controls, this was turned into a free occupation. The government retained the right to license non-guild members to practise a particular trade where otherwise there might be severe shortages. The government was often lax (at least to judge from guild complaints) on regulating demarcation disputes; the evasion of guild rules by some guild masters (e.g. employing more workers than they should); the illegal establishment of workshops by nominally dependent journeymen; the smuggling of guild-controlled goods from the rural hinterland, the suburbs or from outside the state; and many more such offences. The reason was that the complex society of Hamburg could not be run under the strict observation of a corporate ideology and, in any case, the governing elite did not believe in the economic case implicitly represented and sometimes explicitly put by guildsmen. That was an ideology of producer-oriented regulation whereas the merchant elite was committed to the idea of trade-oriented and 'natural' economy. Rather the elite supported the guilds as agents of control.

The role of discourse

Thus far it would appear that the tension between the dualist arrangements of Hamburg's institutions can be understood in terms of an inherent contradiction. On the one hand, the trading city lived and breathed through unregulated entrepôt trade – hence its *laissez-faire* position on trade. On the other hand, the autonomous city-state had to maintain control over its growing and often dangerously pauperised population – hence its corporate policing of the domestic economy.

There is a great deal of truth in this argument but it does not go far enough. It is frequently asserted that 'interest' itself is something that has to be constructed as a matter of language and values. Without taking the 'linguistic turn' to the extreme of denying the idea of interest as something distinct from the language in which it is expressed, nevertheless I would argue that these notions of 'interest' are bound up with certain underlying assumptions. Challenge or undermine the assumptions and the way in which interest is constructed alters.

First, there are the underlying assumptions associated with the free-trade position. I have referred to the constant invocation of a 'natural' division of labour. Protectionism was denounced as artificial interference with this natural state of affairs. Economic growth came about through the release of resources by means of abolishing such artificial constraints, through the addition of population understood as an external factor of demand (e.g. the argument that British demographic growth is good news for German farmers – especially, of course, if German farmers do not increase at the same rate), and occasionally through the one-off discovery of some fresh resource (such as the opening-up of a new part of the world or a major technological breakthrough). Absent from all this is any idea of the economy as inherently dynamic, a source of perpetual innovation and growth. Hamburg interests were very slow to pick up on railway construction and did so more for defensive reasons than any others – it was not so much that railways would generate economic growth as that they would alter the geography of trade. Free trade itself was based upon the particular location and position in the international division of labour of Hamburg, not upon an optimistic view of economic growth. In this sense, List was more growth-oriented than the Hamburg free-traders.[26]

This seems to me to be very different from the free-trade case put by Cobden and the ACLL. It may well be that some of the interests behind the repeal movement were concerned with one-off gains, such as increased demand for manufactured goods from agrarian interests that were able to sell their products to Britain, or even – despite Cobden's denials – the prospect that free trade in corn could enable a lowering of wages. But by 1843–4 the propaganda of the ACLL had gone much further than that, for example in the arguments for agrarian modernisation through extra investment and secure long-term tenures.

The Hamburg free-trade case is also not associated with a broader vision of social change. Indeed if anything the Hamburg vision is of a fairly static and fixed geographical division of labour. What is more, when one probes further, the Hamburg free-trade position is associated with an anti-industrial ideology, at least in terms of 'not in my backyard' arguments. Hamburg merchants had pursued policies which, to a limited extent, 'de-industrialised' Hamburg in the first half of the ninteenth century. The continuation of *Polizei* combined with a lack of protection for any sector producing for an extra-local market contributed to a decline in the shipbuilding, sugar-refining and brewing industries, which had grown to considerable dimensions by the end of the eighteenth century.

In the later nineteenth century Hamburg would re-industrialise, most notably through the location of industry in the free port area. But this was not something that the merchant elite of the 1815–70 period regarded positively. The primacy of trade was not merely an argument about how trade drives production, it was about the superiority of the trading economy and society over other kinds of economy and society. In the 1830s and 1840s Hamburg public opinion was regaled, along with much of the rest of western Europe, with literature on the social question. First, there was the distress of agricultural districts in the wake of crop failures or even, at the other extreme, over-production and low prices. Many commentators of the time were quite aware that poverty, although more visible in cities, was in fact worse in rural areas. Second, the growth of the early industrial cities provided a shocking example to the Hamburg elite. Hamburg merchants may have welcomed Cobden, but in the early 1840s press reports as well as private correspondence within the merchant elite make it clear that they had no wish to take the road they believed was being taken by Manchester.

Partly this was an aesthetic revulsion. Partly it was a concern that a producer interest could develop which might challenge and even overshadow trading interests. Partly it was a concern that an industrial city could not preserve its autonomy in the way that a trading city-state could. Corporate controls, guild powers, etc. would clearly have no place in such a society. There was a fear that a mass of dependent wage-labourers would be beyond control of anything less than a territorial state with a standing army and other powerful governmental agencies, and would constitute a homogenous mass which, particularly at times of depression and mass unemployment, could prove politically explosive. Hamburg recognised that it profited from the products of Manchester and the cotton towns, and from the work of landless labourers on east Elbian estates, but trusted that it would never be forced to share the structures and problems of these societies.

Much of this attitude was associated with a certain pessimism. In the mid-1830s the senator in charge of police affairs, Hudtwalcker, was wrestling with the problems of altering definitions of citizenship for the kinds of reasons I have already outlined. Hudtwalcker, who was an evangelical Lutheran and not, admittedly, typical of much of the Hamburg elite, but who on the other hand had to obtain elite support for his proposals, wrote a fascinating memorandum on the problems he confronted.[27] He noted that under modern conditions there was an irreversible shift from a society of ranks or orders to a society of contract. The policy of categorising and controlling people by birth or status was becoming increasingly difficult to carry out.

However, Hudtwalcker saw this process as a specifically economic one and considered it from a particular Christian perspective. Man is fallen. If men are given greater freedom in one part of their life, to prevent anarchy and collapse it is essential that compensating controls be imposed in other parts of their life. In Hamburg *Polizei* complemented rather than contradicted free trade. The development of greater economic freedom needed to be balanced by the construction of more effective forms of surveillance and control. Just as in Hamburg the free-trade vision was based upon a zero-sum conception of the economy, so Hudtwalcker's social vision was based upon a zero-sum conception of moral capacity. Sustained moral growth was as impossible as sustained economic growth.

Compare that with Cobden's vision. For Cobden free trade was a metaphor for and a major cause of the growth of freedom in other aspects of human life. His departure point was that of an already mobile and fairly unregulated national society but he still saw in Britain's political, religious and educational institutions, above all in the persistence of land-ed, aristocratic power, many obstacles to the fullest expansion of freedom. Hudtwalcker drew precisely the opposite political, religious, social – for want of a better summarising word: moral – conclusions from increasing economic freedom.

Most of the merchant elite of Hamburg did not share Hudtwalcker's specifically Christian world-view. They tended to more sympathy for rationalism, enlightenment ideas and an assumption of cosmopolitan superiority. Yet in their conduct of affairs and in the arguments they used to justify the apparently contradictory commitments to free trade and *Polizei*, they did in effect concur with his views.

That brings me full circle to Ruperti's toast at the banquet held for Cobden: 'Free trade, the source of all other freedoms.' Can we now dismiss this as hypocrisy? I think not. For Cobden the toast had a transparent meaning –

free trade as both model and agent of expanding freedom. For the merchant elite of Hamburg, free trade is rather the necessary condition of political autonomy. But such autonomy additionally required the maintenance of corporate controls and merchant domination.

Conclusion: what is the connection between freedom and trade?

Some narrow speculations

Free-trade ideas relate to certain interests but these interests are also constructed through discourse. Hamburg merchants did not just have different interests from Cobden and the membership of the ACLL. They also thought and talked about the world in a different way. For them free trade was an obvious necessity to preserve the autonomy and civilised forms of life they had managed to construct and defend in their city-state. For Cobden free trade was a good in itself and a way of projecting a new, more ideal way of life throughout Britain and Europe.

This raises bigger issues which are related to the title of the conference (and indeed the present volume) – 'Freedom and Trade'. Schonhardt-Bailey in Chapter 5 suggests we think of ideology as 'road maps' and that institutions (more broadly, collectively organised patterns of action) embody ideologies. Lloyd-Jones in Chapter 7 brings out vividly the way Manchester was an 'open' society in ways quite unlike Hamburg. There was no population movement controls. (The principle of returning paupers to their parish of origin did not seem to have great practical significance.) There was not even a unified system of government. (It has been argued, from a *laissez-faire* perspective, that this was a positive advantage economically.) Indeed the dominant merchant and manufacturing interests were divided not just by political and religious beliefs but also about the institutional framework in which those different beliefs should be pursued. Notions of interest and related policies were not therefore embodied in any institutional structure. The idea of *Polizei* was unthinkable. The liberal bid for power did envisage unified government for the city (incorporation), but above all was based upon the notion of agitation for policy change, making a virtue of lack of institutional control, an attack on remaining institutional restrictions (the Corn Laws but also such things as church establishment). The lower orders were not to be controlled by means of corporate categorisation and regulation but through a combination of cultural reform and preventive policing of a modern kind.[28]

There were optimists and pessimists, evangelical Christians and secularists who saw the balance of cultural reform and policing, the limited or the expanding benefits of repeal, in different ways. But operating within this common institutional framework itself created a good deal of consensus. The political economy arguments of the ACLL also provided the core of a 'road map' which could be used both by 'narrow interests' and by those for whom repeal was the beginning of a broad push for a society of greater freedom.

The institutional framework in Hamburg was very different – its own city-state with established political institutions; its policing of its boundaries; and corporate regulation of its internal economy and population. This in itself embodied the core ideas of the merchant elite. They had greater 'internal' control than their Manchester counterparts but far less 'external' control (less economic weight, not part of a powerful territorial state). Their internal illiberalism reflected the control they had there; their external liberalism reflected their lack of control (whereas in Britain it was seen actually as a policy which could induce change elsewhere). Their 'road map' was based on the assumption that society was not self-regulating. So whereas Hilton can argue powerfully that evangelical Christianity can be associated with a *laissez-faire* view of economy in Britain; I can see just as easily, in a different institutional context, how it can be associated with *Polizei* in Hamburg.[29]

Some broader speculations

The term 'economic liberalism' was widely used only from the 1860s. So far as Germany is concerned, and possibly elsewhere, this indicates to me two things: on the one hand, a conflating of free-trade positions with more general policies of economic liberalisation; on the other hand, a distinction between economic and political liberalism. Already for some time political liberalism had frequently combined with the defence of *Mittelstand* interests against the bureaucratic state but also the property-less and the outsiders, and this often included notions of economic and social regulation.[30] When some of these liberals did advocate economic freedom, for example Rotteck and Welcker in that bible of early German liberalism, the *Staats-Lexikon*, they did so more because of its implications for reducing governmental power and promoting national unity than because of its specifically economic attractions. Although the majority in the Frankfurt Parliament in 1848 generally leaned towards economic liberalism, it remained uncommitted on German tariff policy and the consitution it drew up left to the future the precise way in which freedom of movement, settlement and occupational choice was actually to be regulated. Partly this was because at a popular level there was much more support for protectionist and regulatory policies than for policies of low tariffs and full internal economic freedom.[31]

On the other hand, the strongest advocates of a less regulated and low-tariff economy were often wedded to authoritarian forms of government, partly because economic illiberalism seemed to have popular roots. Examples include Rhenish entrepreneurs and east Elbian farmers. Often governments most committed to creating greater economic freedom – as in Prussia – had to use great concentrations of authoritarian state power in order to impose that freedom (e.g. land reform measures such as division of commons) and created a new kind of policing (e.g. in Berlin) to cope with some of the consequences of producing greater freedom of movement, settlement and occupational choice. This was different from Hamburg in certain respects because the much greater territory involved as well as the monarchical–bureaucratic form of government did allow for greater economic liberalisation.

Apart from these variations in 'interests' and institutional context, there is also the question of varying 'economic visions'. I have already argued how static was this vision in Hamburg, linked to notions of a 'natural' division of labour.[32] Actually it was not very different in its basic assumptions from those underlying many protectionist interests which criticised the Hamburg view. What is interesting is how and why there develops an optimistic economic vision based on ideas of sustained growth, sometimes wedded to notions of 'development', and later associated with an 'urban-industrial' model of the economy. I am not sure that in certain respects one could even say that most advanced spokesmen of the ACLL had such 'future-oriented' visions which took on the second and third of these ideas.

But raising these issues points to complex and varying ways in which notions of freedom (e.g. as a function of material well-being or as constrained by the development of new class structures) are linked, through economic visions, to the particular concern with free trade. Generally until well after 1848 it seems to me that the growth of political freedom and of economic freedom and prosperity were not closely linked in German states (and one could extend the argument to most other parts of Europe) outside certain minority groups. I would suggest that in the period c.1820–60 this can be linked to arguments Keith Tribe has put forward about how 'National Economics', rather than being understood as the introduction of classical political economy in Germany to replace that of Cameralism, rather represents a continuation of older 'policing' views juxtaposed with aspects of political economy.[33]

For a brief period in the 1860s there appeared to be a shift towards a broader notion of economic liberalism and a connecting of this to political liberalism. In a period of economic expansion, development and optimism, it was now possible to think of constitutional liberalism and a shift to a much freer market economy going together. Hence the popularisation of the term 'economic liberalism'. That can be linked to Anthony Howe's Chapter 13, which depicts the shift away from unilateral economic liberalism in Britain to bilateral agreements with European states although that also has multilateral components (e.g. through most-favoured-nation clauses). A British 'narrowing' of the free-trade position was linked to a European 'widening'.

Even then, German liberalism had to work with the 'strong state' which had, by means of successful war, provided it with the unified territory and institutions that enabled it to envisage liberalisation as a practical ideal. This link between authoritarian state and economic liberalisation was also demonstrated in the way in which it was the government of Louis-Napoleon, not a liberal republican regime, which concluded the free-trade agreement with Britain. Furthermore, even this particular kind of economic liberalism was faltering in Germany with the onset of crisis and price depression in 1873–4.

Concluding speculation

Most of this chapter has focused on the specific and special case of Hamburg, comparing it to the 'vision' of Cobdenite liberalism. However, the way in which a trading liberalism in Hamburg was associated with concerns about control and regulation in other spheres of life suggests to me that the ACLL arguments about the relationship between free trade and a broader set of freedoms was peculiarly British. This was not only because it uniquely suited British interests (the critical point made by List) but also because it was related to a peculiar institutional context and set of social and political conflicts. Other, perhaps more influential models have sought to hedge the dangers of economic freedom about with many other forms of control or have associated the growth of democracy with dangers to economic liberalism.[34]

This is a commonplace in our era, where free trade liberalism has often been associated with authoritarian conceptions of politics and morality, and where claims to defend the freely chosen ways of life of particular communities have been used to justify extensive interference with market freedom. The relationships between free-trade principles, economic liberalism and broader conceptions of freedom have always been complex and problematic. I have been able to argue this only with reference to one small example. I would not argue that this example is typical in the sense that the particular relationships established there are to be found in many other cases. However, I would argue that it is typical in showing that one must connect the principle of free trade to interests, institutions and discourse; that one should expect this principle to have very different meanings in different cases; and that the equation of free trade with freedom is but one, perhaps very unusual, such meaning.

Notes

1 For Cobden's visit to Hamburg see M. Taylor (ed.) *The European Diaries of Richard Cobden 1846–1849* (Aldershot, 1994); Hinde 1987; *Hamburger neue Zeitung und Addreß-Comptoir-Nachrichten*, 237 (6 October 1847) and 238 (7 October 1847); *Deutscher Freihafen*, 10 October 1847: 'Das Freihandelfest in Hamburg'.
2 For further details on Ruperti see P.E. Schramm, *Hamburg, Deutschland und die Welt. Leistung und Grenzen des hanseatischen Bürgertums in der Zeit zwischen Napoleon I und Bismarck: Ein Kapitel deutscher Geschicht* (Hamburg, 1943), *passim*.
3 M. Taylor, *The European Diaries of Richard Cobden 1846–1849* (Aldershot, 1994) *passim*.
4 *Manchester Guardian*, 31 October 1835; quoted in N. Edsall, *Richard Cobden: Independent Radical* (London, 1986), pp. 37–8.

5 For example, the *Manchester Guardian*, 9 February 1842, describes the bazaar currently operating in Manchester as doing well, with a high turnover, much of it in useful articles at moderate prices with quick returns on capital. These 'have been the distinguishing features of the fair 'free-traders' mode of transacting business. Would that our merchants and manufacturers were permitted by the monopoly-interest to follow out similar principles of commercial intercourse with every country, and in every market of the world.'

6 P. Aycoberry, 'Freihandelsbewegung in Deutschland und Frankreich in den 1840er und 1850er Jahren', in D. Langewiesche (ed.) *Liberalismus im 19.Jahrhundert. Deutschland im europäischer Vergleich* (Göttingen, 1988); J.R. Davis, *Britain and the German Zollverein 1848–66* (London, 1997).

7 For a general account of Hamburg in English, with further references to relevant literature, see my essay 'Liberalism in mid-nineteenth century Hamburg and Manchester' in J. Breuilly *Labour and Liberalism in Nineteenth-Century Europe* (Manchester, 1992).

8 A. Schulze, 'Weltbürger und Geldaristokraten. Hanseatisches Bürgertum im 19.Jahrhhundert', *Historische Zeitschrift*, 259, 1994, pp. 637–70.

9 J. Bossmann, 'Primat des Handels oder Industrialisierung? Hamburger und Stettiner Wirtschaftsbürger und ihre Herausforderung durch süddeutschen Fabrikanteninteressen 1814–1849', unpublished Magisterarbeit, University of Bielefeld, 1992; R. Walther, 'Wirtschaftlicher Liberalismus' in R. Koselleck *et al.* (eds) *Geschichtliche Grundbegriffe*, 3 (Stuttgart, 1982).

10 For a good characterisation of this in English see R.J. Evans, *Death in Hamburg: Society and Politics in the Cholera Years, 1830–1910* (Oxford, 1987), esp. pp. 1–27.

11 R.J. Evans, 'Family and class in the Hamburg grande bourgeoisie', in D. Blackbourn and R.J. Evans (eds) *The German Bourgeoisie: Essays on the Social History of the German Middle Class from the Late Eighteenth to the Early Twentieth Century*, (London, 1991).

12 J. Breuilly and W. Sachse, *Joachim Friedrich Martens und die deutsche Arbeiterbewegung* (Göttingen, 1984).

13 K. Gröwer, ' "Wilde Ehen". Zu einer Lebensform der sozialen Unterschichten im 19.Jahrhundert am Beispiel Hamburgs', unpublished Magisterarbeit, University of Hamburg, 1989.

14 H. Krohn, *Die Juden in Hamburg 1800–1850. Ihre soziale, kulturelle und politische Entwicklung während der Emanzipationszeit* (Frankfurt, 1974).

15 P.E. Schramm, *Hamburg, Deutschland und die Welt. Leistung und Grenzen des hanseatischen Bürgertums in der Zeit zwischen Napoleon I und Bismarck: Ein Kapitel deutscher Geschichte* (Hamburg, 1943), p. 251.

16 W.O. Henderson, *Friedrich List: Economist and Visionary 1789–1846* (London, 1983).

17 J. Bossmann, 'Primat des Handels oder Industrialisierung?'

18 For an account of this encounter in October 1841 see Staatsarchiv Hamburg 614–1/11: Turner Verein 1840–1842. This contains extracts of the minute book of the Hamburg Gymnastic Association, a most detailed description of the events, and an analysis of newspaper reports.

19 L. Gall, 'Liberalismus und "Bürgerliche Gesellschaft". Zu Charakter und Entwicklung der liberalen Bewegung in Deutschland', *Historische Zeitschrift*, 220, 1975, pp. 324–56.

20 *Nachrichten*, 18 April 1848.

21 W. Schmidt, *Die Revolution von 1848/49 in Hamburg*, (Hamburg, 1983) p. 40.

22 For more detailed presentations of these and other debates and arguments, see J. Bossmann, 'Primat des Handels oder Industrialisierung? Hamburger und

Stettiner Wirtschaftsbürger und ihre Herausforderung durch süddeutschen Fabrikanteninteressen 1814–1849', unpublished Magisterarbeit, University of Bielefeld, 1992; H. Best, *Interessenpolitik und nationale Integration 1848/49* (Göttingen, 1980).

23 The article was published in the *Hamburger Nachrichten*, 31 August 1848. I am indebted to Frank Uekötter for bringing this to my attention in an essay he wrote in a course I taught at the University of Bielefeld in 1992–3. See F. Uekötter, 'Freihandel in Hamburg: Seine Bedeutung für Politik und Gesellschaft am Beispiel der Revolution 1848/49', unpublished Referat, University of Bielefeld, 1993.

24 A. Krause, *Die Unterschichten Hamburgs in der ersten Hälfte des 19.Jahrhunderts* (Stuttgart, 1965).

25 Gröwer, 'Wilde Ehen'.

26 These arguments about conceptions of the economy are developed in Bossmann, 'Primat des Handels oder Industrialisierung?', but are most elaborately worked out and applied in Boch's study of Rhenish economic interests of this period. See R. Boch, *Grenzenloses Wachstum? Das rheinische Wirtschaftsbürgertum und seine Industrialisierungsdebatte von 1814–1857* (Göttingen, 1991).

27 The memorandum appears in Staatarchiv Hamburg files Bestand 332–8: Meldewesen, B12: concerned with the revision of the 1833 law on servants and is dated 24 January 1837. Hudtwalcker also refers to various of these issues in his autobiography. See M.H. Hudtwalcker, *Ein halbes Jahrhundert aus meinem Lebensgeschichte* (Hamburg, 3 vols, 1862–4, III, pp. 412–24).

28 M. Hewitt, *The Emergence of Stability in the Industrial City: Manchester, 1832–1867* (Aldershot, 1996); S.J. Davis, 'Classes and police in Manchester 1829–1880', in A. Kidd and K. Roberts (eds) *City, Class and Culture* (Manchester, 1985).

29 B. Hilton, *The Age of Atonement: The Influence of Evangelicanism on Social and Economic Thought* (Oxford, 1988).

30 For examples of such liberalism, see P. Nolte, *Gemeindebürgertum und Liberalismus in Baden 1800–1850* (Göttingen, 1994).

31 Gall, 'Liberalismus und "Bürgerliche Gesellschaft"', p. 324–56; H. Sedatis, *Liberalismus und Handwerk in Süddeutschland. Wirtschafts- und Gesellschaftskonzeptionen und die Krise des Handwerks im. 19.Jahrhundert* (Stuttgart, 1979); M. Walker, *German Home Towns: Community, State, and General Estate, 1648–1871* (Ithaca, NY, 1971).

32 For Hamburg, specifically, this argument is heavily indebted to Bossmann, 'Primat des Handels oder Industrialisierung?'; more generally to R. Boch, *Grenzenloses Wachstum? Das rheinische Wirtschaftsbürgertum und seine Industrialisierungsdebatte von 1814–1857* (Göttingen, 1991).

33 K. Tribe, 'Cameralism and the science of government', in *Strategies of Economic Order: German Economic Discourse 1750–1950* (Cambridge, 1995), p. 29. Tribe focuses on territorial states and links his argument to the 'state-building' measures begun in the Napoleonic period. This makes it especially interesting that the combination of *Polizei* and political economy is also encountered in the very different setting of Hamburg.

34 The celebrated book by Fukuyama on the 'end of history' presents yet another model relating market economics to liberal democracy. See F. Fukuyama, *The End of History and the Last Man* (London, 1992).

9

COMMENTS ON LLOYD-JONES AND BREUILLY

Alon Kadish

That the repeal of the Corn Laws, and freer trade or indeed total free trade, would serve the economic interests of the Manchester business community was a common accusation made by the critics of the Anti-Corn Law League, and one frequently echoed by the supporters of the Factory Movement. Roger Lloyd-Jones shows that free trade was indeed a sensible strategy adopted by a 'variegated, dynamic and open' business system keen to ensure its prosperous survival. Lloyd-Jones does not overlook the involvement of Manchester businessmen in political and municipal reform and their socio-cultural activities. Indeed in the chapter's final paragraph he underlines their 'notion that the common interest of capitalists and workers, their jobs, their prosperity and their future was threatened by the continued operation of the Corn Laws.' It seems, however, worth stressing that the economics of the Manchester free traders reflected not only profit seeking, but also their wider social, political, and religious concerns, an issue which I have developed in my chapter on the League's economics.

The Manchester free traders accepted high wages as desirable. High wages would increase the home market's purchasing power in a way which would boost producers' profits, improve the material and moral state of the working classes, and ensure greater social and political stability in an age fearful of the consequences of radical agitation among the lower classes. They rejected protection, either by means of Corn Laws or factory legislation, as a policy incapable of securing high wages. The prosperity of industry would not only benefit the rest of society in a general way. High wages and free trade, they argued, were closely and causally linked. Their advocacy of free trade was not only a strategy for economic survival but also one of political and social progress, hence its enormous appeal and rapid ascendancy as one of the principles of mid-Victorian political culture.

John Breuilly's chapter raises the interesting issue of the relation between policy and rhetoric. To the standard debate on whether trade followed the flag or the flag followed trade, one might add the question of the relation between economic policies and the rhetoric employed in their service. To take the matter a step further, the question might be viewed as part of the process of the transference of ideas, that is did free trade rhetoric and the adoption of free trade as an external economic policy eventually influence economic and political thinking in internal policies? Seen from the perspective of 150 years it might be interesting to examine whether free trade has indeed acted, as Cobden believed it would, as 'both model and agent' of expanding internal social, political, and religious freedom; whether the adoption of free trade as a technical means to a concrete end did not, in retrospect, influence other policies and ideologies.

10

THE RECIPROCITY DEBATE IN PARLIAMENT, 1842–1846

Douglas A. Irwin

The English classical economists were known not just for their success in developing a lasting body of economic theory, but also for their keen interest in economic policy. This interest in policy was not confined solely to exchanges in the leading journals of the day, but spilled over into Parliament as well, where many economists served as members during the first half of the nineteenth century. Although their influence on legislation can be questioned, that their way of thinking about economic issues permeated many parliamentary debates cannot.[1]

Above all, the classical economists were noted for their advocacy of free international trade. The cogent criticism of mercantilism by Adam Smith, reinforced by the theoretical developments of David Ricardo and others, established free trade as their common creed. During the parliamentary debates over protection that were drawn out over much of the early nineteenth century, those who struggled to shift Britain's commercial policy toward free trade looked to political economy for support for their position. Even new theoretical developments about trade were discussed, if only to support one position or another.[2]

Yet, curiously, one respected economist who contributed much to the intellectual case for free trade, and who briefly served as a Member of Parliament, developed a theory which purported to show how free trade could actually harm a country that undertook such a policy unilaterally. The economist, Robert Torrens, argued in favor of reciprocity, that any changes to Britain's tariff be contingent upon similar reductions in foreign tariffs. Torrens publicized his arguments in a series of pamphlets addressed to prominent politicians in the early 1840s – precisely the time when Parliament was considering the enactment of tariff reductions. The result was a spirited debate between leading economists and, as the controversy gained attention in Parliament, among leading politicians.

This chapter traces how Torrens's heretical contentions filtered into the House of Commons debate over tariff reductions from 1842 to 1846, focusing on how his theory was utilized by opponents of tariff reductions and countered in turn by advocates of liberalization. Because of his reputation as a serious political economist, Torrens put free traders on the defensive by providing an economic basis for reciprocity.[3] Torrens's call for reciprocity ultimately failed, however, because disagreements about the policy were based on differing judgments – which Torrens's theory could not assist in resolving – as to the response of foreign countries to changes in British commercial policy. Furthermore, the negative consequences that Torrens envisioned seemed remote in comparison with what appeared to be the more palpable benefits of free trade. At the end of the debate, those advocating reciprocity failed to undermine the view that reciprocity was problematic and that unilateral free trade would be beneficial to Britain.

Torrens's position on free trade

Torrens's most original work in economics concerned international trade theory. For example, he deserves at least joint credit with Ricardo for developing the theory of comparative costs, which confirmed to many the unqualified virtues of free trade.[4] However, Torrens was also more eclectic than other contemporary economic thinkers of the day in his view of free trade as an economic policy. Initially a conventional proponent of free trade, Torrens became over the course of his career an unorthodox economist who gave comfort to those resisting a liberalization of Britain's commercial policy.[5] One of the first explicit statements that revealed his heterodoxy on free trade came in Parliament. Torrens rose in Parliament on July 3, 1832 to express reservations about free trade. 'Whatever might be the advantages of free trade,' he said, 'these advantages were in some degree counterbalanced by an enhancement in the value of money, and a general fall in the prices not merely of the goods imported, but also of British goods.'[6]

A unilateral tariff reduction would set in motion the specie-flow mechanism described in David Hume's classic exposition on the balance of trade in the mid-eighteenth century. Such a reduction would create an incipient trade deficit, leading to an outflow of gold and thus a fall in the price of British goods. This decline in price would, in turn, stimulate foreign demand for British exports and naturally eliminate the trade deficit and bring an end to the gold outflow.

Torrens disagreed with the standard free-trade view that it mattered not whether foreigners imported Britain's goods or money. He also departed from standard Ricardian doctrine in viewing foreign demand as a factor determining the exchangeable value of Britain's traded commodities. These issues had been 'wholly overlooked by the advocates of free-trade principles, though it was obvious they had . . . only to be stated to be at once recognised.'[7] As a result of these considerations, Torrens was prepared to advocate that tariffs be reduced only on goods coming from countries with which Britain had a favorable specie balance.[8]

Torrens reinforced his reputation for controversy again in 1841 when, in a series of pamphlets directed at Britain's political leadership, he expressed more clearly and enunciated more forcefully his objections to unilateral tariff reductions.[9] Torrens again began his analysis with the specie-flow mechanism as described by David Hume, David Ricardo, and Nassau Senior, and again introduced the concept of international demand as determining the prices of traded goods. According to Torrens, a unilateral tariff reduction by Britain would increase the quantity of imports demanded without initially altering foreign demand for British exports. A flow of precious metals from Britain to finance the trade imbalance would generate deflationary pressures, exacerbating economic distress and dislocation in Britain by inflating the real burden of debt and taxation.

In addition, the price of British exports would fall and the price of British imports would increase, meaning that a greater quantity of British labor would be required to purchase a given quantity of imports. This adverse terms-of-trade effect, although somewhat set in the background by Torrens's stress on the monetary costs of unilateral tariff reductions, was quickly recognized by economists as a novel claim.[10] As the terms of the international exchange of goods were closely related to the distribution of the gains from trade, Torrens had successfully noted a possible tension between cosmopolitan and national justifications for free trade, with unilateral free trade possibly being at odds with national welfare. Torrens remained a free trader in that he never lost sight of the fact that free trade would be best for the world as a whole. But national welfare, he argued, should be the priority for British policy makers and this made him a qualified free trader. His conclusion for Britain was clear: 'the sound principle of commercial policy is, to oppose foreign tariffs by retaliatory duties, and to lower our import duties in favour of those countries who may consent to trade with us on terms of reciprocity.'[11]

Partly because Britain was on the verge of adopting free trade, Torrens incurred sharp criticism from many prominent economists for questioning the benefits of that policy.[12] He firmly rejected such criticism, stating that he was working within the logical framework of Ricardian analysis. What perhaps galled free-trade economists most was Torrens's decision to direct his views to prominent politicians and not to more theoretically minded economists through more obscure outlets in some form of peer review. By so promoting his views, Torrens clearly intended his theories to be immediately applicable to British economic policy. Other economists feared that politicians might indeed find his analysis plausible and act on its advice by slowing the move to free trade.

Reception of Torrens's ideas in Parliament

Although Torrens framed his ideas to influence the ongoing political debate over trade policy, there is little doubt that his opinions played a relatively minor role in the drama surrounding the repeal of the Corn Laws and other tariffs. As Fetter (1980, p. 79) noted, 'the few protectionist-oriented economists thought more in terms of maintaining the unity of the empire, or the social and political leadership of the landed gentry, than in developing the subtleties of Torrens's analysis.' Yet a significant theme of the debate concerned whether Britain's tariff reductions should or would be reciprocated by other countries. Torrens's writings were important to this discussion, and how his ideas arose and in what context are questions worth pursuing.

A brief description of Britain's commercial policy during this period helps set the context for the tariff debates of the 1840s. At the end of the Napoleonic Wars in 1815, Britain increased the protection given to agriculture by enacting a more restrictive version of the Corn Laws. Parliament later enacted some tariff reforms in the 1820s based on the principle of reciprocity, meaning that bilateral treaties were negotiated with foreign governments amenable to reducing duties on trade. During the 1830s, however, trade liberalization languished as foreign countries spurred Britain's efforts to negotiate reciprocity treaties. By the early 1840s, when sentiment in Britain for tariff reductions (and even Corn Law abolition) was growing, many free traders came to believe that reciprocity was only delaying the arrival of free trade for Britain and that it should ignore the trade barriers of other countries and adopt free trade unilaterally.

To this end, John Lewis Ricardo (David Ricardo's nephew) introduced a resolution in Parliament in April 1843 that 'it is not expedient that any contemplated remission of Import duties be postponed, with a view of making such remission a basis of commercial negotiations with foreign countries.'[13] In submitting the proposal, Ricardo argued not only that the move would benefit Britain through an extension of commerce (greater imports would be paid for by greater exports), but also that Britain should not pretend that advantage could arise from retaliation against foreign tariffs in an effort to reduce those duties.

Benjamin Disraeli spoke against the proposal and revealed traces of Torrens's influence with his opening remarks.[14] He denied J.L. Ricardo's assertion that it was generally acknowledged that the initial loss of precious metals as a result of a unilateral tariff reduction caused no injury. Disraeli expressed his belief that 'anything that could cause a sudden abstraction of the precious metals from this country must necessarily affect the commercial transactions of this country at the same time.' When such outflows had occurred in the past, they produced the 'most serious consequences,' including currency disruptions and downward pressure on wages and prices.

Furthermore, 'until [the governments of Europe] accepted our high notions of political economy' and also wished to liberalize their trade,

> was it not the natural course to adopt the happy medium which was always followed by practical men – that system of reciprocity by means of which, through negotiations, they might obtain those benefits which they all acknowledged increased commerce, and avoid those dangers that might possibly attend a less cautious and prudent course?[15]

Viscount Sandon also stood to deplore the 'fallacy constantly put forward . . . that all imports were paid for in manufactures. . . . On the contrary, vast quantities were occasionally paid for in gold, to the great derangement of our circulating medium, and the injury of the many interests in this country.'[16] Prime Minister Robert Peel also opposed the resolution and advised 'the House to reserve to itself the power of applying sound principles to particular cases, as they arise.' Peel also directly injected Torrens into the debate:

> since I came into the House I have read a postscript of a letter, addressed to me by a gentleman, a zealous free-trader, whose authority cannot well be disputed on the other side of the House. I see hon. Gentleman opposite turn away from Colonel Torrens now as a gentleman of no authority at all – but I refer to his opinion for the purpose of showing that upon this subject even strenuous advocates of free-trade are not united.

After quoting a representative paragraph from Torrens, Peel said that Torrens 'calls, too, in aid of his opinions other high authorities' such as Nassau Senior, James Pennington, and David Ricardo, 'in whose chapter on trade the doctrine is involved.' 'Whatever may be the connection of the hon. Member opposite with [David Ricardo],' Peel added, 'he cannot feel greater respect than I do.' Peel argued:

> If, then, these differences of opinion exist – if these speculative doctrines upon which even free traders are not agreed – I hope the House of Commons will not make itself party to an abstract resolution embodying these views without much more mature consideration.[17]

J.L. Ricardo responded that 'as far as he recollected the opinions of Mr. Ricardo, he did not think it possible that he would have advocated the principle of reciprocity.' (J.L. Ricardo did not understand Torrens's claim, which was not that David Ricardo and others were advocates of reciprocity like himself, but that his conclusions were derived from a theoretical framework created by Ricardo and others.) With regard to Torrens, whose 'pamphlet had attracted considerable attention,' J. L. Ricardo said that Peel had merely 'stated what Colonel Torrens intended to prove, and not what he had proven, so that this mathematical demonstration was *in nubibus* . . . at present.' Ricardo attempted to recall a mathematical demonstration by Benjamin Franklin, which he claimed was in support of the proposition that reciprocity and retaliation were harmful. If country X has three manufactures (cloth, silk, and iron) and trades with countries A, B, and C, then should X protect (say) silk, others will retaliate, forcing X to counter-retaliate by putting on duties on clothing and iron imports, and so on. In the end, Ricardo said that Franklin questioned 'what benefit these four countries would gain by these prohibitions, while all four would have curtailed the sources of their comforts and the conveniences of life?' Ricardo insisted this was a true demonstration of the consequences of reciprocity, whereas Torrens had only threatened to give a demonstration.[18] In fact, Ricardo's confused exposition was nothing of the sort but merely an assertion that trade restrictions beget trade restrictions.

The defeat of this resolution did not dissuade J.L. Ricardo from repeating his efforts. In March 1844, he submitted a proposal requiring Britain 'not to enter into any negotiations with foreign powers, which would make any contemplated alterations of the tariff of the United Kingdom contingent on the alterations of the tariffs of other countries.' Britain's commercial interests, he thought,

> will be best promoted by regulating our own Customs' duties as may be most suitable to the financial and commercial interests of this country, without reference to the amount of duties which foreign powers may think it expedient, for their own interests, to levy on British goods.[19]

One MP (Sir J. Hanmer) objected on grounds that Torrens had developed and revealed a clear understanding of a tariff's impact on the terms of trade. If Britain lowered duties on Bordeaux wines while its cloth was forced to pay duties in France,

> We should have to pay increased quantities of the cloth in order to buy the wine. . . . The noble Lord talked of imports and not exports being the measure of national prosperity, but surely the rate at which we were to buy the imports was of some consequence in this argument.

The fact that the enjoyment of the wine-drinker was enhanced while the cloth manufacturer was taxed

> was the answer (well put in a number of the *Foreign and Colonial Quarterly Review* last autumn), to those who said . . . that broad

considerations of public and general advantage dictated a disregard of foreign tariffs, and the adoption of some such vague and sweeping propositions as was then before the House, by which all means of even moderating those [foreign] Tariffs would be thrown away.[20]

In reply, Joseph Hume conceded that 'it had never been said that we were not placed at a disadvantage by the conduct of those foreign nations who levied high duties on our exports, nor that a treaty of complete reciprocity would not be beneficial.' But Hume insisted that another method must be tried to extend British commerce: as many foreign countries would not consent to reduce their duties, Britain must therefore act independently on its own economic interests.[21]

It is important to note that nearly all economists both in and out of Parliament sought free trade as the ultimate outcome for British policy. Agreement as to the end of policy, however, was equally matched by disagreement as to the means by which the policy was to be achieved. Those committed to free trade differed on which tactics Britain should adopt in establishing the policy, with economic opinion aligned on a spectrum depending on whether foreign tariffs were viewed with indifference, concern, or alarm. Four broad categories of beliefs can be identified.

At one extreme, J. L. Ricardo and his followers believed that Britain's free trade policy should be determined independently of foreign tariffs, either because such tariffs were irrelevant to Britain's economic gains or because they were beyond Britain's control. Unilateral free traders like Viscount Palmerston rejected the view that Britain should 'continue to submit to an evil which we have the power to put an end to, because, forsooth, another country chooses to continue to subject us and themselves to another evil of a similar kind, which is beyond our control.'[22]

A second group of unilateralists conceded that foreign tariffs might be a cause for concern, but believed that they would be eradicated because other countries, observing Britain's success with free trade, would be compelled to follow its example. The success of the 'demonstration effect' of British free trade in reducing foreign tariffs was assured and, for these MPs, dispelled any worries about the harm those tariffs might have. One Member, for example, 'felt assured that our good example would be everywhere followed, and that an extension of peace and civilization would be the consequence.'[23] By contrast, Torrens had no faith that Britain's free-trade example would induce other countries to lower their trade barriers: that 'America would forthwith imitate our example, and relax her tariff . . . is utterly fallacious.'[24]

Another group thought that foreign tariffs were important enough that negotiations to reduce them should be tried first, with recourse to unilateral free trade only should they fail. Britain's failed attempts at reciprocity in the 1830s had pushed some of these MPs into the unilateral free-trade camp, although a fully fledged Corn Law repeal was not on the bargaining table during that decade. Peel justified the unilateral nature of the Corn Law repeal by stating that

> it is only because we have continued these attempts for the last ten or fifteen years, and have made no progress [in securing reciprocity treaties], that we at last came to the resolution that we would exclusively study our own advantages; and that we would no longer injure the people of this country by debarring them from foreign articles, because foreign countries would not enter into reciprocal treaties with us.[25]

Finally, those in sympathy with Torrens believed in strict reciprocity: there should be absolutely no reductions in British tariffs until foreigners agreed to do the same with their tariffs. Disraeli insisted that 'before we come to settle this great question, we must grapple with the important point of waging war against hostile tariffs,' ridiculing the notion that it was possible to fight hostile tariffs with free imports.[26] Of course, those opposed to unilateral free trade were both qualified free-traders like Torrens and crude protectionists with whom Torrens disagreed. The crude protectionists were especially prone to latch onto the monetary aspects of Torrens's theory in an effort to rehabilitate mercantilist doctrine. In this vein, one Mr Spooner recited the Torrens line on the loss of gold that would follow tariff reduction and sweepingly concluded 'that protection to native industry was essential to the prosperity of all classes in the country.'[27] Disraeli and other politicians who agreed with Torrens's concerns about foreign tariffs also tended to emphasize the more dramatic monetary consequences of tariff reduction rather than the more abstract terms-of-trade argument.

The classical economists, by contrast, concentrated on the more intricate terms-of-trade aspects, as Torrens eventually did himself. As a prominent political economist, Torrens's name arose in Parliament at various times in a variety of circumstances. Part of what was culled from Torrens's thought was not related to his theory of trade. Some drew attention to Torrens for his work on distribution, in which he predicted (as did many other economists) that Corn Law repeal could not be expected to improve the condition of the working classes because nominal wages were regulated by the price of provisions. J.C. Colquhoun stated that 'Colonel Torrens, a political economist, to whose opinions hon. Gentlemen opposite would be disposed to pay respect, asserted that . . . such a measure would not produce any improvement in the condition of the working classes, or in the rate of wages.'[28] In addition, his pamphlets were cited as evidence that repeal would ruin agriculture and yet provide no compensating benefit to labor and manufacturing. For example, defenders of the Corn Laws opposed a sudden shock to landed interests, saying that any drastic policy change would cause distress between agricultural laborers and farmers. Adam Smith and David Ricardo were frequently invoked to support the call for a gradual introduction of free trade. When one MP stamped Smith's views as 'antiquated,' James Graham decided to quote from a pamphlet printed 'within the last fortnight' by Torrens saying that free traders 'close their understanding against the equally indisputable facts, that the immediate effect of free-trade would be to create agricultural distress.'[29]

But Torrens was most frequently mentioned for his concern about foreign tariffs, as when J.C. Colquhoun warned that

> This country ought not to shut its eyes to the fact, that following whatever course of policy you might, as had been shown by Colonel Torrens in his recent pamphlet, that we meet with every impediment to exclude us from foreign markets.[30]

Torrens was also cited as an important writer who had changed his mind on these important issues. One MP

> could name a gentleman of great talent, to whom he was once opposed at an election, on the very ground of the Corn-laws, that gentleman being then a strong advocate for repeal – he meant Colonel Torrens – but what was not the opinion of Colonel Torrens, as expressed in some letters which he had recently published, addressed to the right hon. Baronet at the head of the Government. That gentleman was now convinced, and stated in those pamphlets, that the effect of such a measure would be ruinous to the agricultural interest of the country, and be productive of no good effect to the manufacturers; that it would limit labour and reduce the rate of wages.[31]

It is hard to conclude that MPs deliberately misrepresented Torrens's views in the House of Commons to win debating points. Instead, members took his views under thoughtful consideration and tried to evaluate the possibility that his concerns merited attention.

Victory of unilateral free trade

The debate over unilateral free trade and reciprocity reached a new urgency in early 1846 when Prime Minister Peel proposed to repeal the Corn Laws. Part of the debate over the measure was concerned with the non-reciprocal nature of the proposed repeal. While Torrens's pamphlets had been available for over a year, the issues they discussed were bound to arise again as Britain considered enacting the policy he opposed. Peel defended the unilateral nature of the repeal on the grounds that other countries would eventually follow Britain's example and adopt free trade. George Bentinck, by contrast, thought Peel to be in a 'fool's paradise' for anticipating 'such flattering results from the reciprocity system.'[32] Peel responded by saying 'I never promised, knowing, as I do, the strength of the protecting interests in the French Chambers, that France would at once yield to the influence of reason.' However, he reiterated that Britain's example 'will ultimately prevail' in France and elsewhere. And if gold were to be exchanged for the additional imports? Peel dismissed the dire consequences foreseen by Torrens and his parliamentary advocates: there would be 'no wound whatever on the commerce of this country.' The gains would be greater if France were to adopt a more liberal commercial policy as well, Peel conceded,

> but if the double benefit cannot be obtained, let us not deny ourselves the benefit of the single one. Let us not pay a greater price for interior articles because we cannot induce France to buy good articles at a low price.[33]

John Russell chimed in as well, calling the alarm about parting with gold 'really preposterous.'[34] At this point in the debate, Disraeli jumped in to protest 'three or four common-places – the prostitutes of political economy whom Gentlemen on each side in turn embrace, in order to show that you may fight hostile tariffs with free imports.' He called these issues 'amongst the most difficult problems' of political economy and 'one which ought to be most gravely considered by any Minister.'

> If a country submits to the imposition of unequal import duties, does she become tributary to the countries by which such unequal duties are imposed? . . . And if in consequence of these hostile tariffs we give more of our labour for the produce of foreign countries, what effect will this interchange have on the distribution of precious metals which are foreign produce? . . . I remember a gentleman, an authority on matters of political economy, Colonel Torrens, who for some time had a seat in this house, bringing the noble Lord (Lord J. Russell) in a series of very ingenious essays, to account for the doctrines which he held upon the interchange of commodities between nations.

While this was some years ago, Disraeli said, he

> read as so recently as last night a very elaborate analysis and a very careful application of the laws which regulate interchange between nations [authored by a] man free from any bias of party feeling; who has given up his time to abstract studies; is known to possess a high order of intellect; and may be considered in the light of an hereditary

political economist – I mean John [Stuart] Mill, the son of the historian.[35]

Disraeli noted that 'certainly it will at once be admitted that the author has no bias in favour of the doctrines which I have endeavoured on this occasion to support.'

> After investigating the subject with all the power of logical analysis for which he is remarkable, and with all the knowledge of econom-ical science for which he is distinguished, he arrives at the conclusion that hostile tariffs must be met by hostile tariffs – that reciprocity should be the principle upon which an exchange should take place between nations . . . I think I heard a Gentleman say "No," . . . I have not the book with me, but I am sure that I have not overstated the argument.

Disraeli concluded with a warning:

> you can only carry on your system of fighting hostile tariffs with free imports, by requiring more labour for the effort, and thus involving the further depression of wages, and the further degradation of the labourer.[36]

Because Disraeli did not finish his discourse on the topic, four days later Mr Roebuck reminded Disraeli 'to enlighten the House on all this doctrine of political economy.' Roebuck warned of the dangers of 'dipping' into a book and, citing chapter and verse with Mill's book in hand, insisted that Mill rejected protecting duties and duties on necessaries of life, both of which applied to the Corn Laws. As he could not believe Disraeli possible of misquotation, Roebuck sarcastically added that he 'should in charity conclude that the hon. Member had never read the book at all.'[37]

Disraeli immediately rose and exclaimed, 'All I can say is, that the hon. and learned Gentleman speaks upon a subject of which he knows nothing.'

> I think, if he will lend me the book, as I dare say he will, I could quote some passages, if the leaves are cut and open, and the book has been read – quite as germane to the matter as any which he has read to the House. [The book was handed to the hon. Member.]

Disraeli then quoted from the preface, where Mill stated that he substantially agreed with Torrens's analysis.

> I am sure that the Prime Minister recollects, because I remember his speaking to me on the subject in the lobby of the House . . . that the

principle of reciprocity was the basis of the argument used by Colonel Torrens.

Disraeli quoted again from Mill on specie and price movements resulting from tariff changes, and concluded with biting sarcasm that Roebuck's contentions of misrepresentation were 'futile.'[38]

Mr. Herbert indicated that while he believed Disraeli could show Mill to be a supporter of reciprocity,

> the question the House had to decide was not whether reciprocity was the most favourable system on which commerce could be carried on, but whether they, who were in advance of other countries in the principles of commerce, could induce other countries to assist us by establishing perfect freedom.

Herbert did not want to go into details, but added regarding the fear of losing specie that 'nothing had been better put on that subject than it was by Mr. D. Hume in his Theory of Commerce . . . , and he had destroyed the theory, which had been resuscitated for use on the present occasion.'[39] Mr C. Wood 'did not think that the House was a good arena for a discussion of political economy' and tried to show that a large volume of imports had coincided previously with the importation of specie in contradiction to Disraeli's claims.[40]

This clash over political economy and Mill's views on reciprocity attracted the attention of the press. The *Spectator* chided Disraeli for his use of political economy in his speeches opposing repeal:

> With immense labour he is piling up a long speech, full of all the crude misconceptions and half-knowledge, the inevitable fruits of a hasty perusal of elementary books in a science the technical language of which is new to him, while the enormous, widely ramified, and ever-varying operations to which it relates, are perfectly unfamiliar.

The paper specifically criticized Disraeli's recruitment of Mill as a supporter of reciprocity, writing that a 'more entire perversion of an author's meaning it would be difficult to imagine.' It quoted Mill's hostility to protective duties and concluded with regard to Disraeli: 'Wilful misrepresentation we put out of the question; but how dense must be the obtuseness that could read the passage we have just quoted, yet take Mr. Mill for an advocate of the reciprocity system!'[41]

The problem with Disraeli's reading of Mill was that two important qualifications were omitted. While in his preface Mill agreed that his 'opinions [were] identical in principle with those promulgated by Colonel Torrens,' he immediately added in parenthesis that 'there would probably be considerable difference as to the extent of their practical application.'[42] As to his view of the tariff-induced specie-flow, Disraeli did not mention Mill's view that it gives 'rise, as a general fall of prices always does, to an appearance, though a temporary and fallacious one, of general distress.'[43]

Just weeks later, Parliament endorsed Peel's plan for repeal of the Corn Laws, thereby setting the precedent for adopting unilateral free trade. The repeal, of course, was largely decided on factors other than the reciprocity issues raised by Torrens. But those other factors had to act through the voting MPs, who felt compelled to justify their rejection of reciprocity. This justification fell into three categories: those MPs who were pure unilateral free traders, those who put their faith in the success of the 'demonstration effect,' and those who thought reciprocity had failed for Britain in the recent past. Regardless of their different evaluation of foreign tariffs, all three agreed that unilateral free trade would prove beneficial. This consensus dominated the opposing view that formal negotiations should precede any British tariff liberalization. A potential obstacle to tariff reform was thereby removed.

An evaluation of the debate

It is exceedingly rare to see a good portion of a political body so attuned to developments in economic theory. The parliamentary appetite for advice from distinguished authorities can surely be described as high if members are found citing pamphlets by Torrens just as they are being advertised and published. The spectacle of members passing around a copy of Mill's *Essays upon some Unsettled Questions of Political Economy* and debating its message for economic policy is perhaps the most vivid illustration of this point. A reading of the debates leaves the impression that the ability to invoke authority – preferably Adam Smith or David Ricardo or John Stuart Mill, settling for Torrens or someone else of his caliber depending on the circumstances – contributed to the scoring of a debating point or to the appearance of literacy in political economy, if not to the actual persuasion of anyone.

This research has not uncovered evidence that the issues raised by Torrens changed the final outcome of the debate over tariff reductions. Because political economy was so frequently invoked in parliamentary debates, however, Torrens's thought forced unilateral free traders, such as J.L. Ricardo and J.D. Hume, to discuss not the merits of free trade in general, but the merits of unreciprocated free trade. Torrens raised the question of how free trade should be implemented, a question the unilateralists sought to close lest it delay the adoption of free trade.

Although he successfully initiated an important debate and controversy, Torrens ultimately failed to have the impact he sought. This was not because the intricacies of his theory necessarily eluded even the economically literate in Parliament. Torrens was understood by others. The failure was partly due to the fact that a judgment had to be made about Britain's influence over foreign tariffs. Past experience suggested that Britain could not influence those tariffs through bargaining; Torrens recommended a continuation of Britain's tariffs until negotiations could succeed. But mindful of Britain's decade-long failure to negotiate trade treaties, other MPs took foreign tariffs as immutable, meaning Britain should pursue free trade alone and making the debate over reciprocity moot. Still others believed that Britain's success with free trade would serve as an example and thus subtly induce others to follow, transforming unilateral into multilateral free trade.

The overriding reason for Torrens's failure, despite the attention his ideas received, was that Parliament was wedded to the notion that political economy in general implied that free trade would assuredly result in gains for Britain, regardless of the tariff policy pursued by other countries. This perspective, staunchly supported by the unilateralists, proved to be the dominant theme in the trade policy debates over the remainder of the nineteenth century.

Acknowledgements

I wish to thank Cheryl Schonhardt-Bailey and Andrew Marrison for helpful comments.

References

Brown, Lucy (1958) *The Board of Trade and the Free Trade Movement, 1830–1842* Oxford: Clarendon Press.

'Disraeli on Mill' (1846) *The Spectator* 19 (May 9): 444–5.

Fetter, Frank W. (1975) 'The Influence of Economists in Parliament on British Legislation from Ricardo to John Stuart Mill,' *Journal of Political Economy* 83: 1051–64.

Fetter, Frank W. (1980) *The Economist in Parliament: 1780–1868*, Durham, NC: Duke University Press.

Hansard's Parliamentary Debates (HPD), various volumes 1842–46.

Irwin, Douglas A. (1988) 'Welfare Effects of British Free Trade: Debate and Evidence from the 1840s,' *Journal of Political Economy* 96: 1142–64.

Irwin, Douglas A. (1989) 'Political Economy and Peel's Repeal of the Corn Laws,' *Economics and Politics* 1: 41–59.

Irwin, Douglas A. (1996) *Against the Tide: An Intellectual History of Free Trade*, Princeton, NJ: Princeton University Press.

James, Scott, and David A. Lake (1989) 'The Second Face of Hegemony: Britain's Repeal of the Corn Laws and the American Walker Tariff of 1846,' *International Organization* 10: 1–29.

Mill, John Stuart (1844) *Essays on Some Unsettled Questions of Political Economy*, London: Parker.

O'Brien, Denis P. (1977) 'Torrens, McCulloch and Disraeli,' *Scottish Journal of Political Economy* 24: 1–18.

Political Economy Club (1921) *Centenary Volume*, London: Macmillan.

'Reciprocal Free Trade' (1843) *Foreign and Colonial Quarterly Review* 2: 526–51.

Robbins, Lionel (1958) *Robert Torrens and the Evolution of Classical Economics*, New York: St Martin's Press.

Torrens, Robert (1833) *Letters on Commercial Policy*, London: Longman.

Torrens, Robert (1844) *The Budget: On Commercial and Colonial Policy*, London: Smith, Elder & Co.

Viner, Jacob (1936) 'Professor Taussig's Contribution to the Theory of International Trade,' *Explorations in Economics: Notes and Essays Contributed in Honor of F. W. Taussig*, New York: McGraw-Hill.

Notes

1 See Fetter (1975) and (1980). Economic thought was so frequently invoked in Parliament that one member promised to speak 'without referring to those English political economists of whose opinions the House must be satiated.' Hansard's Parliamentary Debates, third series 83 (February 17, 1846): 1089. Hereafter cited as HPD with volume and column number.

2 Jacob Viner (1936, p. 3) has written in reference to the classical theory of international trade, 'The main lines of its evolution can indeed be adequately traced in the pages of Hansard's Parliamentary Debates.'

3 Torrens also provided a theoretical backing for those Liberal Tory reformers of the 1820s, such as Huskisson, who had sought to link trade liberalization with reciprocity, but whose views had become less influential by the early 1840s. See the discussion in Brown (1958), for example.

4 See the discussion in Irwin (1996), pp. 88–90.

5 This evolution is vividly described by Robbins (1958).

6 HPD 14 (July 3, 1832): 17–20.

7 HPD 68 (April 25, 1843): 937.

8 He apparently never realized his intention to introduce a resolution based on this recommendation. See Financial Resolutions Intended to be Moved by Colonel Torrens on Thursday, 29th March 1832, a printed item held in the Kress Collection at Harvard University. Similar views are expressed in a series of letters to his Bolton constituents, later collected and published as Torrens (1833). Torrens served as an MP for three separate constituencies from 1826–27, 1831–32, and 1833–35.

9 These pamphlets were later collected in Torrens (1844).

10 Torrens's discovery eventually paved the way for the theory of the optimum tariff. See Irwin (1996), ch. 7.

11 Torrens (1844), p. 50.

12 For a review of this debate, see Irwin (1988) and (1996), pp. 101–110. The Political Economy Club gave an early indication of the reception Torrens's ideas were to receive. According to J.L. Mallet's diary entry for May 8, 1835: 'The first question discussed was a question of Torrens, which was unanimously voted to turn upon an impossible case. He claimed the right to discuss any abstract proposition with a view to the establishing a principle, but it was over-ruled in the present case which did not go to *establish* but to *disturb* a principle, that of Free Trade upon grounds altogether hypothetical.' Political Economy Club (1921), p. 270.

13 HPD 68 (April 25, 1843): 902ff.

14 Torrens had close political ties to Disraeli, which may account for his familiarity with political economy. See O'Brien (1977).

15 HPD 68 (April 25, 1843): 944, 947.
16 HPD 68 (April 25, 1843): 935.
17 HPD 68 (April 1843): 967. The postscript referred to by Peel is in Torrens (1844), pp. 329–356.
18 HPD 68 (April 25, 1843): 970. Ricardo apologized for not being fully informed because Torrens's pamphlet, 'though advertised yesterday, was not published till that evening, and it was curious that when he went to the library to look for the book, written by a near relative of his own . . . that was also absent.'
19 HPD 73 (March 19, 1844): 444–5.
20 HPD 73 (March 19, 1844): 1301. The reference is to 'Reciprocal Free Trade' (1843), a review article of Torrens's publications and one of the few to support his claims.
21 HPD 73 (March 19, 1844): 1303.
22 HPD 85 (March 27, 1846): 257.
23 HPD 85 (March 23, 1846): 1472.
24 Torrens (1844), p. 405. James and Lake (1989), however, contend that a liberalization of US tariff policy was linked to the Corn Law repeal.
25 HPD 84 (March 9, 1846): 818.
26 HPD 78 (March 17, 1845): 1023.
27 HPD 84 (March 13, 1846): 1017.
28 HPD 69 (May 10, 1843): 155.
29 HPD 66 (February 16, 1843): 689–90.
30 HPD 66 (February 16, 1843): 746.
31 HPD 69 (May 9, 1843): 94.
32 HPD 86 (May 4, 1846): 44.
33 HPD 86 (May 4, 1846): 68–9.
34 HPD 86 (May 4, 1846): 78.
35 Disraeli was referring to the essay 'Of the Laws of Interchange between Nations; and the Distribution of the Gains of Commerce among the Countries of the Commercial World,' published in Mill (1844).
36 HPD 86 (May 4, 1846): 87–9.
37 HPD 86 (May 8, 1846): 277–8.
38 HPD 86 (May 8, 1846): 279, 281–2.
39 HPD 86 (May 8, 1846): 282.
40 HPD 86 (May 15, 1846): 625.
41 'Disraeli on Mill,' (1846), pp. 444–5.
42 Mill (1844), p. v.
43 Mill (1844), pp. 40–1.

11

THE RECEPTION OF A POLITICAL ECONOMY OF FREE TRADE

The case of Sweden

Lars Magnusson

In his survey of Swedish economic thought from the middle of the nine-teenth century onwards Eli Heckscher emphasised how 'mercantilism' – as a system of thought – especially during the 1860s was replaced by liberal and free-trade ideas. The change was in fact so tremendous and rapid, he wrote, that the 'main cause of this must have been outside influences and not internal change within our own community'.[1] This outside force was the free-trade liberal doctrine, which had finally arrived in Sweden. At the same time, however, Heckscher noted that the main influence behind this breakthrough did not originate 'from where one should have expected', that is from England. In fact, as Heckscher argued: 'As far as I am acquainted with the Swedish economic discussion and our popular economic literature of the 1860's and 1870's, there is almost no trace of any influence from English writers.'[2] Hence almost no translations of English economic texts were carried out during this period – not even Richard Cobden's writing was translated into Swedish. Instead the new ideas were imported from France, and especially from Bastiat, and the harmony economists. Apart from Bastiat, Heckscher mentioned writers such as Ambroise Clément, Courcelle-Senueil, Blanqi and others for having a profound influence on the Swedish discussion.

Moreover Heckscher built up an argument implying that the *laissez-faire* ideas of the harmony economists became the main driving force behind the trade reforms and tariff reductions that took place in Sweden during the middle of the 1850s. Such ideas also served as the main intellectual argu-ment behind the Swedish signing of the Cobden Treaty in 1865, he argued. Heckscher as well as many other Swedish economic historians would draw the conclusion that the liberalisation of Swedish foreign trade in its turn triggered off an export-driven industrial breakthrough which had its origin in the 1840s with the introduction of free trade in England – as England was one of the main buyers of Swedish timber and planks as well as iron and steel. Moreover, after the signing of the Cobden Act in 1865 Sweden was ready for yet another upsurge of industrialisation during the 1870s. According to Heckscher and the prevailing orthodox interpretation of nineteenth-century Swedish economic history, Sweden was really the success story *par excellence* of free-trade economics.

To what extent this linking of events gives us an adequate historical picture of the Swedish industrialisation process I shall not deal with in this context.[3] Rather, I shall discuss the development of political economy in Sweden during the first half of the nineteenth century and the role of English 'classical political economy', as well as of free-trade ideas in general, in this development. Discussing 'influence' it is important to emphasise that the incorporation of ideas from another discursive context takes the form of a process of 'translation'. Hence, concepts and meanings are not passively received but are interpreted within a specific discourse which has its roots in particular historical circumstances. Historians of economic thought seem up to now not to have taken enough notice of this process of translation and not to have dealt explicitly with how meanings and concepts are changed through such a process of translation. Instead, they often tend to read the history of economic thought backwards from the standpoint of modern theorising and misinterpret the actual spreading and transformation of economic discourse over time. Hence in the Swedish case it was possible for Heckscher to interpret the situation as a drastic shift – from 'mercantilism' to Adam Smith or rather Frédéric Bastiat – occurring in the middle of the century. Moreover, and for the same reason, it has been possible for later Swedish scholars of the history of economic doctrines to downplay the impact that Adam Smith in reality made – also in Sweden![4]

However, the crucial question is: which Adam Smith was imported into Sweden? From our point of view it seems clear that the image of Smith as a 'doctrinaire' (Heckscher) free-trader, a Manchester liberal of the Cobden kind, was created from the middle of the nineteenth century onwards. Without doubt, the campaigning abilities of Manchester economists here played an important role as well as the lively discussion on free trade and protectionism which became especially heated in the 1840s and then reappeared over and over again in the discussion during the rest of the century.[5] Hence in much recent scholarly debate – especially in the UK – the link between Adam Smith and 'classical political economy' as well as between these two and 'free trade' or *laissez-faire* economics has put in question. That Adam Smith in fact was not a dogmatic *laissez-faire* advocate in the modern sense of the term is nowadays widely recognised in most modern scholarly works.[6] Although forcefully arguing against the 'commercial system' and in favour of 'free trade' in general, Smith pointed out several instances when free trade could not be recommended. Hence, as we argued, it was only from the middle of the nineteenth century that Smith became a 'doctrinaire' free trader advocating *laissez-faire* as a general principle for international trade. This 'invention of a tradition' of free trade, originating with Smith and followed up by disciples such as Cobden, was to a great extent the consequence of the political debate that raged from the halcyon days of the repeal of the Corn Laws in the 1840s to the 'fair trade' discussion in the 1880s. In this discussion Smith was increasingly used by Richard Cobden and other free-traders within or outside the Manchester school to bolster their case against a varied group of writers whom they labelled as 'protectionists'. However, like the 'classical' economists, the 'protectionists' differed in their attitudes and theoretical approaches. It was only late in the nineteenth century that 'protectionism' became a 'school' of its own with its own distinct 'nationalistic' creed which could be contrasted to the gospel of a cosmopolitan 'free trade'. Thus neither the repeal of the Corn Laws in 1846 nor the Cobden Treaty some years later can be immediately interpreted as a victory of 'classical political economics'. First, this would be to make all too simple the very complex relationship which in general occurs between economic policy and economic theory. Furthermore, it is true that the politicians and ideologues who carried through these reforms were partly influenced by classical economics. However, the classical economists themselves tended to disagree on the matter and many of them proposed gradual reform rather than a radical abolition of all kind of duties. Hence for example Ricardo recommended a gradual reduction of the duties on corn over a ten-year period. Also the great admirer of Smith, John Ramsey McCulloch, was able at the same time to advocate free trade as well as accept protection in the form of duties and tariffs. Hence on the one hand he would state in his best-known work, *Principles of Political Economy* (1825), that 'Under a free commercial system, labour would be distributed as best suits the genius and capacities of different nations.'[7] On the other hand he defended the introduction of protection and tariffs, especially for revenue purposes: 'when such duties are imposed on proper articles, and are confined within moderate limits, they are among the most unexceptionable that can be devised.'[8] Thus import duties up to 25 per cent were permitted for revenue purposes, according to McCulloch. He would even state that: 'Hence it is plain that in commercial policy, as in most other things, there are no absolute principles, and that they must in every case be subordinated to the *salus populi*.'[9] Although he was generally against protection for the sake of the infant industry argument he could see some instances when it might be applied: 'it may sometimes be expedient to restrain the too great or rapid development of branches of industry, the success of which mainly depends on our dealing with a peculiar people or territory.'[10]

Another, perhaps even more interesting, example is Robert Torrens and his defence of duties relying on the principle of 'reciprocity'. Torrens was from the 1820s a politician and a highly influential economic journalist as well as the founder of the Political Economy Club. Although he was the author of *Essay on the External Corn Trade* (1815) in which the eventually famous comparative cost theory – often believed to be Ricardo's invention – appeared for the first time, Torrens became increasingly critical of unilateral tariff reduction. This measure could not be defended as long as foreigners continued to impose duties on British wares, he argued.[11] Instead he recommended reciprocity as a golden rule – as modern scholarly discussion has made clear this is a recommendation which is not as totally incompatible with Adam Smith as was once believed.[12] Moreover, Torrens's adoption of more 'protectionist' views from the 1830s onwards did not simultaneously involve any rejection of Smith or his own and Ricardo's comparative cost approach.

Hence, in general, it seems wise not to draw an immediate line of causation between 'classical political economy' and Smith on the one hand and the policies of free trade on the other. This is certainly also true when we come to the specific case of Sweden and the translation of new ideas of this species into that country. As we shall see Smith and his 'system' were to a large extent accepted by the Swedish economic writers – but perhaps in a peculiar way. Clearly, the message of Bastiat and the harmony economists was translated and took a different form when it became popular within the Swedish discussion from the 1850s. A stern follower of Bastiat such as the extremely influential finance minister J.A. Gripenstedt – the mind behind the tariff reforms and the adoption of the Cobden system – was able to reconcile the *laissez-faire* gospel of Bastiat with a positive view of the regulatory orders of the state to intervene in the economy.

Nor is it true that 'mercantilists' prevailed in the economic discussion in Sweden up until the middle of the nineteenth century. To some extent this was reconciled by Heckscher, who argued that 'mercantilism' by 1860 had lost its former position although it had not yet been replaced by something else. Not even German 'romanticism' à la List had filled up this void, or 'jerkiness' according to Heckscher, occurring in economic thought in the middle of the nineteenth century in Sweden. Quite rightly so: there is little traceable influence in the Swedish economic discussion from the school of 'national economists', that is from Americans such as Alexander Hamilton, Matthew Carey or Henry Carey or from Friedrich List, the Swabean adventurer, writer, cosmopolitan and railway enthusiast. In the middle of the nineteenth century this 'school' had been formed around a positive programme of national industrial protection. Although quite distinct in temper and style each shared the view that an agricultural economy was always inferior to an industrial economy – hence it was necessary for every striving nation to take this step. Moreover, the 'cosmopolitanism' developed in much English economics during this time was false and in reality concealed the fact that free trade was a tool for preserving England's superiority as an industrial nation and as the 'workshop of the world'. With regard to protection and free trade for example Henry Carey argued, first, that British free trade was injurious to less developed countries and, second, that economic theory and practice should be relative to the particular stage of economic development at which a certain nation was situated. Such ideas of 'national economics' were even more pronounced with Friedrich List.

However, nothing of this sort can be traced in the Swedish discussion. This might be regarded as peculiar given the historical and intellectual contacts between Sweden and the German states, especially as economic discourse in Sweden during the eighteenth century – particularly in the universities – was heavily influenced by German cameralism. To a large extent Sweden was a latecomer in the industrialisation race and for the same reason its public, as the German one, might fall prey of infant-industry or import-substitution arguments. Instead, the response to the English initiative to abolish the Corn Laws and to establish free trade seems to have been much more positive in Sweden. Without doubt, this positive response fits well with the general political and economic situation prevailing in Sweden at the time, as we shall see below.

In Sweden the first chairs in the economic discipline were inaugurated in Uppsala in 1741, Åbo in 1747 and Lund in 1750. In Uppsala the first professor Anders Berch was heavily influenced by German cameralists such as Dithmar and he lectured on a mixture of policy, economic legislation and practical husbandry. His textbook, *Inledningen till Almänna Hushållningen* (1747) was even translated into German in the 1750s. In Åbo and Lund the emphasis on husbandry and agriculture was even more strongly marked. The first professor in Åbo was Pehr Kalm, who was a student of Linnaeus and as such lectured mainly on natural history and practical husbandry. In Lund the first professor was Johan Henrik Burmeister, who gave lectures in zoology, botany and practical husbandry. He was succeeded in 1758 by Claus Blecher Trozelius, a former clergyman and reader in economics in Uppsala. He adopted Berch's textbook in his lectures, but spent most of his time teaching husbandry and the improvement of agriculture. During the 1760s Trozelius presented a number of dissertations at Lund, which according to the custom of the time he probably wrote himself, with titles such as 'The advantage of building stone-houses' or 'On Scanean bee-keeping'.[13]

Hence according to Trozelius 'economics' was an applied natural science in the service of agricultural improvement. This approach became even more pronounced when Carl Adolph Agardh was appointed to a chair in Practical Economy and Botany in Lund in 1812. Agardh's main interest was botany, where he made some important scientific discoveries by trying to improve Linnaeus' sexual system. But he also lectured on economic legislation and during the 1820s and 1830s he attended many Diets as an expert on economic policy, especially concerning monetary issues.[14]

Outside the academic sphere the eighteenth-century discussion was very much influenced by English 'reform mercantilists' and in particular French *économistes*. Hence during the 1750s and 1760s many writers appeared who were eager to attack old mercantilist regulations and use natural law language in order to plead for more freedom of trade. Among these we must especially mention the writer and politician Anders Nordencrantz and the vicar from the distant *Österbotten*, Anders Chydenius, crowned by Carl G. Uhr as a 'predecessor of Adam Smith' especially with his short tract *Den Nationale Winsten* (1767).[15] Nordencrantz on his part was heavily influenced by the contemporary moral philosophical discussion and in his political and economic views he relied very much on the Scottish enlightenment school. Also the French physiocrats made some impact in Swedish, especially during the 1760s and early 1770s. Their main propagator in Sweden was the baron and tutor of Gustavus III, Carl Gustaf Scheffer, who translated Quesnay's *Maximes* as well as Du Pont de Nemours' *De l'origine et du progrès d'une science nouvelle* and some texts by Mirabeau into Swedish.[16] As has been painstakingly researched by Lars Herlitz it is clear that Scheffer's translation of central physiocratic texts cannot be regarded merely as pure translation. Hence in order to use the French texts in a Swedish political context Scheffer omitted some parts of the texts and added 'improvements'. Thus the introduction of physiocracy in Sweden during the 1760s is a clear example of 'translation' in the sense that we talked about earlier.[17] This was even more pronounced with the 'last of the Swedish physiocrats' (Heckscher), Anders Wappengren, the humble spice merchant from the city of Gävle. To some extent his *Grunderna till den borgerliga hushållningen* (1798) was influenced by the physiocratic vocabulary. However, the contexts in which Wappengren put these ideas were strikingly different. He imported the vocabulary of physiocracy in order to mount a massive attack – with proto-socialist overtones – against all 'usurpers' who lived on the labour of others, including all landowners.[18]

It is symptomatic that most of these new influences appeared outside the academic world, where economics retained its character as a science of householding and cameralism well into the nineteenth century. Hence, it is often stated that whatever intellectual influence Adam Smith and the new classical political economics may have had in Sweden after 1800, the universities were certainly not involved. Smith's *Wealth of Nations* first appeared in Swedish in 1800 – in a highly abridged translation from Sartorius' German edition. Against this background it is typical that the leading Swedish writer on economic issues during the 1790s – the merchant Christian Ludvig Jöransson, who in 1792–8 published a long work (1,450 pages) in several parts, *Försök til et systeme i Sveriges allmänna hushållning och penning-väsende* – were influenced by Sir James Steuart but seem to have been unaware of Smith's work.[19] During this period the only writer who directly referred to Smith was the politician and physician David von Schulzenheim, who in his *Bref om rikets penninge-werk och allmänna hushållning* (in two parts, 1794, 1796) set out to criticise Jöransson's text. He mainly used Smith in order to criticise the view that the accumulation of bullion made a country rich and thus echoed Smith's assault against the mercantile system. However, according to Heckscher, von Schulzenheim may have been citing Smith but seems not to have understood him properly and thus on the whole remained quite unaffected by Smith's general conceptions and views.[20]

Hence both Heckscher and other commentators have tended to play down the influence of Smith both outside, and certainly within, the Swedish academic milieu during the first half of the nineteenth century. Hence, as we saw, the breakthrough of the new liberal ideas occurred only in the 1850s and 1860s. However, this is certainly an exaggeration. In fact already in the 1790s several writers were aware of Smith but either did not regard him as the founder and originator of a totally novel system of economics or, at least, interpreted him in a different manner to writers of later generations. Hence for example von Schulzenheim in the 1790s discussed Smith on a par with other writers such as Hume and, to Heckscher's astonishment, the obscure writer John Sinclair. In this context it must be remembered that much of what Smith said in *The Wealth of Nations* on trade, the invisible hand, etc., was common parlance during this period. As already argued we can even trace parts of his general approach – including the invisible hand argument – in the writings of Chydenius and Nordencrantz during the 1760s.

This would change from 1820 onwards, when several Swedish writers – also within the academic community – began to hail Smith as an originator of a new system of political economy. However, they would 'translate' his views in a way that may sound unfamiliar to us – but not perhaps to the public at the time. It is to these translators and interpreters that we now turn.

An important example in this context is Lars Georg Rabenius, who held the chair in jurisprudence, economics and commerce in Uppsala 1807–37. In 1829 he published a new textbook of economics, *Lärobok i Nationalekonomien*, which replaced Berch's by now extremely dated book published more than eighty years earlier. In this treatise, which introduced a Swedish public to the German word *Nationalökonomie*, Rabenius set out to build a bridge between new and old political economy. In his introduction he presented 'three different economic systems': the 'mercantile system', 'physiocracy' and the 'industrial system' (for the last he mainly referred to Adam Smith). After harshly criticising the first two systems, he hailed the 'industrial system' for being the most logical and providing a 'true' picture of the economic system. His esteem of Smith is also evident from one of his student's notebooks (probably compiled in 1827). According to this student Rabenius in his lecture said that 'Smidt [sic] had laid a proper foundation for the study of his subject.'[21] In his textbook Rabenius provided an outline dependent upon Smith's (and Say's) discussion of growth and wealth, the importance of the principle of division of labour, and so on. 'The Smithians,' he said, 'have without doubt laid a true foundation of the subject when emphasising Land,

Labour and Capital, as the source of production and ... wealth.'[22] At the same time he defined his subject, *Nationalekonomi*, as

> a scientific outline regarding the means by which, given the preser-
> vation and growth of national economic self-maintenance, every
> individual may through industry lawfully gain what he can and
> enjoy what he wants, while the state at the same time may receive
> necessary means for the general requirements of the society.[23]

He was ready to defend different regulations in order to defend state intervention designed to strengthen the *Nationalekonomi*. Hence, he argued that
private and public interest were not always identical. 'Private gain may be
accomplished by selling *Brännvin* [acquavit] at a great profit but is the
Nation really a gainer as well?' he asked rhetorically.[24] Thus although men
had a number of innate rights the state had the right to defend itself and
protect the interest of all. It was highly typical when he stated: 'Freedom is
of course the most valuable right Man possesses, but it must be regulated by
law so that it does not degenerate and become pernicious.'[25]

Much the same can be said with regard to Carl Adolph Agardh, who held
the chair in economics at Lund from 1812 to 1834. Like his predecessors
in the chair his main interest was botany. However, as noted above, mainly
as a delegate to several Diets he served as an economic expert and adviser to
the government on monetary, financial and other subjects. In his economic
views he was heavily influenced by Smith and – especially – Jean Baptiste
Say. In 1821 and 1822 he even followed Say's lecturing courses in Paris and
was probably involved behind the scenes when Say's *Traité d'économie politique*
was translated into Swedish in 1823. In his main theoretical work in economics, *Granskning af Statseconomiens grundläror* (1829) Agardh is ready to
accept the 'liberal' system of Smith – but only to a degree. Thus he states
that Smith's system has been 'rejected by the experience of practical men as
well as by an instinct which makes statesmen reluctant to carry it out.'[26] His
most important argument against Smith – or rather against the conclusions
that most people tended to draw from *The Wealth of Nations* as this work,
according to Agardh, was more often cited than thoroughly read – was the
passive role it provided for the state in economic life. Second, he argued that
Smith overestimated the role of labour and underestimated the role of natural resources as a main progenitor of economic wealth and growth. Hence,
in his role as economic expert he would often argue for state intervention. He
was a bitter opponent of the decision to sell state-owned forests and he
defended the Swedish version of the Navigation Acts, *Produktplakatet*, as well
as calling for an expansionary fiscal policy in order to encourage the agricultural sector. However, to say that he was a protectionist is to exaggerate.
At times he would defend custom duties for the same reason as Torrens had
done – following the rule of reciprocity. However, particularly after 1840 he

seems to have become more critical towards them. The main point here, however, is that he was ready to ask for state intervention at the same time as he, by and large, accepted the 'systems' of Smith and Say. Hence it seems quite accurate when one of Agardh's biographers, Eskil Wadensjö, argues that:

> Some writers have referred to Agardh as a mercantilist and physio-crat. However, he can not be described as a mercantilist just because he asks for a more active role of the state in the economy or as a physiocrat just because he feels sympathy for the physiocrat's high esteem of agriculture.[27]

When Agardh resigned from his position in 1834 to became a bishop, his chair in economics and botany was withdrawn. However, two years later a new chair was inaugurated, but now in Cameral and Economic Juris-prudence. Its first holder was the lawyer Johan Holmbergsson, who was fol-lowed in 1844 by the economist and historian Jacob Lundell. As Agardh had done, Lundell accepted classical political economy and Smith. He was also ready to accept free trade and freedom of enterprise as well as arguing for the abolition of the guild system. However, he warned against too much freedom as this might lead to the rise of 'big capital', a decline of competition and the establishment of monopoly. He does not give the state such an important role in economic development as Agardh and Rabenius. Its main role is to provide a regulatory order in which industry can thrive. He says: 'freedom in trade both allows for and necessitates a reasonable organisation which can minimise the dangers which stem from the abuse of freedom.'[28] And further:

> Free enterprise is to be understood as a means for each and all to freely choose an own occupation to support themselves, without any restrictions besides such which are necessary for the well-being of the state. However, its defenders can surely not go so far as to demand total freedom or limitless discretion; instead they admit that the individual's natural liberties or his ability to work can be restricted and organised according to reason so that it does not violate the general interest or is set against a purposeful state.[29]

Besides these three examples it is possible to add a number of other writers who by and large accepted Smith and the classics but at the same time were hesitant to become 'doctrinaire' free-traders, as Heckscher called them. Hence the Swedish author and history professor, Erik Gustaf Geijer – for long a leading Tory but becoming a stern liberal after his famous 'downfall' in 1834 (not least influenced by his reading of the *Edinburgh Review*) – remained convinced that the economy must be regulated to some extent, especially in order to defend the poorer strata of the population. His wavering between freedom and regulation was especially evident in his discussion of the Swedish poor law system. Here he would occasionally argue that the 'social question' necessitated state intervention and sometimes he rather stressed the need for voluntary philanthropy – explicitly referring to the principle of benevolence – as a means to solve this issue.[30]

A final example should suffice. In 1839 Anders Stenkula, a lecturer in finance and law at Lund in the 1830s as well as a devoted follower of Geijer, published his *En blick från stats-ekonomien på Sveriges handel och näringsflit*. It provided an argument in favour of Smith and the classical political economy school, which is seldom explicitly mentioned but seems to be implicit in much of the literature we have referred to here. Hence, like Rabenius, Stenkula refers to Smith's system as 'the industrial system'. In *The Wealth of Nations*, Stenkula says, is outlined a new theory of state economy (*statsekonomien*) which depicts how modern industry is the basis of the modern state. According to Stenkula, Smith's brilliance lay mainly in the explication of this system and how it operated. Hence, we must accept Smith's 'industrial system' because it provides Sweden as a state with an effective means to prosper and grow (and to introduce it the state undoubtedly must play an important role!).[31]

According to Heckscher, as we saw, the introduction of Smithian economics – particularly in the form of harmony economics – occurred only 1850 and especially in the 1860s. As we have seen, however, this is a highly dubious conclusion. Rather, it seems clear that the new 'industrial' or Smithian system was accepted by a majority of leading Swedish economists during the first half of the nineteenth century. The conclusions they draw from Smith were, however, different from the ones a later generation would draw. Above all, many of them were ready to mix these new ideas with a quite positive view of the state and some scepticism against 'doctrinaire' *laissez-faire* views. As we have argued, this view of Smith – also in an international setting – became dominant only after 1850 and can perhaps be seen as a consequence of the amalgamation of Smith with the gospel of free trade especially from the 1840s onwards.

Furthermore, it has been stated by many Swedish economic historians that here was a causal link between the intrusion of 'foreign' liberal ideas of a free-trade stance and the breakthrough of more liberal policies in Sweden especially in the field of duties and tariffs. Also, on the whole it has been common to argue that the establishment of the new liberal policies in Sweden implemented especially from the mid-1850s onwards can be explained as an outcome of such an influence. Hence it was especially at the Diet of 1853/4 that a great number of prohibitions against free importation and exportation were lifted and duties were lowered on more than two hundred items.[32] However, more recent historical works have questioned to what extent these liberal politics really implied a radical break with the past. The argument has been put forward that there was a clear continuity in which new liberal ideas were mixed with a positive view of state intervention.[33] For one thing it seems clear that protectionist policies remained a popular alternative – especially at a time of crisis – and never totally disappeared during this period. Thus after a period of liberalisation, protectionism once again came back in full force at the end of the 1850s and at the Diet of 1859/60 some of its members went so far as to plead for a more general prohibitive act against importation. The severe crisis of 1857 played the pivotal role in the reappearance of strong protectionist opinions.[34] Another telling fact is that when Sweden in 1865 suddenly and without warning took the step of aligning itself with the Cobden system this stirred up much controversy afterwards and would never have gained a majority had it not been pushed through by ruthless methods. Moreover, without the great prestige of one person, the finance minister J.A. Gripenstedt, this step would certainly not have been possible. The general view in the 1860s seems to have been that protection was a method that must be utilised in order to achieve economic growth, to preserve stability during periods of trade crisis and to serve as a welcome source of income for the state.

Born in 1813, Johan August Gripenstedt became a member of the Swedish government in 1848 – a position which he would maintain mainly as a finance minister during the next two decades. According to his biographers he had early on been influenced by liberal economic ideas, especially by Bastiat. At times he would express rather doctrinaire liberal ideals – at least in theory. In his politics, however, he was often ready to make compromises and admit exceptions to the general rule.

The 'Gripenstedt system' has given name to the liberal reform programme in Sweden which set the tone of the political discussion during the late 1850s and 1860s. Gripenstedt was not merely the architect of the Free Trade Act of 1865 but also of the establishment of the partly state-run and partly privately run railway system established in the late 1850s, the inauguration of a modern banking system (which introduced privately owned finance banks) – a field in which he co-operated with the finance tycoon A.O. Wallenberg – the establishment of domestic free trade in 1864, etc. To this should be added his efforts to reform the Swedish monetary system and to introduce the decimal system in Sweden. Hence, the reform activity of Gripenstedt was far-reaching and was to have important consequences for the future. It is not too much to say that these reforms provided the necessary institutional framework for further industrialisation and growth in Sweden.

On the one hand the 'Gripenstedt system' can be seen as the result of one man's liberal economic ideas. Often Gripenstedt would provide general statements which seemed very close to Bastiat's natural rights-based free-trade gospel, especially articulated in *Harmonies économiques* (1850). Gripenstedt wrote in 1851: 'Free trade is one of the main pillars upon which human society and culture resides.'[35] However, there is also another side to his personality as well his political system which rather seems to reflect a disposition towards some kind of continuity argument to which we referred earlier. Hence, at the same time as he presented himself as a true disciple of Bastiat he was ready to defend – for particular purposes – state intervention-ism. This duality is perhaps most clearly envisaged in the heated discussions during the 1850s regarding the establishment of a Swedish railway system. In the public debate on this matter in the early 1850s – especially using the liberal newspaper *Aftonbladet* in their campaigning – several in the radical camp argued for a free and privately owned railway system. Gripenstedt on the other hand was determined to see to it that the state would play a leading role in the building-up of a railway system.[36] In a speech in 1853 he argued that 'in a society there are certain tasks which are of a kind that necessitates public steering and intervention.'[37] Another typical example of his positive view of state-interventionism regards the banking sector. While introducing laws and regulations which made possible the introduction of a system of private finance banking in Sweden he tended to view the state as the true guarantor of this system. Hence in the crisis of 1857 when a number of the newly established finance banks were experiencing severe troubles he set out to save these banks – among them A.O. Wallenberg's *Stockholms Enskilda bank* - by ways of state-loans.[38] By this measure it was made clear that the Swedish state would not allow any of the major financial institutes to go bankrupt; this policy would be carried out in practice several times during the latter half of the nineteenth century. Gripenstedt defended his measures with the argument that 'nobody can with a good conscience just leave the fate of the different industries to themselves.'[39] From someone who was held to be a convinced disciple of Bastiat this might seem a bit surprising, to say the least.

Against this background it is clear that the 'Gripenstedt system' above all can be characterised as a 'pragmatic, nationalistic liberalism which recog-nised both the free interplay of the market forces as well as the overall duty of the state.'[40] It gave recognition to freedom of trade and pursued a policy of deregulation while it admitted that the state had an important role to play. Hence, the function of the state was not merely to provide a suitable insti-tutional framework for modern industrialisation and further growth – in accordance with Bastiat and the post-1840 interpretation of Smith. Apart from this, according to Gripenstedt, the state must play a direct intervening role in a liberal economy. Without doubt, this ideology became the corner-stone of Swedish economic policy from the mid-nineteenth century onwards.

Also in a more general sense the first half of the nineteenth century was characterised by changes in the economic and administrative system. This process has often been described in terms of deregulation; against the back-ground of the 'Gripenstedt system' it is however more appropriate to talk of a system of economic modernisation and 're-regulation'. Back in the eighteenth century the strategy of administered industrialisation had been propounded by a *dirigiste* state. Reforms in order to improve agriculture were launched in order to increase population and contribute to increased production and productivity. At the same time the establishment of manufactures was strongly supported. According to this view only a prosperous agriculture and a modern manufactory sector could provide the means for a powerful and happy commonwealth. Moreover, in order to support the manufactures a policy of regulation was introduced. At the core, this policy implied that each occupation should be protected from interference by others. Hence it was made manifest that the manufactures – especially those in textiles – should be protected against competition from peasant handicrafts and proto-industries.[41]

However, after the end of the Napoleonic Wars Sweden experienced a more distinct phase of deregulation and liberalisation. As a consequence, many of the restrictions upon production and free enterprise were gradually lifted. From the 1820s onwards the so-called *Bergverks-lagarna* (laws for the protection of the mining and iron industry) were abolished; up to then they had limited the production of iron and steel (with the aim of preserving the supply of charcoal). In the same vein the specific privileges of the manufacturing sector were removed as well as the system of state-supported manufactures originally introduced in the 1720s. Such reforms made entry easier for embryonic entrepreneurs. Of even more importance in this context was the abolition of the guilds in 1846 and the gradual establishment of free enterprise in 1864. At the same time the labour market was gradually 'liberalised' and other laws and regulations were lifted in order to facilitate industry and production for the market.[42]

However, this did not imply that the state withdrew from all interference in the evolving industrial market economy which began to flourish especially from the 1850s. On the contrary, the vindication of the old governance structure laid the ground for the establishment of a new set of institutions which served to promote and bolster modern economic growth and development. Hence, development from 1840 onwards was very much characterised by the introduction of new principles of state governance which aimed explicitly towards such modernisation. Certainly, the departmental reform of 1840 served such a cause. Through this an old and quite inefficient state apparatus building upon privilege and the independence of old *collegiums*, academies and, especially, the locally based *länsförvaltningen* (county administration) was replaced by a much more efficient and tightly knit state administration. By the establishment of specially designed departments with their own exclusive functions the state became a much more powerful machine for direct rule and governance. Previously, with the looser 'feudal' structure, the possibility to implement policies had been very limited. Nor did this process of deregulation imply that costs for state administration were reduced. To the extent that figures can be computed it seems rather that overall costs for state administration – in real terms – increased during most of the nineteenth century. Although the tax system was reformed in different steps during the same century – for example the abolition of the old land-based taxes – there is no positive indication that the total tax burden decreased during the period. Rather, the opposite seems to be the case.[43]

Heckscher's statement that mercantilism prevailed until the middle of the nineteenth century and was then replaced by liberalism is misleading for the reasons we have argued. As we have seen Smith and his system were to a large extent accepted – at least partly – during the first half of the nineteenth century. However, in general neither Smith nor the classical political economists were primarily regarded as radical advocates of free trade. Instead, they were interpreted as proponents of an 'industrial system' which indeed allowed for more freedom of trade and industry than before but at the same time was compatible with state intervention. Thus, in the Swedish context a specific discourse of political economy was developed in the beginning of the nineteenth century in which 'liberal' ideas were mixed with a positive view of the state and its orders to promote economic growth and preserve social and economic stability. Most certainly, this blend of ideas cannot be regarded as '*laissez-faire* economics' or 'protectionism', nor as *Nationalökonomie* in the German-cameralist tradition and even less so as 'mercantilism'. Without doubt, the economic discussion in Sweden was highly influenced by French – but also British – political economy. However, when translated within a Swedish context the languages of these schools changed into something quite distinct. Although the tone of the economic discussion would change after the 1860s when *laissez-faire* and harmony ideas would prevail – and particularly after the founding of *Nationalekonomiska föreningen* in 1877, which, as Heckscher pointed out, were dominated by 'doctrinaire' free-traders – a positive view of the state would survive over the years. In spite of the breakthrough of neo-classicism in Sweden with leading names such as Wicksell, Cassel and Heckscher at the turn of the century, radical *laissez-faire* economics would never dominate in Sweden – at least not for a very long period. Hence, it is perhaps not far-fetched to argue that the establishment of a specific language of economics in Sweden during the nineteenth century, in which liberalism and state interventionism were blended, serves as a main reason underlying the acceptance of the Stockholm school of economics and later on Keynesianism – both with a positive view of state intervention – in Sweden during the inter-war period.

Notes

1 E.F. Heckscher, 'A Survey of Economic Thought in Sweden 1875–1950', *Scandinavian Economic History Review* 1: I 1953.
2 Ibid., p. 108.

3 L. Magnusson and M. Isacson, *Proto-industrialisation in Scandinavia*, Leamington Spa: Berg 1987.
4 H.T. Vallindet, 'Adam Smith's genombrott: Sverige', *Ekonomist Debatt* 3 (1987), pp. 229 f.
5 L. Magnusson, 'Introduction', in Magnusson (ed.) *Free Trade and Protection*, vols I–III, London: Routledge 1996.
6 D.P. O'Brien, *The Classical Economists*, Oxford: Clarendon Press 1971, p. 32; R.H. Campbell and A.S. Skinner, *Adam Smith*, London: Croom Helm 1982, p. 183.
7 J.R. McCulloch, *Principles of Political Economy*, 5th edn 1864, New York: Augustus M. Kelley, p. 91.
8 Ibid., pp. 111f.
9 Ibid.
10 Ibid., p. 111.
11 L. Robbins, 'Introduction' in Robert Torrens' *Letters on Commercial Policy*, London: London School of Economics and Political Science 1958, p. vii.
12 See for example Smith's discussion on the right to protect its domestic industry, in A. Smith, *The Wealth of Nations*, Oxford: Oxford University Press 1976, p. 463. See Magnusson, 'Introduction', pp. 3f.
13 G. Johannesson, *Lunds universitets historia, II, 1710–1789*, Lund 1982, p. 216. On early economists in Sweden in general, see E.F. Heckscher, *Sveriges ekonomiska historia*, II:1, Stockholm 1949, p. 812ff; K. Petander, *De nationalekonomiska åskådningarna i Sverige 1718–1765*, Stockholm 1912; L. Magnusson, 'Mercantilism and reform-mercantilism: the rise of economic discourse in Sweden during the eighteenth century', *History of Political Economy* 19:3 1987; J. Lönnroth, *Minervas uggla*, Stockholm: Arbetarkultur 1985; S.-E. Liedman, *Den synliga handen*, Stockholm: Arbetarkultur 1986.
14 E. Wadensjö, 'Carl Adolph Agardh', in C. Jonung and A.-C. Ståhlberg (eds) *Ekonomiporträttet: Svenska ekonomer under 300 år*, Stockholm: SNS 1990.
15 C.G. Uhr, *Anders Chydenius: A Finnish Predecessor to Adam Smith*, Turku: Åbo 1963.
16 L. Magnusson, 'Physiocracy in Sweden 1760–1780', *Economies et sociétés, La Diffusion internationale de la Physiocratie*, Cahiers de l'ISMÉA P.E. no. 22–23, Paris, 1995.
17 Ibid.; L. Herlitz, *Fysiokratismen i svensk tappning 1767–1770*, Göteborg 1974.
18 Magnusson, 'Physiocracy in Sweden', p. 398; Heckscher, *Sveriges ekonomiska historia*, pp. 873ff.
19 Heckscher, *Sveriges ekonomiska historia*, pp. 878f.
20 Ibid., pp. 884f.
21 J. Linell's lecture notes from Rabenius lectures (1827?), B.142 a:2, Huppsala University Library.
22 L.G. Rabenius, *Lärobok i Nationalekonomien*, Uppsala 1829, p. 25.
23 Ibid., p. 5.
24 Ibid., p. v.
25 Ibid., p. vf.
26 C.A. Agardh, *Granskning av stats-ekonomiens grundläror*, Lund 1829, p. 11.
27 Wadensjö, 'Carl Adolph Agardh', p. 79.
28 J. Lundell, *Om hantverksskrån och näringsfrihet*, Lund 1844.
29 Ibid.
30 C.A. Hessler, *Geijer som politiker*, II, Stockholm: Gebers 1947, s. 218f.
31 A. Stenkula, *En blick från stats-ekonomien på Sweriges handel och näringsflit*, Helsingborg 1839.

LARS MAGNUSSON

32 A. Montgomery *Svensk tullpolitik 1816–1911*, Stockholm 1921, s. 73.
33 G.B. Nilsson, *Ett namn att försvara: André Oscar Wallenberg 1866–1886*, III, Stockholm: Norstedts 1994, p. 11f, 533f.
34 A. Montgomery, p. 89.
35 P.T. Ohlsson, *100 år av tillväxt: Johan Gripenstedt och den liberala revolutionen*, Stockholm: Brombergs 1985, s. 85. See also O. Gasslander, *J. A. Gripenstedt, Statsman och företagare*, Lund: Gleerups 1949.
36 Gasslander, p. 146.
37 Ohlsson, p. 101.
38 Gasslander, pp. 218f.
39 Ohlsson, p. 119.
40 Ibid., p. 112.
41 Magnusson and Isacson, *Proto-industrialisation in Scandinavia*; L. Magnusson, 'Proto-industrialization in Sweden', in S.C. Ogilvie and M. Cerman (eds) *European Proto-industrialization*, Cambridge: Cambridge University Press 1995.
42 L. Magnusson 'Les institutions d'une économie de marché: le cas de la Suede', *Revue du Nord* 76: no. 307 (1994).
43 Ibid.

12

COMMENTS ON IRWIN AND MAGNUSSON

Keith Tribe

That economic theory all too often provides window-dressing for economic policy is a familiar complaint (from economists). The discrepancy between economic theory and the policies executed in its name is a constant one, although of course the conditions vary. The relationship is generally thought to be a one-way affair: economists expound the theoretical principles, politicians select some portions that appeal to them, and they might or might not be applied with or without understanding or insight. Irwin and Magnusson describe an era when this rhetorical relationship had not become well established, although they write of an issue at the heart of economic policy-making and economic theory: the welfare effects of free trade.

In each chapter the relationship between theory and policy is not clear cut, but for rather different reasons. Both Torrens, the originator of the comparative advantage argument, and David Ricardo, the name with which it is most often associated, were themselves at some time Members of Parliament. Ricardo's nephew, John Lewis Ricardo, spoke in the free-trade debates, albeit rather incoherently, as Irwin notes. Joseph Hume, a regular speaker in the House on economic matters, is not usually counted as an 'economist' in these discussions, but the example of Torrens, and to a lesser extent Ricardo, just goes to show how restrictive such a demarcation between 'economists' and 'politicians' in the mid-nineteenth century is. We are, after all, still dealing with an entity called Political Economy.

Magnusson's perspective is rather different, but goes to show how the path of attributable influence never runs smooth. Instead of the respectable theoretical genesis of which British free-trade enthusiasts could boast – from Smith to Torrens to Ricardo and the Mills – the Swedish 'Gripenstedt system' seemingly drew its inspiration from Bastiat, a 'populariser'. This meant in effect that the adoption of a free-trade system was not based upon an elaborated economic argument which linked the structure of national production to an international division of labour, but instead upon a vague endorsement of the idea of economic freedom. And this in a country which had had established chairs of economics for over one hundred years, unlike in Britain, where university chairs in the subject had been in existence for at most twenty years. Of course, as Magnusson demonstrates, what might be understood by 'economics' for this purpose in the eighteenth century was quite at odds with the tradition emerging in contemporary Britain. The link to Bastiat is quite possibly explained by the impact of Say upon one of the leading professors, Carl Adolph Agardh. Furthermore, the understanding of Smith common among Swedish professors in mid-century was one distinct from that in Britain – a greater readiness to ascribe the state a role being a significant difference. But the presence of a more firmly established academic economic tradition made little difference to the policy argument.

In both Britain and Sweden the debate over the introduction of free trade or the adoption of a policy of systematic protection was carried out in abstract terms: proponents of free trade argued the general benefits of free movement of goods, persons and capital; opponents pointed to the loss of national sovereignty involved. Neither side advanced any relevant empirical evidence to support their claims. Clearly we have come little further one hundred and fifty years later. Perhaps the sole mark of the limited progress made is that protectionists, for long without any substantive economic legitimation, can today gain some limited theoretical succour from New Trade Theory, an edifice constructed around some basic theorems concerning gains from trade plus elements of basic oligopoly theory. (It is *inter alia* a curiosity that Ohlin's *Interregional and International Trade*, built as it is upon a model assuming perfect competition in factor and product markets, was published in the same year by the same publisher in the same series as Chamberlin's *Theory of Monopolistic Competition*, which showed why these assumptions of perfect competition had to be abandoned; and with them went the story about comparative advantage on a national basis.)

Today, loose talk of globalisation is rife and everywhere innocent of a simple distinction between the volume of trade and its structure, and the recognition that even for relatively open economies only a small proportion of economic activity is traded internationally. Measured by the usual scale, relating the volume of the external sector to the total GDP, Japan has for example become steadily 'less global' throughout the twentieth century, although the increasing closure of the British economy is rather less marked. These are broad-brush arguments, of course, but they rest upon an elementary acquaintance with relevant basic statistics which, unfortunately, are neither mentioned nor recognised in contemporary debate. And so it was in the 1840s, as both Irwin and Magnusson demonstrate. The advantages and disadvantages of free trade were debated upon all sides without either party apparently resorting even to speculation over, for instance, the structure and composition of Baltic trade, or the changing pattern of Atlantic trade. Although statistics were of course not readily available to the protagonists, these matters were the commonplace concern of merchants, shippers, bankers and insurers. None of this practical knowledge was adduced in debate; argument upon both sides rested upon the dogmatic assertion of general principles and the derivation of possible future scenarios. Here, again, little changes. The rhetoric of 'crisis', and the consequent pressing need for 'reform', is endemic in both politics and economics. Once this condition is recognised perhaps historians can begin to write a different story.

13

FREE TRADE AND THE VICTORIANS

Anthony Howe

Amidst a voluble debate concerning Victorian values, the importance of free trade has been strangely neglected.[1] Yet there is a good case for arguing that free trade was the most commonly held of all Victorian values. It formed part, as Adelman has suggested, of 'the mental furniture of every educated Victorian', furniture whose sheen was so resplendent that from the repeal of the Corn Laws in 1846 until the opening of Chamberlain's Tariff Reform campaign in 1903 it scarcely needed dusting or repolishing.[2] Such a pervasive hold upon the Victorian mind owed its strength to free trade's origins in the two most fundamental pillars of the Victorian age, long ago identified by G.M. Young, those of utilitarianism and evangelicalism.[3] Both bodies of dogma have been expertly dissected, especially as we have been boldly counselled to locate the roots of economic policy-making more in evangelical religion than in secular models of free trade.[4]

But whether it owed its moral impetus more to Bishop Butler and the doctrine of Atonement than Richard Cobden and the Anti-Corn Law League, the repeal of the Corn Laws by the Conservative administration of Sir Robert Peel in 1846 marked a decisive turning-point in fiscal, imperial, and foreign policy whose implications were only gradually worked out after 1846. For the Tories who now opposed repeal (it is misleading to call them protectionists for many were Huskissonites believing in freer, not free, trade) Britain in 1846 was entering upon a 'great and hazardous experiment' whose outcome was more likely to be harmful than beneficial.[5] For the Anti-Corn Law League, on the other hand, repeal opened the way to the millennium, the world republic in which commerce would ensure peace.[6] It was only gradually, from betwixt the poles of such divergent views, that free trade emerged as part of a liberal consensus within domestic politics and perhaps the single most distinctive feature of the British state in an international perspective in the nineteenth and early twentieth centuries.[7]

Not surprisingly therefore in the immediate aftermath of the repeal of the Corn Laws, support for free trade, deriving from both the secular and

164

evangelical models outlined by Hilton, expressed itself in a variety of policy formulations.[8] In this way, the application of free trade after 1846 gave rise to a complex amalgam of ideas and policies, not to a simple 'stern and unbending Cobdenism'. Too often later nineteenth-century free trade has been identified with its twentieth-century epigones such as F.W. Hirst or defined through the simplifying lens of the tariff reformers in the early twentieth century.[9] Notions of 'Cobdenism', 'Manchesterism' and 'the Manchester School' have typically been inherited from opponents rather than from the supporters of these creeds, with 'free trade' normally dismissed as a mere vulgarisation of Smith's ideas but without reference to the different ways in which ideas were translated into policy.[10] Attention to differing political applications of 'free trade' allows us however to help understand the longevity of free trade in Britain, for its propagation and later defence showed it to be neither unbending nor narrow; rather free trade proved one of the most versatile and malleable of Victorian doctrines. For what in the 1840s had appeared the creed of the evangelical Liberal Tories and Lancashire's cotton masters was to become a central belief of the progressive defenders of early twentieth-century social democracy.[11]

Tory interpretations of free trade

Repeal in 1846 represented a fundamental breach within the Tory free-trade tradition for although the tendency in party history has been to emphasise a simple ideological division between Peelites and protectionists within the Tory party, the novel development in the 1840s was that Peel and his followers moved from Huskissonite freer trade towards what became at its extreme point 'universal free trade'.[12] It was in this respect that Peel himself may now be seen as approaching the cosmopolitanism of Cobden, abandoning Huskisson's attachment to reciprocity and the empire in favour of unilateral free trade, in the belief that 'hostile tariffs' were best countered by free imports, and that improved trade between nations provided 'a bond of peace . . . that will control the passions of those European governments who indulge themselves in the vision of war.'[13] This optimism, which now countered some of Peel's earlier evangelically based caution, culminated in Peel's famous paean to Cobden in June 1846, not simply a lapse of political taste as it has often been judged but a genuine acknowledgement of a new ideological element in Peel's thought.[14] Perhaps the most poignant recognition of this came from Sir John Gladstone, who believed that the Peelites, including his son William, had now abandoned 'real free trade' in favour of a Cobdenite chimera.[15] This critical view was shared by many in the provinces and above all in the City of London as many gentlemanly capitalists contemplated with alarm the ending of their shelter from storms of international competition which Peel now encouraged them to ride or sink under, just as he urged landowners to rely upon their own resources not those of state privilege via tariffs.[16] Peel

165

himself had earlier reduced but not abandoned imperial preference but its abolition was a logical culmination of repeal. For repeal ended the possibility of preference for colonial corn, a prospect encouraged as recently as 1843 by the Canada Corn Bill, although interestingly the Colonial Office had already refused to extend preference to Australian corn, and in that neglected part of the British Empire, to Ionian currants. Oddly, this aspect of Peelite policy is rarely stressed by historians although it was well brought out by Peel's grandson, George Peel (who, incidentally, lived to rehearse the lessons of repeal on its centenary in 1946) in his summary of the 'Life of Peel' included in Parker's three-volume biography in the 1890s.[17]

Yet this aspect of free trade was vitally important in the mid-nineteenth century, for it provided the essential bulwark against the revival of Huskissonite reciprocity. This was both intellectually defensible and politically powerful in the late 1840s and early 1850s.[18] For the Tory government of 1852 came near to securing a bilateral treaty with France which, if successful, would not only have pre-empted the Cobden–Chevalier treaty of 1860 but would have purposefully undermined Peelite free trade and provided a more plausible alternative to it than that offered by the agricultural protectionists.[19] Tories including Disraeli continued to valorise this type of freer trade as the proper Tory model, for example, later criticising the 1860 treaty as merely a less successful version of Pitt's 1786 Anglo-French treaty of commerce. But the Peelite model of universal free trade also barred the way back for the 'Fair Traders' in the 1880s, for Peel had made it clear that free trade was benefical for Britain whether or not other countries reciprocated; this was an unconditional policy of free imports.

The international dimension of Peelite policy in the 1840s is often the least considered one for this was rarely central to parliamentary debate.[20] More pivotal here was the preoccupation with the fiscal face of the battle between land and industry. Here it is far more easy to see in the 1840s the culmination of Huskissonite policies, with Peel himself taking up ideas he had already aired in the 1820s.[21] The crucial simplification of the tariff relied upon Peel's revival of income tax in the short term but in the longer term upon a few highly productive sources of indirect taxation. This fiscal model aimed at maximum revenue with least artificial distortion of the economy, and the minimal creation of interest groups dependent upon state favour. This model of fiscal reform attracted not only liberal Tories but also Whigs such as Parnell in 1830 (even C.P. Villiers attributed his free-trade ideas to Huskisson) and in the 1830s became entwined with the elimination of 'Old Corruption'.[22] Whether or not Peel derived his ideas from the Report of the Select Committeee on Import Duties in 1840, his goals were again perceived to be increasingly akin to those of the Radicals, especially as the latter were won over to an acceptance of direct taxation, a conversion made much easier by the abandonment of protection (for no longer could taxes on industry be said to pay for protection for land).[23] That 'public economy was an essential part of public virtue' became a truism uniting Peel, Gladstone, and Cobden, as well as a generation of Radical critics who aspired to the 'free breakfast table' and even the abolition of all customs houses.[24] Hence as Matthew has shown, Gladstone took to the fullest extent consonant with revenue-raising the abolition of tariffs, in his budgets of 1853 and the 1860s, culminating in 1869 with the abolition of the corn registration duty, left in place after repeal but now exposed as 'the final shred of protection' within the British tariff.[25] In this process principles originated by Peel were carried forward by Gladstone and Cobden, seeking to enforce economy on governments by cutting off permanently its fiscal resources.[26]

It was this model of fiscal free trade whose longest-term advocates were found within the civil service itself. For example, the Peelite Fremantle abandoned Parliament for the Board of Customs, becoming a crucial ally of Gladstone in cutting down the tariff, and as he noted on his retirement in 1873, 'constant and extensive reductions and abolitions of import duties' had afforded relief to the taxpayer to the extent of £20 million per annum.[27] Fiscal free trade became an integral element in Treasury thinking under Gladstone's sway, imbibed by officials such as Lingen, Hamilton, and Mowatt and through them carried forward into the twentieth century. It provided a ready-made defence against later attempts to subvert orthodoxy, for example during the Boer War, the policy of preference for Australian wines was rejected as portending 'the most important change in our trade policy since Sir Robert Peel's Tariff Reforms.'[28] Above all, this bureaucratic interpretation of free trade, linking it to the 'knaveproof state', provided a model of resistance to increased government expenditure, the fear that expenditure opened the state up to the threat of vested interests, both of tariff-seeking economic interests but also the demands of a class-based elect-orate. These arguments also continued to be made by Unionist free traders in the early twentieth century, for example, by Balfour of Burleigh, Arthur Elliot, and others who traced their free-trade beliefs back, not to Cobden, but to Peel.[29] Conversely, we should note that this model also ensured that when the demand for increased state expenditure was irresistible, it was met by increased direct taxation by the Liberal governments after 1906. Only in the 1930s was customs revenue once more to rise relatively as a component of government finance.[30]

Free trade and the Whigs

In some ways a Whig version of free trade is more difficult to identify than a Tory one; Peter Mandler, for example, has emphasised the style of thought shared by liberal Tories and Whigs, deriving from both secular influences and evangelical ones, although Hilton has also pointed out the difficulties inherent in identifying consistently the theological-politico-economic positions of individual politicians.[31] In the 1830s clearly the Whigs were identified more strongly than Tories with the ideological version of free trade diffused through the *Edinburgh Review*, and with the Radical brand of free trade which was held within the Board of Trade.[32] Yet leading Whig finance ministers such as Sir Charles Wood were open to many of the same influences as Peel, for example education at Oxford under the influence of Copleston.[33] Brent too has interestingly argued that there had emerged, especially among the Drummond Professors at Oxford, a new form of optimistic political economy, which may have informed the intellectual background to Whig moves towards free trade in the 1840s.[34] But as is well known, the Whigs had conspicuously failed to evolve a successful economic policy in the 1830s: on the one hand, they had been diverted by the social interventionist gestures of the Foxites, while on the other they had failed to overcome the vested interests of land, timber, and sugar; in disgust, C.P. Thompson, the Whig-Radical MP for Manchester, resigned, recording 'there is no chance of carrying the House with one of any great commercial reforms, timber, corn, sugar etc. . . . party and private interests will prevent it.'[35] Belatedly the Whigs attempted to run on freer trade (a fixed duty on corn) in 1841 but too late to convince the electorate: as T.F. Lewis put it, the Whig government

> had only to propose what is just and right for it to become utterly contemptible and unpopular . . . a Conservative government was to be created in order to uphold and maintain all that rational people have for years shown to be at variance with the true interests of the publick.[36]

Under Anti-Corn Law League pressure in the 1840s, however, the Whigs continued to push towards free trade; Cobden's strategy, although purportedly a non-party one, aimed in the first place to drive Whigs, not Tories, to repeal. First, despite distaste for aspects of League politics, Russell, Grey, and others by 1843 were ready to abandon the Corn Laws, deeming the regulation of food supply as no longer within the power of government. Grey more dogmatically urged the 'sweeping away of all restrictions upon the freedom of trade except those duties which we impose simply and exclusively with a view to revenue.' Grey also now demanded 'free trade on the ground of justice to the working classes', although others equally saw the necessity of repeal if the Whigs were to regain their hold on the urban selectorate they had created in 1832.[37] Second, the Whigs in opposition attacked more strongly than the Peelites the issue of imperial preference, seeking to draw a line between Peelite tendernesss for colonial interests and Whig embrace of a self-governing empire. Third, the Whigs espoused earlier than Peel the idea of unilateralism in commercial policy, the view to which Peel and Gladstone were converted in 1845 but in which J.L. Ricardo, Howick, Villiers and others preceded them in debates on commercial policy in 1843 and 1844.[38] In all these policies, little separated Whig and Peelite free-traders: the Whigs merely enjoyed the freedom of opposition while Peel was constrained by the dictates of governing with a party largely wedded to protectionism. Yet the Whigs had set themselves implicitly an agenda for office to which their Radical allies would hold them against the residual protectionist hankerings of aristocratic Whiggery. Cobden himself in July 1846 announced the goals to which Whig government should aspire:

> Do not lose the *free trade wind*. Your countrymen can only entertain one idea at a time. There is much to do yet. All anomalies of the tariff must be removed . . . February 1849 must be the doomsday of all Protectionists.[39]

How well did the Whigs heed Cobden's advice? Here although the Whig ministry of 1846–52 is commonly seen as 'timid and maladroit', it actually achieved a great deal in terms of the lasting systematisation of free trade within British policy.[40] Arguably, it was the success of the Whigs in this respect, conjoined perhaps as Vincent has argued, with the spectre of the revival of Chartism in 1848, which made the world (or at least Britain) safe for free trade.[41] Yet the importance of Chartism was more in deterring the protectionists from their advocacy than in winning over the Whigs, whose own protectionists were largely impotent despite the occasional glimmer of a Whig–protectionist alliance.[42] Moreover, the Whigs' moves preceded the revival of Chartism, for immediately on entering office in July 1846 they had set out to abandon imperial preference. Grey at the Colonial Office had quite clearly embraced the doctrine of unilateral free trade, and the Whigs moved speedily to equalise the duties on foreign and colonial sugar, rejecting Tory claims that the moral issue of slavery removed sugar from 'the ordinary and regular principles applicable to free trade'.[43] In the event, the Commercial Crisis of 1847 which hit most strongly the West Indian interest forced the Whigs to moderate this policy but not to abandon its principles. Clarendon was adamant on this point: 'That [reversion to the old system]', he wrote, 'would be retaxing the whole community for the benefit or the supposed benefit of a particular class . . . it would be a complete triumph to the Protectionists and beyond all doubt lead again to a Corn Law agitation.' The Whigs therefore held to equalisation, with its liquidation of many of the City of London's most 'gentlemanly capitalists'.[44]

The Whigs also moved but much more slowly towards the equalisation of the timber duties. Russell was retrospectively to single out the timber interest as 'one of the powerful colonial interests' hostile to Whig reform but in the late 1840s the Whigs were held back in part by the crisis in Canadian trade 'occasioned', as 'Bear' Ellice put it, 'by our recent Revolution in our fiscal and financial policy' but also by anxiety as to growing sentiment in favour of annexation with the United States.[45] Wood was also prepared to retain this remnant of protection while it proved fiscally lucrative. Even so by

1851 the timber duties, for Grey 'the last remaining example of a system of the very worst protection', came under renewed Whig attack although it was left to Gladstone first (in 1853) to reform and then in 1866 to extinguish this budgetary resource.[46]

Second, the abandonment of preference also necessitated the abandonment of the mother country's entitlement to receive preference from her own colonies; hence in the Colonial Possessions Act of 1846, Britain abandoned its right to benefit from differential duties within the empire, although failing to ensure that the colonies might not impose duties against Britain as well as others; in this many contradictions of later imperial economic policy were begotten. Above all Grey was to lament that colonial autonomy was to undermine imperial economic unity, while Gladstone in the 1870s was appalled to discover the extent of colonial tariffs and their increasingly pro-tectionist nature.[47] The issue as to whether the self-governing colonies were parts of the British Empire, bound by its commercial treaties, or independent economic units, confused British commercial diplomacy right up until 1902. In some ways Chamberlainite Tariff Reform was the ultimate, if draconian, attempt to unravel the Whig colonial legacy of 1846.

Third, the Whigs more directly confronted the prescriptions of Smith in tackling the second fundamental pillar of protection, the Navigation Acts, and their supposed beneficiaries, the shipping interest. The Navigation Acts, as Sarah Palmer has reminded us, were no mere antiquarian survival: over 40 per cent of imports to Britain still entered under their aegis in the early 1840s, while the shipping interest itself, still strongly based on the City of London, was an essential political bastion of protection.[48] Protectionism was in some ways far more prominent among the City's gentlemanly capitalists than was loyalty to the vulgar Northern creed of free trade. Abolition of the Navigation Acts was immediately attractive to many Whigs, including Clarendon (at the Board of Trade) and Grey (at the Colonial Office), but it was also expected to lead to strong opposition, for as Clarendon noted, 'in the minds of many they are an institution, a bulwark, bound up with Church and State, and [the] 40th article of the National Creed.'[49] In the event the opposition proved even stronger than the reformers expected. For repeal divided the Whigs themselves, with many, including Palmerston and Brougham, mindful of Smith's support for the Acts, and reluctant to follow the path of unilateral repeal. Together with the protectionist backlash, this came near to toppling the Whig government in 1849. As a result, repeal of the Navigation Acts has not redounded to the credit of the Whig ministry. Yet compared with Peel's earlier equivocation on this issue, the Whigs acted with some speed and purpose in a direction which was the logical comple-ment to their abolition of differential duties and colonial preference. Despite the protectionist fears that repeal would remove the basis of British power, repeal arguably encouraged the revival and modernisation of British ship-ping. Thus many opponents of repeal in the 1840s such as W.S. Lindsay

170

recognised by 1860 that free trade was the necessary basis of shipping's prosperity, even if shipowners still had some legitimate grievances to be remedied.[50]

Fourth, the Whigs wrestled with the international promotion of free trade; the desire that while Britain had abandoned tariff bargaining, it wished still to encourage other nations to follow its own example. On the one hand, therefore, Cobden toured Europe disparaging the efforts of the Foreign Office (but not those of the Board of Trade) while seeking to propagate the League vision of a free-trade Europe; on the other hand, in more guarded fashion, Palmerston urged his ministers abroad to encourage where possible the movement of European nations towards tariff liberalisation; for example, in Spain, Portugal, Italy, and the Zollverein.[51] Thus in 1847, Lord Howard de Walden in Brussels welcomed the Free Trade Congress of 1847 as disseminating 'the extreme benefits which would result to the community in general of all nations from the abandonment of the restrictive system in matters of commerce.'[52] But British diplomacy was confined to moral exhortation and did not extend to tariff-bargaining. This unilateralism remained the keynote of British foreign policy and the Whigs, for the most part, had no wish to resume the Tory search for a bilateral treaty with France, urging rather that 'a change in the commercial policy of France . . . could only be the result of conviction on the part of the French Government and nation.'[53]

Finally we may note that the Whigs, with the enthusiastic free-trader Granville in charge, promoted the Great Exhibition of 1851 in a very real sense as a propaganda device for the benefits of free trade, the proclamation to the world of the British model of commercial prosperity and liberal state. Here was a distinct reminder, against the background of the 1848 revolutions, of Smith's most important lesson, that political liberty was possible only in commercial societies, with the implicit rider that the greater the commercial prosperity the greater the potential for political liberty.[54]

Despite therefore the inconsistencies in practice of the Whigs – their undoubted timidity on Corn Laws and irresolution on fiscal policy – they were by no means the 'bourbons of the fisc' as they have been presented. They had made in some ways a bold attempt to pick up the Peelite mantle; to bid, if Peel would not, for Radical middle-class support, and in some ways to become the 'party of the middle-classes', the goal which Cobden had mapped out for Peel in 1846.[55] If this was, as Parry has described it, 'anaemic Peelism', it had a lot to be said for it in terms of rallying the middle-class electorate at a time of Protectionist resurgence, while Whig policy could be positively portrayed as a social policy designed to 'promote the comfort and the health of the labouring portion of our community.'[56] We may therefore detect a consistent purpose behind the occasional vagaries of Whig policy, the view that the community was not to be exposed to the exactions of monopolists and that the economy, including the empire, was to be freed from artificial restraints. The British state, strengthened by the reduction of the demands upon it, would be controlled by Whig politicians, but would be responsive to the guidance of enlightened bureaucrats, to an electorate to be selectively extended, and mindful of working-class needs for cheap food and healthy dwellings. This ideal failed to pull together the fragmenting forces of the Whig aristocracy in the late 1840s but it was one which both Palmerston and Gladstone would subsequently seek to fulfil.

Finally in terms of the continuities of British policy in the nineteenth century, it is worthwhile to draw attention back to the Board of Trade, whose importance in the 1830s Lucy Brown so admirably analysed. For in the later 1840s the Board recruited a talented group of free-traders, including Edgar Bowring, the son of Sir John, Louis Mallet, the son of one of the founders of the Political Economy Club, Lord Hobart, a long-term admirer of Cobden, and perhaps most influentially Sir Thomas Farrer, the ultimate embodiment of later nineteenth-century free-trade orthodoxy. The Board also included the young Sir Stafford Northcote, whose own later views as a leading Disraelian Conservative remained close to those of his early friends. In some ways not only the Whig implementation of economic policy in the late 1840s but also the subsequent interpretation of free trade in Victorian Britain owed much to this influential group of mandarins.[57]

'Gladstone–Cobdenism' (Overstone)[58]

The 1852 election ended the hopes of a protectionist revival in Britain, yet the advance of free trade was more equivocal. On the one hand, as Hilton has argued, the secular model of free trade rapidly replaced the evangelical model in the 1850s.[59] Gladstone's budget of 1853 took forward the simplification of the tariff set out by Peel and Wood, removing many 'engines of taxation' and heralding a permanent decline in the number of resources available to the state. Commercial diplomacy also achieved some successes, for example the elimination of the Sound Dues in the Baltic and the Anglo-Russian Commercial Treaty of 1859.[60] On the other hand, the Crimean War had demoralised the Cobdenites with Cobden largely renouncing the apostolate of free trade. From the Sussex Weald he contemplated with deepening gloom the ascendancy of Palmerston: symbolically, in 1856 it was Palmerston, not Cobden, who was fêted at the new Free Trade Hall in Manchester.[61] Yet fiscal reform was never wholly forgotten: France had renewed its interest in a commercial treaty in 1855 and Lord Clarendon at the Paris peace negotiations of 1856 had suggested to Palmerston the idea of a European free-trade congress.[62] Even so, the legacy of war finance largely ruled out fiscal experimentation in the late 1850s.

This changed rapidly and completely with the renewal of Gladstone's chancellorship in 1859. Gladstone not only took up the reins of Peelite finance but now much more readily sought to use British fiscal change as the lever to free trade abroad. The Cobden–Chevalier treaty, which linked the budget of 1860 to fiscal reform in France, was thus conceived not as an exporters' treaty but as 'a victory for humanity' designed to ensure peace between Britain and France at a time of growing tension but also to boost European commerce as a whole.[63] In a sense this was a return to tariff-bargaining of the type abandoned in 1846 although as the defenders of the treaty urged this was a multilateral treaty on Britain's behalf, and therefore quite distinct from the earlier retrograde model based on exclusive dealing between two nations alone. This rationale was insufficient to convince the treaty's many Whig and Peelite critics, including strong free-traders such as Villiers, Clarendon, Grey, and W.R. Greg, who lamented the return to pre-1846 commercial diplomacy, and feared an increase in direct taxation to follow in its wake.[64] Yet the Cobdenites now set out a fundamentally new vision of the international order; for them 1860 was no simple return to reciprocity, but fiscal changes deemed to be in Britain's interest were timed to coincide with movements abroad, in order to ratchet tariffs downwards. This did involve detailed bargaining yet for Gladstone this was a defensible role for a responsible power, seeking both fiscal benefits and the enhancement of the prospects of peace which commercial treaties brought. Gladstone therefore not only was willing in 1860 to prepare his budget with France in mind but also in 1866 prepared his budget largely with the needs of the Anglo-Austrian Commercial Treaty in view. Between 1860 and 1866 Great Britain therefore negotiated treaties not only with France but also with Belgium, Italy, Germany, and Austria, while initiating negotiations with Spain and Portugal.[65]

This was a conscious attempt to reconstruct Europe on a free-trade basis, not as Gladstone put it 'for mere increase of trade [but] for those blessings which increase of trade brings with it: peace, security, goodwill.'[66] For others, including Cobden's leading official ally Mallet, European trade also provided a deliberate counterweight to the swing of Palmerstonian policy towards the east in the 1850s.[67] Self-conscious 'disciples of Cobden' such as the diplomat Sir Robert Morier now set out their vision of a free-trade world, one of peace, prosperity and democracy, based on free exchange between nations and between property-owning individuals within them.[68] This was a counter both to socialism in Europe and to protection and monopoly in Britain. But importantly free-traders had moved from a vision of commerce leading spontaneously to peace to a view of the necessity of agreements between nations concerning tariffs, a form of regulatory liberalism, in which governments had a part to play in securing common interests, rather than relying upon the natural harmony of interests between states. This in a sense prefigures the forms of international rules and institutions developed after 1945.[69] It was, however, at this time an ideal shared by only a minority of diplomats and businessmen, if also by a number of leading European intellectuals and statesman, for whom Cobden rather than Palmerston or Peel epitomised their international ambitions. Thus, for the Prussian minister

Bunsen, Cobden was 'the first diplomatist of the world' while the creator of Napoleon III's Liberal Empire, Emile Ollivier, confided 'To be Cobden would be greater and would suit me better than to be Robert Peel.'[70]

This internationalist perspective, however, was eroded relatively quickly. Already by the late 1860s, it had run up against important opposition within the Liberal Cabinet with Lowe, above all, asserting the need for the autonomy of the Treasury in its fiscal policy, the idea that only national fiscal ends should be considered. Even so, the idea of concurrent fiscal change throughout Europe via a tariff congress was periodically revived, including, as Gaston has shown, by Northcote when Chancellor of the Exchequer in 1875.[71] The obstacles to its success lay primarily in the lack of support for such a policy in a Europe already turning back to protection rather than in the lack of enthusiasm in the Foreign Office, whose contempt for trade can be too easily exaggerated.[72] Within British policy-making, the real constraint on future tariff treaties lay in the perceived lack of bargaining counters, with the British tariff already confined to relatively few articles whose further erosion the Treasury was reluctant to countenance.[73] Nevertheless, the Cobdenites regularly urged forward commercial negotiations, urging flexibility in wine duties to revive negotiations with France, Spain, and Portugal, and flexibility on spirits duties to attract Germany. They thus aimed for a stable fiscal system in which the European states would seek by limiting tariffs to drive down government expenditure and to enhance the prospects of a peaceful democratic order. How far there was scope for a new bout of treaties in the late 1870s is perhaps doubtful but this policy dispute well reveals the divisions of opinion among free-traders, with the 'Cobdenites' still seeking free exchange, to perfect the world market and to release democracy from the power of vested interests and militarism. To this end they advocated commercial treaties and other international institutions, for example agreements to outlaw sugar bounties, in order to perfect the institutional setting of economic progress; and briefly in the early 1880s these were ends to which Gladstone himself would lend important if lukewarm support.[74] On the other hand, for the Foreign Office, the Treasury, and the Board of Trade commercial treaties increasingly gave rise to more problems than they solved; above all, as Farrer urged, they almost invited movements for 'Fair Trade' and retaliation.[75] By 1885, therefore, the model of 1860 remained a distant and exceptional measure, a vestige of briefly 'Liberal Europe' rather than a prescription for policy-making in the age of Empire.

Cobdenism after Cobden

Palmerstonian Britain, which had proved unenthusiastic yet surprisingly favourable towards Cobdenite diplomacy, had often seemed to marginalise Cobden's domestic influence.[76] Free trade itself as an emerging consensus owed its strength as much to Peelite/Gladstonian loyalties within the bureaucracy and to the legacy of Huskissonite free trade as much as to the influence of Cobden and the League. Yet this fundamentally altered in the generation after 1865, especially as in the wake of the Second Reform Act, Cobden's posthumous importance to the Liberal party became fundamental. For Cobdenite radicalism now developed as a central strand within Liberalism, remaining powerful until 1931, and sustaining a vigorous popular loyalty to free trade.[77]

First, within the Liberal party, a much neglected part was played by the Cobden Club set up in 1866 as the political equivalent of the National Association for the Promotion of Social Science; historians have enthusiastically written up the latter while almost wholly ignoring the former save occasionally to confuse it with the Political Economy Club.[78] The Cobden Club, with strong support among all sections of the Liberal party, developed as an important propaganda branch of Liberalism sustaining a vast range of publications devoted to the ideas of its eponymous hero.[79] Its influence extended to Europe, the United States, and Australasia but at home the Club provided the standard Victorian defence of free trade, integrating the works of Giffen, Farrer, and Fawcett and 'vulgarising' these in the rhetoric of affluence expounded in the works of Augustus Mongredien and George Medley.[80] This was an educational role comparable in some ways to that played by the League in the 1840s.[81] But the Club also acquired a considerable political appeal as threats to free trade emerged briefly in the late 1860s, and more persistently from the late 1870s. At this point the Club sought to work through forging working-class alliances, such as with the Trades Union Congress (TUC) and Arch's Agricultural Labourers' Union in order to counter incipient attacks on free trade. Here the Club importantly sustained popular loyalties to free-trade which Biagini has well described, with for example 'plebeian' free-traders such as John Noble or Thomas Briggs seeking inspiration in Cobden.[82] The Club also complemented well the emergence of a wider cult of Cobden expressed in mid-Victorian England, for example in several public busts and statues and numerous popular biographies: arguably this cult of Cobden was far stronger and certainly more long-lasting than that of Bright in Victorian and Edwardian Britain.[83]

In this way, therefore, just as Victorians might have been tempted by fears of depression back towards protection, the shade of Cobden rose to caution and reprove them. It did so with marked success. For in two major respects the Cobdenite message struck home to lasting effect. First, the Liberal defence of free trade between 1866 and 1886 largely deprived 'Fair Trade' of an audience; wherever it emerged for example, as a creed of unemployed workers in London in the late 1860s, it was rapidly cried down as the tool of reactionary landowners and vested interests; or in Lancashire in 1881, its temporary success induced a counterattack of immense proportions in the election of 1885.[84] Elsewhere in the world, as many pointed out, protection was associated with democracy, for example, the USA, France and Australia;

the Cobdenite strength within the Liberal party ensured that in England, protection would become neither a Liberal nor a popular cause.[85] Above all in the election of 1885, when there were widespread fears of the emergence of popular protectionism, the Club's national campaign in association with groups such as the National Reform Union, and even Bradlaugh's secular societies, helped ensure the loyalty of the new democratic electorate to free trade. This was of vital long-term importance in inoculating the late Victorian electorate against both Fair Trade and Tariff Reform.[86]

Second, while 'Cobdenism' remained a potent force in the popular Liberalism of the 1880s, this does not mean, as some historians have assumed, that free trade remained exactly as Cobden had left it: the view that every attack on free trade merely produced a sheaf of pamphlets from the 1840s, sufficient to draw the sting of protection. On the contrary, by the 1880s a clear faultline had developed within the free-trade camp which derived from the ambiguous legacy of Cobden. This was well defined by one of Cobden's critics, Maine, when analysing the 'Church of Cobden' in 1872 (*Pall Mall Gazette*).[87] For Maine discerned that Cobden himself had been poised between his desire to minimise the power of the state and his desire to depose the 'privileged classes'. It was the latter objective which Maine detected as the key to Cobden's successors, to be achieved through the power of the state wielded by the democratic electorate. This fault-line led directly towards the split between individualist and collectivist free-traders in the 1880s. For on the one hand, individualist thinkers such as Mallet held that the distinctive character of Cobden's economic policy lay in the

> belief that the social problem (by which I mean the reconciliation of the interests of property with those of the proletariat) was to be solved by Peace and Free Trade in the largest sense, of Free Exchange, between all nations . . . and by the steady adoption of the principles of personal liberty and personal responsibility.[88]

This may be seen, guardedly at least, as a development of the 'market view' of free trade which Hilton has identified in Peelite survivors such as the Duke of Argyll, and which carried its adherents in an individualist, anti-socialist direction.[89] Yet this increasingly isolated Mallet and like-minded free-traders within the Cobden Club, which they saw as veering towards invoking the power of the state to right the balance between property and poverty. Typical of this new direction was Joseph Chamberlain but Chamberlain's views did not discomfit other free-traders, for example Farrer, who claimed to find nothing in Chamberlain 'contrary to the best political economy'.[90] Significantly, it was Farrer who in the 1880s emerged as Mallet's successor as the leading intellectual influence within the Cobden Club, while in an important secession in 1882 many founders of the Club withdrew, including W.C. Cartwright, Odo Russell, Morier, and Goschen, arguably 'a revolt of the Peelites/Whigs' which left the Club's Radicals to defend free trade in the later nineteenth century. Given the failure of 'free exchange' internationally by the 1880s, this group was above all to emphasise a 'rights' view of free trade, that is to say the right of consumers to cheap food and of the community to be free from the oppressive power of vested interests. This was in some ways a retreat from free trade in its largest international sense towards national domestic goals.

These conflicting interpretations of free trade may perhaps best be illustrated by two important, if recondite, policy debates in late Victorian Britain, those concerning sugar bounties and bimetallism. For Mallet, action against sugar bounties was desirable, in a sense on Smithian grounds for they were clearly an artificial interference with trade which it was within the power of international diplomacy to remove.[91] Likewise, the bimetallic standard, he believed, was also a proper institutional mechanism which would sustain, and not subvert, free trade. Yet both policies were anathema to Farrer and many other free-traders; action against bounties was now held to conflict with the rights of consumers, a revival of Peelite 'free imports' but now associated with a 'rights', not a market interpretation of free trade. Yet this was a policy which, its free-trade critics thought, elevated 'national independence' above 'international dependence'.[92] Similarly bimetallism, while not equated with protection, was seen as likely to raise prices and diminish real wages, an attack on the power of consumers upon which the health of the economy depended. Mallet's 'Cobdenism' with its support of countervailing duties and of a bimetallic standard now drew him into 'queer company for a free trader', that of covert protectionists and bounty-seeking West Indian producers, yet he upheld the consistency of his creed of free exchange and individual property-ownership.[93] This ultimately carried him into the camp of the Liberty and Property Defence League, with other formerly staunch 'Cobdenites' such as Levy, Grant Duff, and Mackay. Yet it was the fewness of such individualist free-traders by the 1890s which led many to lament the 'end of the Manchester School' and the 'decline of Cobdenism', including Gladstone, who saw in the Cobden Club's *Jubilee of Free Trade* 'a great act of gallantry for the Cobdenian faith is in all points at a heavy discount, Peace, Retrenchment, Free Trade and all the rest of it.'[94]

Yet this view was at once accurate and misleading. For while free trade had increasingly become detached from *laissez-faire*, the 'Cobdenites' had correspondingly gravitated towards the 'collectivist camp'. For the 'New Liberalism ' of the 1900s had its origins in the split already detected within the Cobdenite camp in the 1880s; for example, Arnold Toynbee, while not a member of the Cobden Club, avidly defended free trade as a right of the community to be defended against the claims of uncompetitive industries.[95] Similarly, Toynbee's Balliol friend, B.R. Wise, produced an influential reconciliation of free trade and state intervention in his book, *Industrial Freedom*

(1892), which Farrer acclaimed as 'just the book I would have liked to write'. Wise made his career in Australia, where in 1898 he met Sidney Webb, who saw in Wise's book 'a good modern statement of fiscal free trade. . . . In England, he would have inevitably developed into a refined Collectivist.'[96] But this reconciliation between free trade and collectivism may be detected in a range of authors in the 1890s, such as Atherley-Jones, F.J. Shaw [Brougham Villiers], J.M. Robertson, E. Adams (in Scotland), and in the Georgeite movement for land nationalisation, all of which contributed to a cumulative and powerful reinvigoration of the arguments for free trade.[97] It was to this form of Cobdenism that influential recruits were won during the Boer War, for example, Hobson and Hobhouse, although others were won back to 'Manchesterism' by its foreign policy. In this way, the intellectual as well as the political ramparts of free trade had been rebuilt well in advance of Chamberlain's thrust against them.

As a result of this rejuvenation of free trade, Chamberlain's attack upon outdated 'Cobdenism' was itself already out of date when it was launched in 1903.[98] As the celebration of the centenary of Cobden's birth in 1904 would show, the radical hero of the 1840s had already secured his place within the Edwardian progressive tradition.[99] This was well recognised by surviving Edwardian individualists. For as the free-trade Unionist Strachey announced, developing the ideas of Mallet (of whose son Bernard he was a close friend) by 1908 'Cobdenism' was dead, killed off by the latterday Cobdenites.[100] On the other hand, as other chapters in this volume show, free trade remained at the heart of a renewed Liberalism, which proved both intellectually vigorous and politically insurmountable within Edwardian Britain.[101]

Notes

1 For example, J. Walvin, *Victorian Values* (London: Deutsch, 1987); E.M. Sigsworth (ed.) *In Search of Victorian Values: aspects of nineteenth-century thought and culture* (Manchester: Manchester University Press, 1988); T.C. Smout (ed.) *Victorian Values* (Proceedings of the British Academy, 78, Oxford: Oxford University Press, 1992).

2 P. Adelman, *Victorian Radicalism* (London: Longman, 1984), 25.

3 G.M. Young, *Victorian England: Portrait of an Age* (London: Oxford University Press, 1936), 5–11.

4 On political economy, most recently, D. Winch, *Riches and Poverty: an intellectual history of political economy in Britain, 1750–1834* (Cambridge: Cambridge University Press, 1996); and most originally, B. Hilton, *The Age of Atonement: the influence of evangelicalism on social and economic thought, 1785–1865* (Oxford: Clarendon Press, 1988).

5 J. Gladstone, *Plain Facts intimately connected with the intended Repeal of the Corn Laws* (London, 1846), 30; R. Stewart, *The Politics of Protection* (Cambridge: Cambridge University Press, 1971), 70.

6 For Cobden's views, *The Political Writings of Richard Cobden* (2 vols, 1867), now included in P.J. Cain (ed.) *The Political and Economic Works of Richard Cobden* (6 vols, London: Routledge, 1995); P.J. Cain, 'Capitalism, War and International-

ism in the Thought of Richard Cobden', *British Journal of International Studies* v (1979), 229–47; R.F. Spall, 'Free Trade, International Relations and the Anti-Corn Law League', *International History Review* 10 (1988), 405–32.

7 A. Howe, *Free Trade and Liberal England, 1846–1946* (Oxford: Oxford University Press, 1997).

8 Hilton, *Atonement*, 64–70 and *passim*.

9 F.W. Hirst, *From Adam Smith to Philip Snowden: a history of free trade in Britain* (London: Thomas Fisher Unwin, 1925); W. Cunningham, *Richard Cobden and Adam Smith* (London: Tariff Reform League, 1904).

10 E.g. R. Walther, 'Economic Liberalism', *Economy and Society* 13 (1984), 193–5.

11 A. Howe, 'Towards the "Hungry Forties": Free Trade in Britain c.1880–1906', in E. Biagini (ed.) *Citizenship and Community* (Cambridge: Cambridge University Press, 1996), 193–213.

12 Hilton, *Atonement*, 326.

13 *Hansard*, 3rd ser. 83, cc. 276–8 [27 Jan. 1846].

14 *Hansard*, 3rd ser. 87, c. 1053 [26 June 1846].

15 Sir John Gladstone, 'Free Trade' (draft), 23 July 1846, Glynne–Gladstone papers, 1187, Clwyd Record Office; *The Gladstone Diaries* ((ed.) M.D.R. Foot and H.C.G. Matthew, 14 vols, Oxford: Oxford University Press, 1968–94), vol. iii, xxxviii–xxxix.

16 A.C. Howe, 'Free Trade and the City of London, c. 1820–1870', *History* 77 (1992), 391–410; P. Harling, *The Waning of 'Old Corruption'* (Oxford: Clarendon Press, 1996), 228–54.

17 C.S. Parker, *Sir Robert Peel from his Private Papers* (3 vols London: John Murray, 1891–9), iii, 587; cf. [Free Trade Union] *The Centenary of the Repeal of the Corn Laws* (London: Free Trade Union, 1946).

18 For Torrens's case for reciprocity, L. Robbins, *Robert Torrens and the Evolution of Classical Economics* (London: Macmillan, 1958); D. Irwin, *Against the Tide: an intellectual history of free trade since 1776* (Princeton, NJ: Princeton University Press, 1996), 101–15; Stewart, *Protection*, 208.

19 This episode can be traced in Malmesbury to Disraeli, 28 Dec. 1851 to 24 Sept. 1852, Disraeli Papers B/XX/99, Bodleian Library, Oxford; Cowley–Malmesbury Correspondence, 1852, Cowley papers, FO519/196, Public Record Office (PRO).

20 Cf. S.C. James and D.A. Lake, 'The Second Face of Hegemony: Britain's Repeal of the Corn Laws and the American Walker Tariff of 1846', *International Organisation* 43 (1989), 1–30; P.K. O'Brien and G.A. Pigman, 'Free Trade, British Hegemony, and the International Economic Order', *Review of International Studies* 18 (1992), 89–113.

21 A.J.B. Hilton, *Corn, Cash and Commerce: the economic policies of the Tory Governments, 1815–1830* (Oxford: Oxford Historical Monographs, 1977).

22 Harling, *The Waning of 'Old Corruption'*, *passim*.

23 For one Radical view, A. Prentice, *The Pitt–Peel Income Tax* (1842) in A. Kadish (ed.) *The Corn Laws* (6 vols, London: Pickering and Chatto, 1996), v, 359–70.

24 Gladstone to Welby (Treasury), 26 Oct. 1887, Murray Papers, 1678, Blair Castle.

25 H.C.G. Matthew, 'Disraeli, Gladstone and the Politics of Mid-Victorian Budgets', *Historical Journal* 22 (1979), 615–43; J.S. Mill to A. Lalande, 2 May 1869, in *The Collected Works of J.S. Mill* (ed. F.E.L. Priestley, J.M. Robson *et al.*, Toronto, University of Toronto Press, 1963–) vol. xvii, 1595–6; for the lucrativeness of this duty, J. Prest, 'A Large or a Small Amount? Revenue and the nineteenth-century corn laws', *Historical Journal* 39 (1996), 467–78.

26 L. Mallet to M.E. Grant Duff, 4 Nov. 1868, Grant Duff Papers, Ms Eur. F234/37, India Office Library.

27 Fremantle to Gladstone, 26 Nov. 1873, Gladstone Papers, Add. Ms. 44139 f. 299, British Library.
28 H. Roseveare, *The Treasury* (London: Allen Lane, The Penguin Press, 1969), esp. 183–234; A.E. Bateman, 'Wine Duties', 29 Apr. 1899, CAB/37/49/27, PRO.
29 For the Unionist free-traders, R.A. Rempel, *Unionists Divided* (Newton Abbot: David & Charles, 1972), and Sykes, Chapter 14 in this volume; Northbrook to Elliot, 25 Sept. 1903, Arthur Elliot Papers, Ms. 19493, National Library of Scotland.
30 P. Mathias, *The First Industrial Nation* (London: Methuen, 1969), Table 12, p. 469; *Statistical Abstract for the United Kingdom* (Cmd. 5627, London: HMSO, 1938), 170–1.
31 P. Mandler, *Aristocratic Government in the Age of Reform* (Oxford: Clarendon Press, 1990); B. Hilton, 'Whiggery, Religion and Social Reform: the case of Lord Morpeth', *Historical Journal* 37 (1994), 829–59.
32 B. Fontana, *Rethinking the Politics of Commercial Society* (Cambridge: Cambridge University Press, 1985); L. Brown, *The Board of Trade and the Free-Trade Movement 1830–1842* (Oxford: Clarendon Press, 1958).
33 Among Wood's friends there had been Sir Thomas Fremantle, Gladstone's customs expert. For Fremantle's octogenarian reflections on the 'palmy days of Oriel', Cottesloe to Halifax, 12 Oct. 1883, Hickleton Papers, A4/136.
34 R. Brent, 'God's Providence: liberal political economy as natural theology at Oxford, 1825–60', in M. Bentley (ed.) *Public and Private Doctrine* (Cambridge: Cambridge University Press, 1993), 85–107.
35 Journal, 21 Sept. 1839, in G. Poulett Scrope (ed.) *Memoir of Lord Sydenham* (London, 1844), 102.
36 T.F. to G.C. Lewis 13 May 1841, Harpton Court Papers, C/1706, National Library of Wales. I am most grateful to Peter Mandler for this reference.
37 Howick (later Grey) to Russell, 18 Jan. 1845, Russell Papers, William Perkins Library, Duke University; Mandler, *Aristocratic Government*, 217–19, 223–4, 228–31.
38 *Hansard*, 3rd ser. 68, cc. 902–73 [25 Apr. 1843]; 73, cc. 1270–304 [19 Mar. 1844]; for an extra-parliamentary view, 'A Manufacturer', *Reciprocity* (n.d. c. 1843) in Kadish, *Corn Laws*, v, 83–155.
39 Cobden to Russell, 4 July 1846, Russell Papers, PRO30/22/5B.
40 For a typically adverse judgement, D. Southgate, *The Passing of the Whigs* (London: Macmillan, 1962), 161.
41 J. Vincent (ed.) *Disraeli, Derby and the Conservative Party: journals and memoirs of Edward Henry, Lord Stanley, 1849–69* (Hassocks: Harvester Press, 1978), xii–xiv.
42 Stewart, *Politics of Protection*, 160–1.
43 Ibid., 130–3.
44 Clarendon to James Wilson, 15 Jan. 1848, Wilson Papers, William Perkins Library, Duke University; Howe, 'City', 401–4.
45 John, Earl Russell, *Recollections and Suggestions, 1813–1873* (London, 1875), 210; Ellice to Russell, 30 May 1849, Russell Papers, PRO30/22/7F.
46 Grey to Russell, 18 Nov. 1848, Russell Papers, PRO30/22/7D; Gladstone, 'Timber Duties', 12 Sept. 1865, memo in Layard Papers, Add. Ms. 39117, ff. 94 *et seq.*, British Library.
47 Grey, *The Colonial Policy of Lord John Russell's Government* (2 vols, London: Richard Bentley, 1853), 1, 281–2; cf. Grey, *The Commercial Policy of the British Colonies and the McKinley Tariff* (London: Macmillan, 1892); Gladstone to Kimberley, 16 May 1871 in *Diaries* vii, 496; P. Knaplund, *Gladstone and Britain's Imperial Policy* (London: Allen & Unwin, 1927), 104–21, 247–51.

48 S. Palmer, *Politics, Shipping and the Repeal of the Navigation Laws* (Manchester: Manchester University Press, 1990), 40; Howe, 'City', 402–4.

49 Clarendon to Grey, 9 Jan. 1847, Papers of 3rd Earl Grey, Department of Paleography and Diplomatic, Prior's Kitchen, University of Durham.

50 W.S. Lindsay, *Our Merchant Shipping: its present state considered* (London: Longman, 1860).

51 M. Taylor (ed.) *The European Diaries of Richard Cobden, 1846–51* (Aldershot: Scolar Press, 1994); D.C.M. Platt, *Finance, Trade, and Politics in British Foreign Policy, 1815–1914* (Oxford: Clarendon Press, 1968), 143.

52 De Walden to Palmerston, no. 27, 21 Sept. 1847, FO10/133.

53 Clarendon to Walewski, 7 Sept. 1853 in E. Hertslet, 'Attempts since 1830 to accomplish commercial arrangements with France', 3 Mar. 1860, FO97/207, PRO.

54 For another Whig enthusiast for the Exhibition (and free trade), D. Spring, 'Earl Fitzwilliam and the Corn Laws', *American Historical Review*, 59 (1953–4), 300.

55 J. Morley, *The Life of Richard Cobden* (2 vols, London: Chapman and Hall, 1882), i, 390–401.

56 J.P. Parry, *The Rise and Fall of Liberal Government in Victorian Britain* (London: Yale University Press, 1993), 173–4; *Hansard*, 3rd ser. 115 [Wood, 4 Apr. 1851].

57 Brown, *Board of Trade*; E.A. Bowring, Diaries, 1841–52, William Perkins Library, Duke University; B. Mallet, *Sir Louis Mallet: a record of public service and political ideals* (London: James Nisbet, 1905); Mary, Lady Hobart (ed.) *Essays and Miscellaneous Writings of Vere Henry, Lord Hobart* (2 vols, London: Macmillan, 1885); T.C. Farrer, (ed.) *Some Farrer Memorials: being a selection from the papers of Thomas Henry, first Lord Farrer, 1819–1899* (printed for private circulation, London: George Sherwood, 1923).

58 Overstone to Granville, 20 Jan. 1871, in D.P. O'Brien (ed.) *The Correspondence of Lord Overstone* (3 vols, Cambridge, 1971), iii, 1205–6.

59 Hilton, *Atonement*, ch. 7.

60 C.E. Hill, *The Danish Sound Dues Question and the Command of the Baltic* (Durham, NC, 1926), 241–68; G. de Bernhardt, *Handbook of Commercial Treaties* (1912), 743–52.

61 *Manchester Guardian*, 3 Nov. 1856, p. 3; Bright to Cobden, 8 Aug. and 2 Nov. 1856, Bright Papers, Add. Ms. 43384, British Library.

62 Clarendon to Palmerston, 6 Apr. 1856, Clarendon Deposit, c.135, Bodleian Library, Oxford.

63 A.L. Dunham, *The Anglo-French Treaty of Commerce of 1860* (Ann Arbor: University of Michigan Press, 1930) remains the standard account; O'Brien and Pigman, 'Free trade', 99–100; cf. Cobden to T. Thomasson, 2 June 1861, Thomasson Letters, British Library of Political and Economic Science.

64 E.D. Steele, *Palmerston and Liberalism, 1855–65* (Cambridge: Cambridge University Press, 1991), 97ff; W.R. Greg, 'The Budget and the Treaty in their Relation to Political Morality', *National Review* 10 (1860), 313–21.

65 See especially A. Iliasu, 'The Role of Free Trade Treaties in British Foreign Policy, 1859–1871', unpublished PhD thesis, University of London, 1965.

66 Gladstone to Lacaita, 1 Dec. 1860, Gladstone Papers, Add. Ms. 44233 f. 156.

67 Mallet to Cobden, 21 Sept. 1861, Cobden Papers, Add. Ms. 43666 f. 140, British Library.

68 'A Disciple of Cobden' [Morier], *Commercial Treaties. Free Trade and Internationalism. Four Letters* (Reprinted from the *Manchester Examiner and Times*, 1870).

69 For this perspective, R.O. Keohane, 'International Liberalism Reconsidered', in J. Dunn (ed.) *The Economic Limits to Modern Politics* (Cambridge: Cambridge University Press, 1990), 165–94.

70 For Bunsen, *Memoirs, by his wife* (2 vols, London: Longman, 1868), ii, 526; E. Ollivier, *Journal, 1846–1860* (eds) T. Zeldin and A. Troisier de Diaz (2 vols in 1, Paris, Julliard, 1961), i, 424.
71 J.W.T. Gaston, 'The Free Trade Diplomacy Debate and the Victorian European Common Market Initiative', *Canadian Journal of History* 22 (1983), 122–56.
72 See, for example, *Free Trade and the European Treaties of Commerce* (London: Cobden Club, 1875).
73 See for example, 'Wine Duties', memo. Aug. 1878, FO881/3683.
74 For example, Gladstone's 1880 budget included financial provision for a new commercial treaty with France based on the reduction of wine duties, *Hansard*, 3rd ser. 252, cc. 1625–31 [10 June 1880].
75 T.H. Farrer, *Free Trade versus Fair Trade* (London: Cobden Club, 1885 edn), 207–8.
76 See, for example, N. McCord, 'Cobden and Bright in Politics, 1846–1857', in R. Robson (ed.) *Ideas and Institutions of Victorian Britain* (London: G. Bell and Sons, 1967), 87–114.
77 Howe, *Liberal England*, ch. 4; E. Biagini, *Liberty, Retrenchment and Reform; Popular Liberalism in the Age of Gladstone* (Cambridge: Cambridge University Press, 1992), esp. 93–102.
78 But see H.J. Hanham, *Elections and Party Management: Politics in the time of Disraeli and Gladstone* (Hassocks: Harvester Press, 1978), 101.
79 C.J.L. Brock and G.H.B. Jackson, *A History of the Cobden Club* (London: Cobden Club, 1939); Howe, 'Free Trade in Britain', 196–201.
80 E.g. A. Mongredien, *History of the Free Trade Movement in Britain* (London: Cassell, 1881); G. Medley, *Pamphlets and Addresses* (London: Cassell, 1899).
81 For the League and popular economics see A. Kadish (ed.) *The Corn Laws*, i, xxvii–xli and Chapter 1 in this volume.
82 Biagini, *Liberty*, 103–19.
83 Howe, 'Free Trade in Britain', 194–96; cf. P. Joyce, *Democratic Subjects: the self and the social in nineteenth-century England* (Cambridge: Cambridge University Press, 1994).
84 S.H. Zebel, 'Fair Trade: an English reaction to the breakdown of the Cobden treaty system', *Journal of Modern History* 12 (1940), 161–85; B.H. Brown, *The Tariff Reform Movement in Great Britain, 1881–1895* (New York: Oxford University Press, 1943).
85 A.S. Milward, 'Tariffs as Constitutions', in S. Strange and R. Tooze (eds) *The International Politics of Surplus Capacity: Competition for market Shares in the World Recession* (London: Allen & Unwin, 1981), 57–66.
86 Howe, 'Free Trade in Britain', 196–8.
87 'The Church of Cobden', *Pall Mall Gazette*, 10 Jan. 1872.
88 Mallet to T.B. Potter, 10 June 1883, enclosed in Mallet to Lord Odo Russell, Ampthill Papers, FO918/54; for this line of thinking, see too M.W. Taylor, *Men vs the State: Herbert Spencer and late Victorian individualism* (Oxford: Clarendon Press, 1992).
89 Hilton, *Atonement*, 261, 363–5.
90 Farrer to Chamberlain, 31 Oct. 1885, Chamberlain Papers, JC5/30/1, Birmingham University Library.
91 For further details, see Howe, 'Free Trade in Britain', 201–6.
92 Mallet to Potter, 24 May 1889 in minutes of the Cobden Club, 25 May 1889, Cobden Papers, 1186, West Sussex Record Office.
93 Mallet, *Sir Louis Mallet*, 130.
94 Gladstone to T. Fisher Unwin, 23 June 1896, Cobden Papers, 981, West Sussex Record Office.

95 A. Kadish, *Apostle Arnold: the life and death of Arnold Toynbee* (Durham, NC: Duke University Press, 1986), 73–7, 96.

96 Farrer to Wise, 11 July 1892 in Cobden Club Minutes, 6 Aug. 1892, Cobden Papers, 1186, West Sussex Record Office; A.G. Austin (ed.) *The Webbs' Australian Diary, 1898* (Melbourne, Melbourne University Press, 1965), 27. But Wise became a Protectionist in Australia and Tariff Reformer in England.

97 M. Freeden, *The New Liberalism: an ideology of Social Reform* (Oxford: Clarendon Press, 1978) provides a good guide to this breach with *laissez-faire*, if less concerned to portray the retention of free trade.

98 For the most recent appraisal, E.H.H. Green, *The Crisis of Conservatism: the politics, economics and ideology of the Conservative Party, 1880–1914* (London: Routledge, 1995).

99 E.g. H. Samuel, 'The Cobden Centenary and Modern Liberalism', *The Nineteenth Century* June 1904, 898–909.

100 *Spectator*, 8 Aug. 1908, 184–5; J. St Loe Strachey, *The Adventure of Living: a subjective autobiography* (London: Hodder and Stoughton, 1922), 158–66, 262–3.

101 See Sykes and Cain, Chapters 14 and 16 in this volume.

14

'TIME IS BEARING ANOTHER SON'

Tariff reform and imperial apocalypse

Alan Sykes

Tariff reform has been described as 'a multi-faceted policy structure [which] seemed to the bulk of the Conservative party to offer solutions to a set of difficulties which reached their peak in the Edwardian period'.[1] Difficulties there certainly appeared to be, although not everyone saw them as such. In the long late-Victorian depression, Britain's share in world trade declined as its industries failed to keep pace with growing foreign competition; much of British agriculture was ruined and the bulk of its food was imported, especially that of the working classes,[2] and over 70 per cent of the population lived in towns; unemployed riots in the mid-1880s and industrial confrontation in the 1890s, raised doubts about future social stability; social investigations uncovered widespread poverty and deprivation which recruiting for the Boer War confirmed.

The falling birthrate, especially among the middle and upper classes, raised social-Darwinist fears of racial deterioration; the war itself revealed military and administrative inefficiency while the demands for troops left an isolated Britain dangerously denuded of home defence in a hostile world; the navy remained the front line of imperial defence, but Germany was poised to challenge British naval supremacy, raising the question of Britain's ability to finance a response. Peacetime expenditure had been rising steadily for some years, and even a small colonial war obliged the Chancellor of the Exchequer, Hicks-Beach, to resort to the expedient of a 3d. per cwt registration duty on imported corn. The late Victorian and Edwardian state appeared to be suffering from a generalised crisis, at once economic, social, racial, military, diplomatic and fiscal.

The Conservative government had its own political difficulties, manifested in a series of by-election defeats. Association with tarnished imperialism, and the passage of an Education Act which fanned the dying embers of political nonconformity into white-hot outrage while embarrassing Liberal Unionist allies, made a dramatic new policy initiative an attractive proposition.

Despite Balfour's tepid response, the opposition of a minority in the parliamentary party and some regions, notably Lancashire, tariff reform was greeted with considerable enthusiasm by the majority of the Conservative party's constituency activists, who recorded their support at successive annual conferences of the National Union. A few Liberals and some Fabians were also seduced by tariff reform but not enough to alter its party political affiliation.

What Unionists understood by 'tariff reform' is more problematic, simply because it was a 'multi-faceted policy structure', changing its image according to the light in which it was depicted, the angle from which it was seen, and the disposition of the observer. Tariff reform was neither a simple, nor an agreed, policy at any time, and both its objectives and its details, such as they were, changed over time. Moreover, despite Chamberlain's attempt to present tariff reform as outside party politics,[3] the political alignment of the policy with the Conservative party could itself dictate support for political reasons which had nothing to do with tariffs. As Peter Clarke observed of Lancashire, 'far from fiscal attitudes dictating party allegiance, it would be truer to say that party allegiance dictated fiscal attitudes.'[4]

Chamberlain's initial proposal was to give the colonies preference by remitting Beach's registration duty in their favour. This was a gesture dictated by imperial sentiment arising from discussions at the Colonial Conference of 1902, not an economic policy, still less 'a multi-faceted policy structure' directed at resolving Britain's difficulties. Nor did it survive Chamberlain's absence in South Africa during the winter of 1902–3. Ritchie's repeal of the registration duty in his budget of 1903 provoked the tariff reform campaign that Chamberlain launched in the autumn, and ensured that it would be launched not as a small amendment to an existing tax, albeit with far-reaching implications, but as a proposal for new duties that amounted to a revolution in fiscal policy.[5]

Chamberlain based the campaign for tariff reform on four hypotheses: that the relative decline in Britain's foreign trade, and the even greater decline within that trade of finished manufactured goods, was caused by protective tariffs; that it was accordingly essential to Britain's prosperity to maintain the growth in imperial trade; that imperial trade could be maintained only by a system of reciprocal preference; and that the survival of the empire depended upon the expansion of imperial trade. Even before the campaign proper began in October 1903 the confusions of tariff reform became evident. Chamberlain responded to the abandonment of the registration duty on 15 May with the argument that imperial trade should be kept 'even at some present sacrifice',[6] because of its importance to imperial unity, and gave retaliation an imperial gloss as the means to defend Canada against Germany's threatened reprisals rather than as the way to improve the prospects for British industry in foreign markets. 'I am perfectly certain,' he announced, 'that I am not a protectionist.'[7]

Despite this, when he finally admitted openly on 28 May what everyone already knew, that reciprocal preference entailed food duties, he added the justification of domestic protection both for industry against foreign dumping and unfair competition, and for agriculture. Food taxes might not be 'intentionally protective' but 'if you were to put a considerable duty on corn that would be to a certain extent protection for the farmer.' This raised the crucial question of the reaction of the working classes to duties which might increase the price of bread. Chamberlain, at this stage, accepted that food duties would raise the cost of living, but suggested that wages would rise to meet the increased costs, and linked the 'very large revenue' the duties would produce to social reform, in particular old age pensions.[8] Tariff reform was from the outset a producers' policy,[9] and Chamberlain tried to treat the working classes in this light.[10] The resulting economy might have high costs, but it would also enjoy high wages and high living standards. Too much attention had, according to Chamberlain, been paid to cheapness. 'Increased wages are even more important to the working classes than reduced cost of living.'[11]

But although he continued to repeat his criticism of cheapness in subsequent campaign speeches,[12] neither Chamberlain nor other tariff reformers had the courage of their convictions. They quickly succumbed to the general belief that the working classes still thought of themselves primarily as consumers, and that food duties constituted an electoral difficulty. From June 1903 it became axiomatic that tariff reform must be achieved 'without increasing the cost of living to the working classes of this country.' Old age pensions now had 'no part whatever in the question of a reform of our fiscal policy.'[13] The taxation of food was no longer even incidentally 'to increase our home food supply' but, as Chamberlain stressed to the lifelong agricultural protectionist, Henry Chaplin, in September, 'only needed and useful for *preference*.'[14]

In order not to increase the overall cost of living, Chamberlain's revised policy from June 1903 was to propose that the revenue raised from such taxation should be used to reduce other 'food' duties on tea, sugar or tobacco thus compensating for any increase in the price of bread.[15] Adopting this approach was a tactical decision, both to meet free-trade critics 'on their own ground',[16] and to avoid totally alienating the agricultural interest. By accepting that grain prices would rise, Chamberlain hinted that there might still be some incidental protection for agriculture from tariff reform; by compensating for that rise with reductions elsewhere, he attempted to side-step the potential clash between urban consumers and rural producers.

Chamberlain was not really concerned about agricultural decline: 'Our existence as a nation depends upon our manufacturing capacity and production. We are not essentially or mainly an agricultural country.'[17] It was one area where Chamberlain and Balfour were in basic agreement. 'If this country is to increase its wealth and population,' Balfour argued, 'the increase must in the main be looked for in other regions than agriculture.'[18] The fate of agriculture did, however, concern other tariff reformers. 'The fundamental historic principle upon which all tariffs that I am acquainted with have been framed,' wrote Professor W.A.S. Hewins, the leading theoretician of the tariff reform movement, 'is to safeguard the position of agriculture.'[19] To this end, the Agricultural Sub-committee of the Tariff Commission, of which Hewins was secretary, recommended the imposition of a 1/- duty on colonial imports, although the intention was less protection than to provide revenue for non-fiscal assistance. Tariff reformers never squared the circle of safe-guarding British agriculture effectively within a non-protective system of preferential tariffs.

There were still further problems. Chamberlain assumed in June 1903 that 'any alteration of our fiscal system must necessarily increase the sums received in the shape of indirect taxation',[20] but in any effective scheme of preference, food duties would not produce much revenue. To 'square the budget', Chamberlain was forced to take into account 'some tax on manu-factured goods', that was nominally for retaliation, but practically for rev-enue and, incidentally at least, protective.[21] A considerable proportion of this revenue, he argued, would come not from the British consumer, but from 'the foreigner', who would accept reduced profits, in effect paying part of the duty, to retain access to the British market.[22]

Undefined and redefined as his ideas were during the summer of 1903, Chamberlain had already gone too far for Balfour. Balfour admitted that reciprocal preference was a desirable goal, but considered food duties, and hence preference, had 'not yet come within the sphere of practical politics.'[23] His own reasoning, elaborated in *Economic Notes on Insular Free Trade*, took him only as far as 'liberty of fiscal negotiation' backed by the option of retaliation against countries which maintained tariff barriers against British manufactures. It was on the basis of this differentiation between aspirations and possibilities that he conducted his complex manoeuvres during the summer of 1903 to effect the resignations of both the committed free-traders and Chamberlain from the cabinet, and it was a policy of retaliation without preference that he announced as official Conservative party fiscal policy to the National Union at Sheffield on 1 October.

Retaliation was, as Balfour argued, a self-contained policy with its own rationale, not a half-way house between Chamberlain and his opponents.[24] Its adoption as Conservative party policy was nevertheless almost wholly the product of political calculation in response to the disruption occasioned by Chamberlain's initiative. The anticipated hostility of the electorate was only one part of Balfour's reservations; he also feared that 'to make it part of the Government Programme would be to break up the Party.'[25] Chamberlain had to resign because he both insisted on the necessity of preference for imperial reasons, and accepted that it was 'for the moment politically impracticable.'[26] He left believing that Balfour was sympathetic to his cause, and would advocate it once he had demonstrated the degree of support in the country. The free-traders were removed to preserve the balance of the government. The policy was devised to secure these political objectives.

Balfour's was the first attempt to state a fully rounded, albeit single-faceted, policy of fiscal reform, but it was soon followed by Chamberlain's multi-faceted structure, which was unveiled at Glasgow on 6 October. The proposed duties were not high, and in the case of food almost symbolic, so difficult was the task of reconciling the interests of an electorate of consumers with the interests of colonial and British farmers as producers: a tax not exceeding 2/- per quarter on imported foreign corn, excluding maize, 'a corresponding tax' on foreign flour, 5 per cent on foreign meat and dairy produce, excluding bacon, to which was added 'a moderate duty on all [foreign] manufactured goods, not exceeding 10% on the average.'[27] Apart from food duties and preference, Chamberlain's policy differed from Balfour's in the manner of its proposed retaliation, modifying the general revenue tariff after negotiation with foreign powers, rather than imposing specific retaliatory duties if negotiations failed. The entire programme was deceptively simple, no more than 'a transfer from one item to another' of indirect taxation, turning 'profitless taxation' into 'scientific taxation'.[28]

With the possible addition of the Tariff Commission's proposed 1/- duty on colonial wheat, although this was abandoned in 1910 because so few supported it,[29] this outline of what Chamberlain regarded as a tariff reform budget remained throughout the Edwardian period the full, 'wholehog', tariff reform programme. The pattern of the succeeding years was one of tariff reform pressure on Balfour to move official Conservative policy closer to the 'Glasgow programme'. Under such pressure, Balfour made two minor advances. First, in the autumn of 1904 he converted his original indefinite postponement of preference into a commitment to summon a colonial conference after the next election and, if that conference decided in favour of preference requiring food duties, to put the question of preference to a second general election. Second, after the humiliating election defeat in 1906 when he lost his own seat and only 157 Unionists were returned, he agreed that neither a non-protective general tariff on manufactured goods nor 'a small duty on foreign corn' were 'in principle objectionable, and 'should be adopted if shewn to be necessary for . . . more equal terms of competition for British trade and closer commercial union with the Colonies . . . or for the purposes of revenue.' Typically Balfourian in its negative, abstract and qualified expression, it was far removed from the Glasgow programme.[30]

Nevertheless the Glasgow programme was no single point of light. Chamberlain steadfastly maintained that his underlying purpose was the realisation of his imperial vision,[31] but the emphasis had to be reorientated to appeal to the British electorate. In the Glasgow programme, the first aim of tariff reform became 'the maintenance and increase of the national strength and prosperity of the United Kingdom.'[32] Prosperity, however, meant not only more than, but also something different from, mere money. Much of the criticism in Asquith's celebrated destruction of Chamberlain's Glasgow speech in fact missed the point. Asquith noted that in the past thirty years income tax receipts had doubled; interest upon foreign investments had more than doubled, as had savings, and bank deposits and the amount in cleared cheques had greatly increased. None of this mattered. The only telling point was the increase in real wages, and real wages were to fall in the Edwardian period.[33] In direct contrast, Chamberlain took little account of

> a greater aggregation of national wealth which, for aught we know, may never be properly distributed. It is not the amount of the income tax, not the number of cheques that pass through the clearing houses that marks the progress of a nation.[34]

Chamberlain cared 'very little whether the result [of tariff reform] will be to make this country, already rich, a little richer. The character of a nation is more important than its opulence.'[35]

'Character' had a double meaning. In one sense it meant 'the character of the individual' which, according to Chamberlain, depended 'upon the greatness of the ideals upon which he rests', as did 'the character of the nation'.[36] The empire 'made us what we are – it has taught us the virtue of national sacrifice.'[37] Tariff reform was not intended to make either the British people or Britain rich, but to make them great, to ensure

> that this people shall rise to the heights of its great mission . . . show themselves worthy of the leadership of the British race and, in cooperation with our kinsmen across the seas . . . combine to make an Empire which ought to be, greater, more united, more fruitful for good than any Empire in human history.[38]

In another sense, however, 'character' referred more to socio-economic structure. Chamberlain predicted that without tariff reform

> we shall lose not only our commerce, but the whole character of the country will be changed; and, in the course of another generation, this will be much less an industrial country, inhabited by skilful artisans, than a distributive country with a smaller population consisting of rich consumers on the one hand, and people engaged in the work of distribution on the other.[39]

The country was, Chamberlain argued, 'richer than ever, and yet weaker. We may have more millionaires and fewer working men and that is the direction in which we are tending.'[40] The objective of tariff reform was to ensure 'to every willing and industrious workman in this country continous employment, full employment at fair wages',[41] which, in turn, could be realised only

189

by maintaining imperial trade and strengthening imperial unity.[42] 'Trade with the colonies and British possessions [was] larger in amount . . . and very much more valuable' because it consisted of manufactured goods.[43] The altered balance of foreign trade resulting from lower exports and higher imports[44] was, according to Chamberlain, a loss of 330,000 jobs, or subsistence for over 1.5 million people.[45] Imperial trade gave employment to 615,000 workers, or subsistence to just over 3 million. Adding to that the proportion of foreign trade with British colonies that might be taken by Britain under preferential agreements, Chamberlain concluded that colonial trade under tariff reform would provide employment and wages for 'three-quarters of a million of workmen, and subsistence for nearly four millions of our population.'[46]

From this point of view, Asquith's figures on the returns from foreign investments, presented to demonstrate Britain's wealth, were, for Chamberlain, indicators of something approximating to Ruskin's idea of 'illth', giving employment to foreign workers and producing goods to compete with Britain. A country's 'wealth', properly understood, meant population, the 'product in men, and the number and proportion of its population which it can keep in comfort and happiness, and for which it can find remunerative employment.'[47] Protection was essential to sustain living standards, wage levels and existing industrial regulations.[48] Tariff reform was thus part of a wider protective reaction that also included the campaign for the exclusion of pauper aliens that culminated in the Aliens Act of 1905. Immigration control was supported by Chamberlain, and by East London MPs like Evans-Gordon, for the same reasons that they supported tariff reform.[49]

Yet, despite dropping his specific references to old age pensions, pledging the revenue from the general tariff to making good lost revenue and recommending that the surplus should be applied to the reduction of ordinary taxation,[50] Chamberlain still continued to promise the extension of social reform and also rating reform to placate agriculture.[51] George Wyndham, whom Chamberlain considered sufficiently sympathetic to his cause to invite him to join 'an agitation for tariff reform',[52] described the programme expounded by 1905 as

> practically protection of manufactures plus a surplus revenue to be devoted to conciliating agriculture by *doles*, and fostering advanced Domestic legislation. . . . The Imperial aspiration scarcely appears, and is not more than an aspiration quite irrelevant to what he actually puts forward.[53]

Wyndham also saw the problem:

> Employment is more important than cheapness even at some cost.
> Imperial Unity is vital even at some cost. Retaliation is necessary,

190

even at some cost. Yet the machinery for effecting these objects, at the risk of three separate occasions for cost, is, in addition, to extract surplus millions.[54]

On the domestic front, multiple facets brought multiple contradictions; in so far as each was effective, preference, protection, retaliation and revenue were exclusive not compatible goals.[55]

Even the imperial ideal was not without its complications. Chamberlain saw protection as an incremental process which was gradually destroying British trade but which could, like any process, be interrupted. In America, the process was completed; no further trade could be done because 'she produces everything; she excludes everything'. The colonies, however, were at various stages in the process, and Britain might still intervene to prevent, by agreement, the development of colonial industries.[56] Chamberlain's vision was not surprisingly apocalyptic. This was 'the parting of the ways', 'the last time' that the empire might be bound together, an opportunity that might never recur; 'We must either draw closer together or we shall drift apart.'[57] His inclination towards what Salisbury called 'the catastrophic theory of politics'[58] sprang from his ideas, not from his temperament, and was, as Salisbury believed, inherent in tariff reformers. Garvin in 1904 echoed the doctrine of imminent imperial disaster:

> As a result of reversals of fortune it is still possible that Canada might cease to be Canadian, that Australia might become a yellow continent, that South Africa might even yet be German-Dutch, that India might pass to who knows what new masters, that England herself might become the Holland of the twentieth century.[59]

Unless tariff reform was to be simply a delaying tactic in the process of exclusion and decline, the opportunity to avert future catastrophe meant that the empire had to be moulded to Britain's interests before colonial development took the process too far.

Chamberlain's grand design clashed with rising colonial nationalism. Officially, the colonies welcomed Chamberlain's initiative, but they offered preference to allow the substitution of British for foreign imports. Relaxation of the protection of native industries was never considered. Chamberlain's reference to Canada as 'the granary of empire' raised a storm of protest as implying that Canada was not suited to manufacturing.[60] But Chamberlain certainly did intend that Canada should not have a manufacturing future in a decently organised empire. The colonies, he argued at Glasgow, 'will arrange for tariffs in the future in order not to start industries in competition with those which are already in existence in the Mother Country.' According to Amery, Chamberlain recognised the mistake, and the sentence was deleted from the official text of his speech.[61] It was nevertheless what he meant.

Chamberlain's vision of the future unity of the empire created ambiguities even between his seemingly compatible strategies of retaliation and preference. His conclusion that America could be exclusive because of the size of the domestic market also applied to the empire, which contained not only a white population of over 50 million, but 350 million 'people under our protectorate, under our civilisation, sympathising with our rule, grateful for the benefits we accord to them, and all of them more or less prospective or actual customers of this country.'[62] Because of its

> variety . . . we have an Empire which with decent organisation and consolidation might be absolutely self-sustaining. . . . There is no article of food, there is no raw material of your trade, there is no necessity of your lives, no luxury of your existence which cannot be produced somewhere or other in the British Empire.[63]

But if, in the 'great reserve in the sons of Britain across the seas', there was 'nothing we want that they cannot supply; there is nothing we sell that they cannot buy',[64] then retaliation against protected competitors was both pointless and impossible. Once the empire was decently organised, which was the point of the tariff reform campaign, then Britain would not need foreign trade, or indeed, have anything left to sell to foreigners.

All this confusion of thought was not necessarily a political disaster. Chamberlain had a peculiar, circumstantial, definition of 'protection',[65] and used the term to mean 'Protection . . . against unfair foreign competition'.[66] His notion of 'unfair' seemed to include all competition that enjoyed protection, so that in his programme retaliation and protection were compounded into a single idea that allowed tariff reform, despite all its confusions, to tap into popular chauvinism. Wyndham, in November 1905, did some 'reconnoitring' in his Dover constituency, and found that after two years of campaigning,

> they have not given any serious thought to the question of Fiscal Reform. They do not distinguish between Retaliation, High Protection, Low Protection, Preference to Colonies, Tariff for Revenue etc. etc. But they want a change. They talk of the Imperial Idea; want to 'pal' with the Colonies; are annoyed – this above all – with Foreign countries for taxing our goods unfairly. . . . A little quiet talk reveals that no two of them agree on anything. . . . But do let us do something; *hit* somebody. . . . They do not want protection, or a general Tariff, or much taxation of any kind! But they often call themselves protectionists. By that they mean . . . that they resent the treatment given to us by Foreigners and grudge them our open market.[67]

In the aftermath of the electoral defeat of 1906, however, tariff reform underwent a further reorientation that placed less stress on imperial and international relations and more on domestic taxation. The unexpected appearance of the Labour party; the belief that the party had lost the election because it had lost the 'Tory Democracy', and the assumption that the electorate would insist on costly social reform which the Liberal government would meet with 'spoilatory taxation' all combined to focus attention on the fiscal crisis, and force Balfour into a more positive outlook. Disenchantment with Balfour's silence on tariff reform during 1906 went so far that Sandars, Balfour's private secretary, and Acland Hood, the Chief Whip, both feared the drift of members from party constituency organisations to the local branch of the Tariff Reform League (TRL), the latter becoming, in effect, an alternative party. They recommended 'a speech . . . at the National Union meeting on February 15th' reaffirming commitment to all aspects of tariff reform, imperial unity, revenue for social reform and retaliation. 'The fortunes of the party . . . depend on this speech.'[68]

After attempting to avoid the issue at Hull by stressing the danger of party divisions, Balfour capitulated to the demand, which was more broadly based in the party than he had realised. He outlined a 'safe, sound, sober policy' of fiscal reform centred on four points: broadening the basis of taxation; safeguarding industry from unfair foreign competition; recapturing foreign markets; and the maintenance of colonial markets.[69] Balfour was reverting to Chamberlain's original suggestion of providing preference by the remission of revenue duties imposed for purely domestic purposes. For Balfour in 1907, 'some revision of our fiscal system – some broadening of our basis of taxation – would be absolutely necessary if we were the only commercial nation in the world, and did not have a single colony.'[70] The Savoy Hotel speech formed the basis for both Balfour's speech to the National Union Conference at Birmingham in November 1907, and the Conference resolution on tariff reform. By that time, Labour victories at Jarrow and Colne Valley, Asquith's budget of 1907 differentiating between earned and unearned incomes, and the onset of a sharp depression increasing unemployment, had aggravated the conditions that provoked the Savoy Hotel speech. The party, with the exception of a small minority of doctrinaire free-traders, reunited behind the 'Birmingham programme'.

Lloyd George's budget of 1909 confirmed all the worst Conservative fears about Liberal finance, and tariff reform accordingly grew in prominence as the alternative source of revenue for social reform. The revenue argument, however, obscured, and conflicted with, the revival of economic activity that tariff reform, as protection, was expected to bring, and the increase in receipts from existing taxation that would follow. Even the general tariff that Chamberlain included in his original scheme was of doubtful necessity, given that the remitted 'food' duties cost under £3 million.[71] The actual, as distinct from political, need for state-sponsored social reform for which the revenue was theoretically required, was equally unsubstantiated. The predicted reduction of unemployment and higher wages would enable the working classes to make their own voluntary provision. At a stroke, the most common causes of poverty, low wages, unemployment, old age and ill health, would be removed or remedied without any direct state intervention. The working classes would also be able to provide for their own children and their own housing. Social reform need amount to no more than regulation, if necessary, taking advantage of the security provided to industry through tariffs to coerce employers into the payment of fair wages, along the lines of Australian 'new protection', and of parents to make satisfactory provision for their children's health and education.

Here, too, tariff reformers lacked the courage of their alleged convictions. Following, but accentuating, Chamberlain's linkages, 'tariff reform' after 1906 came increasingly to symbolise a whole 'constructive' programme of social measures resting upon tariff-generated revenue in response to the reorientation of Liberalism towards interventionist welfare provision. In a memorandum of 24 October 1907, Austen Chamberlain included some 'thoughts' which reinstated old age pensions to their place in the tariff reformers' repertoire and added land purchase, housing and sweated industries.[72] This Milnerite elaboration was, indeed, the product of conversations with Milner, who always saw tariff reform as 'an element of a larger policy . . . a policy of constructive Imperialism, and of steady, consistent, unhasting and unresting Social Reform.' Under Milner's influence, tariff reform became 'social imperialism' not just in the sense of attaching the working classes to empire by providing welfare reforms as a bribe, but because the empire itself depended upon 'a healthy, thriving, manly people at the centre.'[73] Milner's starting point was organic: 'the different classes and section of the community are members of that body . . . when one member suffers, all the members suffer.' From this point of view, 'the attempt to raise the well-being and efficiency of the more backward of our people . . . is not philanthropy; it is business.'[74]

The conclusions of a small Milnerite committee, which emerged from a dinner hosted by Arthur Lee to discuss a 'programme of a constructive policy' in 1907 even before Balfour spoke at Birmingham, were published in the *Morning Post* in 1908. It began with tariff reform

as the only means of protecting employment, of increasing production and of equitably providing revenue for national defence and social reform [and] of meeting the proposal unanimously put forward by the self-governing Dominions for promoting closer Imperial relations

irrespective of implicit contradictions, and went on to elaborate a raft of social reforms that the tariff would pay for: wages boards and a minimum wage in industries where workers were unable to organise effectively for their own protection, state-assisted rural reconstruction in the form of smallholdings, co-operation and 'the dissemination of technical information', and the reform of local taxation.

But despite a sophisticated extension of the principle of 'unionism' from the usual usage of the union with Ireland to an all-embracing integrationist concept of the 'union of classes' at home and the 'union of the empire' overseas, the programme revealed the limitations of tariff reform radicalism. The *Morning Post* gave most attention to old age pensions, but it did so as 'part of the bigger question of State insurance against the incapacity to work, from whatever cause the incapacity may arise.' It was a question 'of national organisation' rather than humanitarian relief or social justice, and, like Austen Chamberlain in his memorandum of October 1907, it concluded that the 'solution will be found in a contributory system.'[75] Contributory insurance served the double purpose of reducing the drain on the Exchequer, even though tariff reform at times seemed to promise a deluge of money, and ensuring the respectability of the recipients. Insurance was the obvious means to avoid the creation of a dependency culture, and formed, with the tariff, the twin pillars of constructive Conservatism.

The Reveille programme of 1910, which saw tariff reform as 'an essential element' of its 'National Policy', but 'far from the whole of it', brought all the elements of this expanded 'tariff reform' together, linking insurance to the anticipated benefits of a protected home market and economic revival.

> With tariff reform to induce the greater investment of capital here, insurance, and other measures of social reform become practical under the conditions of a rising market for labour. . . . Destitution will gradually be abolished but without the loss of industrial initiative.[76]

This argument for the practicability of social reform behind tariff walls restored tariff reform to its protectionist function. Social reform was feasible because less was required, and it was contributory. Revenue, whether from a Chamberlainite general tariff or Balfour's vague priorities, was once again no longer pivotal, even though the general tariff was in origin and essence a revenue and not a protective tariff.

The Reveille programme, however, also laid significant stress on defence. The revenue anticipated from tariffs urged for their protective function was, to say the least, uncertain, and there were other demands upon it which might entail the reduction of social reform costs. The navy had played its part in provoking Lloyd George's 'revolutionary budget', and was arguably a greater priority, especially for imperialist advocates of a mighty 'sea-state'. Garvin estimated that tariffs would provide sufficient money to pay for three dreadnoughts annually, with the added spice that the foreigner would pay for his own subordination.[77] Focusing on the navy was a promising line of argument in relation to food duties and their alleged unpopularity. With food imports at such a high level the navy was the nation's 'insurance premium to secure the supply of food', and the 'benefits of Free Trade' had to be 'set against the cost of naval supremacy.' After 1894 those benefits declined sharply as naval costs rose far more sharply than grain prices.

> Free Trade no longer came free. The cost of naval power became a *subsidy* for food not different in principle from the tariffs imposed by Continental states during the same period and similar in its distorting effect on the economy. . . . As far as grain was concerned, the cost of naval power ate deeply into the benefits of Free Trade.[78]

This was not an argument greatly exploited by contemporaries. Balfour's restructured programme had the purely political aims of reducing division in his own party and providing a policy alternative which would save the rich in Britain from increased direct taxation. It was a tactical manoeuvre and the prominence it gave to tariff reform in the Conservative programme was illusory. The general election of January 1910 that followed the Lords' rejection of the 1909 budget left the Liberal government still in office, albeit dependent on Irish and Labour votes, and revealed that 'tariff reform' was still not 'practical politics'. Worse still, Irish support for the budget was achieved only by a deal that made reduction of the Lords veto powers and the introduction of Home Rule inevitable.

After January 1910, doubts about tariff reform's electoral appeal even as a source of revenue resurfaced, and it became the victim of further Conservative re-prioritisation. The Conservative party did regain many of the seats lost in 1906, but the class polarisation evident in the election suggested that this was less because Balfour's modification of tariff reform had made the programme acceptable than because Liberal experiments in 'socialism' had frightened property owners back to Conservatism despite tariff reform. Certainly Balfour and the Balfourites in the party thought this. In November 1910 Balfour promised to submit tariff reform to a referendum in a desperate attempt to make it palatable, but without success. The Conservatives lost in December by virtually the same margin as the defeat in January. Balfour's replacement in November 1911 by Bonar Law, reputedly a wholehog tariff reformer, aroused hopes that tariff reform might be restored to its nominal place as the 'first constructive work', but these too were short-lived.

The announcement that the referendum on tariff reform was to be abandoned led to such protests, especially from Lancashire, that Bonar Law was forced to withdraw into yet another variant of tariff policy, again determined by party and electoral considerations. At Ashton-under-Lyne on 16 December 1912 he stated that food duties would not be imposed unless they were required by the colonies. When this failed to placate the Lancashire rebels, he announced in Edinburgh that a Conservative government would proceed immediately with tariffs on manufactured goods, but that food duties would be subject to a second general election.[79] This modification of the double election policy that Balfour had adopted, also in Edinburgh, some nine years earlier, managed to combine the worst of both worlds. It openly sacrificed both preference and British agriculture to urban interests, but would do no more for British industry than the retaliation Balfour had proposed at Sheffield unless it was to be naked protection.

This is what agriculturalists automatically assumed. They protested against the prospect of higher machinery prices, and perhaps even more out of a sense of betrayal.[80] Bonar Law's policy, however, had no economic intention. It was a purely political manoeuvre to keep the party together by retaining duties on manufactured goods to placate the 'wholehoggers' while abandoning food duties to placate the timid. Even the attitude of the electorate was relegated to the background. Bonar Law's Edinburgh programme threw the tariff reform movement into disarray. Already desperately short of funds, the TRL now found itself also short of a policy. Whether it supported the new party programme or remained 'wholehog', it risked being outflanked by a new League. It compromised by supporting both. Having considered and rejected 'bounties' (subsidies), it was, like the Conservative party, also short of a tariff policy for agriculture. Hewins, who was supposed to devise a formula for speakers in the new situation, found the farmers' case unanswerable, and was 'laughed down at Canterbury' when he tried to defend the new tariff reform policy.[81]

The dilemma of the TRL in 1913 highlights the historical difficulty surrounding tariff reform in the Edwardian period, the variety of meanings that it embraced as a result of political necessities and the logical confusions introduced by those necessities. The incidence of tariffs, the revenue anticipated, and the social reform proposals to be supported by that revenue were characterised by a necessary but unconvincing vagueness. Chamberlain defended himself from accusations of imprecision by pointing out that negotiations with other governments were central to the idea of both preference and retaliation, and that the final incidence of the tariff would depend on their outcome.[82] The primacy Balfour gave to revenue raising for domestic purposes simplified this issue. Hewins believed in 1909 that a Unionist government 'could at once proceed to introduce a tariff which would satisfy the four conditions laid down in the Birmingham resolutions.'[83] But despite an expert committee headed by Milner and including both Hewins and the shadow chancellor, Austen Chamberlain, which began to meet at the end of 1908,[84] no such tariff was ever devised. In February 1910, when the remote possibility of office loomed, Austen Chamberlain still noted that 'a Tariff Reform Budget cannot, in spite of all Hewins may say, be produced at a moment's notice.'[85]

Tariff reformers could not avoid being caught in a conflict of interests, or perceived interests, between producers and consumers, between industry and agriculture, between different industries, and even within the same industry or the same firm.[86] In such a national system of economics, political priorities not the market determined the structure of the tariff. Chamberlain understood this because he knew his own motives for raising the issue, motives that relegated economic factors to the sidelines. 'I don't wish to underestimate the economic side of the question,' he noted in 1904, 'only I say it is secondary, it is not vital.'[87] It was British and imperial security in terms of manpower that was vital. 'The true question is not,' as Chamberlain constantly reiterated, 'whether this country is richer or poorer, the question is whether this country provides sufficient employment at remunerative rates for all who seek it.'[88] Implicitly for Chamberlain, explicitly for Milnerite social reformers, the population was to be healthy, fit, disciplined, organised and trained not solely, or even primarily, for its economic advantages, although these would be a by-product, but for reasons of defence.

Underpinning the tariff reform outlook was a Darwinian view of international relations, a 'race for existence that has been going on ever since the world began',[89] which Britain was losing.[90] This was not simply the 'bolt from the blue', but an inevitable confrontation. 'I want to prepare you,' Chamberlain told his audiences, 'now, while there is still time, for a struggle . . . from which, if we emerge defeated, this country will lose its place, will no longer count among the great nations of the world.'[91] National strength and national prosperity went hand in hand, 'ships, colonies and commerce are the inseparable links of a single chain',[92] but colonies needed defending, as did shipping, and apparently, markets.

At this point, tariff reform dreams and tariff reform nightmares tended to fuse into a single vision. For security, the empire that might become self-sustaining also required to be hermetically sealed. 'The only markets in which modern nations can make themselves secure,' as Garvin revealingly observed, 'are their own.'[93] Chamberlain made the same point about the security of essential supplies of food. In the future, whether from natural disaster or home demand, foreign sources of corn would fail and prices soar. The only remedy was to 'increase your sources of supply . . . call in the colonies.'[94] Intervention to halt the protectionist process was required before it was too late. 'Whether we can do it with any effect or at all in twenty years hence I am very doubtful.'[95] The imperial apocalypse was visible on the horizon.

The key to Chamberlain's anxieties, and thus to tariff reform, lay not in a blinding realisation of Britain's worsening trading position, or in the shimmering crisis that appeared to confront Edwardian Britain, but in Chamberlain's 'weary Titan' speech delivered to the Colonial Conference of 1902.[96] Britain could not continue to bear the burden of governing and defending the empire alone. Chamberlain found inspiration in the colonial contingents sent to South Africa during the Boer War,[97] alarm in the decline of Britain that the war displayed. Based on the fate of the Dutch and

Venetian empires in the past, and the examples of America and Germany in the present, he saw a future of large states and large integrated markets,[98] and no future for little England. The basis of great states was 'commercial union which in some shape or another, must precede or accompany closer political relations, and without which, as all history shows, no permanent co-operation is possible.'[99] Economic unity was the foundation of political unity, and imperial unity the only source of security.

Psychologically, the empire represented a way for imperialists to cheat history. Concerned with the precedent of Rome and trapped in a cyclical view of history in which 'all history is the history of States once powerful and then decaying', a belief that although Britain was 'old', the empire was 'new', nourished the dream that a phoenix might be conjured from the ashes.[100] In what became his valedictory speech to his Birmingham constituents in 1906, Chamberlain expressed his basic fears:

If the ties of sympathy which have been gradually woven between ourselves and our children across the seas ... were weakened or destroyed ... then this England of ours would sink from the comparative position which it has enjoyed throughout the centuries. ... It would be a fifth-rate nation, existing on the sufferance of its more powerful neighbours.[101]

Against this, he held out an alternative prospect for the future:

the creation of an Empire such as the world has never seen. We have to cement the union of the states beyond the seas; we have to consolidate the British race; we have to meet the clash of competition, commercial now – sometimes in the past it has been otherwise – it may be again in the future. Whatever it may be, whatever danger threatens, we have to meet it no longer as an isolated country; we have to meet it fortified and strengthened, and buttressed by all those of our kinsmen, all those powerful and continuously rising states which speak our common tongue and glory in our common flag.[102]

Tariff reform was about modifying an economy by political means, within political constraints, to achieve a political end, the rescue of an embattled empire as the basis of Britain's great power status before both empire and nation were overwhelmed. If that entailed economic loss, then the economic loss would have to be met. The campaign opened with a quotation from Adam Smith: 'Defence is greater than opulence', and wholehogger tariff reform, if not Balfourite tariff reform, never departed from that view.

Notes

1 E.H.H. Green, *The Crisis of Conservatism: The Politics, Economics and Ideology of the British Conservative Party 1880–1914*, London, Routledge, 1995, p. 11. A similar expression, 'many-faceted', was used earlier by Peter Cain, 'Political Economy in Edwardian England: The Tariff Reform Controversy', in Alan O'Day (ed.) *The Edwardian Age: Conflict and Stability 1900–1914*, London, Macmillan, 1979, p. 35.
2 Avner Offer, 'The Working Classes, British Naval Plans and the Coming of the Great War', *Past and Present*, 1985, 107, p. 204.
3 Charles Boyd (ed.) *Mr Chamberlain's Speeches*, London, Constable, vol. 2, p. 141.
4 P.F. Clarke, *Lancashire and the New Liberalism*, Cambridge, Cambridge University Press, 1971, p. 274.
5 Chamberlain to Devonshire, 25 August 1903, in J. Amery, *Joseph Chamberlain and the Tariff Reform Campaign*, London, Macmillan, 1969, vol. 5, pp. 372–4.
6 Boyd, op. cit., p. 131.
7 Ibid., p. 137.
8 Amery, op. cit., pp. 233–5. Chamberlain had already linked higher wages, old age pensions and fiscal reform on 19 and 22 May. Ibid., pp. 226–7.
9 Boyd, op. cit., p. 205. See also pp. 172–3, 268.
10 Ibid., p. 200.
11 Amery, op. cit., p. 226.
12 Boyd, op. cit., pp. 201, 205, 280.
13 Amery, op. cit., pp. 265–8.
14 Ibid., p. 440.
15 Ibid., pp. 265–8.
16 Chamberlain to Devonshire, 25 August 1903, in ibid., pp. 372–4.
17 Boyd, op. cit., p. 146.
18 Copy, Balfour to Collings, 7 May 1908, Balfour Papers, 49859, ff. 251–2.
19 Hewins to Steel-Maitland, 17 November 1913, Hewins Papers.
20 Chamberlain's speech at the Constitutional Club, 26 June 1903, in Amery, op. cit., p. 267.
21 Chamberlain to Devonshire, 25 August 1903 in ibid., p. 373. In July 1905, Chamberlain claimed that the general tariff 'will be a tariff principally for revenue . . . which . . . may be turned at a moment into a penal tariff.' Ibid., vol. 6, p. 725.
22 Boyd, op. cit., pp. 159–60, 310–11. This again represented an evolution in Chamberlain's thinking. On 28 May 1903, he still believed that the working classes would pay 'three fourths' of taxes on food. Amery, op. cit., vol. 5, p. 233.
23 Balfour to the King, 15 September 1903, in ibid., p. 397.
24 Balfour to Austen Chamberlain, 10 September 1904, in Austen Chamberlain, *Politics from Inside*, London, Cassell, 1936, p. 28.
25 Balfour to the King, 15 September 1903, in Amery, op. cit., p. 397.
26 Chamberlain to the King, 21 September 1903. Ibid., p. 419.
27 Boyd, op. cit., pp. 158–9, 162.
28 Ibid., pp. 162–3.
29 Alan Sykes, *Tariff Reform in British Politics, 1903–1913*. Oxford, Oxford University Press, 1979, pp. 216–17.
30 Balfour to Chamberlain, 14 February 1906, in Amery, op. cit., vol. 6, pp. 846–7.
31 J.W. Mackail and Guy Wyndham, *Life and Letters of George Wyndham*, London, Hutchinson, n.d. vol. 2 pp. 520.
32 Boyd, op. cit., p. 143.
33 H.H. Asquith, *Trade and the Empire: Mr. Chamberlain's Proposals Examined in Four*

Speeches and a Prefatory Note, London, Methuen, 1903, p. 17. (Speech at Cinderford, 8 October 1903.)
34 Boyd, op. cit., p. 368.
35 Ibid., p. 255.
36 Ibid., p. 367.
37 Ibid., p. 190; see also p. 154.
38 Ibid., p. 255.
39 Ibid., p. 192; see also p. 224.
40 Ibid., p. 313.
41 Chamberlain regarded fair wages as 30/- per week, well above Rowntree's subsistence wage in York (*Poverty: A Study of Town Life*, p. 110), and the upper margin used in the Fabian Women's Group investigation into the respectable poor in Lambeth as described by Maud Pember Reeves in *Round About a Pound a Week*. Boyd, op. cit., pp. 152–3, 175.
42 Ibid., p. 185; see also p. 189.
43 Ibid., p. 147.
44 Ibid., pp. 146, 168.
45 Ibid., p. 175.
46 Ibid., pp. 152–3.
47 Ibid., p. 280.
48 Ibid., pp. 171–2; see also pp. 318–24.
49 Ibid., p. 208; see also B. Gainer, *The Alien Invasion*, London, Heinemann, 1972, pp. 138–43, 185–90.
50 Boyd, op. cit., p. 162.
51 Amery, op. cit., vol. 6, p. 726.
52 Mackail and Wyndham, op. cit., p. 518.
53 Ibid., p. 520.
54 Ibid., p. 510. Chamberlain did realise these contradictions to the extent that he admitted on one occasion that benefits would accrue through either retaliation or protection, not both, but still did not indicate how either was compatible with what was a revenue tariff. Boyd, op. cit., p. 163.
55 Cain, op. cit., p. 43.
56 Boyd, op. cit., pp. 148–51.
57 Ibid., pp. 151, 140, 164, 155.
58 Salisbury to Selborne, 10 August 1904, Selborne papers, 5, ff. 88–91.
59 J.L. Garvin, 'The Principles of Constructive Economics as Applied to the Maintenance of Empire', in *Compatriots Club Lectures*, London, Macmillan, 1905, p. 55.
60 John Eddy and Deryck Schreuder (eds) *The Rise of Colonial Nationalism*, London, Allen & Unwin, 1988, p. 41.
61 Amery, op. cit., vol. 6, p. 463.
62 Boyd, op. cit., p. 179.
63 Ibid., p. 153; see also pp. 247, 333.
64 Ibid., p. 178.
65 Ibid., p. 279.
66 Chamberlain to Devonshire, 28 September 1903, in Amery, op. cit., vol. 5, p. 433.
67 Mackail and Wyndham, op. cit., pp. 521–2.
68 Sandars to Balfour, 22 January 1907, Balfour Papers 49765, ff. 11–16.
69 Sykes, op. cit., p. 131.
70 Ibid., p. 131.
71 Boyd, op. cit., p. 161.
72 Copy, Austen Chamberlain to Balfour, 24 October 1907, Austen Chamberlain Papers, 17/3/23.

73 Sykes, op. cit., p. 137.
74 Ibid., p. 122.
75 *Morning Post*: Proof Copy, Bonar Law Papers 18/4/75; Austen Chamberlain's memorandum: Austen Chamberlain to Balfour, 24 October 1907, Austen Chamberlain papers, 17/3/23.
76 *Morning Post*, 19 October 1910.
77 Garvin, op. cit., p. 36.
78 Offer, op. cit., pp. 205–7.
79 Sykes, op. cit., pp. 264–73.
80 Ibid., pp. 281–2.
81 Ibid., pp. 275–7. Austen Chamberlain, op. cit., p. 532.
82 Boyd, op. cit., pp. 163, 158.
83 Hewins to Balfour, 19 September 1909, Balfour Papers, 49779 ff. 221–31.
84 Milner to Steel-Maitland, 6 December 1908, Steel-Maitland Papers, G.D. 193/88/3.
85 Austen Chamberlain, op. cit., p. 209.
86 A. Marrison, 'Businessmen, Industries and Tariff Reform in Great Britain, 1903–1930', *Business History*, 1983, 25, pp. 148–64. Even then, businessmen might have little comprehension of the policy. Wyndham reported

> two brothers, partners in a Brewery, one is against Joe and is a Free-trader, but would like to make the Foreigner treat us better; the other calls himself a 'Chamberlainite' and a protectionist; but would not tax food, raw materials, partly manufactured articles, and so on, with an endless list of exceptions.
>
> (Mackail and Wyndham, op. cit., p. 522)

87 Wolfgang Mock, *Imperiale Herrschaft und nationales Interesse: 'Constructive Imperialism' oder Freihandel in Großbritannien vor dem Ersten Weltkrieg'*, Stuttgart, Klett-Cotta, 1982, p. 186.
88 Boyd, op. cit., p. 266; see also p. 267.
89 Ibid., p. 258.
90 Ibid., p. 369.
91 Ibid., p. 145.
92 Garvin, op. cit., p. 12.
93 Ibid., p. 47.
94 Amery, op. cit., vol. 6, p. 484. The fear was not wholly unreasonable. See Offer, op. cit., pp. 205–6.
95 Chamberlain at Glasgow in Boyd, op. cit., p. 149.
96 Amery, op. cit., vol. 5, p. 31. See also Boyd, op. cit., p. 300.
97 Boyd, op. cit., pp. 153–4.
98 Ibid., pp. 144, 189–90, 217, 268.
99 J. Chamberlain, *Imperial Union and Tariff Reform. Speeches delivered from May 15 to Nov. 4 1903*, London, Grant Richards, 1903, p. ix.
100 Boyd, op. cit., pp. 181, 129; see also p. 148.
101 Ibid., pp. 367–8.
102 Ibid., p. 143; see also p. 180.

15

COMMENTS ON HOWE AND SYKES

Andrew Marrison

In his fascinating chapter on free trade after 1846, Anthony Howe enters into a subject which has been heavily neglected by historians, who until recently seem to have taken the position that there was scarcely a story to tell. He also rescues the doctrine of free trade from the accusation, made for instance by Chamberlain's tariff reformers after 1900, that it was a fossilized and sterile anachronism which had outlived its usefulness. Stressing the depth and strength of Victorian Britain's attachment to free trade, his essay shows the doctrine to have developed: it proved 'neither unbending nor narrow but rather . . . one of the most versatile and malleable of Victorian doctrines.' In the immediate post-repeal period, he reveals the triumph of Peelite universal free trade over an (all-too-often overlooked) Huskissonite as well as a protectionist opposition within the Tory camp, and a consolidation of the support for a 'fiscal free trade' which brought the Peelites closer to the Whig-Radicals and which found ready favour in the Civil Service. He also restores the reputation of the Whigs on imperial preference and unilateralism in the post-repeal period, uncovering their 'in some ways . . . bold attempt to pick up the Peelite mantle' and their role in consolidating middle-class support against a possible protectionist reaction in the years before 1852.

Howe also examines the longer-term Cobdenite legacy to the Liberal party, and the role of the Cobden Club in cementing a widening democracy and free trade so firmly together in the late nineteenth century. But free trade did not remain 'exactly as Cobden had left it'. Within the Cobdenite legacy was the potential for a rift between a 'market' and a 'rights' view of free trade. The latter, enshrining the right of consumers to cheap food and of the community to protection from rent-seeking vested interests, became the glide in free-trade ideology that allowed a compatibility with Liberal collectivism and the 'New Liberalism'. In this sense, Mallet and the Liberal adherents of a 'market' view found themselves strangely close to those agitating for reciprocity, countervailing duties, and bimetallism.

Howe thus enriches our understanding of the position and the role of free trade ideology in the second half of the nineteenth century. He leaves the story at the turn of the century, with Liberalism renewed, 'intellectually vigorous and politically insurmountable'. But what sort of consolidation was this? Was the triumph of the 'rights' version perhaps a poor victory for a political ideology, more obviously the product of the 'vested' interest of the majority – as much a pragmatic electoral device as a consistent element of Liberal political philosophy? Huskisson, it appears, had been reborn in both political parties. Scholars seldom ask, and would get no answers from the historical record if they did, whether supporters of Chamberlain were 'protectionists' (the assumption is always that they were) or 'true free-traders' more close to the 'market' version (the assumption is always that they were not). This is particularly relevant in regard to those tariff reform manufacturers who were very often lukewarm on food duties.

Furthermore, the longer-term consequences of the victorious 'rights' version of free trade on the survival of the Liberal Party itself invite speculation, and here I hope we shall learn more from Howe's *Free Trade and Liberal England, 1846–1946* (Oxford, 1997). Liberal concentration on free food and graduated direct taxation was clearly 'progressive' in its appeal for the working class and held it in good stead in the Edwardian period. But what of the middle classes? Earlier, without strong trade unions, and with taxation and government expenditures still conforming strongly to Gladstonian principles, the 'rights' version of free trade would have had implications little different from Peelite unilateralism. But by the Edwardian years, the middle classes sensed lighter tax burdens abroad, and inexorable pressure on the public purse at home in future, pressure that they, not the working class, would have to meet. Business and maybe other middle-class Liberals were deserting the party in some numbers before the First World War, largely because of that very position on taxation and public spending. Furthermore, the 'rights' version could be no Liberal monopoly, and found fertile ground in the Labour party. Did it, in the longer run, serve to polarise political opinion between labour and capital, accelerate the demise of the Liberals, and thus contribute to the consolidation of the Conservatives as the most successful political party in twentieth-century Britain?

In outlining the 'generalised crisis, at once economic, social, racial, military, diplomatic and fiscal' that appeared to be facing Edwardian Britain, Alan Sykes's chapter gives an excellent and panoramic sweep across the difficulties of constructing a tariff reform policy to the liking of all its supporters. Those difficulties involved, at the same time, avoiding internal 'contradictions'; reconciling the different objectives of different tariff reformers; and accommodating different strategies for the purpose of persuading the electorate – strategies which might not only cause some dispute among the tariff reformers but might also demonstrate instability of emphasis and the related tendency to change over time.

There were certainly a seemingly impossible number of policy objectives – Empire unity; imperial trade; retaliation and reciprocity with non-Empire countries; protection at least to some degree (because foreign tariffs would never have fallen to zero and because Britain was more heavily taxed than abroad); revenue; the protection of capital from despoilatory taxation; social reform; employment at decent wages; regeneration in those various social and spiritual aspects which hovered around insubstantially in the ether of national efficiency. Now, some tariff reformers could doubtless take all these on board serially and additively, working on the premise that if you say something quickly enough, loudly enough, and often enough in politics you are likely to persuade somebody. Others would have their preferences, their ranking. But working out what they would have settled for by what they said at any one time is not always easy. Most of the evidence we have on the tariff reformers' objectives comes from a myriad of speeches, or from private letters which laid out what in effect were ideal or opening positions. There was not an immediate 'brain's trust' discussion after each speech, a conference after each letter, to hammer out differences of emphasis and differences of expression. The evidence may serve to conceal an underlying unity, a potential for compromise.

Contradictions and conflicts were inevitable when a policy with a single core – the manipulation of a blueprint of a yet unborn tariff – was designed to achieve so many different objectives. As a policy prescription, tariff reform was probably not unique in that. But politically, the more immediate problem was that Unionist disunity forced tariff reform to become too decentralized. If party unity was a precondition for a tariff reform government with any chance of gaining a mandate, then it is arguable that all those hundreds of tariff reformers who tried to help by speaking and writing endlessly on tariff reform fragmented the lesson, clouded the beacon. What tariff reform needed was stronger leadership and presentational clarity – fewer arguments, each repeated identically and more often, rather than widening in the hope of gaining new recruits at the margin! Ideally, conflicting, or semi-conflicting, agendas should have been kept hidden. Tariff reform broke, was perhaps forced into breaking, a cardinal rule of popular politics. Keep it simple.

The inevitable contradictions in a large and ill-defined policy like tariff reform were also particularly difficult for a country with Britain's unique fiscal legacy. Elsewhere, the implementation of policy in advanced industrial countries was pragmatic. Most countries never moved away completely from the trade controls of the seventeenth and eighteenth centuries. The trade controls that remained could be marginally adjusted, tampered with, experimented with, reversed. Hence mistakes could be reviewed, internal conflicts could be either minimized or met by the political subordination of one interest group by another. Britain's unique problem was starting a tariff blueprint from scratch. It was a situation not totally unlike that encountered by today's political parties when drawn into discussing their tax proposals in advance of a general election.

That tariff blueprint never emerged. After 1915, the McKenna and Key

Industry Duties gave experience of empirical tinkering, of a learning process in the implementation of tariffs and of living with their effects. Furthermore, the objectives of interwar tariff reformers were narrower than those of their radical-imperialist predecessors. Even so, these two factors were insufficient for a National Government with a mandate for protection and imperial preference to introduce a predetermined tariff designed around a blueprint. The Import Duties Act of 1932 was not, as its advocates had hoped, a complete structure, and it was only semi-complete in the sense that it was a stop-gap. Protection and preference involved sucking it and seeing, involved the Ottawa Conference and the Import Duties Advisory Committee. Of course, in the Ottawa negotiations, many of Sykes's most central contradictions were only too evident, though *politically*, as a beacon, preference did endure long enough still to be a problem when Britain's relations with Europe came onto the agenda.

Whether tariff reform was politically a success or a failure depends on two things – one's time scale and one's definition of victory. Those who regard the repeal of 1846 as a 'victory' and tariff reform as a 'failure' do rather overlook that tariff reform (dated 1903–32) was achieved slightly more quickly than repeal (dated 1815–46). Yet the tariff reform of 1932 was one of shrunken ideals, even if most tariff reformers who were still around in 1932 proclaimed it as a victory. While this suggests that they were prepared for something less than their ideal, it is nevertheless true that victory had been achieved by a narrowing of objectives, a process in which industrial safeguarding was pushed through the 1920s and preference and social reform relegated to the background. This was the tariff reform that made headway in the 1920s and which was possible in 1932. If the rhetoric of politicians allows partial success to be portrayed as total success, I am not sure politics ever achieves much more than that.

16

FREE TRADE, SOCIAL REFORM AND IMPERIALISM

J.A. Hobson and the dilemmas of Liberalism, 1890–1914

Peter Cain

Free trade was one of the foundation stones of Britain's nineteenth-century social order. As the first industrial country, Britain had also become the first major exporter of manufactures and had followed this by becoming the world's leading international service centre. As a result, the vested interests of business in free imports of food and raw materials were far more varied and powerful in Britain than elsewhere and free trade was a key element in reconciling business to the social order in mid-Victorian Britain. Free trade also had a wider cross-class appeal. It was immensely popular with skilled working men not just because it brought cheap supplies of food but also because protectionism was associated in Britain with the defence of landed privilege and with the aristocratic, 'tax eating', warmongering state which Cobbett and Paine had railed against as 'Old Corruption'. Anti-aristocratic feeling was also the basis of Cobden's and Bright's middle-class, free-trade cosmopolitanism, which, in its turn, underlay the Spencerian distinction between traditionally 'militant', or aristocratic-authoritarian, states which were perpetually at war with each other, and modern 'industrial' or small-scale, market-driven ones. Industrial societies were becoming steadily more involved in a global division of labour which radicals believed was materially beneficial to all who participated in it and also created an interdependence that would eventually make war between nations unthinkable.[1] This ideology of 'industrialism', uniting capitalists and workers in a 'producers' alliance' against inherited privilege, was central to Gladstonian liberalism in its heyday in the 1870s with its emphasis on the 'free breakfast table' and the small state: and its power was widely diffused enough to ensure that, despite its strong aristocratic connections, the Conservative party was forced to accept these central precepts of Gladstonianism.[2]

From 1880, as world economic development took a new turn, Gladstone's consensus came under severe pressure on both the domestic and the international fronts. Its ideological assumptions were severely challenged and some were overthrown. Free trade, of course, survived into the Edwardian era to become a vital part of the thinking of the reconstructed Liberal party of 1906 and, on the ideas front, 'New Liberal' thinkers like J.A. Hobson[3] were keen to show that they were the true inheritors of the free-trade faith, frequently invoking not only the authority of Cobden and Spencer but also employing their language. But the economic and the intellectual context in which free trade flourished after 1900 was different to that of the 1870s. A reconciliation between Hobson's own ideas and those of his liberal predecessors was achieved only after much struggle and confusion and some dalliance with the heresy of protection, as this chapter will demonstrate.

The free-trade, anti-state tradition of Gladstone was put in question by increasing disquiet about the extent of 'unearned' income in free-trade, capitalist Britain and by the dire poverty that the famous social surveys of the 1880s and 1890s brought to public view. The clamour for what contemporaries called 'collectivist' solutions to social problems began to grow; and the movement towards a democratic franchise in 1884–5 encouraged reformers to believe that, as the representative of the nation rather than the exclusive possession of the wealthy, the state could legitimately interfere in the market for the social good. The gap between those liberals, like Spencer, who stood by the free market and those who came to believe, as Hobson and L.T. Hobhouse did, that true liberty could flourish only if the state created genuine equality of opportunity, grew wide. Britain's dependence on foreign trade and, increasingly, on markets for its capital exports in a world becoming ever more competitive, also brought problems in the shape of imperial expansion, both formal and informal, to embarrass the adherents of Gladstonianism. Gladstone's occupation of Egypt in 1882, four years after he had condemned such a project as immoral and unnecessary, illustrated the dilemma of reconciling cosmopolitan ideas with international reality. By the 1890s, the Liberal Imperialists such as Rosebery frankly accepted the need for what was later termed 'free-trade imperialism' in order to prevent territory in 'backward' areas from falling into the hands of protectionist European rivals; Chamberlain, who had broken with Gladstone over the issue of home rule for Ireland on the grounds that this was the first step towards the dismemberment of the empire, led his breakaway Liberal Unionist faction in the same direction as Rosebery. Free-trade imperialism and social reform were often yoked together and expansion in Africa and Asia was frequently sold to the electorate as a means of providing jobs and maintaining living standards. It caused bitter divisions within liberal ranks with Cobdenites condemning it as the antithesis of their master's philosophy and a sure recipe for massive state expenditures which, besides reducing economic growth, would eventually provide an excuse to reintroduce tariffs to finance revenue needs.

Indeed, traditional liberals saw the emerging Fair Trade movement of the 1880s and 1890s as the inevitable outcome of the attempt to resurrect the paternalist, imperially aggressive state. Fair Traders saw matters rather differently. They made great play with the fact that, despite Cobden's confident assurances, Europe and the United States had not followed Britain's lead in fiscal policy and that the latter was therefore saddled with unilateral free trade. The outcome of such a one-sided bargain was increased competition in British and empire markets, lower domestic investment and the flow of capital abroad. For the Fair Traders, unilateral free trade was the obvious cause of the 'overproduction' which so exercised businessmen of the time,[4] and of the unemployment which underlay poverty and social distress. The remedies they proposed were protection, imperial preference and the extension of empire and, by the late 1880s, they had significant support in the Conservative party.[5] The protectionist contagion spread faster in the 1890s: Chamberlain, who had joined forces with the Conservatives, actively canvassed the idea of an imperial Zollverein in 1896. Gladstonianism was in disarray by the 1890s at both the level of ideas and of practical politics and the Grand Old Man was well aware of this, writing to Bryce in his retirement that 'I am fundamentally a dead man: one fundamentally a Peel-Cobden man.'[6] And as Hobhouse wrote dolefully in 1899, Cobden's name was in such bad odour among social reformers that they were inclined to be for anything Cobden was against, including imperialism.[7] Yet, within a few years, free trade and social reform were combined triumphantly by a revivified Liberal party. Hobson's work on free trade and protection between 1890 and 1914 – its contradictions and *bouleversements* as well as its insights – is interesting not just because of Hobson's fame as a radical economic liberal but also because it illustrates some of the difficulties that had to be faced in trying to reconcile Cobdenism with the New Liberalism and how that reconciliation was eventually achieved.[8]

Hobson did not come to New Liberalism easily. As a young man, he had some exposure to the 'unearned increment' radicalism of J.S. Mill but it appears to have left little trace by the mid-1880s, when he first began to live in London and to write a 'London Letter' for his father's newspaper, the *Derbyshire Advertiser*.[9] His stance then was Liberal Unionist and his attitudes to poverty and the poor were decidedly orthodox, as were his views on foreign policy. He was also a vigorous imperialist. In 1887, for example, he could be found advocating 'commercial advances' on China arguing that 'the opening up of the vast Chinese Empire to European trade would be the greatest event since the discovery of America. . . . Think what a market for English manufactures if it could be opened!'[10] One of his objections to Gladstone's policy of home rule for Ireland was that it would bring about the disintegration of the empire;[11] in 1888, he admonished John Bright for objecting to the idea of imperial federation, which he felt was necessary in view of the imperial hostility of France and Russia.[12] In the late 1880s, however, Hobson combined his imperialism with an adherence to free trade though he warned against 'fetish worship' in this regard.[13]

Hobson's theoretical novelty began with *The Physiology of Industry* (1889), written with the businessman A.F. Mummery.[14] The authors argued that Say's Law was incorrect: supply did not necessarily create its own demand and produce full employment of resources, because of the problem of over-saving, which they thought endemic to advanced capitalist economies.[15] The *Physiology* was clearly the *fons et origo* of the New Liberal economics which later made Hobson famous; the authors showed some leanings in this direc-tion when they concluded that taxation should fall mainly on savings and that higher wages would be beneficial to economic health. On the other hand, diagnoses of oversaving, overinvestment and even underconsumption were common at the time and were susceptible to fairly conservative inter-pretations. The origins of the economic malady could be traced to unilateral free trade with protection and imperialism recommended as solutions.[16] Indeed, rather than moving smoothly from the theoretical heresies of the *Physiology* to the radical underconsumptionism of *The Problem of the Unemployed* (1896), Hobson's views followed an erratic course. At first he appeared to forget his heresy altogether and then moved towards the kind of social imperialism espoused by some Fair Traders and later adopted by Chamberlain.

The *Physiology* itself gave some support to the growing attack on free trade. Hobson and Mummery recognised that existing defences of free trade relied on the idea that 'over-supply' was impossible.[17] Their most radical suggestion was that the problem of underconsumption could be alleviated by a rise in wages and that one way of protecting any increase in wages, whether achieved by trade unionism or other means, was to exclude cheap foreign labour through an alien law.[18] They also showed some sympathy with the idea of a shorter working day with wages maintained at existing levels and argued in this case that the measure would only be effective if it were adopted internationally or if Britain were protected by tariffs; otherwise, foreign competition would 'ruin its capitalists, and so reduce the quantity of labour demanded as to force either a general emigration, the repeal of the law, or its systematic and general evasion.'[19] At the same time, they claimed that a tariff would not reduce industrial output.[20]

After this partial endorsement of protection in the cause of social reform, Hobson then went into retreat in the following year when, in the Conservative-inspired *National Review*, he attacked Sidney Webb's Fabian plea for a shorter working day at existing wage levels. Webb claimed that the cost, where not compensated by productivity increases, would come out of profits.[21] Hobson replied that a shorter working day would reduce profits, discourage exports and investment, encourage imports and reduce real wages. Protection could stem imports but it would also raise prices, stimulate for-eign investment and reduce aggregate output. His conclusion was that the working class could raise its real incomes only via increased productivity or if capitalists became satisfied with lower rates of return on capital in the long run.[22] Hobson made no reference here to his work with Mummery nor did he mention the fact that he had claimed that tariffs could not affect industrial output. The *Physiology* might never have been written.

Similar arguments about the difficulties of an eight-hour day, though more cautiously expressed, were deployed in his Boothite book on poverty published in the following year.[23] But Hobson now reverted to his original argument that the prohibition of foreign labour could help to maintain wage levels among the poor and to eliminate 'sweated' trades and, while being careful to avoid any open advocacy of protection, he clearly thought that free trade was in jeopardy as worker power increased.

> Whether such new and hazardous changes in our national policy are likely to be made depends in large measure upon the success of other schemes for treating the condition of the oversupply of low-skilled labour. If no relief is found for these, it seems not unlikely that a democratic government will some day decide that such artificial prohibition of foreign labour, and the foreign goods which compete with the goods produced by low-skilled English labour, will benefit the low-skilled workers in their capacity as wage-earners more than the consequent rise in prices will injure them in their capacity as consumers.[24]

In *Problems of Poverty*, Hobson was careful to avoid any open commitment to tariffs but, in the same year, he took his thinking about the links between the problem of poverty and the international economy a dramatic stage further.[25] Again occupying the pages of the *National Review*, he argued that, with modern means of communication, the inevitable result of free trade would be the export of capital from the high-wage economies of Europe to India and to China, where labour was cheap and abundant, bringing in its wake mass poverty and undermining progress towards industrial democracy in the West. Hobson posed the possibility of the British Empire acting as one market but then claimed that, under a regime of free trade, the empire would also be subject to destructive competition: 'there would be no guarantee that trade and population should not pass from the British Empire, as we know it now, to lands which lie undeveloped in their natural resources.'[26] Free trade had to go: 'if we are not content that Britain should lose her trade, we shall be driven to a policy of Protection.'[27] Although in his father's newspaper he wrote that an Imperial Zollverein was 'one of the great possibilities for the future',[28] in the *National Review* he tried to show that conventional tariffs against imported goods were not the answer since they would only raise prices and wages and accelerate the outflow of capital. 'If we should be determined to defeat the tendency of trade to leave England and seek a land of cheaper subsistence, we shall be compelled to seek some means of placing a prohibitive tariff on the migration of English capital.'[29] That rather than restricting immigration, which would act only as an 'early palliative' against cheaper European production, was the key to retaining an industrial population in Britain despite what the 'fanatical Free Trader, jealous for his fetish', might think.[30]

Hobson's assumption in 1891 was that free trade, while maximising world wealth, could reduce average incomes for the masses in some parts of the world, worsen the distribution of income and have disastrous consequences for welfare and for individual freedom because urban democracy would be destroyed and replaced by a 'revived feudalism' governed by those who controlled international finance.[31] The overall result of the process of industrialisation under free trade in what we now call the Third World would be an increase in world income: but there was an irresistible tendency for that income to become more unevenly distributed and to bring social disaster in its wake. Since he now saw cosmopolitanism as a threat to industrial civilisation, Hobson's approach at this time took him beyond the bounds of free-trade imperialism and outside the Liberal fold. At this point, his position was closer to Fair Trade thinking and to the Chamberlainite 'constructive imperialist' ideology which emerged after 1900. Hobson's appearance in the *National Review* may be indicative of his sympathy for this kind of radical conservatism.[32] His claim that free trade would inevitably create a plutocracy in the West, made wealthy through the ownership of overseas assets and at the expense of the indigenous industry of Britain, was certainly nearer to Fair Trade than it was to the conventional Cobdenism of the Liberal party in which he had grown up and where it was always assumed that free trade was an unmitigated benefit to all members of the international community.

After 1891 Hobson never repeated his argument about prohibiting capital exports but he reprinted *Problems of Poverty* in 1895, 1896 and 1899 and did not change the views on free trade expressed therein. By 1895, however, he had developed the idea of oversaving so far as to argue that most of it arose from capitalist monopolies, which resulted in underconsumption and poverty for the masses, and that the solution was 'a general policy of economic and social reform' involving redistribution of income and wealth via taxation, welfare provision and support for organised labour.[33] However, although he now recognised the fact that capital export could provide relief for oversaving he drew no radical conclusions from it;[34] his global frame of reference remained imperialist. He showed some sympathy with an aggressive policy in China in 1895 and gave tentative support to Chamberlain's explicitly protectionist ideas on imperial federation.[35]

By 1895–6, Hobson could be described as a radical in terms of economic and social policy but he had yet to adopt the Cobdenite anti-imperialist stance for which he is best known today. Indeed, he feared that Cobdenism could be self-defeating in the long run and, in thinking this, he was in good company, as C.H. Pearson's *National Life and Character*, which caused a considerable stir in liberal circles, demonstrated. Pearson's formative experiences were mid-Victorian and his last book was an elegant and ironic funeral oration for the free-market liberalism of his youth. He was convinced that the pressure of democracy would inevitably lead to a demand for social reform and for protection of living standards from foreign competition. But the tendency to protection and to socialism would be quickened by the rise of Asian and African industry, based on cheap, submissive labour and galvanised by free trade and European capital, which would eventually drive European trade back behind its own borders, undermine empires and check emigration. No longer able to expand globally, the white nations would be forced to solve their social problems through state socialism, a sharp levelling of incomes and a nationalistic militarism partially excused by the hostility of the rising Asian and African powers as they threw off the yoke of imperialism. In such a manner, the 'militant' state would re-emerge and European liberal civilisation decline.[36] Pearson's views were critically received in some liberal circles: the *Edinburgh Review* thought Pearson's vision too clouded by his Australian experience and continued to put its faith in Britain's ability to stay ahead technologically.[37] But many older liberal intellectuals such as Bryce, Frederic Harrison and Henry Sidgwick, disquieted by the collectivist tendencies of the time and by the pace and nature of world economic development, felt that Pearson's gloomy predictions might eventually be realised.[38] The demonstration that Cobdenism could produce its own inevitable antithesis must also have confirmed Hobson's own suspicion of unmitigated free trade.[39]

National Life and Character certainly touched a nerve in Britain and it was the forerunner of a great deal of agitated *fin de siècle* speculation about the future of industry and of the welfare of the working class in an age of eager and growing global competition. In the latter part of the 1890s, the heavyweight periodicals which circulated widely among the educated middle class carried numerous articles warning that British trade was under threat, that new methods and new markets were needed, that if they were not forthcoming then Britain's days as a great power would soon be over. Most, however, did not accept Pearson's fatalistic prognostications but believed instead that, through protection or imperialism or both, Britain could retain its internal stability and its status in the world in the twentieth century. There is no doubt that most commentators saw imperial expansion and protection as a way of forestalling social and political change; even those who recognised the need for reform often saw it in the context of a struggle for world markets involving large increases in military expenditure and an aggressive policy of expansion.[40]

Typical of this latter response were the immensely popular writings of Benjamin Kidd, especially *Social Evolution* (1894) and *Principles of Western Civilisation* (1902). Kidd's overexcited, repetitive and vague lucubrations were a world away from the cool and measured forecasts of Pearson, but Kidd clearly regarded the latter's predictions as the *reductio ad absurdum* of 'Manchester' economics, a surrendering to the brute forces of the market which allowed the 'unearned increment' and capitalist monopoly to flourish. Yet his social reforming zeal was not designed to emancipate the individual in traditional liberal fashion but to strengthen the nation in its Darwinian struggle for pre-eminence in the world. The 'destiny' of the British Empire lay 'in upholding throughout the world the conditions of development, and the standard of life won with such effort in our civilisation'; and to hold onto these standards in the future inevitably presaged 'rivalry . . . between a few, great, clearly defined systems of social order.'[41] When Chamberlain finally abandoned free trade in 1903 and launched the Tariff Reform Campaign, Kidd's adherence was a logical step because for him the new policy was

> that of the living nation standing for its own ideas and ideals in the world, aggressive, progressive, as far as possible self-contained and self-sufficient, and therefore necessarily stretching ever outwards towards the widest possible basis of production organised towards its own aims.[42]

Hobson's radical economic liberalism was far enough advanced by 1895 for him to protest at the militancy of Kidd's position. He also objected strongly to the way in which Kidd expected the individual to subordinate himself to society in the struggle for imperial dominance.[43] On the other hand, his concrete proposals for social reform were similar to Kidd's and he still showed some interest in Chamberlain's plans for imperial federation so his stance and Kidd's were not easy to distinguish. Indeed, dissension among radicals on imperial matters was acute in the later 1890s and many shared a sympathy with Liberal Imperialists and with Chamberlain. The Rainbow Circle, the intellectual forcing house of much New Liberal thinking, was riven with disputes between those like Herbert Samuel, who saw imperialism as necessary to create the wealth for social reform, and others, including William Clarke, who opposed it in Cobdenite fashion as a social and economic disaster.[44]

At some time in 1896–7 Hobson's opinions on imperialism must have gone through a dramatic revolution wherein, like Clarke and J.M. Robertson in the late 1890s, he came to believe that imperialism and protection were antithetical to social progress. The great issue which, despite the common ground they shared over the need for social reform, separated out the emerging New Liberal group from Chamberlain's supporters, their Roseberyite Liberal colleagues and from the Fabians and reunited them with traditional Cobdenite Liberals like John Morley, was the aggressive, jingoistic imperialism of the late 1890s in China and in South Africa. There was a long tradition in British radicalism, running through from Cobbett to Cobden, which associated high finance with aristocracy and aggression overseas.[45] The struggle for 'spheres of interest' and financial concessions in China, and the apparent connection between Chamberlain's and Milner's aggressive position towards the Transvaal and the machinations of mining capitalists such as Rhodes, dramatically reactivated that tradition, dormant since the Egyptian crisis of 1882.[46] The same phenomena also convinced Hobson that imperialism was driven by the needs of financiers eager for new markets and capable of any excess to obtain them and that imperialism was part of a wider attempt to preserve an inherently diseased form of capitalism and the economic and political status quo.

In order to explain his new conviction in ways which were consistent with his developing social radicalism, Hobson transformed the theory of underconsumption he had developed by 1895 into a theory of imperialism, arguing now that overseas expansion provided an outlet for oversaving, avoided the need for domestic redistribution of income and wealth and, by stirring up antagonism with other capitalist powers in search of territory, reactivated militancy and reinforced social conservatism. In creating a demand for increased armaments it also swelled state expenditure, simultaneously diverting attention from social reform and increasing the pressure for new forms of taxation which could most easily be met by tariffs. Protection was thus a natural ally of reactionary imperialism and, by making the distribution of income in capitalist countries even worse, it aggravated the oversaving crisis, reinforced the tendency to export capital and added a new twist to the vicious circle of imperialism.[47] These free-trade/anti-imperial views brought Hobson much closer to the traditional Liberal position: a common hostility to what was happening in China and in South Africa was an important element in forging an emotional and intellectual alliance between old and new liberalism and in recreating the Liberal party as an electoral force after 1900. Hobson now associated himself very closely with the traditional liberal anti-imperial tradition, frequently invoking Cobden by name and often using the language of Spencer.

But how was Hobson, the born-again cosmopolitan liberal, able to reconcile his new position with the argument that Britain's dependence on foreign trade was so great that protection and imperialism were inevitable in the interests of all classes in the community? There is no doubt that he continued to believe that, if present trends were allowed to continue, the predictions about Asian imperialism he had made in 1891 might come to pass. In 1902 in *Imperialism: a Study* he expressed this with great force:

We have foreshadowed the possibility of . . . a European federation of great Powers which, far from forwarding the cause of world civilisation, might introduce the gigantic peril of a western parasitism, a group of advance industrial nations, whose upper classes draw vast tribute from Asia and Africa, with which they supported great tame masses of retainers, no longer engaged in the staple industries of agriculture and manufacture, but kept in the performance of personal or minor industrial services under the control of a new financial aristocracy. Let those who scout such a theory as undeserving of consideration examine the economic and social condition of districts in southern England today which are already reduced to this condition, and reflect upon the vast extension of such a system which might be rendered feasible by the subjection of China to the economic control of similar groups of financiers, investors, and political and business officials, draining the greatest reservoir of profit the world has ever known, in order to consume it in Europe.[48]

Free trade under existing conditions clearly promoted imperialism: yet, from the late 1890s, Hobson could no longer rely on any Chamberlainite remedy, which he now saw as part of the problem rather than its solution. Caught in this dilemma, Hobson produced a wonderfully ingenious solution in an article of 1898 which later supplied the economic backbone for the far more famous *Imperialism*.[49] Here, Hobson first made the link between oversaving, underconsumption, foreign investment and imperialism. Removing oversaving by redistributing income in favour of the mass of the population, however, would inevitably mean a curtailment of foreign investment and would also result in a rise in domestic demand and a shift to the home market, reducing the need for foreign markets drastically.

In *Imperialism*, Hobson developed the idea in a way that was compatible with his evolving collectivism. Radical redistribution of income, reinforced by other social reforms such as improved education, would eventually mean that consumer demand would shift from the mass-produced goods, which were the staple commodities of foreign trade and the basis of international economic rivalry, to individually crafted, culture-specific commodities not tradable internationally. In this new moral world, free trade would reign everywhere and bring with it an element of civilising cosmopolitanism: but, since foreign trade would be very limited, it could not have the effect, predicted in 1891, of undermining living standards in Britain nor could it seriously disturb its social structure or its culture. Similarly, those underdeveloped countries previously subject to disruptive economic imperialism and forced industrialisation would now be free to develop in a way consistent with their traditional culture and beliefs because imperialism was no longer a necessity. The limited influence of international trade and factor movement in the new order would mean that each entity, whether it be an advanced country like Britain or a 'backward' one like China or India, could retain its cultural integrity while avoiding the perils associated with protection.

Unfortunately, Hobson's frequent mention of Cobden's name at this point in his career could not hide the fact that his attitude to the international economy was not the same, since Cobden had always assumed that the ideal world would be one in which the international division of labour was taken as far as possible. In fact, his own views had disturbingly anti-Cobdenite implications. Leonard Courtney, the Cobdenite Liberal MP, felt that Hobson was over-reacting to those who had exaggerated the importance of foreign trade and reminded him that his own argument could be used to justify protection.[50] As proof, Courtney cited the recent plea for protection made by Andrew Carnegie, the businessman and philanthropist, on the grounds that the home market was far more important than the foreign and had to be safeguarded.[51] Hobson's position did not square with the common-sense Cobdenism of liberal tradition.

Characteristically, Hobson never officially repudiated the views he had set out in *Imperialism* but he soon began to publish articles and books which carried a rather different, more orthodox, message. The substance of this new strain of thinking can be detected as early as 1903 in a piece which he wrote in response to Chamberlain's opening shots in the tariff campaign.[52] Here, Hobson repeated much of what he had written in 1891, agreeing with the protectionists that 'Free Trade makes no provision to secure that industry and an industrial population shall remain attached to any particular piece of earth' and admitting also that protection was 'an endeavour to struggle against certain dangers inherent in the world economy of Free Trade, and to keep within the territorial limits of the nation a sufficient volume and adequate variety of industry.'[53] He also reaffirmed that, if movement of this kind was to be prevented, tariffs on goods would be insufficient and a drastic prohibition of capital export would have to be effected. But, in contrast to the position he had taken up in 1891, he now argued that the rise of foreign competition under free trade had been accompanied by increased trade and rising living standards and that foreign competition had been important in stimulating change. Hobson also assumed that any capital and labour forced out of particular industries by foreign competition would find employment elsewhere. He then went on to say that the pressure for protection was simply a political manifestation of the fundamental problem of maldistribution of income and wealth which forced the search for foreign markets and encouraged imperialism and war. The solution was political and economic democracy. But whereas in 1898 and in 1902 Hobson had concluded that, in the new moral world, international trade would have a small role to play in economic life, in the 1903 article he now took up a much more explicitly Cobdenite position claiming that

> the civilisation of the future demands the maintenance of strong independent nations – fearless of aggression – *entering into ever closer commercial intercourse with one another*, and, in the practice of mutual aid upon the plane of physical life, laying the foundations of a higher spiritual fellowship.[54]

In *Imperialism*, international trade was important to an economy when it was suffering from the diseases of oversaving and underconsumption. In the 1903 article, the argument is much more explicitly Cobdenite: even a healthy capitalist organism was dependent on foreign trade.

Given his sympathy for some of Chamberlain's policies as late as 1896, Hobson appears to have undergone something of a Pauline conversion to anti-imperialism by 1898, a conversion which made it impossible for him any longer to advocate protection. At first, however, his support for free trade was equivocal since it was to operate in a world where most international transactions had been abolished. This was hardly consistent with the liberal cause Hobson was now enlisted in, as Courtney politely pointed out. It is not surprising, therefore, that faced with the threat of tariff reform and social imperialism, Hobson's views on free trade moved nearer to liberal orthodoxy as the 1903 article indicates. Unfortunately, the rapid shift in his allegiance left him with an intellectual puzzle which he never resolved thereafter and may not even have appreciated. In 1898 and in *Imperialism* he contended that, given the endemic problem of oversaving, Say's Law would work only in a reformed economy with a fairer distribution of rewards. In 1903, however, his arguments in favour of free trade, particularly his assertion that factors of production displaced by foreign competition would find alternative employment, seemed to imply that Say's Law operated in the unreformed economy also. This assumption of an automatic adjustment process was emphasised even more strongly in his book *International Trade* (1904), where he asserted categorically that international transactions raised income for all factors of production. Because he had become convinced that protection supported imperialism and that the latter inhibited social change, Hobson was desperate to prove that free trade was beneficial to all parties in the economy and did not have the ill effects on production or distribution that the protectionists claimed. But, in defending free trade, he had to fall back upon orthodox positions which either contradicted his radical economics or at least sat very uncomfortably with it.

In considering Hobson's rather erratic intellectual progress, one should also remember that, like many other radicals, he was extremely optimistic about the long-term progress of mankind, which he saw as inevitable, even if that progress could frequently be halted or temporarily reversed. So, given the collapse of Conservative protectionist strategies at the 1906 election and again at the two elections in 1910, together with the beginnings of what appeared to be a serious social reform programme in Britain and a rapid expansion in world trade, Hobson convinced himself, as did Hobhouse, that the new moral world was about to appear.[55] He never stopped worrying that imperialism or war might retard progress as it had done between 1880 and 1902, but he became increasingly confident that the good effects of international trade and investment were outweighing the bad and his analysis of the international economy became steadily more mainstream as a result.

What is striking about his work just before the war is not just the extent to which he argued that a global trading and finance network was important to general living standards, but how far he was willing to go in saying that it could bring benefits to the masses even before any fundamental change had been made in the distribution of income. Between 1909 and 1911, at the beginning of a huge overseas investment boom which peaked in 1913 and which provoked a widespread debate on the merits of sending so much capital abroad, Hobson's retreat towards orthodoxy reached its climactic. Writing in the *Financial Review of Reviews* – not the first publication a radical would be expected to refer to – Hobson's claims that foreign investment was surplus to domestic requirements and that it brought benefits to all classes by cheapening imports and boosting exports were little more than cross-party commonplace.[56]

What is more, he applied the same reasoning to imperialism, presenting imperial expansion as a stage in world economic development which, by opening up underdeveloped countries to the world economy, had initiated a process of convergence that would bring the poorer nations nearer to the economic levels of the rich. Hobson also claimed that the growing tendency for the major powers to co-operate in international investment projects was creating an interdependence between nations that was the best guarantee against major wars in future and, in an atmosphere of permanent peace, the movement towards radical reform and economic justice within nations would be accelerated. The contrast with the analysis of 1902 was stark: under-developed nations did not need to be protected against foreign economic invasion because that invasion was part of their process of development, the path to progress. This was an analysis which contradicted Cobden, who was never less than hostile to imperial expansion in any guise, though it could be argued that the kind of imperialism which Hobson appeared to justify was an inevitable outcome of the internationalism championed by the former. Indeed, Hobson's position in 1911 was consistent with the kind of free-trade imperialism broadly acceptable within the Liberal party. He became so enamoured of this rather bland, almost Panglossian, internationalism that, just before the war and even in the early days of the conflict, he wrote further articles for the *Financial Review of Reviews* which would not have been out of place on the City page of a newspaper with a conservative bias.[57]

Hobson's dilemmas in regard to the international economy and its effects, and his various attempts at solving them, have a broad interest because they illustrate the perpetual problems faced by reformers and revolutionaries who must act in a world where openness offers many tempting economic benefits but also exposes nations to disasters imported from abroad and threatens to wrest control of their nation's destiny from their hands. His early, conservative fears about the impact of a relentlessly changing world economy on the welfare of Britain and industrial Europe have, of course, been echoed frequently by business and trade union interests ever since. The most recent example, the late Sir James Goldsmith's tirade against the long-term consequences of the latest GATT agreement, was written in a manner uncannily reminiscent of Hobson's *National Review* article of 1891 and carried the same apocalyptic message.[58] Again, when in the late 1890s he decided that tariffs and empire were incompatible with radical economic reform, Hobson retreated into a form of self-sufficiency that had much in common with the ideas of a host of radicals and socialists in the twentieth century such as Stalin, Mao, and dependency theorists like Frank or Wallerstein, who felt that reform or revolution was possible only when nations were isolated from the international mainstream.[59] Given the dependence of Britain on the international economy by Hobson's time, this approach proved neither intellectually nor practically satisfying; between 1903 and 1914, he fell back to the position that the maximum development of the international economy was the key to promoting beneficial social change. This, of course, has been the predominant idea in the developed world since Ricardo's time and is implicit in most orthodox economic theory and policy in the late 1990s. It is not necessarily incompatible with a radical critique of capitalism and imperialism: Hobson could have argued, as Marx had done, that the maximum exposure to liberal capitalism and its attendant imperialism was important in bringing the system to fruition more speedily and, therefore, destroying it sooner.[60] But between 1903 and 1914, Hobson adopted the line that imperialism was a stage on the road to the more harmonious development of a true capitalism rather than a means to its destruction. Although he never admitted it, and was perhaps even unaware of it, Hobson's solution to the vexed question of free trade and its implications involved him in surrendering or severely compromising, his famous theory of imperialism. Whether he should be condemned for inconsistency and for betraying the radical cause or whether, on the contrary, he deserves praise for his flexibility in responding to intellectual challenges and a changing environment is another question altogether.

Notes

1 For background see P.J. Cain, 'Capitalism, War and Internationalism in the Thought of Richard Cobden', *British Journal of International Studies* V (1979); M. Taylor, 'Imperium et Libertas? Rethinking the Radical Critique of Imperialism during the Nineteenth Century', *Journal of Imperial and Commonwealth History* 19 (1991); and M.W. Taylor, *Men Versus the State: Herbert Spencer and Late Victorian Individualism* (Oxford, 1992).

2 E.F. Biagnini, *Liberty, Retrenchment and Reform: Popular Liberalism in the Age of Gladstone, 1860–1880* (Cambridge, 1992).

3 The most prominent works on the New Liberalism are: P.F. Clarke, *Liberals and Social Democrats* (Cambridge, 1978); M. Freeden, *The New Liberalism: an Ideology of Social Reform* (Oxford, 1978); S. Collini, *Liberalism and Sociology: L.T. Hobhouse and Political Argument in England* (Cambridge, 1979); and A. Vincent and R. Plant, *Philosophy, Politics and Citizenship: the Life and Thought of the*

British Idealists (Oxford, 1984), ch. 5. On Hobson as economist in this context see J. Allett, *New Liberalism: the Political Economy of J.A. Hobson* (Toronto, 1981).

4 A. Kadish, 'The Non-Canonical Context of *The Physiology of Industry*', in J. Pheby (ed.) *J.A. Hobson After Fifty Years: Freethinker of the Social Sciences* (London, 1994).

5 The Fair Trade movement is in urgent need of modern scholarly attention. The best introduction remains J.H. Zebel, 'Fair Trade: an English Reaction to the Breakdown of the Cobden Treaty System', *Journal of Modern History* 12 (1940). Their own best statement of their case is in the *Minority Report of the Royal Commission on Depression in Trade and Industry,* PP 1886, C4893.

6 Quoted in Vincent and Plant, *Philosophy, Politics and Citizenship*, p. 35 from a letter of December 1896.

7 L.T. Hobhouse, 'The Foreign Policy of Collectivism', *Economic Review* 9 (1899), pp. 199–200.

8 What follows is a revised version of arguments first put forward in P.J. Cain, ' J.A. Hobson, Cobdenism and the Radical Theory of Economic Imperialism, 1898–1914', *Economic History Review* 31 (1978); and Cain, 'International Trade and Economic Development in the Thought of J.A. Hobson before 1914', *History of Political Economy* 11 (1979). See also P.F. Clarke, 'Hobson, Free Trade and Imperialism', *Economic History Review* 34 (1981) and my reply, 'Hobson's Developing Theory of Imperialism' in the same issue of the *Review*. It should be noted that Hobson was quite capable of contradicting himself at every stage in his career as well as changing intellectual gear at various stages of his life. Here I concentrate on the major temporal shifts in his thinking rather than dwelling on the contradictions within each phase of his thought.

9 For insights into Hobson's early years, so carefully obscured in *Confessions of an Economic Heretic* his autobiography of 1938, see A. Kadish, 'Rewriting the *Confessions*; Hobson and the Extension Movement', in M. Freeden, (ed.) *Reappraising J.A. Hobson: Humanism and Welfare* (London, 1990).

10 'A London Letter', *Derbyshire Advertiser and Journal*, 21 Oct. 1887, p. 8.

11 Ibid., 2 Dec. 1887, p. 8.

12 Ibid., 7 April 1888, p. 8.

13 Ibid., 4 April 1887, p. 8.

14 *The Physiology of Industry* is now available in R. Backhouse and P.J. Cain (eds) *J.A. Hobson: A Collection of Economic Works* (Bristol, 1992).

15 The best introduction is R. Backhouse, 'Mummery and Hobson's *The Physiology of Industry*', in Pheby, *J.A. Hobson After Fifty Years*.

16 For a careful argument that overproduction, unemployment and capital export offered at least *prima facia* evidence in favour of protection, see C.A. Cripps, 'Competition and Free Trade', *National Review* 10 (1887) and the same author's 'Free Trade and the Economists', *National Review* 11 (1888). See also Kadish, 'The Non-Canonical Context', pp. 56–7, 60–1.

17 *Physiology*, p. ix.

18 Ibid., pp. 209–13.

19 Ibid., p. 214.

20 Ibid., pp. 205–9.

21 S. Webb, 'Limitation of the Hours of Labour', *Contemporary Review* 56 (1889).

22 J.A. Hobson, 'The Cost of a Shorter Working Day', *National Review* 15 (1890).

23 J.A. Hobson, *Problems of Poverty* (London, 1891), pp. 127–32.

24 Ibid., pp. 126–7.

25 'Can England Keep Her Foreign Trade?', *National Review* 17 (1891). This article

is reprinted in P.J. Cain (ed.) *J.A. Hobson: Writings on Imperialism and Internationalism* (Bristol, 1992).

26 Ibid., p. 9.

27 Ibid., p. 10.

28 *Derbyshire Advertiser*, 10 April 1991, p. 2.

29 'Can England Keep Her Foreign Trade?', p. 10.

30 Ibid., p. 3.

31 Ibid., p. 11.

32 For an approach to constructive imperialism see E.E.H. Green, *The Crisis of Conservatism: the Economics, Politics and Ideology of the Conservative Party, 1880–1914* (London, 1995); and P.J. Cain, 'The Economic Philosophy of Constructive Imperialism', in C. Navari (ed.) *British Politics and the Spirit of the Age: Political Concepts in Action* (Keele, 1996).

33 The first clear expression of his radical underconsumptionism is in 'The Economic Cause of Unemployment', *Contemporary Review* 67 (1895).

34 J.A. Hobson, *The Problem of the Unemployed* (London, 1896), pp. 86–8.

35 *Derbyshire Advertiser*, 22 Mar. 1895, p. 8; 4 Oct. 1995, p. 8.

36 C.H. Pearson, *National Life and Character: A Forecast* (2nd edn, London, 1894), pp. 122–33. The book was first published in 1893.

37 See *Edinburgh Review* 178 (1893), pp. 277–304. Cf. *Quarterly Review* 177 (1893), pp. 105–30.

38 C. Harvie, *The Lights of Liberalism: University Liberals and the Challenge of Democracy, 1860–86* (London, 1976), pp. 232–5; F. Harrison, 'The Evolution of Our Race' *Fortnightly Review* ns 54 (1893), p. 35. Sidgwick was disturbed by Pearson's methodology but felt that his predictions might possibly come true. See H. Sidgwick, 'Political Prophecy and Sociology', in *Miscellaneous Essays and Addresses* (London, 1904), pp. 219–22.

39 Pearson's baleful view of the outcomes is tersely expressed in his 'The Causes of Pessimism', *Fortnightly Review* ns 54 (1893), p. 446.

40 For examples of the literature see J.B.C. Kershaw, 'The Future of British Trade', *Fortnightly Review* ns 62 (1897): H.S. Hallett, 'British Trade and the Integrity of China', *Fortnightly Review* ns 63 (1898); Brooks Adams, 'The Commercial Future: the New Struggle for Life amongst Nations', *Fortnightly Review* ns 65 (1899); H. Birchenough, 'The Imperial Function of Trade', *Nineteenth Century* 46 (1899).

41 B. Kidd, *The Principles of Western Civilisation* (London, 1902), pp. 465–6. For his attack on Pearson and Manchester see also pp. 21–9, 449–50. Kidd was encouraged to write by Alfred Milner, his boss at the Inland Revenue in the early 1890s, who later became a strong supporter of tariff reform and constructive imperialism.

42 B. Kidd, 'Imperial Policy and Free Trade', *Nineteenth Century* 54 (1903), p. 36.

43 J.A. Hobson, 'Mr. Kidd's "Social Evolution"', *American Journal of Sociology* 2 (1895–6).

44 Compare Samuel's approach with Clarke's in M. Freeden (ed.) *Minutes of the Rainbow Circle, 1894–1924* (Camden Fourth Series, vol. 38, London, 1989), pp. 71–4. Kidd was once invited to join the Rainbow Circle and later was invited by the Compatriots Club, the main intellectual vehicle of tariff-reform imperialism. What both bodies had in common was a hostility to free-market liberalism. See Green, *The Crisis of Conservatism*, pp. 160–1.

45 For a brief introduction to this tradition see P.J. Cain, 'Hobson, Wilshire and the Capitalist Theory of Capitalist Imperialism', *History of Political Economy* 17 (1985).

46 Collini, *Liberalism and Sociology*, pp. 77–88.

47 On finance and protection see *Imperialism: A Study* (1988 edn), pp. 94–109.

48 Ibid., pp. 364–5. For similar predictions see J.M. Robertson, *Patriotism and Empire* (London, 1899), pp. 181–2 and W. Clarke, 'The Social Future of England', *Contemporary Review* 78 (1900), reprinted in J.A. Hobson and H. Burrows, *William Clarke: a Collection of his Writings* (London, 1908). Clarke makes a direct reference to Pearson.

49 The seminal article is J.A. Hobson, 'Free Trade and Foreign Policy', *Contemporary Review* 74 (1898), reprinted in *Writings on Imperialism and Internationalism*. Without endorsing Hobson's drastic solution to the problem, Hobhouse did suggest that 'healthy' industry would have less need for foreign markets. See 'The Foreign Policy of Collectivism', p. 209. Etherington's claim that Hobson took his main idea from Wilshire, the American socialist, is misleading. See N. Etherington, *Theories of Imperialism: War, Conquest and Capital* (London, 1984), chs 2, 3; and P.J. Cain, 'Hobson, Wilshire and the Capitalist Theory of Capitalist Imperialism', *History of Political Economy* 17 (1985).

50 L. Courtney, 'What is the Advantage of Foreign Trade?' *Nineteenth Century* 53 (1903), p. 811.

51 A. Carnegie, *A Rectorial Address* (Edinburgh, 1902). See also 'Expansion and Expenditure', *Edinburgh Review* 197 (1903), pp. 348–51.

52 'The Inner Meaning of Protectionism', *Contemporary Review* 84 (1903), reprinted in *Writings on Imperialism and Internationalism*.

53 Ibid., pp. 365, 367.

54 Ibid., p. 374.

55 L.T. Hobhouse was at his most optimistic about the future just before the First World War: Collini, *Liberalism and Sociology*, pp. 120–1.

56 Hobson's essays were reprinted in 1911 as *The Economic Interpretation of Investment*. See also W.S. Churchill, *The People's Rights* (London, 1909: 1970), pp. 104ff. and P.J. Cain and A.G. Hopkins, *British Imperialism: Expansion and Innovation* (London, 1993), pp. 215–16, for more general opinion at that time.

57 See, for example, his articles 'Investment Safeguards under Changing Conditions' in the June 1914 issue, and 'Investment under War Conditions' of March 1915. The war did eventually force Hobson to rethink his views. See P.J. Cain, 'Variations on a Famous Theme: Hobson, International Trade and Imperialism, 1902–38' in Freeden, *Reappraising J.A. Hobson*, pp. 31–53.

58 J. Goldsmith, *The Trap* (London, 1994) and *The Response* (London, 1995)

59 When politicians like Tony Benn and many socialist intellectuals, including E.P. Thompson, opposed British entry into the Common Market in the 1960s and 1970s, they used more moderate versions of the isolationist argument.

60 Marx displays this line of thinking most obviously in his writings on British India in K. Marx and F. Engels, *Collected Works,* XII (London, 1979 edn). Invoking Marx, Tom Nairn used the same argument to attack those socialists who opposed British entry into Europe in *The Left Against Europe?* (London, 1973).

17

INSULAR FREE TRADE, RETALIATION, AND THE MOST-FAVOURED-NATION TREATY, 1880–1914

Andrew Marrison

A belief that Britain's chief trading partners were 'returning' to protection in the late nineteenth century, after some mid-Victorian tendency towards trade liberalization,[1] played its part in conditioning the two Edwardian challenges to fiscal orthodoxy – Balfour's argument for retaliation, as advocated in his famous pamphlet of September 1903, and Chamberlain's scheme of imperial preference, sketched in outline in his Glasgow speech in October.

As is well known, Balfour's sought to avoid electorally unpopular food duties while at the same time holding his party together. His prescription, deliberately vague, was to 'plead for freedom to negotiate that freedom of exchange may be increased. . . . The precise manner in which we should use our regained liberty is an important, yet after all only a secondary issue.'[2] In arguing that Britain *already had* such a liberty, and that Balfour had already exercised it on the European sugar bounties, Harold Cox emphasized the ambiguity in Balfour's policy,[3] and there was much speculation about what the Prime Minister meant. Was his a policy of *ad hoc* specific and temporary retaliation, the intention and the satisfactory outcome of which would be a continuing, though not a pledged, free-trade policy? Or was it a scheme following that pattern which had shown such development in Europe since 1870, involving a two-tier tariff, in which negotiating countries gained access to each other's 'conventional' or 'minimum' tariff by reciprocity?

In the opinion of informed contemporary Heinrich Dietzel, Hicks Beach and the majority of Balfour's supporters sought the first alternative, less reprehensible to free-traders because its ultimate objective was the reduction of tariffs, whereas Balfour inclined towards a two-tier tariff, and would 'probably allow the principle of Protection . . . a certain influence on tariff policy.' 'Hicks Beach . . . wants merely a policy of retort; whereas Balfour seems to

224

aim at one of reciprocity.'[4] Balfour, however, specifically denied this in his speech at Sheffield in October 1903, confining himself to 'informing any foreign country which we thought was treating us with outrageous unfairness that unless they modified their policy to our advantage we should feel ourselves compelled' to retaliate on some of their exports to Britain, a statement which Hicks Beach found acceptable.[5] Whether such a policy, retaliation held as a threat to prevent foreign tariffs against Britain from getting even higher, that is to preserve the *status quo ante*, would have been effective is doubtful. It would at least have been tested for bluff by foreign trading partners, and it clearly stood in danger of developing into a two-tier tariff if seriously pursued.[6]

Chamberlain's scheme also raises problems of ambiguity and uncertainty, though lesser ones. As developed by his Tariff Commission,[7] it involved three tiers – a preferential tariff, a permanent 'general' tariff, and a 'maximum' tariff. The normal formulation of a two-tier tariff, say in Europe, was to start with the 'general' or 'maximum' tariff, as specified by the legislature, and then construct a lower tariff through some tariff-making or tariff-negotiating body, often (but not always) within a 'conventional' or 'minimum' limit that had been previously laid down by the legislature. But this was not always the case; less frequently, the lower-level tariff was specified and the higher-level tariff derived subsequently.[8] This latter practice, modified by the need for an imperial tariff, was the one envisaged by Chamberlain.

Confusingly, what the Chamberlainites called their 'general' tariff was in fact their 'conventional' or 'minimum' tariff, the tariff which would meet commercially friendly nations. It would still disadvantage friendly nations relative to the colonies. A 'maximum' or 'fighting' tariff was to be reserved for those unwilling to meet the conditions demanded for access to the 'general' tariff.

In May 1904, Chamberlain and his Commission sketched out their blueprint for a three-tier tariff. The general tariff, based loosely on proposals first aired at Glasgow, would lie in the range 5–7½ per cent on agricultural products and would *average* 10 per cent on manufactures, graded from about 5 per cent on crude semi-manufactures to something like 15 per cent on highly finished goods. Later, for domestic political reasons, the Commission developed cold feet, and the proposals as published were for a *maximum* of 10 per cent on finished goods.[9]

But what of the conditions for foreign access to the Tariff Reformers' 'general tariff'? In June 1904, Chamberlain mentioned two different criteria. The first was that such countries 'must make a proportional reduction in their own'. But then, in contradiction of this, he continued that 'as a general thing' foreign countries should be required to 'reduce their Tariff to the level of our normal [i.e. general] Tariff.'[10] These criteria, especially the second, would have had profound implications for the treatment of foreign goods. As some Commission members pointed out forcibly during their discussions, few foreign countries would, or probably could, have met the strict condition of a reduction of their duties on British goods to the level of a British tariff of 5–10 per cent, and would have been forced onto Britain's yet-unspecified 'fighting' tariff.

Tariff reformers put relatively little emphasis on the 'maximum' or 'fighting' tariff. Hence the 10 per cent 'general' (= 'conventional' or 'minimum') tariff is usually what historians have in mind when they characterize Chamberlainite Tariff Reform as moderate.[11] However, if access to Britain's 'general' tariff was to be made so difficult, the implication is that the *real* Chamberlainite tariff was the 'fighting' tariff – Tariff Reform held the prospect of developing into a considerably higher tariff regime than we generally recognize. Though retaliation was common currency in Tariff Reform speeches, the 'fighting tariff' was an aspect seldom emphasized or specified, but the intention did endure, and it resurfaced in Chamberlain's speech on the cotton trade at Preston in January 1905.[12] The occasion was of course significant: the only hope of producing a policy attractive to export-orientated Lancashire lay in the prospect of getting foreign tariffs down. But, like the main Commission, its Textile Committee was also sceptical about the prospect of successful retaliation, as were witnesses and respondents to its questionnaires.[13]

The very moderacy of Chamberlain's proposed 'general tariff' suggests that its implementation would probably not have provoked a violent reaction from protectionist co-trading states, whose tariffs were generally distinctly higher. If this low level of duties had been introduced on the basis of the *status quo ante*, and extended widely through the most-favoured-nation (MFN) treaties, protectionist countries would have had difficulty opposing it on the basis of righteous moral indignation. Equally, it would scarcely have been worth the trouble and uncertainty involved in retaliating, and thereby running the risk of goading Britain into applying her 'fighting' tariff, at a time when other nations continued to receive MFN access to the 'general tariff'. If, however, Chamberlain's ideas of the foreign concessions necessary to secure access to that 'general tariff' had been rigorously enforced, foreign retaliation might have become much more likely as foreign countries encountered Britain's 'maximum' tariff.

Imperial preference adds another dimension. Three-tier tariffs were relatively unusual, and were typically installed to give preference to overseas colonies or dependencies, as in the case of France and Belgium. However, unlike in those cases, Chamberlain's scheme involved colonies which were populous, high-income countries important and growing in world trade. Furthermore, dominion possession of fiscal autonomy made preference vulnerable in a way that its French and Belgian counterparts were not. As Pigou observed of the German reaction to Canadian unilateral preference:

> It might be said that Canada and Great Britain were parts of a single State, whose domestic arrangements were nobody's business but

their own. But is not Germany's reply conclusive, that, 'if the English colonies are to be in a position to follow out their own Customs policy, other countries must be allowed to treat them as separate Customs territories'?[14]

Would this legalistic or 'constitutional' argument have weighed heavily with foreign diplomats, or would they have adopted a pragmatic approach? When Canada extended unilateral preference to Britain in 1897, Britain had to abrogate its treaty with Germany, thus exposing Britain to the danger that it might find MFN treatment replaced by 'least-favoured-nation' treatment as Germany implemented its fighting tariff. Interestingly, this never happened. The most plausible reason is that Britain was by far the largest import market in the world – it had far more latent strength in negotiation than free-traders recognized. Germany was in fact careful not to ruffle British sensibilities over the Canadian issue. Technically, British imports lost MFN status in Germany, but the Reichstag continued to pass a yearly decree extending MFN treatment to British goods until the German–Canadian dispute was settled. When, in the new century, the sentiment for imperial preference gathered force, Baron von Richthofen told the British Ambassador in Berlin that if '*large portions* of the British Empire were to give preferential treatment to Great Britain, it would be very difficult to obtain the consent of the Reichstag to the prolongation of most-favoured-nation treatment to Great Britain herself.'[15] Even this suggests a pragmatic qualification. Furthermore, the German–Canadian dispute did not deter other dominions from granting Britain unilateral preferences in the years before 1914, and it is noticeable that Germany did not implement Richthofen's threat and react similarly in these later cases.[16] It was probably sensible not to do so. For the most part, dominion tariffs on all manufactures were substantial, and set against these the preferences to Britain were small.

Like Germany, unhappy about Canada's granting of preference to British manufactures, the USA reacted differently. Rather than enter a tariff war, the US administration stepped up attempts to promote a US–Canadian reciprocity treaty. Of course, long-standing political motives of pan-Americanism underlay the attempt, and it cannot be assumed that a belief in serious damage to US exporters was a significant component. Furthermore, the USA did not retaliate either against Britain or against Canada. Indeed, it might well have found it difficult to justify such retaliation when it imposed what was in effect its 'maximum' tariff against all except those with whom it had concluded a specific commercial treaty outside the orbit of the MFN clause.[17]

Unilateral preference was one thing. Chamberlainite Tariff Reform, however, involved British admission of dominion goods at preferential rates. Here, manufactures were of negligible importance. More significant was the proposed preference on wheat. Chamberlain's original Glasgow proposal was for free admission of colonial wheat, compared with a duty equivalent to about 7 per cent *ad valorem* on foreign wheat (two shillings per quarter). But modifications by the Tariff Commission's Agricultural Committee, endorsed by Chamberlain, introduced a one shilling duty on colonial supplies. The resulting preference would therefore have been 3.5 per cent of c.i.f. (cost, insurance and freight) import price. While this sounds small, it is to be remembered that the late-nineteenth-century international wheat market is often cited as approximating to conditions of perfect competition. Furthermore, there were some in the Tariff Reform League who were unhappy with the Commission's scheme and clung to free admission of colonial wheat – clearly, the 7 per cent differential would have been more significant. While we need to remember that 'constitutional' considerations might have ranked alongside pragmatic ones, our suspicion that pragmatic considerations were paramount in the eyes of foreign negotiators before 1914 suggests that the USA, more interested in wheat exports to Britain than the European powers, would have been more likely to be antagonized by colonial preference than would the rising manufacturing powers of western Europe. Apart possibly from wheat, it is not clear that the scale of protection envisaged by prewar Tariff Reformers was large enough to provoke a major trade war, except in the event of Britain resorting to the widespread implementation of a high 'fighting' tariff in any attempt to secure wholesale reductions in the tariffs of its trading partners.

So far, it has been argued that a Chamberlainite 'general tariff' would probably not have provoked large-scale retaliation as long as its administrators had not been too ruthless in insisting that trading partners made unrealistic tariff reductions in order to gain access to it. Much the same can probably be said of Balfourite retaliation. The policies were elastic and capable of adjustment to avoid major tariff wars. On a practical level, furthermore, Chamberlainite imperial preference should not have unduly antagonized European industrial powers. However, there was still the 'constitutional' position, the matter of principle, and the question of the US response to imperial preference on wheat and animal products, apart from the possibility that Britain's departure from free trade would have provoked precipitate and even irrational reactions. Thus, there was clearly some threat to Britain's existing enjoyment of MFN treatment in the markets of the world. How did contemporaries evaluate this threat?

Free-traders did not deny that European moves towards protectionism disadvantaged Britain, but were unshakeable in their conviction that 'onesided Free Trade' remained Britian's best policy. They put great faith in the MFN clause.[18] It was assumed that any attempt at retaliation or preference by Britain would bring into jeopardy its access to MFN treatment from foreign countries.[19] A.M.S. Methuen, publisher and later Liberal MP for Godalming, used appropriately colourful language:

But – and mark this – if we, through Retaliation or Preference, make an exceptional arrangement with a Power which the other powers do not enjoy, we are removed forthwith from all the privileges of the 'most-favoured-nation'. Who shall say how many millions of pounds you will sink into the fathomless abyss, how many traders you will ruin, if in your reckless haste you expose us to the heavy hand of the foreign retaliator?[20]

J.M. Robertson, Liberal MP and prolific free-trade publicist, saw MFN footing as an 'immense advantage'. To sacrifice it, 'on the alleged chance of a gain from "retaliation", which has never been seen to accrue in human experience, would be the extremity of national folly.'[21]

What free-traders were slower to recognize is that the presence of MFN arrangements allowed big players to defect, by preventing exclusion. As Conybeare points out,

Although free trade maximizes world income, some countries may do better by utilizing the MFN clause to free-ride on the rest, raising their own tariffs, while receiving the benefits of the tariff reductions of other countries via the MFN norm. The United States attempted this strategy during the 1920s.[22]

One might add that there are signs that this was also US practice in the period 1880–1914, especially before the Payne–Aldrich Tariff of 1909. The USA persisted in signing bilateral commercial treaties which it then refused to generalize through MFN arrangements. Apart from such treaties, the USA in effect had a single tariff structure. Since the treaties were mostly with South American states whose role in the system was as suppliers of primaries,[23] it could be argued that, for most of the period before 1914, the USA had a non-discriminating tariff as regards trade between manufacturing nations (hence extending Conybeare's point about 'free-riding' to the prewar period). Arguably, however, even among industrial exporters Britain was particularly disadvantaged by US policy. US tariffs on manufactures were high, and Germany, Austria-Hungary, France, Portugal, and Italy were all included in US reciprocity treaties at various dates.[24] Furthermore, the Latin American treaties were connected with a US design to reduce British influence in Latin America, an area whose 'neutral market' status gave it particular strategic importance for British traders.

Britain had some forty-four MFN treaties around 1900.[25] Free-traders invoked the general principle of the MFN arrangement, arguing that thereby British industry was insulated from the worst effects of increasing foreign protectionism. To counter the free-trade case would involve empirical investigation of whether the principle was achieved in practice. Only one such attempt was made during the Edwardian years, again by Chamberlain's

Tariff Commission, which provided the only detailed empirical information on foreign tariff structures and MFN arrangements available in the campaign.[26]

Commission member Sir Charles Follett, recently retired from the Customs and Excise,[27] had two broad criticisms of MFN arrangements. The first (he put it second) was that arising from the US interpretation of the MFN treaty, which allowed reciprocity treaties to be concluded outside its orbit.[28] Such evasion, which we might style 'evasion by interpretation', was known to contemporaries, though usually overlooked by polemicists in the fiscal controversy. According to the standard work on American treaties, the USA was the only important trading nation to adopt it, though at the turn of the century Japan showed signs of favouring the American approach.[29]

Follett's second method of evasion he termed 'evasion by classification', whereby splitting a product into (often artificially) different sub-groups, and subjecting each to very different rates of duty, could be used as a method of penalizing or favouring selected countries, or could have the same result without design. The German–Swiss Treaty, Follett instanced, had resulted in Swiss duties on German earthenware being half those on British.[30]

Though most polemical free-traders paid little attention to this accusation, Alfred Marshall did not:

> It is, of course, true that the existence of a most-favoured-nation clause sometimes deters an astute German or other diplomatist from pressing for specially low duties on goods in the production of which England happens to have some advantage over his country, and that in that case England gets no benefit from the efforts of that particular diplomatist. But she is not dependent on any one such diplomatist. Nearly everyone who is trying to get any taxes on imports lowered on behalf of his own country is likely to be working for England's good under this clause, *unless he gives himself a great deal of trouble to avoid doing it.* The few cases in which he takes the trouble are quoted over and over again in the English controversial literature; while little is heard of the far more numerous cases in which England's masterly policy of quiescence is rewarded by her reaping the fruits of other people's excitements, quarrels, and worries. *The clause, in fact, gives England nearly all she could obtain by interminable tariff wars, and at no cost.*[31]

We might pause to consider what Marshall meant by this last sentence: apparently, persistence with 'interminable tariff wars' could have yielded Britain small advantages that under the operation of the existing MFN system were denied to it, but these would have to be set against the short-term disruptions of tariff war. Yet there is no elaboration of this argument, and we could, perhaps, accuse him of employing the same rhetorical and polemical devices as did the 'controversial' literature which he so despised.

The Tariff Commission found it difficult to ascertain British business opinion on the operation of the MFN clause.[32] In the 'tariff committees' of the chambers of commerce, though there was an intense hostility towards foreign tariffs, specific comment on MFN arrangments was sparse. In part this may be because the merchant members of the chambers favoured free trade, whereas the manufacturing members knew little of the actual operation of the clause. In Harold Cox's volume on British industry under free trade, none of the nineteen business authorities even mentioned MFN treatment.[33] The Commission's inquiry into cotton was nearly as unilluminating. There were only four complaints about MFN arrangements printed in the *Report on the Cotton Industry*,[34] and though the Commission received others,[35] Secretary W.A.S. Hewins had to admit that 'we have not got very much about the most favoured Nation clause.'[36]

The Commission treated the MFN issue gingerly; only in 1910 did it make a determined attempt at investigation. In September Hewins drafted a list of seven questions to be sent to leading manufacturers, a list which recognized the complexity of the issue by omitting its potentially confusing imperial aspects.[37] The questionnaire did not elicit a large response, but, given the almost entire absence of other sources, it does something to remove the paucity of information available to historians, and the replies were printed in a memorandum published in November. Twenty-one out of twenty-four firms considered that direct negotiations with foreign countries would be preferable to the existing system of indirect 'bargainings in which British representatives have no part'. Only nine out of forty-one firms considered that MFN arrangements resulted in British exporters receiving parity of treatment with their rivals. Ten out of twelve thought foreign goods were charged at lower rates of duty than the British goods with which they competed.[38] The respondents to the questionnaire were of course self-selecting, but their responses do at least give some empirical ground for the belief that there was dissatisfaction among British businessmen. Furthermore, the Commission laid emphasis on the increased scope for 'evasion by classification' as European tariffs had become more complex since 1880.[39]

The most important element of the memorandum of 1910 was an attempt to assess the quantitative importance of MFN treaties to British trade. The Commission's statistical staff went to considerable trouble scrutinizing the trade returns of the various countries with which Britain had MFN treaties, in conjunction with the tariff schedules relevant to those treaties.[40]

Taking the six countries which absorbed the great bulk of Britain's exports to countries employing a two-tier tariff – France, Germany, the USA, Austria-Hungary, Italy, and Japan – the Commission demonstrated that the MFN clause resulted in a reduction of tariffs for only 18.9 per cent (by value) of British exports.[41] Since British exports contained a significant proportion of (non-taxed) raw materials, and also some goods which attracted the same, undifferentiated rate under both general and conventional tariff schedules, some £121 million out of total exports to these countries of £149.5 million were unaffected by MFN treaties. Only £28 million of British exports to these nations came within the orbit of such treaties.

Some 70.5 per cent (£66.1 million out of £93.7 million) of British dutiable exports to the six countries paid the highest rate of duty. The Commission's complaint was that many of these goods had to compete in the importing market with similar (though not identical) goods imported from rivals at a *lower* rate of duty. This was because the third country's exports had benefited from direct negotiations and the reduction so obtained was then incorporated into the importing country's conventional tariff. Though this conventional rate was then generalized through the MFN treaty, the good Britain actually exported was unaffected, since Britain had not been involved in the direct negotiations as to *precisely* which goods were to be reduced from the general to the conventional rate. Essentially, the UK's problem was that the MFN treaty secured to it only the concessions on the precise types of good in which *other* people traded.

An attempt was made to show more precisely the magnitude of such discrimination, by a highly detailed examination of German figures (see Table 17.1). Cotton yarns and manufactures were singled out for special attention. Only 18 per cent of British exports to Germany qualified for the conventional tariff, whereas 60 per cent of Switzerland's did so. Whereas £1.34 million of Britain's total cotton exports to Germany of £1.64 million were in categories where no treaty provision had been made, only £218,000

Table 17.1 Treatment of German imports by group (% by value), 1909

	Conventional rate = General rate	Conventional rate = General but binding rate	No treaty rates
Total imports			
From UK	15	48	37
France	27	38	35
Austria-Hungary	50	41	9
Switzerland	41	47	12
Manufactured imports			
From UK	28	29	43
France	28	34	39
Austria-Hungary	38	44	18
Switzerland	51	36	13

Source: "Most Favoured Nation Arrangement and British Trade", *Tariff Commission Memorandum* 43, 28 November 1910, pp. 10, 12.

out of the Swiss total of £531,000 were treated similarly. The Commission also found similar features in the structure of Austro-Hungarian imports.[42]

The conceptual point is well-taken. Even Saul, otherwise a moderate supporter of the MFN system, agrees that 'when two countries framed a tariff agreement among themselves . . . the concessions granted often did not have the same value for Britain even if she enjoyed most-favoured-nation rights with both.'[43] What is harder to gauge is the extent to which this occurred on a global scale. Germany's close relations with central European neighbours were indeed something of a problem for Britain, as was later to be demonstrated in the alarms caused by the rumours of a *Mitteleuropa* alliance in 1915–16.[44] But in one sense Britain was less interested in Austro-Hungarian or Swiss competition in the German market than it was in the treatment of goods from the rising industrial nations – France, Belgium, Italy, the USA, and shortly Japan. The only one of these rivals whose position relative to Britain in the German market can be plotted is France, and it can be seen from Table 17.1 that those positions were similar, except for the inversion of the proportions entering under the first two columns of that table, a difference whose significance is neither defined nor explained in the memorandum. Of the US position in the German market, for instance, we are left uninformed. In general, German tariffs, especially compared with US tariffs, were relatively modest, and considerable revisions in the German Customs Law of 1902, coming into effect in 1906, were on the surface quite favourable to British interests. A conventional tariff below the higher general tariff, resulting from Germany's trade negotiations with central European countries, was generalized through Germany's twenty-eight formal MFN treaties. Indeed, for Dietzel, a main purpose of the revision of 1902 was to allow retaliation against the high tariffs of Russia and the USA.[45] Even the Tariff Commission had to admit that 'in practice the [German] conventional tariff is extended to almost every other country, and the general tariff becomes a penalty tariff.'[46] All this was in sharp contrast to the McKinley and Dingley tariffs, and the US interpretation of the MFN clause. Nevertheless, the Tariff Commission study apart, there is still a paucity of information about how precisely, in a tariff structure which on the surface looked relatively benign, the particular design of the German classification reacted specifically upon imports from Britain.

The Commission more or less admitted that the six mentioned countries – France, Germany, the USA, Austria-Hungary, Italy, and Japan – constituted the bulk of the problem posed by the two-tier tariff system.[47] We can see differences in the way these countries treated Britain. France and Japan seem to have treated imports from Britain fairly evenly, and even Austria-Hungary was less harsh than Germany. The ratio of imports of British goods which enjoyed concessionary rates to imports of those which did not[48] was 1.34 : 1 for France; 1.14 : 1 for Japan; 0.96 : 1 for Austria-Hungary; 0.40 : 1 for Italy; and 0.32 : 1 for Germany. In this relative sense, it is also noteworthy that there was strong opposition in France to any kind of commercial treaties.[49] In any case, the French 'maximum' and 'minimum' tariff system, adopted in 1892, tended to give smaller concessions to all countries than the difference between the earlier 'general' and 'conventional' tariff structure that it replaced. Accordingly, 'the "bargaining power" and threats of foreign countries have had very little effect upon the French tariff. . . . In no case were the concessions made by the French considerable.'[50]

This nevertheless tends to minimize the potential threat of dual-tariff systems. A single general tariff was often difficult to maintain intact. Norway found it necessary to change to the 'maximum' and 'minimum' system. It was Taussig's view that the US reciprocity treaties 'had never been of any substantial importance', and that their repeal in the 1909 Tariff Act was 'of little significance except as indicative of the disappearance of any intention to deal with tariff questions in this way.'[51] But US adoption of the 'maximum' and 'minimum' system in the Payne–Aldrich Tariff of 1909 suggests that his epitaph on the reciprocity sentiment was premature. Belgium found it necessary to conclude commercial treaties and extend MFN treatment, even under what apart from the colonial tariff approximated to a single tariff system. Even in the Netherlands, essentially a free-trade country with a 5 per cent revenue tariff on manufactures, the government supported a graduated protective tariff, though it was thwarted by a referendum in 1913.[52] The maintenance of the single tariff in its pure form was, at the least, unstable. Indeed, the Commission's examination of the two-tier system was scarcely complete – to the six countries which were held up in the 1910 memorandum as the major examples, there are to be added Norway, Switzerland, Spain, Russia, Greece, Persia, Turkey, and Brazil.[53]

Lord Lansdowne, Unionist Foreign Secretary between 1900 and 1905, thought the Tariff Commission's memorandum on MFN treaties 'most important', while *The Times* enthused over it.[54] When Unionist leader Arthur Balfour spoke at the Albert Hall in May 1911 he was strongly influenced by the Commission's argument.[55] The free-traders were not to be convinced. As Enever Todd put it, the argument that direct bargaining was more powerful than indirect, 'attractive as it sounds, remains nevertheless a theory.'[56]

As we have noted, Saul accepts that a certain amount of 'evasion by classification' took place. He cites the 'famous clause 103 of the German tariff of 1902 which placed a low duty on "imports of large dappled mountain cattle reared at a spot at least 300 metres above sea-level and which have at least a month's grazing at a spot at least 800 metres above sea-level".' However, mirroring Marshall more or less precisely, he adds that 'other examples are very hard to find.'[57]

Such a conclusion may be unsafe. The example cited was an obvious and deliberate discrimination, such a parody of 'evasion by classification' that it is scarcely surprising that similarly obvious examples were not widespread – tariff war would have been even more endemic to continental Europe than it was! The labyrinthine complexities of product listings in the US tariff of 1913, for instance, suggest that cases would be hard to spot. Vandegrift's *Handbook* lists 600–700 separate cotton products at seventeen different rates of duty, from zero to 60 per cent.[58] The historian simply cannot use the British official trade returns to work out what duties British cotton exports to the USA attracted, since the British product classification does not tally with that in the US tariff. Furthermore, the likelihood of discrimination without deliberacy, but still with consistent bias, would be higher.

Our conclusion must be that, the Tariff Commission exercise apart, there is precious little evidence available on which to assess the real value of the MFN clause to Britain in the decades before 1914. Saul's approach, which rests on sources which are mostly British government publications, stands in danger of missing all but the *obvious* cases in a situation where there was arguably a motive, for foreign negotiators, in striking deals which were *not obvious*. At the same time, the Tariff Commission study does not appear to provide sufficient information about its methods or its sources to allow us to attempt to replicate its findings. There is a need for further study at the level of archive sources of the actual tariff negotiations of different countries.

Clearly, retaliatory tariff warfare consequent on the introduction of Tariff Reform would have been a possibility. But the degree of damage to Britain depends heavily on an assessment of the value of the MFN system to British exporters, an assessment which cannot be made safely given the present level of historical research. If free-traders were correct that MFN arrangements conferred large benefits, Tariff Reform stood in danger of exposing large numbers of British exports, which had hitherto had access to foreign markets under 'conventional' tariff rates, to the corresponding 'maximum' tariff rates. If, on the other hand, the Tariff Commission study is to be believed, it follows that, even with its MFN treaties, Britain was already trading nearer to the 'maximum' tariff levels of countries with two-tier tariffs, and further from the 'conventional' levels, than scholars have generally thought the case, and had much less to lose.

This final section offers some additional thoughts on where the balance of advantage in such a retaliationist struggle would have lain. Saul regards Britain as having been particularly ill-placed, and he mobilizes Marshall in his support:

> Marshall pointed out how vulnerable Britain was to retaliation on the part of her neighbours: 'England is not in a strong position for reprisals against hostile tariffs, because there are no important exports of hers, which other countries need so urgently as to be willing to take them from her at a considerably increased cost; and because none of her rivals would permanently suffer serious injury

through the partial exclusion of any products of theirs with which England can afford to dispense.'[59]

Certainly, Marshall shared the orthodox free-trade distaste of tariffs as negotiating weapons. Nevertheless, elsewhere in the Marshall's memorandum there seems to be a fairly clear indication that he did not regard the welfare gains from trade in manufactures with Britain's European neighbours as substantial. Even if *all* industrial countries subjected British manufactures to high import duties, the damage would be small. Britain would be

> unable to market abroad any great quantity of those refined machines and other implements, for which there is little demand except in highly advanced countries; and, therefore, she would be a little restricted in the economies of production on a large scale in this important group of manufactures. But her own market would afford scope in almost every branch of such work for several establishments of the largest size which can advantageously be controlled by single management; and therefore her loss under this head, though considerable, would not be very great. She would give more attention to the products suitable for sparsely peopled countries; and this would help her in obtaining such crude mineral and agricultural products as she needed.[60]

Marshall may here have been underestimating the speed at which 'intra-industry' trade between advanced industrial nations[61] or import-substitution in less industrialized countries[62] would develop, but he evidently considered that the major gains from trade were to be found in the different factor endowments of manufacturing and primary-producing economies. This suggests that his belief in the harmful potential of Chamberlainite policy hung mainly on the dangers of agricultural protection and on the capacity of a British tariff to damage British exports to less developed countries.[63] True, there seems a strong similarity here between Marshall's ideas and Saul's analysis of tariff policy in the light of the multilateral system of settlements, but Marshall's point is in fact different from Saul's. Saul is saying that Britain was vulnerable to European retaliation, whereas Marshall thought the effect would be relatively small and largely confined to short-term dislocation effects. Marshall's real point, that a British tariff would be ineffective in reducing European tariffs, was in fact shared by protectionist British industrialists.

Under this Marshallian regime, the greatest danger would have lain in retaliation from the 'sparsely peopled countries'. Since Marshall must have realized that British duties on raw materials were unlikely, and that British duties on manufactures would not threaten such countries, the implication is that they would have been provoked by the duty on wheat and (where appropriate) other foodstuffs. Would primary producers really have retaliated against British manufactures (and therefore in favour of German or French manufactures) when German and French duties on wheat were so much higher than those proposed by Chamberlain? This seems unlikely.

There was also, however, the possibility of foreign reaction on 'constitutional' grounds to imperial preference on wheat, which perhaps prompts consideration of the US case in more detail. The view that Britain would be damaged more by US retaliation than by retaliation by the industrial powers of Europe rests on the assumption that the USA was itself not vulnerable through its large export of wheat to the UK. But the market possibilities for US exporters were largely confined to the industrial economies of north-west Europe. With the exception of Britain, these were already protected by tariffs considerably higher than the proposed British duty on wheat. Of course, Germany (more than France) still imported considerable amounts of US wheat, and some switching would have been possible here. In theory, the effect of a British tariff in increasing wheat imports into Germany and displacing rye would require the incorporation of the elasticity of substitution between wheat and rye into the analysis, in itself a difficult and uncertain historical exercise. But the real world outcome would have been even more complex, in view of two institutional factors. First, German rye production was aided by a concealed export subsidy whereby the exporter of rye was granted an import certificate allowing importation of a specified amount of wheat free of duty. Such certificates were tradable (and must have traded at a price between zero and the prevailing duty on the equivalent amount of wheat), but their average market price in the Edwardian period is unknown. Second, increased imports of wheat into Germany would have most probably provoked pressure for a raising of the German tariff. While some switching would have taken place, it seems distinctly likely that US exporters would have taken the view that it was better to tolerate the lower tariffs of the British market, and that there would have been attempts to disguise the origin of US produce by passing it through Canada. Reflecting afterwards upon his Boer War Corn Registration Duty, Hicks Beach admitted that the duty had caused reductions in US railway rates so that the full cost of the tariff was not passed to the British consumer.[64] Indeed, scholars point to the high foreign elasticity of demand for American grain. According to Williamson, in the world wheat market of the 1860s and 1870s the USA was still a small country, a price taker rather than a price maker.[65] Rothstein's classic article argues that 'by the mid-1880s there was almost universal acknowledgement of the crucial rôle of the British market in fixing prices.'[66]

This raises explicitly the 'optimum tariff', the ability of a country to use a tariff to affect its terms of trade.[67] In McCloskey's words: 'By analogy with the optimal behavior of a monopolist, a nation whose purchases and sales abroad have a discernible effect on world prices is well advised to restrict its purchases and sales to some degree.'[68] Though it is difficult to discern the elasticity conditions first laid out by Johnson from historical data, it is accepted that GNP stands as a proxy for them. Large economies tend to possess the elasticity characteristics which predict gains from retaliation, while small countries tend to suffer those which foretell losses.[69]

Contrary to the opinions of most contemporary classical economists, some work on the effects of the repeal of the Corn Laws has stressed the importance of recognizing that Britain was a large country, whose own tariff policy had the power to influence its terms of trade.[70] McCloskey's well-known 'optimum tariff' calculation yielded the result that a small (but not 'trivial') mid-Victorian welfare loss of about 4 per cent of national income was incurred by the move to free trade in the years after 1846, and Douglas Irwin has produced similar results.[71] After 1880, however, industrialization abroad reduced Britain's scope for benefiting from its relative size: 'In the 1930s Britain herself finally did abandon free trade, but by then, alas, the dominant position that would have enabled her over the preceding century to exploit the rest of the world was gone.'[72] Indeed, a British retaliatory tariff would probably have been more effective in the 1880s, the decade of Fair Trade, than in the 1900s. Nevertheless, before 1914 Britain remained a large international player, both by virtue of its GNP ranking and by virtue of its being by far the world's largest market for imports of raw materials and of manufactures. According to German official figures, in 1913 the value of British imports was 15,704.5 million *Reichsmarks*. The corresponding figure for the USA was 7,523.3 million; for France 6,521.3 million; and for Russia 2,967.9 million.[73] Conybeare has no doubt about the inclusion of Britain as a large player. Less expected, perhaps, is that he excludes the United States.[74]

Those who object that McCloskey's demonstration of the smallness of the income loss from adopting free trade in the mid-Victorian period suggests that the later income gain from a Chamberlainite 'optimal tariff' would be equally small, or smaller, might be correct – though it should be remembered that the 'optimal tariff' is a static concept measuring static benefits from changes in the terms of trade, and these might remain and be compounded over time as long as other conditions remained unchanged. But the point at issue here is that, contrary to a common and enduring view, Britain was not under some unique disadvantage relative to other industrial nations in its ability to impose tariffs. Retrospectively supported by Saul, contemporary free-traders used the fear of retaliation to dissuade the British public from a policy which, its advocates would have claimed, had dynamic benefits. Those dynamic benefits might have been illusory. But, as a real objection to the attempt to realize them, the threat of retaliation was probably highly exaggerated.

Notes

1 In contrast to traditional belief, Forrest Capie has questioned whether the late-nineteenth-century rise in nominal tariff levels was fully reflected in the real incidence of protection, stressing that this was also a period in which import duty revenues fell as a proportion of total imports, and the ratio of total imports to total output (a measure of 'openness') increased. Three case-studies measuring 'effective protection' – Hawke for the USA, Toniolo for Italy, and Webb for Germany – suggest a similar result. See F.H. Capie, *Tariffs and Growth: Some Insights from the World Economy, 1850–1940* (Manchester, 1994), ch. 5.

2 A.J. Balfour, *Economic Notes on Insular Free Trade* (London, 1903), p. 31.

3 H. Cox, *Mr. Balfour's Pamphlet: A Reply* (London, 1903), pp. 4–5.

4 H. Dietzel, *Retaliatory Duties* (trans. D.W. Simon and W.O. Brigstocke, London, 1906), pp. 11, 19–20. See also Burrell, in *Westminster Review*, 1904, p. 165.

5 Hicks Beach to Balfour, 11 October 1903; quoted in Lady Victoria Hicks Beach, *Life of Sir Michael Hicks Beach* (London, 1932), II, 198–9.

6 It is for this reason that I am reluctant to accord the same significance to the differences between supporters of 'retaliation' and 'protection' in the Tariff Reform campaign as do some other writers. If, for instance, a 'retaliationist' would not have been satisfied until foreign tariffs were reduced to zero, he would in effect have supported a standing British tariff. Cf. F. Trentman, 'The Transformation of Fiscal Reform: Reciprocity, Modernization, and the Fiscal Debate within the Business Community in Early Twentieth-Century Britain', *Historical Journal*, 39, 1996.

7 A fifty-nine-strong unofficial body of important businessmen set up early in 1904, and guided by the central academic thinker of the movement, W.A.S. Hewins. For the Commission and its origins, see A. Marrison, *British Business and Protection, 1903–1932* (Oxford, 1996), chs 1–2, 4–7.

8 Usually, the maximum–minimum system involved the drafting of a high maximum tariff and a lower, but fixed, minimum tariff for each commodity, whereas the more widespread general–conventional system involved negotiated reductions in the higher general rate being extended to third parties through the MFN clause. See T.E. Gregory, *Tariffs: A Study in Method*, (London, 1921), pp. 69–71, 77–79; J.A.C. Conybeare, *Trade Wars: The Theory and Practice of International Commercial Rivalry* (New York, 1987).

9 *Report of the Tariff Commission*, vol. I, *The Iron and Steel Trades* (London, 1904).

10 Tariff Commission Minutes (Verbatim Typescript), 28 June 1904, pp. 3–4; 2/1/8, Tariff Commission Papers (hereinafter TCP).

11 'The movement away from free trade proposed by the Tariff Reformers was probably too small to change either the pattern or the volume of world commerce very much'; P.J. Cain and A.G. Hopkins, *British Imperialism: Innovation and Expansion, 1688–1914* (London, 1993), p. 218.

12 Chamberlain at Preston, 11 January 1905; in C.W. Boyd (ed.) *Mr. Chamberlain's Speeches* (London, 1914), II, p. 293. Even here, Chamberlain's allusion was rather general.

13 Textile Committee Minutes, 15 December 1904, p. 54, 2/3/1, TCP; Textile Committee Minutes, 18 May 1905, p. 39, 2/3/2, TCP.

14 A.C. Pigou, *The Riddle of the Tariff* (London, 1903), p. 57.

15 Quoted in A.C. Pigou, *Protective and Preferential Import Duties* (London, 1906), p. 109 (my emphasis).

16 Gregory, *Tariffs: A Study in Method*, pp. 279–84.

17 See pp. 229–30.

18 Asquith at Cinderford, 8 October 1903; reprinted in *Speeches by the Rt. Hon. H.H.*

Asquith, 1892–1908 (London, 1908), p. 173. See also E. Enever Todd, *The Case Against Tariff Reform* (London, 1911), p. 35.

19 Pigou, *Protective and Preferential Import Duties*, p. 109.

20 A.M.S. Methuen, *England's Ruin, Discussed in Sixteen Letters to the Right Honourable Joseph Chamberlain, M.P.* (London, 1905), pp. 104–5.

21 J.M. Robertson, *Trade and Tariffs* (London, 1908), p. 221.

22 J.A.C. Conybeare, *Trade Wars*, p. 58.

23 See, e.g., *Textile Recorder*, 15 April 1893, p. 335.

24 J.L. Laughlin and H.P. Willis, *Reciprocity* (New York, 1903), Appendix II, pp. 472–539, gives a complete list of such treaties up to 1903.

25 'Memorandum on the New Commercial Treaties and the New German Tariff', *Tariff Commission Memorandum*, 23, 8 April 1905, p. 1.

26 Tariff Commission Minutes (Printed), 3–4 February 1904; 2/1/5, TCP.

27 Solicitor to HM Customs and Excise, 1878–1903. See Follett to Hewins, 22 October 1904; 6/1/8, TCP.

28 Follett, 'The Most Favoured Nation Clause', p. 10 (Follett's emphasis).

29 Laughlin and Willis, *Reciprocity*, pp. 12–15.

30 Follett, 'The Most Favoured Nation Clause', pp. 8–9, 11; 22 October (1904), 6/1/8, TCP.

31 A. Marshall, 'Memorandum on the Fiscal Policy of International Trade (1903)', reprinted in J.M. Keynes (ed.) *Official Papers of Alfred Marshall* (London, 1926), p. 411 (my emphasis).

32 L. Oppenheimer to Hewins, 30 November 1906; 50/27–44, Hewins Papers.

33 H. Cox (ed.) *British Industries Under Free Trade* (London, 1903).

34 *Report of the Tariff Commission*, vol. II, pt. 1, *The Cotton Industry* (London, 1905), paras 2276–7.

35 Hewins to Follett, 8 November 1904; 6/1/8, TCP.

36 Textile Committee Minutes, 30 May 1905, p. 44; 2/3/3, TCP.

37 Hurd to Hewins, 7 September 1910; Hewins to Hurd, 8 and 9 September 1910; 6/1/26, TCP.

38 'Most Favoured Nation Arrangements and British Trade', *Tariff Commission Memorandum*, 43, 28 November 1910, pp. 17–26.

39 Ibid., p. 5.

40 Small inconsistencies exist in their figures, probably due to the use of the import statistics of the foreign countries, rather than the export statistics of the UK, but they are minor. For the general problem, see Y. Don, 'Comparability of International Trade Statistics: Great Britain and Austria-Hungary before World War I', *Economic History Review*, 2nd series 21, 1968, pp. 78–92.

41 Thirty-seven per cent of UK exports to these countries were in categories which were zero-rated. Therefore, British exports which were subject to no duty, or to less than the highest duty in a two-tier tariff, were about 55–56 per cent of the total.

42 'Most Favoured Nation Arrangements and British Trade', pp. 12, 14.

43 S.B. Saul, *Studies in British Overseas Trade, 1870–1914* (Liverpool, 1960), pp. 136–7.

44 Marrison, *British Business and Protection,* ch. 8.

45 Dietzel, *Retaliatory Duties*, pp. 11–12.

46 'Memorandum on the New Commercial Treaties and the New German Tariff', p. 1.

47 'Most Favoured Nation Arrangements and British Trade', p. 6.

48 It should be remembered that this latter figure includes goods for which there were no concessionary rates to *any* country.

49 P. Ashley, *Modern Tariff History* (London, 1904), pp. 332–7, 339–40, 346–8.

50 H.O. Meredith, *Protection in France* (London, 1904), pp. 15, 21–2, 25, 65–6.

51 F.W. Taussig, *Tariff History of the United States* (New York, 5th edn, 1910), p. 407.

52 A. Heringa, *Freetrade and Protectionism in Holland* (London, 1914), pp. 144–6.

53 'The Tariff Systems of Europe and America', *Tariff Commission Memorandum* , 25, 22 July 1905, p. 1; Taussig, *Tariff History*, pp. 403–4; 'Memorandum on the New German Commercial Treaties and the New German Tariff', *passim.*

54 Lansdowne to Hewins, 31 October and 2 November, 1911; Hewins Papers. Also *The Times*, 30 October 1910.

55 Reported in *The Times*, 24 May 1911.

56 Todd, *The Case Against Tariff Reform*, pp. 118–19.

57 Saul, *Studies in British Overseas Trade*, pp. 136–7.

58 F.B. Vandegrift and Co., *Handbook of the United States Tariff, containing the Tariff Act of 1913* (New York, 1913), pp. 450–64.

59 Saul, *Studies in British Overseas Trade*, p. 135, quoting Marshall's 'Memorandum', p. 408.

60 Marshall, 'Memorandum', p. 401.

61 H.G. Grubel and P.J. Lloyd, *Intra-Industry Trade: The Theory and Measurement of International Trade in Differentiated Products* (London, 1975).

62 'Memorandum on the Fiscal Policy of International Trade (1903)', p. 402.

63 Here we exclude Marshall's more general opposition to the introduction of tariffs, made in many standard forms: including the need to obtain raw materials and semi-manufactures at lowest costs, the stimulus to efficiency by remaining open to 'American inventive genius and . . . German systematic thought and scientific training', and the inequity of a policy which would press hardest upon the poor. See ibid., pp. 408–9.

64 Hicks Beach at Manchester, 5 November 1903; reported in *Morning Post*, 6 November 1903, p. 7.

65 J.G. Williamson, 'Greasing the Wheels of Sputtering Export Engines: Midwestern Grains and American Growth', *Explorations in Economic History*, 17, 1980, pp. 189–217.

66 M. Rothstein, 'America in the International Rivalry for the British Wheat Market, 1860–1914', *Mississippi Valley Historical Review*, 47, 1960, p. 406.

67 H.G. Johnson, 'Optimum Tariffs and Retaliation', *Review of Economic Studies*, 21, 1954, pp. 142–53; reprinted in *International Trade and Economic Growth* (London, 1967), pp. 31–61.

68 D.N. McCloskey, 'Magnanimous Albion: Free Trade and British National Income, 1841–1881', in *Enterprise and Trade in Victorian Britain* (London, 1981), p. 168.

69 Ibid. The most important qualification to using size as a proxy for elasticities is where the geographical and commodity composition of a country's exports is concentrated, giving the importer(s) some degree of monopsony power. See Conybeare, *Trade Wars*.

70 J.G. Williamson, 'The Impact of the Corn Laws Just Prior to Repeal', *Explorations in Economic History*, 27, 1990, pp. 123–56. See also Irwin, Chapter 10 this volume.

71 McCloskey, 'Magnanimous Albion', pp. 169–70. Irwin's estimate of the British loss is slightly lower. See his 'Welfare Effects of British Free Trade: Debate and Evidence from the 1840s', *Journal of Political Economy*, 96, 1988, pp. 1142–64.

72 McCloskey, 'Magnanimous Albion', p. 169.

73 See *Statistik des Deutschen Reichs*, vol. 339, 318–20.

74 Conybeare argues that trade strategies and negotiations between large countries are best characterized by a 'Prisoners' Dilemma' game structure, and that the likely outcome is one of conciliation: '[in the late nineteenth century] there were only three large-power Prisoners' Dilemmas that could have occurred – between Germany, Britain, and France. The United States was not yet a major trading nation, supplied only raw materials to Europe, and did not possess the legal institutions that would permit the executive to engage in tariff bargaining.' See Conybeare, *Trade Wars*, p. 182. David Lake sees Britain as a hegemon, albeit a faltering one, before 1912, though its weakening position resulted in the international economic structure being 'transformed from hegemony to bilateral opportunism'. See D.A. Lake, *Power, Protection, and Free Trade: International Sources of U.S. Commercial Strategy, 1887–1939* (Ithaca, NY, 1988), pp. 119–20, 148, 217–18.

18

COMMENTS ON CAIN AND MARRISON

John Maloney

Hobson was everyday prey to Marshallian orthodoxy, Joan Robinson revealing that 'doing a Hobson' became Cambridge code for losing your logic. He was lucky that his work was not more often rifled for statements for undergraduates to shoot down in the Tripos. What Peter Cain's chapter exposes, however, is not lack of logic but lack of consistency. Hobson was attacking free trade in 1889, arguing that it rested on the (false) premiss of Say's Law. He defended it in 1890, ignoring his previous argument and claiming that protection lowered national income. In 1891 he was attacking it again on the grounds that it involved capital export, hence capital shortage, and hence unemployment. After 1896 or thereabouts, he did become a fairly consistent free-trader, not alone in his brief Chamberlainite wobble in 1903. It was the Empire which replaced free trade as the focus of Hobsonian tergiversation, although so did the relationship *between* imperialism and free trade.

Professor Cain unveils a 'vicious circle' analysis by Hobson that I had not seen before. Underconsumption causes lack of aggregate demand causes search for new markets causes conquest causes military expenditure causes tariffs to pay for it causes high prices leading back to underconsumption. It sounds fine until Hobson says, in *Imperialism* (1902), that free trade promotes imperialism. Put that argument into Hobson's vicious circle and free trade undermines itself. But perhaps that is what he meant.

Given that Hobson started by stating that the case for free trade rested on Say's Law, does this mean that his later conversion (or conversions) to the free-trade cause involve an acceptance of Say's Law? Professor Cain's answer is Yes (Hobson argued that workers undercut by cheap imports would find work elsewhere, and this statement is incompatible with underconsumptionism). But Say's Law merely rules out falls in aggregate demand in a closed economy. It says nothing either way about what happens *after* a fall in aggregate demand in an open one. While it is true that Hobson the underconsumptionist was always relatively subdued after his début with

Mummery in 1889, his espousal of free trade is not obviously the cause (or even the consequence) of this.

Economic historians have yet to agree whether the British Empire made a profit. Even if it did, there are serious gaps in Hobson's version of imperialism. Since it makes sense only as a conspiracy theory, why are the conspirators never identified? If trade did not follow the flag, what was the purpose of the whole enterprise anyway? And the colonies' experience of the difficulty of coming by investment capital hardly squares with the Hobsonian picture of huge surpluses flapping round the world desperately looking for an outlet. None the less we can strike out the theory of imperialism and still be left with a lively, well-informed and, *at any one time*, consistent analysis of the free-trade issue from Hobson.

Much as I enjoyed Andrew Marrison's chapter, I am glad that it was not around in 1903. Almost certainly it would have persuaded political waverers that Chamberlainite tariff reform could have been imposed without serious retaliation – though an extension of the paper, or another chapter, might usefully identify who some of these waverers might have been. Marrison's chapter portrays the free-traders, up to and including Alfred Marshall, making brilliant intellectual capital out of fairly slender resources – even if the gains, as well as the losses, from tariff reform were exaggerated by contemporary opinion. Britain never got it right as far as the imperfect competition arguments for tariffs were concerned, persisting with free trade when its share of world exports was large enough for protection to carry some advantage (4 per cent of GNP according to Deirdre McCloskey – I was astounded to learn that some economic historians actually think this striking figure might be too *low*) and then resorting to protection just as its weight slipped below the point where 'optimal tariff' arguments seriously applied. As Marrison emphasizes, the actual effects of going with Chamberlain (or Balfour) in 1903 remain largely a matter for guesswork, though his chapter challenges J.M. Robertson's belief that MFN footing was in practice 'an immense advantage', quite apart from what one might think of Robertson's remarkable dictum that retaliatory tariffs have *never* worked on any occasion.

If one wants protective duties in the first place, Chamberlain's plans come across as more skilful than he has usually been given credit for. To impose a general tariff carefully set a little lower than your rivals', to back this with a genuinely punitive 'last resort' tariff if they should retaliate, and to then favour the Empire with an especially low tariff, to be justified to the rest of the world as a purely family affair, is surely protectionism at its most intelligent. How intelligent that is must remain a matter of contention. But the level of economic debate on both sides was generally high, and not just from the professional economists. Keynes's praise for Balfour's contribution is well known: writing Balfour's obituary in the *Economic Journal* in 1930, he praised *Economic Notes on Insular Free Trade* as 'one of the most remarkable scientific deliverances ever made by a Prime Minister in office', siding with the book against Marshall's critical marginalia of it in his personal copy. Nor did Bickerdike's optimal tariff argument hold any terrors for (at least some) lay-men – one free-trading backbencher understood it, and its contained threat, so thoroughly that he slapped it down by boldly deeming wheat to be a Giffen good. How we have fallen off.

19

THE SOURCES AND ORIGINS OF BRITAIN'S RETURN TO PROTECTION, 1931–2

Forrest Capie

Between the two world wars Britain reversed a commercial policy that had lasted for almost a century. Britain had been the leading exemplar of the free-trade doctrine, and the question, which is the subject of this chapter, is why the reversal? Seeking the sources and origins of protectionism has proved hazardous. For some it is essentially a matter of politics. For others there are clearer economic explanations. In recent times economic analysis of politics has proved both popular and insightful – the economics of public choice. Others have pointed to the need for the appropriate climate within which pressure groups and interest can express themselves with effect.

The theoretical case for free trade has been established for a long time and is overwhelming. Plato set the case out in *The Republic*, and it has been made on many occasions since with increasing elegance, clarity, and refinement. In *The New Palgrave Dictionary* Ronald Findlay called it 'the deepest and most beautiful result in all economics.'[1] Even the high priest of the new international economics, Paul Krugman, who has on occasion found fault with it, recommends it as the best macroeconomic policy stance: 'It is possible then to believe that comparative advantage is an incomplete model of trade and to believe that free trade is nevertheless the right policy. In fact this is the position taken by most of the new trade theorists themselves.'[2]

If this is the case, and free trade is demonstrably such a good thing, why has there been, and is there still, so much protection? The answer lies in the fact that there are gainers and losers, and the gainers from protection can have disproportionate influence on policy-making. But how does that come about?

There is now a large literature in which political economy models are applied to the political economy of trade. Much of this is North American in origin, and there do seem to be good reasons why the American political system encourages the activities of interest groups. Indeed, the Americans gave us the word 'lobbyist' almost coincidental in time with the origins of Ricardian trade theory. It was a term coined in the early nineteenth century for someone who hung around the Capitol lobby seeking favours from the legislators. Nevertheless, the literature does have wide application around the world. At issue for those models is the question: if free trade is the superior policy, why is international trade not free? Indeed, why are trade policies more or less universally biased against trade? The models also seek to say something of the determinants of the different levels of protection across industries and countries.

The basis of these political-economy models is grounded in the Heckscher–Ohlin model of trade. When trade takes place different factors will gain or lose according to their relative factor endowment; the gaining or losing factor may be capital or labour or land. But the losers from trade will have an incentive to resist – that is to seek protection. In other words there will be a demand for protection; and the government has the power to supply protection. The likelihood is that there will be good grounds for a process of exchange between government and organized interests. Legislators provide protection in exchange for some form of support, either financial or electoral. As a monopoly producer of legislation, the government will face a demand curve that is an expression of the payments it will be offered. However, the protectionist outcome will depend on the relative strength of the competing parties and the price will clearly change according to the type of government in power and the nature of those seeking protection.

It is common to think in terms of producers seeking protection, and consumers being less active. Producers are frequently concentrated geographically or industrially in such a way as to give them coherence, with the ability and financial power to do the kind of lobbying that will be productive. Against that consumers are scattered and unable to provide coherent and effective resistance. But it is important to bear in mind that in this model it is the factors that are gainers or losers. The Heckscher–Ohlin model makes the assumption that factors are perfectly mobile between sectors, and economic interest will differ between factors such as labour and capital. However, if this assumption is invalid and factors are not perfectly mobile then economic interest could be organized along industry rather than factor lines so that, for example, labour and land/capital in agriculture may all combine to seek the same policy.

Well-designed political-economy models must therefore take account of these elements, though even if they do, as we argue below, there are other considerable obstacles to their productive deployment. The models should take account of the demand side in providing a description of the preferences available to policy-makers, and of how these preferences are collected and organized through pressure groups into demands. On the supply side they should show characteristic policy-makers' preferences, and set out the institutional context within which the bargaining and policy-making takes place.

For Britain there have been some specific applications of these models. There was growing discussion of protection in the late nineteenth century and there was some action in the formation of pressure groups such as the Fair Trade League and Tariff Reform League. At the same time it is important to note that protectionism was spreading in many countries.

Irwin has employed a model of the kind described above on British experience at the beginning of the twentieth century. He first analysed the nature of voting patterns in the general election of 1906. This was an election that was fought in big part on the issue of tariff reform. The political-economic climate of the time was one in which there was widespread distrust of protection, the British having been won over, over several generations, to the virtues of free trade. This particular analysis posits that 'pecuniary economic interests are assumed to motivate voters to support the trade policy that would alter relative prices in a way that would raise . . . their income.'[3] The results are not overwhelming and Irwin draws attention to some of the non-economic factors that were at work and could explain the less than perfect results. But the conclusion is that there is support for the hypothesis; and we must judge how much weight to put on the results.

In a separate application Irwin analyses the 1923 election. The electorate was considerably enlarged by that date and a number of factors had been at work to change the climate. Irwin argues that in the 1920s the labour market exhibited considerable rigidity and therefore with such imperfect factor mobility interests would be organized along industry lines. His specific test is that the proportion of voters (by county) who vote for free-trade parties will be a function of the occupational characteristics of the constituency in the county. He finds support for the imperfect factor mobility approach and concludes: 'Even in an economy noted for its class stratification, such class sentiments were not sufficient to overcome strong, underlying economic interests when those interests were at stake.'[4]

Again, he goes to some lengths to draw attention to some of the problems associated with this kind of analysis. But they are perhaps worth dwelling on at slightly greater length.

The main problem with this kind of approach is that economic interest seldom falls conveniently into neat and separable boxes. Take for example agriculture in the late nineteenth century. Irwin treats it as one occupational grouping. But at the very least it should be divided into two. In the south of England, in the main there were grain producers. From the 1870s onwards they were suffering from foreign competition. Understandably, they were protectionist, and they also held political power that was highly disproportionate to their economic significance. The other main sector of agriculture comprised the pastoral farmers, predominantly in the north of the country. They did not suffer such competition. There was a considerable increase in the imports of meat but not of a kind that was a serious competitor for the domestic product. Furthermore, grain was an input for these pastoral farmers and they were therefore likely to be opposed to protection.

There were almost invariably great overlaps in interest, and netting out the dominant one would be difficult. Again, nineteenth-century English landowners are an obvious example of a group (or several groups) that had diverse interests. Land, industrial interests, and urban interest were all inextricably mixed. Marrison has provided a detailed account of the complexity of the overlapping interests among industrialists in the late nineteenth and early twentieth centuries, and of the virtual impossibility of seeing how these could be netted out to arrive at a position on fiscal matters. In addition he reminds us of the likelihood of other issues, not strictly economic, that may have dominated. Finally, he raises the possibility that causality may run from interest to fiscal position or from ideology to fiscal position.[5]

There were undoubtedly interest groups at work in Britain in the first third of the twentieth century. They had their nineteenth-century antecedents in such bodies as the Fiscal Reform League (1870) and the National Fair Trade League (1881), not to mention the agitation emanating from some Chambers of Commerce. Benjamin Brown claimed 'it was only a hop, a step and a jump from these early tariff reformers' to the return to protection in the 1930s.[6] But by what means? It may not be possible to measure the extent of interest or to capture the impact of interest group activity in bringing about a shift in policy, but something can be said of the growth of interest group activity.

It does appear that the political life of the country was increasingly influenced by businessmen though there were of course conflicting pressures at work. There was Bonar Law the ironmaker, Baldwin the steelmaker, through to the Chamberlains the screw manufacturers. According to one account in the interwar years on average one-third of the Conservative party in the Commons were employers or managers.[7] And they were aware of their scope for influencing policy. Arthur Chamberlain, Chairman of Messrs Tubes Ltd and director of several other companies, put the case succinctly and powerfully:

> I could make more money in one evening in the House of Commons by arranging for the taxation of my opponent's necessities and for the maintenance of a free market for myself than I could make by honest industry in a month.[8]

Increasing numbers of manufacturers began to support the Conservative party with the avowed intention of securing tariffs. The Unionist Business Committee was founded in 1915 to protect the interests of business in time of war. *The Economist* remarked: 'the obvious truth is that many of our wealthy manufacturers are using their power, funds, and influence to secure the imposition of tariffs.'[9]

The Federation of British Industry (FBI) was formed in 1916 and was protectionist in outlook. In the same year the British Commonwealth Union (BCU) was established 'to form a solid business group in Parliament', to 'press for the protective tariffs and restrictions of imports discussed at the Paris Economic Conference of 1916 and in the Balfour of Burleigh Committee on postwar commercial policy.'[10] The Safeguarding of Industries Bill followed some intense pressure (in October 1921). It would appear to be a case of protection resulting from business pressure.

A key figure in the British Commonwealth Union was Patrick Hannon, a former vice-president of the Tariff Reform League, later secretary of the Industrial Group in the House of Commons (1921–9), and a vice-president of the FBI. Hannon and several others of the BCU were to carry on their activities under a new banner over the next few years, that of the Empire Industries Association (EIA). Hannon even played a part in founding the Association in 1924 for the purpose of lobbying for a tariff. This association had tremendous support from backbenchers, who showed increasing intransigence from 1924 onwards, resenting the decision to drop tariffs that year but comforting themselves with the assurance that no Conservative government would keep such a pledge.[11] If for no other reason, the Association is important in that it has been given much of the credit for the coming of the tariff. For example, Amery remarked of it that it was destined to 'exercise a decisive influence in Parliament when Free Trade was finally swept away.' On the introduction of the tariff in 1932, he commented that 'most of the spadework in Parliament and in the country had in any case been done by my colleagues of the Empire Industries Association.'[12] It is worth looking at the work of this particular organization as an example of how some interests worked to secure their objectives.

The EIA became a powerful pressure group in the course of 1924–30, cultivating the press and public opinion assiduously. Rothermere and Beaverbrook had already shown sympathy, although Beaverbrook differed on one fundamental point, as he wrote to Amery in 1928: 'I am opposed to a special tariff on Iron and Steel . . . I deplore what appeared to me to be an attempt by Baldwin to make the best of both fiscal worlds.'[13] The Association had also established strategic connections within Parliament. For example, the important Safeguarding Committee of the House of Commons (responsible in the 1920s for any protectionist measures imposed) was under the chairmanship of Colonel Gretton, who was invited to be vice-chairman of the EIA and accepted readily. All manner of techniques were adopted in the advancement of propaganda – from the simple financial reward of those who managed to publish letters in the press under their own names advocating protection (2/6d. for a letter in the provincial press, 5/- for one in London) to the employment of paid individuals to draft the letters.[14] Other techniques were to use industries looking for protection to finance huge advertising campaigns. One such operation was carried out with Bryant & May.[15]

There were also requests initiated by British industry for assistance. A letter from the British Brush Manufacturers asked if the EIA could assist them in pressing their application for a Safeguarding Order. Given that Colonel Gretton was vice-chairman of one organization and chairman of the other it must be regarded as obvious that they could, and did, though conclusive evidence is not available.

The role played by the iron and steel industry is also of some significance. It was the single largest industry and was of importance to others. The industry gained early encouragement for a protective tariff from the strong feelings expressed during the First World War about the need to safeguard vital industries. The Board of Trade Committee set up in 1916 to consider the position of the iron, steel and engineering trades after the war was initially under the chairmanship of Sir Clarendon Hyde, a well-known free-trader in the industry; Sir Hugh Bell was also a prominent member. Clarendon Hyde's chairmanship was unacceptable to the industry, for, on matters of protection, 'it is not too much to say that his views are diametrically opposed to those of the vast majority of his fellow manufacturers.'[16] Lobbying by the industry for his removal was successful and the Board of Trade finally replaced him with Scoby-Smith – equally well-known as a protectionist. Not too surprisingly, the Committee's report of June 1918 was strongly in favour of protection.[17]

The evidence presented to this Committee insisted 'almost unanimously that competition through dumping . . . had reached such a pitch that the production of iron and steel in Great Britain was seriously restricted and imperilled.'[18] The Committee was convinced that for 'the future safeguarding of the iron and steel industries it will be necessary to establish system of protective duties.'[19] The Committee went on to make several recommenda-tions. Besides encouraging combinations, it suggested that anti-dumping legislation be introduced, that all imports should show their mark of origin and 'that customs duties be imposed upon all imported iron and steel and manufacturers thereof.'[20]

The iron and steel industry recognized the need to organize, among other things, to campaign for protection. On Armistice Day 1918 the National Federation of Iron and Steel Manufacturers (NFISM) was formed 'in recogni-tion by the industry and the government' that the industry's problems required a stronger central organization.[21] The Federation was made up of the directors of leading companies. The industry continued to seek protec-tion persistently throughout the 1920s. In June 1925 an application was made to the President of the Board of Trade for duties (under the Safeguard-ing Act) on pig iron, wrought iron, heavy steel products and wire. On reject-ing the application at the end of the year, Baldwin as Prime Minister said that safeguarding a basic industry of this magnitude would have repercussions that might have been held to have been in conflict with the government's declaration in regard to a general tariff.[22] Most of the NFISM's executive committee and the director, Sir William Larke, were enthusiastic tariff reformers, and in early 1926 they gave their support to a sub-section of the industry, wire, when it made an independent application. But this application was rejected on the same grounds. The main application was renewed in 1927, but again it was turned down by reference to the original decision.

The iron and steel industry, and particularly the heavy part, was to exert constant pressure on government. Yet the 'key' nature of the industry presented a dilemma: while in one way it was regarded as sensible to safeguard such an industry against destruction by even legitimate foreign competition (given the uncertainty of the international economy), at the same time this meant increasing prices for much of British industry. When it is remembered that the raising of prices (associated with improving confidence) had become an aim of policy by 1930–1, the timing of the introduction of the tariff is perhaps more readily understood.

There clearly was an awareness of lobbying activity and of pressure groups at work. Measuring the impact is more difficult. However, it is interesting to note how, after the decision to introduce protection was made, the tariff structure was designed.

It was the declared intention of the British government to endeavour to remove itself from pressure over the tariff and it therefore created an 'independent and neutral body' in an attempt at keeping the tariff out of politics. To this end the Import Duties Advisory Committee (IDAC) was set up to make recommendations on tariff revision to the Board of Trade. The great bulk of revisions were carried through in 1932, though several amendments were made in each of the years following. A member of the Committee wrote at the end of the 1930s:

> Clearly the principles underlying the tariff must remain a political issue; the government could not divest itself of responsibility for them; but it was felt to be desirable that in the detailed application of the principles so determined there should be no scope for the kind of political activity known elsewhere as 'lobbying' or 'parliamentary log-rolling' . . . . It is, I think, proper to put on record in this place that from the time it came into being until the outbreak of the present war (1940) . . . its refusal from the first to entertain representations from persons or organisations other than those having immediate interest in matters before it made it equally free from any other kind of political pressure.[23]

The procedure followed by the IDAC on the receipt of an application was first, to gather relevant information on the case and then to interview or correspond with the applicant clarifying or supplementing the application. If the Committee was satisfied that a *prima facie* case was made out the application was advertised in the *Board of Trade Journal*, the daily press, and the appropriate trade periodicals. For example, the following notice appeared in the *Board of Trade Journal*:

> The Import Duties Advisory Committee give notice of the following applications for the imposition of increased duties:-
>
> . . .
>
> By the British Hacksaw Makers' Association in respect of Hacksaws
>
> . . .
>
> Any representations which interested parties desire to make in regard to these commodities should be addressed in writing to the Secretary [IDAC] . . . not later than June 20th.[24]

Those opposed to the requested tariff revision were then given an opportunity of commenting (though not a lot of time to prepare) and their case in turn was sent back to the applicant for a rejoinder. There might be a meeting of applicant and opponents, though these were not held in public.[25] According to Ashley this method of tariff making and revision had no parallel in any other country. It should be clear from this brief description of procedure that scope for applying pressure, if it existed, was of a kind wholly different from that in the United States. Of course there would have been opportunities for applicant and opponent to bargain without knowledge of the Committee and for opponents to encourage other potential users to make representations to the Committee. The wool and worsted industry provides an example of an industry which used considerable pressure, besieging its MPs, government departments, and the Committee itself. Hutchinson, Secretary to the Committee, claims that the Committee was not open to such pressure especially from MPs, and while we should be suspicious of such a claim by an involved party this does appear to be a reasonable interpretation.[26]

When a test of the nature of influence on the tariff structure was carried out some interesting results were obtained.[27] The hypothesis was that the effective tariff structure was the appropriate one to use as the dependent variable, and this was a function of (1) industry size captured in a concentration ratio as a surrogate for political clout; but we did not expect a positive sign given the nature of the process, and none was found. (2) Since regionally concentrated industries provided a basis for cohesion plus the fact that regional problems were being sympathetically addressed means we did expect a positive sign on this variable, and this was borne out. (In the light of Irwin's work it may be that what was being picked up was the effect of interest.) (3) Although the IDAC claimed to view severe import competition as a primary consideration there was little support for this in the results, though data problems mean we are left with reservations.

The question we wish to answer is: why was it that in 1931–2, Britain adopted protectionist policies? If the evidence on the impact of interest and lobbying is slender, the principal alternative must be that there was a change in mood, or belief, in the country, of a sufficient size to allow and/or promote the change. It is at this point worth pondering how any change in policy takes place. After all if the explanation for a change in policy was that it was the net outcome of forces expressing economic interest, why is it that we see policy changes sweeping around the world across different types of countries? Take for example the relatively recent experience with monetarism. If we think of the policy expression of this as being tight monetary policy to provide stable prices, then why was it that such policies were almost universally adopted in all kinds of economies? The short answer is that people were tired of inflation and prepared for the sacrifices that were required to correct it. But interest groups are involved. There are losers (creditors) and gainers (debtors) – and the debtors are more likely to be a coherent group – from inflation, and yet the policies were widely adopted. (I am conscious that there is an argument on interest group lines to explain Latin American inflation.) A similar experience on policy change in country after country could perhaps be found in privatization.

And so it would seem to be with protection. The big movements for and against protection have tended to sweep across countries, being adopted and reversed in all kinds of different economies. Thus it was in the 1920s, there was a widespread extension of protectionist policies all round the world. The power of ideas and/or beliefs, and moods must surely play a big part in this.

As David Henderson has put it, the activity of pressure groups is not the only factor:

> if it were, trade policies would now be, and would always have been, highly and unvaryingly interventionist. . . . It is when pressure groups can draw support from widely accepted ideas . . . that their campaigns are most likely to achieve results.[28]

Henderson argues that there are all kinds of ideas (often deep-rooted) that affect policy – ideas on fairness; the need to avoid social disruption; the mercantilist idea that a job saved by restricting imports adds to the total of employment; economic rationalism; and so on. Independently, Krugman has offered the following as an expression of popular views in the USA.

> We need a new economic paradigm, because today America is part of a truly global economy. To maintain its standard of living, America now has to compete in an ever tougher world market place. That's why high productivity and product quality have become essential. We need to move the American economy into the high value sectors that will generate jobs for the future. And the only way we can be

competitive in the new global economy is if we forge a new partner-ship between government and business.[29]

He offers this as a compendium of popular misconceptions about inter-national trade, views of a kind that are heard all the time and expressed even by leading figures in the world of business – 'misleading clichés' as Krugman puts it – but nevertheless powerful in the shaping and introduction of policy.

Of course pinning down what ideas are potent and acted upon is hazardous but it is at least worth trying to say what they were – what ideas were around that seemed to move Britain from being committed to free trade to being sufficiently in favour of protection to adopt it? The rest of this section will seek to do that, with the main elements in the story being war, empire, depression, and employment.

It is a commonplace that war has been a source of new protection. Since the history of much of the world has been one of conflict that is not exactly an adventurous position to adopt. But the fact is that it is a commonplace because of its essential veracity. In wartime a number of elements emerge that improve the possibilities for the protectionist. From governments' point of view there are increased revenue needs. Also, there are goods required that are essential for the military conduct of war and so the idea of protecting key industries gets a fillip. In the absence of certain imports as a result of the loss of the source, for whatever reason, infant industries appear and are then said to need sustaining after the war. Each of these elements was present in the British case in the years 1914–18. And of course in addition there is some-one there to blame and punish – the foreigner. Trade restrictions become patriotic. So the protectionist climate improves enormously.

Duties were introduced by the Chancellor McKenna in the first war budget of 1915 (These were levied at 33 per cent *ad valorem* and covered a range of luxury items – cars, watches, musical instruments, etc.) They were called revenue duties and there is some evidence to suggest that this was the case though equally there must be some suspicion at the very least that they were regarded as a step in the right direction by protectionists. More than this though a great clamouring for protection developed. This often took the form of the claimants pointing to the pivotal nature of their industry and their particular contribution to national security. Ideas on safeguarding such industries were first formulated at the Paris Conference of 1916. They were designed to meet a situation that might arise if Germany was not beaten decisively in battle. After the war those seeking protection were able to use their idea successfully to secure duties in spite of the original requirement having disappeared.

The Balfour of Burleigh Committee of 1918, whose brief was to consider commercial and industrial policy after the war, was strong in its advocacy of a tariff, particularly for 'pivotal' industries. It recommended that 'the imposition of a wide range of tariff duties ... should come into force immediately on the conclusion of war.' Other industries of 'real importance' were to qualify if it were clear that they were in danger of being weakened by foreign competition.'[30] It was in this atmosphere that large parts of British industry were encouraged to seek protection; perhaps this identifies the real beginning of the growth of protectionism, which was to triumph in 1931–2.

Certainly, immediately after the war the protectionists made progress, small but significant. In 1920 the Dyestuffs Act provided for duties on a range of chemicals – 'to close the British market to German competition.'[31] The Safeguarding of Industries Act of 1921 placed duties of 33 per cent on 6,500 items of goods regarded as being of strategic importance – scientific instruments, glassware, ignition magnetos, and so on. On optical glass the duty was 50 per cent. This legislation was renewed in 1926, and the range of goods extended. Thus the war provided the right kind of conditions for protectionists to come out of the closet, and there were many who were more prepared to speak openly for protection.

The role that empire played in the making of British economic policy is also of significance. The role of trade was uppermost in imperial matters. In the late nineteenth century there was much discussion of the relationship between the metropolitan country and the empire countries. The independent dominions (the richest countries in the empire) had strong protectionist tendencies and had for long been providing Britain with preferential treatment. They were pressing for reciprocal treatment in the British market. They already had preference in the capital market. However, it was not so clear how much of their trade could be given preferential treatment. After all they were primarily primary producers and the last thing that wanted taxing from Britain's point of view was food – at least from a political point of view – and raw materials, the taxing of which would damage manufacturing.

But empire had always loomed large in discussions. It was a dominant theme in the late nineteenth century. At its inaugural meeting in July 1903 the Tariff Reform League declared itself 'for the defence and development of industrial interests of the British Empire.'[32] All the leading imperialists could be found in the protectionist camp from Chamberlain down.

We noted above how the pressure group, the EIA, worked assiduously for protection and was given credit by some for achieving its aims; it is difficult to disentangle the influence of the idea of empire and the sympathy it evoked in the electorate on the one hand, and the work of the pressure group that used its name on the other.

The notion is now widespread (and has been for a long time) that economic recession/depression is a breeding ground for protection and there is a good case to be made for that. In the *International Encyclopedia of the Social Sciences* Corden lists depression as one of the causes of protection.[33] It is not surprising to find that depressed economic conditions will allow accusations to be made against foreigners, and their 'unfair' manufacturing/trading practices. Gallarotti attempted to bring precision to this by matching protectionist legislation with the trough of the business cycle through the nineteenth century.[34]

It has certainly been put forward as an explanation for Britain's adoption of protection in 1931–2.[35] But how much of an explanation is it? It is worth considering at a little more length.

First, it is worth emphasizing that the depression in Britain in 1929 to 1932 was not nearly as severe as in most other countries. The fall in output across the whole downswing to mid-1932 was less than 6 per cent. This is not far away from the kind of downswing that was found in the nineteenth century. Of course in 1920–1 Britain suffered a far greater shock and fall in output and yet there was a swift rejection of protectionist proposals soon after.

But in 1931–2 the National Government took advantage of the conditions and misled the people as to the true nature of the conditions, to introduce already well-worked-out schemes of protection. The first part came in late 1931 with punitive duties imposed on a range of goods allegedly because of a flood of imports. There was supposedly an import crisis and urgent action was called for; this was used as an excuse for drastic legislation to stem these imports while a more satisfactory protectionist policy was worked out. This came with the general tariff of April 1932 and was followed later in the year with revisions and with the Ottawa agreements, which gave preferential quotas on some agricultural goods to empire producers over foreign producers.

But were there abnormal imports in October and November of 1931? My own investigation shows that there were not.[36] On the basis of very few, but prejudicial data, which were then manipulated, a case was made at the time. But it does not stand up. There may have been some small increase in the imports of a small number of goods but the likelihood is that causality ran the other way – from tariffs to imports. It was widely rumoured that the National Government would introduce a tariff and so there was some sensible stockpiling in anticipation of that. That played into the hands of those who wished to press ahead with the tariff. Having passed the 'emergency' measures it was but a small step to introduce the formal and wide-ranging legislation in April 1932.

So in Britain there was no such serious Great Depression as there was in other countries, and as there had been in Britain in more recent times. And there was no import crisis. Neither, incidentally, had there been any serious dumping in the 1920s though many complained that there had. (Recent complaints of this kind have been successful in preventing imports legitimately under GATT and they have not been new in that respect.)

Nevertheless, there was a feature of the depression that was undoubtedly important; that was unemployment. Unemployment was fairly steady at around 1 million in the 1920s (about 7 per cent of the workforce) but it climbed to over 3 million at its worst point in the depression, that is about

16 per cent of the workforce. We leave aside here the debate about the causes of this though it is at least worth remarking that a convincing case can be made that it was the sharp rise in real wages that took place with the collapse of the price level in 1929–31 that accounted for a substantial part of it.[37] Leaving that aside, what the increase in unemployment did was allow the protectionist more grounds for accusing foreigners, however falsely, of destroying British jobs. Unemployment was widely used by the protectionists to advance their cause. Free-trade MPs from constituencies badly affected by unemployment kept their free-trade views to themselves at the very least, and even mouthed protectionist sentiments to satisfy local demands.

The argument of this chapter has been in two principal parts. The first has been that while there is less scope in a British context for the application of political-economic models of tariff-making that have proved popular in the USA, they can nevertheless throw light on the policy-making process. Economic interest is universal. But the institutional setting may be more or less conducive to its pursuit. There were pressure groups at work but it is difficult to be clear about their impact. The pressure group models are however different from the approach of Irwin, who has thrown light on how interest could have been expressed in the normal democratic electoral process.

The second part of the chapter has attempted to show that the climate within which protection can flourish changed with the war in 1914–18. That coupled with the work of imperialists and the fact that the war had given protection a huge boost everywhere, encouraged protectionists in Britain to be more vocal and active. A number of steps were taken along the path to full-blown protection between 1915 and 1930, but the real introduction came in 1931 and 1932. There was no serious depression in Britain, but there was a sharp and large rise in unemployment (explained, we would argue, by real wage movements). The world-wide talk of depression together with the obvious unemployment at home were exploited by the protectionists to advance and indeed realize their ambitions.

Notes

1 Ronald Findlay, 'Free Trade and Protection', in *The New Palgrave: A Dictionary of Economics* (London, Macmillan, 1987).
2 Paul Krugman, 'Is Free Trade *Passé?*', *Journal of Economic Perspectives*, 1987.
3 Douglas Irwin, 'The Political Economy of Free Trade: Voting in The British General Election of 1906', *Journal of Law and Economics*, 37, 1994.
4 Douglas Irwin, 'Industry or Class Cleavages over Trade Policy? Evidence from the British General Election of 1923', NBER, WP 5170 (1995), p. 19.
5 Andrew Marrison, 'Businessmen, Industries and Tariff Reform in Great Britain, 1903–1930', *Business History*, 25, 1983.

6 Benjamin Brown, *The Tariff Reform Movement in Great Britain*, (New York, Columbia University Press, 1943).

7 K.W.D. Rolf, 'Tories, Tariffs and Elections', unpublished Ph.D dissertation, University of Cambridge, 1974, p. 254.

8 Quoted in Ronald Findlay, *Britain under Protection* (London, Allen & Unwin, 1934), p.108.

9 *The Economist*, 25 December 1915, p. 106.

10 J.A. Turner, 'The British Commonwealth Union and the General Election of 1918', *English Historical Review*, 93, 1975.

11 John Ramsden, *The Age of Balfour and Baldwin 1902–40* (London, Longman, 1978), p. 297.

12 L.C.S. Amery, *My Political Life*, vol. II, *War and Peace 1914–1924* (London, Hutchinson, 1953–5), p. 291.

13 Beaverbrook Papers (House of Lords), BBK C/5, 12 November 1928.

14 EIA Executive Minutes, 7 April 1925 and 5 July 1927.

15 Ibid., 1 June 1927.

16 *Iron and Coal Trades Review*, 24 March 1916.

17 *Report of the Departmental Committee on the position of the Iron and Steel Trades after the War*, Cd 9071, 1918.

18 Ibid., p. 29.

19 Ibid.

20 Ibid.

21 *The British Iron and Steel Federation* (London, 1963).

22 Public Record Office, CAB 24/224, CP 278.

23 Percy Ashley, 'An Experiment in Tariff Making', *Manchester School*, 11, 2, 1940, p. 5.

24 *Board of Trade Journal*, 2 June 1932, p. 786.

25 Sir Herbert Hutchinson, *Tariff Making and Industrial Reconstruction* (London, Harrap, 1965), foreword.

26 Ibid.

27 Forrest Capie, 'Shaping the British Tariff Structure in the 1920s', *Explorations in Economic History*, 18, 1981.

28 David Henderson, *Innocence and Design: The Influence of Economic Ideas on Policy* (Oxford, Blackwell, 1986), pp. 63, 64.

29 Paul Krugman, 'What do Undergraduates Need to Know about Trade?', *American Economic Review*, 83, 2, 1993.

30 *Final Report of the Committee on Commercial and Industrial Policy After the War*, Cd. 9035, 1918, p. 46.

31 W.J. Reader, *Imperial Chemical Industries* (London, Oxford University Press, 1970), p. 329.

32 *The Times*, 22 July 1903.

33 Max Corden, 'Protectionism', in David Sills (ed.) *International Encyclopedia of the Social Sciences* (New York, Macmillan, 1968).

34 See Forrest Capie, *Tariffs and Growth* (Manchester, Manchester University Press, 1994), p. 29.

35 See, e.g. Peter Lindert, *International Economics*, 9th edn (Homewood, IL: Irwin, 1991).

36 Forrest Capie, *Depression and Protectionism: Britain between the Wars* (London, Allen & Unwin, 1983), ch. 4.

37 Michael Beenstock, Forrest Capie, and Brian Griffiths, 'Economic Recovery in the 1930s', *Bank of England Academic Panel Discussion Paper* (1984).

20

COMMENTS ON CAPIE

Andrew Marrison

As recent work on the Corn Laws themselves has revealed, rational choice models seeking to analyse election results in terms of the economic biases of constituencies can produce weak results that impress few but their practitioners, and here I feel some sympathy with Forrest Capie's chapter. However, though his point about a fundamental cleavage between pastoral and grain farmers is logical on the surface, it is difficult to find an example of a free-trade agriculturalist between 1880 and 1930, and free-trade voting in rural constituencies might rather reflect the 'labourist' free-trade position of the labourers. Extended to the urban constituencies, this might also have implications for interpreting the results of Irwin's examination of the 1906 election, though I think there is strength in Irwin's implicit conclusion, in the two papers cited by Capie, that sectional alignments based on income and direct economic interest were probably stronger in 1923 than they were in 1906.

Though on one level the effects of the war are clear – the McKenna Duties, the Balfour of Burleigh Committee, and the Safeguarding legislation – we should remember the limited extent to which protectionism resulted in extensions of the British tariff after the influence of the wartime fever of 1916–21 receded. As Capie shows, protectionist industrial interests clearly became larger, more organized, more adept at propaganda, in 1916–29. I take the importance of the iron and steel industry, not only as a large trade which affected so many others but also as a rallying point of symbolic importance in the campaign for tariffs. I also agree that the most effective 'business' pressure group was the Empire Industries Association. Yet, as Capie argues, it is difficult to ascertain the effectiveness of such pressure groups: indeed, I would be inclined to credit them with exerting less pressure on politicians than he does, though there is still the question of their influence on public opinion.

What of Capie's handling of the depression of 1929–32? True, the depression was relatively mild by international comparison, but contemporaries had only impressionistic and imperfect evidence to go on, and British observers, by now including many former free-traders, were watching overseas tariff moves like hawks. They were particularly alarmed at the negotiations over Hawley-Smoot, and the possibility of a 'one-sided' tariff truce. To talk of the deception and misleading of the public by those pressing for the tariff is surely too strong? Protectionists like Croft had been preaching their message openly for years – even if retrospective fault can be found with their stat-istical information, were they doing anything that politicians do not do all the time? I have never been sure why protectionists, among all those who have exhibited heterodox beliefs, should be considered uniquely evil and corrupt. Of course the answer lies in the venal pursuit of self-interest, with no compassion allowed for the fact that Britain's manufacturers had to put up with one-sided free trade, higher taxes, and more extensive labour regu-lation than most of their competitors. This being said, however, I would agree with Capie's important point, which has had far too little consideration in the academic literature, of a change in the mood of British public opinion. Some political historians think this is not evident until the summer of 1930, but there is a case for placing it considerably earlier.

I also wonder whether Capie's analysis of 'abnormal imports', first made in *Depression and Protectionism*, entirely hits home? First, the demonstration that imports in 1930–1 were not unusually high compared with the 1920s may be true, but the Tariff Reformers were convinced that imports were abnormal throughout the 1920s – Capie denies dumping, but the historical evidence is pretty hard to marshall either way. More centrally, my reading is that the Abnormal Importations Act of November 1931 was urged upon the public not exactly because of an 'alleged flood of imports' but because of the need to 'forestall [the] anticipatory dumping' which was expected as soon as a British tariff was announced. The decision for the Import Duties Act had already been taken, and was out in the open in the general election.

21

THE END OF FREE TRADE

Protection and the exchange rate regime between the world wars[1]

James Foreman-Peck, Andrew Hughes Hallett and Yue Ma

Two months after being forced off the gold standard, Britain abandoned free trade. Even though protection by then could not support the balance of payments and the fixed exchange rate regime, it introduced a general tariff. But, had Britain temporarily adopted protection eighteen months earlier, it might have saved the gold standard, according to the evidence of this chapter. If it had, the world would have been spared a good number of the trade barriers that were raised in response to sterling depreciation. Moderate and temporary British trade restrictions could have enhanced world trade and welfare by two means. Not only would they have avoided trading partners' policy reactions to the fall of the pound, but also, employed as bargaining counters, they could have reduced foreign tariffs. As it was, for the first half of the interwar period, the world's largest traders could offer no concessions to countries such as France to offset domestic pressure for protection.

In order to substantiate these propositions we first discuss the forces favouring trade barriers. We then show how protectionism, built up during the floating rate period of the early 1920s, was contained during the period of exchange rate stability towards the end of the decade, and was unleashed by the multiple crises of the Great Depression. To quantify the bilateral impacts of the British and US tariffs on the four largest industrial economies we estimate a number of import equations. From these we infer the immediate expenditure-switching effects, as British goods were substituted for French, German and American products (in the case of Britain's 1931 tariff).

The full impact of protection however depends on a range of other, especially monetary, repercussions, which in turn may be influenced by the exchange rate regime. We calculate dynamic tariff multipliers that take these into account for fixed exchange rates, demonstrating how powerful was the British tariff as an instrument of policy. British protection cannot be entirely isolated from the commercial policies of other countries, both because they enhanced or detracted from the desirability of a British tariff and because they may react to it. We address this interaction by simulating what would have happened to British output and gold flows if all tariff protection (in so far as we are able to measure it) by the four principal industrial powers, including Britain, had been removed from 1930. This did not require abandoning gold. Unfortunately the monetary policies of the USA, France and Germany were poor and the British economy suffered accordingly.[2] However, an earlier recognition of these policy shortcomings, with a move to end free trade as soon as Keynes had made the recommendation in 1930, would have markedly improved the British response to the depression.

The supply and demand for policies

Manchester School free-traders and successive generations of neo-classical economists point out that national well-being will be improved by unilateral free trade. But rarely have policy makers' payoffs matched these abstract considerations. Under a regime of multilateral concessions, exemplified by the 'most favoured nation' clause, beneficiaries are tempted to 'free ride'.[3] If my concession to you must be extended to all our trading partners then they have little incentive to liberalize themselves. Doing so will antagonize their import-competing industries without yielding compensating political advantages; gains to their export industries will anyway be achieved by my country's concessions. Of course, if all trading partners think the same way, no liberalization at all will be conceded. Hence bilateral negotiations may lead more effectively to trade liberalization than multilateral stances.[4] Trading partners can link the interests of their export lobbyists with concessions from import-competing industries.

An alternative to protection by tariffs and quotas is an undervalued exchange rate, which also supports export industries. However, it is when exchange rates are overvalued that protectionist lobbying kicks in. Under floating rates quite persistent deviations of the nominal rate from purchasing power parity, or erratic movements in the real exchange rates, are possible. By supporting such deviations, floating rates can trigger protectionist responses. Price movements that are asymmetric between countries – terms of trade shifts – can exercise the same effect. Stable terms of trade and fixed exchange rates thus are a backdrop to the political economy of free trade. Trade barriers are more likely to go up when exchange rates appreciate excessively and/or prices move so as to boost import competition and undermine export sales.

As the well-documented political economy of tariffs reminds us, political changes may independently increase protectionism. Simmons focuses on the interwar rise to power of left-wing parties, unstable governments and politically influenced central banks, emphasizing the incompatibility (actual or perceived) of their policies with stable exchange rates and gold standard membership.[5] She argues that left-wing policy makers were less inclined to chose tariffs as an instrument because such taxes were perceived to hit working-class budgets hardest. On the other hand, stable governments were currency-defenders and tariff-cutters; conservatives and independent central banks favoured raising tariffs. So a shift towards unstable, right-wing governments could be sufficient to release a protectionist wave. But for the key players in the present study, this does not seem to underly policy shifts. The British National Government of 1931 that abandoned free trade may have been right-wing on some definitions but the electoral majority does not suggest instability. Similarly President Hoover, under whom the Hawley–Smoot tariff was raised, may have been right-wing but his authority was not any more uncertain than other presidents'. So political change is not a sufficient explanation for the onset of protection in Britain and the USA. The explanation may fit Germany better, but then currency controls were the principal tool of external economic policy, not tariffs and quotas.

The impact of tariffs and the exchange rate regime

Under fixed exchange rates, tariff increases lower the propensity to import and by switching expenditure to domestic products, raise demand and output. At the same time the balance of payments constraint is eased so that the tendency is reinforced for interest rates to be bid up and to promote a capital inflow. Under floating rates the exchange rate should appreciate to ensure there is an equilibrium at the new higher level of expenditure on domestic products and higher capital inflows. Imposing a tariff switches expenditure from foreign to domestic goods and reduces the demand for foreign exchange. Exports remain unchanged until there is retaliation. In conditions of unemployment and elastic aggregate supply this will appreciate the exchange rate, offsetting some of the impact of the tariff on imports and discouraging exports. Hence, under floating rates trade protection is less beggaring of neighbours than under fixed rates. On the other hand, an appreciation of the exchange rate hurts export and import-competing industries and so encourages the raising of tariffs. Since exchange rate depreciation does not exercise a symmetrical effect, floating rates may encourage protection. With fixed exchange rates none of this happens; the direct effects of a tariff, when raised, are worse for neighbours but the pressures to impose protection will be less.

Since exchange rate appreciation lowers prices and output, the net effect of the tariff on these two variables is uncertain. The output and employment spillovers to trading partners could even be beneficial. Income effects of the tariff can be reinforced by rebating all the tariff revenue, but even then a definite positive impact requires exports, wages and prices not to be affected. Under a managed float, such as conducted by the Bank of England with the Exchange Equalisation Account for most of the 1930s, tariff effects could well resemble fixed exchange rate behaviour when policy was directed to maintaining a stable exchange rate target.[6]

Monetary and price feedbacks

These conclusions about tariff policy are short-run in two senses. First, under fixed rates they do not allow for the longer-term effects of reserve changes. A tariff under fixed rates may improve the current balance and in so doing expand the domestic money supply, which ultimately at least partly counterbalances the initial impact. Second, under both regimes, the conclusion depend upon prices remaining fixed while output is allowed to vary. Long-run models reverse this restriction, fixing output and varying prices. The length of the short run depends on how responsive the economy is and may differ between countries.

Interpreting the impact of past and future policy depends on the time period over which these effects are worked out. An instrument that is highly effective over two years and irrelevant over five may still be of the utmost importance for practical policy. For this purpose therefore, purely theoretical qualitative comparative static analysis must be supplemented with evaluations based on empirical dynamic models.

Retaliation

Since in open economies policy measures spill over to trading partners, those partners may react to them. International regimes and rules, such as the gold standard or the most favoured nation clause, attempt to limit the damage from adverse spillovers and reactions to them.

Interwar commercial policies

Inflation and floating exchange rates in almost all former belligerent countries meant that the interwar period began inauspiciously for free trade. With the big exception of Britain, European economies met the scarcity of foodstuffs and raw materials during the postwar boom and the more protracted currency disorganization with substantial trade restrictions. Britain's 1921 Safeguarding of Industries Act and the continuation of the wartime McKenna Duties were uniquely very minor infringements of the principle of free trade. But elsewhere, exchange controls were the extremely restrictive defence of countries with fluctuating currencies and weak public finances.

As these conditions passed, exchange controls were abandoned and restrictions were replaced by higher tariffs.[7] The US emergency duties of 1921 were followed by the Fordney–McCumber duties of 1922, which raised tariffs steeply, but only on products for which imports were already low. More importantly the USA declared its own tariffs were autonomous; rates would not be reduced in exchange for concessions from other countries. None the less the USA demanded most favoured nation (MFN) status with other countries; that is, it tried to acquire the benefits of concessions bargained between pairs of trading partners. In short the USA, by now equalling Britain in its share of world trade, tried to free ride on the international trading system.[8] France was less rigid but none the less attempted to extract tariff reductions from trading partners. In 1918 it renounced all agreements containing MFN clauses and adopted the principle of reciprocity in 1919 for future treaties.[9] For bargaining purposes the margin between the highest and lowest rates in the French tariff schedule on many items amounted to 400 per cent, compared with the 50 per cent that had been normal in 1910.[10] Moreover, the French introduced country quotas and cartel agreements for Germany, the Netherlands, Belgium and Czechoslovakia in the 1920s.

Meanwhile, increasing monetary stability – with the Schacht Plan of 1924 in Germany and with Britain's return to gold in 1925 – began to create conditions for freer trade. Germany abolished its licensing system in 1925 with full recovery of tariff autonomy. As late as 1927 France, Italy, Spain and a number of other European countries still maintained some foreign exchange controls.

But by the end of that year the franc, the mark and sterling were stabilized and the World Economic Conference created favourable expectations for a cooperative international trading regime – which Table 21.1 suggests were fulfilled at least in part.

Then in 1929 the German industrial tariff was reduced. Certainly agricultural tariffs increased between 1928 and 1929, but a series of French tariff treaties in the same years bound the contracting parties not to raise duties without mutual consent during the period of the treaty. Thus the Franco-German commercial agreement of August 1929 contained many rate reductions that were passed on under MFN clauses.[11]

Unfortunately falling primary product prices dominated commercial policy, disrupting the fragile policy equilibrium in the summer of 1929.[12] With the exception of France, retail prices began to slide in the major economies from 1929 (Figure 21.1), reintroducing the real exchange rate volatility that had temporarily been dispelled in the later 1920s. Then, before the end of the year, agricultural protection intensified in Germany, France and Italy. More importantly, falling agricultural prices in the USA prompted Herbert Hoover to promise during his presidential campaign of 1928 to raise tariffs.

Table 21.1 Decline in number of European tariff revisions, 1925–9

Year	1925	1926	1927	1928	1929
Number	16	16	10	5	2

Source: League of Nations, *Commercial Policy in the Interwar Period: International Proposals and National Policies* (League of Nations, Geneva, 1942), p. 42.

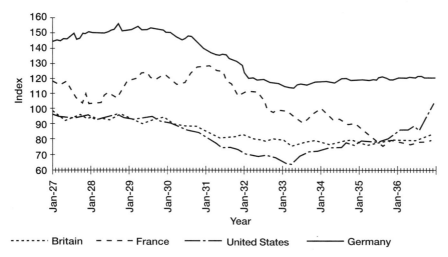

Figure 21.1 Price levels January 1927 to December 1936

By June 1930, when the Hawley–Smoot Tariff Act became law, the political bargaining process had extended increased protection far beyond agriculture.

Adoption of the US tariff was followed by higher trade barriers in Canada, France, Italy, and Spain, and the UK abandoned free trade in November 1931. None the less Eichengreen maintained that only Spain clearly retaliated to the Hawley–Smoot tariff.[13] As an encouragement not to retaliate, the tariff was designed to be non-negotiable, imposing a 50 per cent surcharge on any discrimination against US goods but offering no concessions to economies that favoured US goods. Non-discrimination reduced the interest of export-oriented American sectors in serving as a countervailing influence to the import-competing sectors.[14]

France cut US quotas, probably in response to Hawley–Smoot, while keeping MFN, and the US tariff helped precipitate full empire preference. Chamberlain stated in 1932 that the British Import Duties Act would be used in negotiation with foreign countries. US protection shifted Canada towards the empire and away from the USA.

The financial crises of May 1931 onwards accelerated the upward trend of protection, but now with foreign exchange controls and quotas. To group British and American protectionist measures together is misleading except in so far as, like those of every other country, they hurt trading partners and Britain and the USA were the world's largest traders.[15] The British tariff did not provoke reaction but gave Britain for the first time a bargaining chip to reduce other countries' trade barriers.[16] It was therefore price declines, both autonomous and in response to exchange rate collapses, that triggered the critical responses.

From 1931 commercial policy became the most common instrument chosen to target international monetary disorder. But for the key player in the world economy of 1930, Britain, it might have been a genuine antidote, to the ultimate gain of the world economy. Britain's gold standard difficulties forced it to abandon fixed exchange rates in September 1931 (Figure 21.2). But had a Conservative government won the 1929 election the problem might not have arisen, not necessarily because of particular policies but because of the capital market's perceptions of Labour policies. Indeed assessments of budgetary probity may have been improved by Keynes' tariff proposal, even with a Labour government in office, had the UK not signed a commercial convention in March 1930 binding it not to raise tariffs until April 1931. In February 1930 Keynes recommended a revenue tariff. He and some other economists on a subcommittee of the Economic Advisory Council reported in October that a tariff would both create jobs and save the gold standard.[17] We show he was right (pp. 271–77) and that retaliation would not have offset the potential gains. Anyway, Britain's departure from the gold standard obviously triggered protection abroad. French quotas were extended to protect against sterling depreciation. Retaliation was not merely one country's protectionist response to another's tariff or quota, but also its trade barrier reaction to an exchange rate change (or to an adverse movement in a neighbour's interest rate under a free-floating regime).

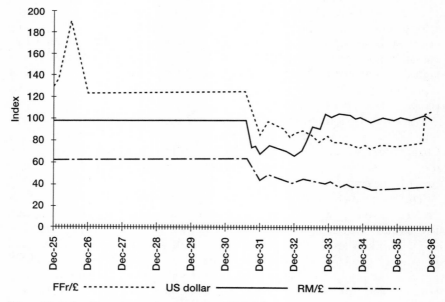

Figure 21.2 Sterling spot exchange rates, 1926–36

British tariff policy

In the Abnormal Importations Act of 1931 Britain allowed *ad valorem* duties of up to 100 per cent. The following year duties were consolidated by the Import Duties Act, which imposed a general 10 per cent tariff and established an Import Duties Advisory Committee to suggest changes in rates. Excluded were empire goods, important industrial materials, and food. After alterations agreed at the Ottawa Conference (which introduced general empire preference) later in 1932, about one-quarter of British imports remained duty-free (though many were restricted by other methods). On one-half, the tariff ranged between 10 and 20 per cent; only 8 per cent of imports were subject to duties of more than 20 per cent and the remainder (including motor vehicles) paid the old duties of the 1920s. Overall this meant that the average tariff including hydrocarbon oil between 1932 and 1937 was 17–19 per cent. For manufacturing the average was 13–15 per cent.[18] Although the £22–£30 million of revenue a year brought in by the tariff[19] was small compared with overall taxation of expenditure (£308 million in 1930), the income was considerable in relation to the budget deficit (£98 million in 1930).

Retaliation

When import price declines accelerated from 1930, existing treaties permitted France to raise most tariffs only after lengthy negotiations. Some duties were 'deconsolidated', such as those on German goods in 1931. In the spring and summer of 1931 a new system of import quotas for agricultural, mineral and industrial products was introduced and progressively extended until by the 1934 3,000 out of 7,000 articles in the customs tariff were importable only in limited fixed quantities over short fixed periods under licence. At first the aim was to reduce German manufactures, which had increased between 1930 and 1931, but after sterling and dollar depreciation, American and British goods were also targeted.

In November 1931 the French imposed a surtax of 15 per cent on British imports to offset the advantage they gained from sterling depreciation.[20] The British complained that the principle was not applied equally to other countries and the French eventually suppressed the tax from the beginning of 1934. But quotas were tightened almost immediately after that. Then, partly as a bargaining device, from 1 January 1934 existing quotas were reduced to 25 per cent and their coverage was extended to include 600 new items. Quotas were somewhat liberalized for the USA and Belgium in return for concessions by those countries. In February 1934 the British imposed a 20 per cent tariff on certain classes of French goods to compensate for the quotas. In July the French gave way. The British made tariff concessions on raw and artificial silk, while the French agreed to take not less than 49.5 per cent of average coal imports into France from all sources in 1928–30. French quotas were clearly intended for bargaining; indeed by 1934, 75 per cent were reserved for political exchange.

Italy responded similarly to Britain over French quotas and the two countries pursued tit for tat strategies until 1933.[21] The French remained undeterred by foreign reactions though. In order to restore its trade balance with Germany, France imposed further quotas during the first months of 1933 on certain German imports.[22]

Having adopted exchange controls in July 1931, Germany raised tariffs by 100 per cent in 1932; imports fell to 1898 levels.[23] But unlike those of the other three major trading economies, Germany's trade controls were actually of little significance compared with foreign exchange restrictions. Without the 1931 financial crisis, Germany's trade would have been relatively unrestricted. Instead German policy operated through exchange controls that at first entitled importers to receive 75 per cent and then 50 per cent (May 1932–February 1934) of the foreign exchange needed for their earlier transactions (July 1930–June 1931). Meanwhile exporters were obliged to declare their exports and give up at least a part of the foreign currency so acquired. Even so, by autumn 1934 the strength of recovery in import demand and the inadequate export performance created a balance of payments crisis. Schacht's New Plan was the remedy, based on the principle that only what could be paid for would be bought, and a dual exchange rate of Sperrmarks ('embargoed marks') set the rate for foreign creditors wanting their money immediately.[24]

Recovery and liberalization

Having abandoned free trade, Britain presented its bilateral trade agreements at the World Economic Conference of 1933 as the only practical route to liberalization. During 1932–3, these treaties brought net demand expansion for Britain, as recovery from the slump began. Agreements also reduced the likelihood of quota retaliation by trading partners.

Depreciation of the dollar in 1933 (Figure 21.2) eased the passage of the 1934 US Reciprocal Trade Agreements Act, which authorized the president to reduce tariffs by up to 50 per cent in bilateral negotiations. On the other hand it did not trigger US recovery. The USA was now in a position to negotiate trade liberalization apparently because fixed rates had been abandoned. But in fact the Bank of England managed the sterling–dollar rate to ensure stability and at a rate similar to that prevailing before 1931 (Figure 21.2). A sort of surrogate gold exchange standard had thereby been partly reintroduced.

Imports and protection

As this chapter has shown, commercial policy in the 1930s was pursued bilaterally. An assessment of the policy's impact should therefore proceed in the same way. With less than full employment, a general tariff in a fixed exchange rate regime will divert resources from export industries to less productive import-competing industries. In a period of heavy unemployment the boost to output is likely to dominate completely the productivity effect. The demand switching effect may be captured by the simplest import demand function, with a tariff, of the form

$$im_{ji} = a_1y - a_2p_m(1 + tariff) + a_4p \qquad \text{(bilateral imports)}$$
$$= a_1y - a_2p_m - a_2p_m \cdot tariff + a_4p \qquad (i,j = 1, \ldots, 4, j \neq i)$$

where im_{ij} = real imports into i from j, p = domestic prices, p_m = import price index, y = GNP
(All variables are in logs except the tariff)

When t rises, import demand falls by more the higher is p_m and the larger is the elasticity b, where p_m is exclusive of import taxes. With a perfectly elastic supply of imports, pre-tax import prices remain unchanged and post-tax prices rise by the amount of the tax. A less than perfectly elastic supply ensures a terms-of-trade response; reduced imports will lower pre-tax import prices.

Monthly bilateral import value series are typically available in the foreign trade sources, but neither bilateral volume nor price indices are. Hence, measurement of aggregate monthly bilateral import prices and quantities either requires a great deal of work or a great deal of approximation. Without disaggregating further to construct such indices, the assumption that country-of-origin price movements are reflected in import prices is a plausible approximation. There may be substantial errors in this measured variable however and the elasticity coefficient may therefore be biased. Hence it is desirable to obtain a tariff impact independent of the coefficient estimate. For that reason our preferred specification is

$$im_{ji} = a_1y - a_2p^* - a_3tariff + a_4p \qquad (1)$$

where p* is a foreign price index, lagged to avoid feedbacks from imports. We take 'tariff' to be a binary (on–off) dummy variable and write

$$a_3tariff = a_2p_m \cdot tariff$$

Exchange rate movements present analogous but more complex problems because, unlike tariffs, they are typically not permanent. In particular the gold standard created expectations of price stability. A given price change under the gold standard was more likely to have been regarded as temporary than after the standard was abandoned. We therefore employ a dummy variable to capture the possibility of greater price responsiveness under the floating-rate regime. In addition we adjust foreign prices to obtain domestic currency equivalent values.

$$im_{ji} = a_1y + a_2(p - p^* - e) - a_3tariff \qquad (2)$$

where e is the exchange rate in domestic currency units per foreign currency unit.

The estimated form of equation, obtained from monthly data over the period 1927–36, shows all British 1931 import tariff coefficients to be statistically significant (see Appendix for the estimated equations and data sources). The US Hawley–Smoot parameters are less well-defined (with t statistics in the range 1.3–2.0). The equations also show that French imports from the UK and USA were reduced by the trade prohibitions of September 1931.

Table 21.2 implies that the 1931 UK tariff on US goods immediately lowered UK imports from the USA by 7 per cent, imports of French goods by 10 per cent, and German goods by 3 per cent. The long-run impacts implied by this table were rather greater – 8 per cent for imports from the USA, 13 per cent for France, and just under 4 per cent for Germany. With an average tariff of 17–18 per cent, but 13–15 per cent on manufactures, these results imply British tariff elasticities (assuming no terms-of-trade effects) of around −0.5 for US products, and perhaps one-third to one-quarter for German goods, which are consistent with other estimates. By way of comparison Kitson and Solomou found a tariff impact coefficient for British manufactured imports of −0.034.[25] Interpreted as a dummy variable as in our model, the finding is broadly comparable. Capie reports Treasury calculations with implied tariff/price elasticities from 0.43 to 1.15 depending on the category of goods.[26] In the presence of a terms-of-trade effect, the import response to a tariff is smaller than when import supply is perfectly elastic. So a given import decline in this instance corresponds to a larger price elasticity of demand.

Import demand equations capture only the first round of a tariff's impact.

Table 21.2 Bilateral tariff coefficients, 1931

	UK 1931	Hawley–Smoot
USA	−0.07	—
UK	—	−0.01
France	−0.10	−0.075
Germany	−0.029	−0.008

Note: Logarithmic real bilateral imports are the dependent variables, the tariff dummies are the independent variables.

Expenditure on domestic goods rises and the balance of trade improves, in both cases with monetary repercussions and at the expense of trading partners. Assessing the full impact of trade restrictions therefore requires a model of the interaction between the principal industrial powers. Williamson and Milner present a succinct analysis of the domestic impact of protection under fixed and floating exchange rates in a Mundell–Fleming macroeconomic model.[27] The simulations in this chapter employ a very similar system, essentially that outlined in Foreman-Peck, Hughes Hallet and Ma (1992) with additional price transmission equations.[28] These link domestic consumer prices with domestic producer prices and rest of the world (producer) prices. The other international linkages modelled, apart from trade volumes, are interest rates. Money demand, price, wage and import equations have also been slightly respecified. Monthly GNP estimates are constructed by interpolations of annual series with monthly indices of industrial activity.[29]

Dynamic tariff multipliers

We can obtain a good idea of the full effects of the tariff from the dynamic multipliers of the full model (Figures 21.3 and 21.4). The output multipliers capture the impact on GNP of all the induced changes at home and abroad in trade, interest rates, and prices. They are calculated for a 10 per cent increase in the tariff dummy from the baseline in 1929. Hence the multiplier depends on the strength of the historical policy measure and on the level of activity, as well as on the model. Fixed exchange rates are imposed over the simulation period.

For the UK GNP is initially apparently raised very substantially, with the

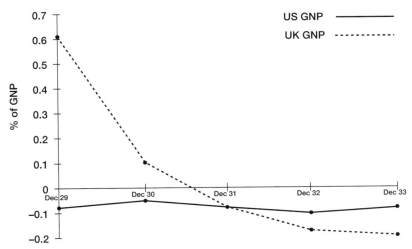

Figure 21.3a GNP impact of UK tariff, 1929–33

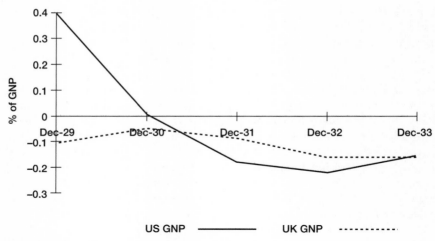

Figure 21.3b GNP impact of US tariff, 1929–33

full tariff boosting GNP by 6 per cent in the first year. By the third year feedbacks are already reducing the initial expansion, an effect which rises with the passage of time – as would be expected with monetary adjustment towards its long-run equilibrium. The Hawley–Smoot tariff also gives a big kick (4 per cent) to US GNP in the first year, with a similar time path to the British tariff, though the impact fades rather more rapidly. After four years the expansion has been neutralized and in the fifth year the cumulative effect has become negative. These conclusions are consistent with the smaller openness of the US economy and the rather larger increases in the US than in the British tariff.

Tariffs under fixed rates also improve the current account with the structures and estimated parameters assumed here. Subsequently capital, gold and price movements only partly offset the initial change. A 10 per cent shock to the British 1931 tariff improves the trade balance by 0.4 per cent of GNP in the first year, and almost half of this improvement persisted five years later (see Figure 21.4a). Britain's actual current account deficit was 2.27 per cent of GNP in 1931. Ignoring repercussions with the rest of the economy for the moment, bringing the 1931 tariff forward by eleven or twelve months would apparently have been sufficient to turn the current balance positive – as it had been in 1930. Similarly, the US trade balance improves by 0.33 per cent of GNP in response to 10 per cent of Hawley–Smoot in the first year, but becomes negative in the second and subsequent years (see Figure 21.4b). Since these negative effects are very small, the trade balance improvement persists. Spillovers to GNP and trade balances of other economies are always initially negative.

Turning to the full model simulations, removal of trade barriers, estimated to begin with Hawley–Smoot, shows that the UK and the USA consistently

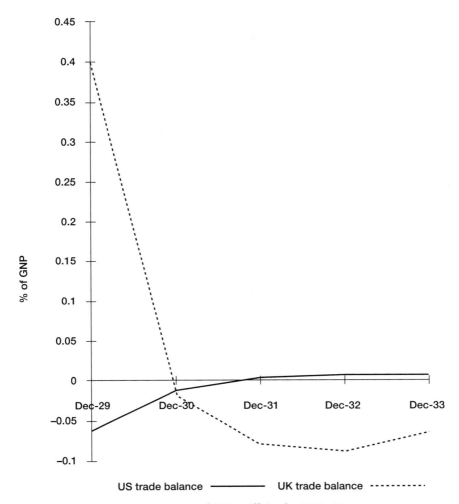

Figure 21.4a Trade balance impact of UK tariff shock, 1929–33

gain from trade restrictions (Table 21.3). France and Germany on the other hand suffer a reduction of GNP and gold losses, the gains from their tariffs being offset by the unfavourable spillovers from foreign protection. That is only part of the story though. France does not give up its quotas nor does Germany abandon foreign exchange control in this scenario. Their 'concessions' do not match those of Britain and the United States.

Subject to that caveat, *under fixed rates*, the UK would have lowered its GNP by almost 12 per cent in 1933 if it and everybody else had abandoned the tariffs and quotas of 1931. But had it chosen protection in 1930 (or earlier), as Keynes recommended,[30] then the severity of the historical

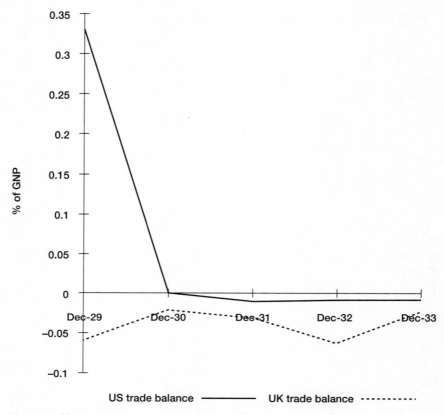

Figure 21.4b Trade balance impact of US tariff shock, 1929–33

downturn in output would have been attenuated, as would the gold losses that eventually forced Britain off the gold standard in 1931. In July of that year the net outflow of gold was $130.8 million, the largest in the period considered; the following month gold exports fell to $24 million. By December 1932 Table 21.3 shows 1931 tariff protection was adding $31 million to Britain's gold inflow (assuming fixed rates). In so far as sterling floated freely when Britain opted for general protection, the actual value to the British economy is much more questionable than these simulations suggest.

Conclusion

Britain abandoned free trade in November 1931 against a background of falling prices, first agricultural and later industrial. These price declines, themselves a product of misguided monetary policies, ignited four years of trade warfare. World trade contracted sharply, even relative to declining world incomes. Measured in depreciated pounds sterling, by 1935 trade had

Table 21.3 Remove trade restrictions from 1930

	GNP %				Gold inflows (GM)			
	30.12	31.12	32.12	33.12	30.12	31.12	32.12	33.12
UK	0.1	−0.4	−7.6	−11.9	0	0.3	−3.1	−12.7
US	−0.3	−0.7	−6.5	−3.4	−1.8	0.1	3.8	2.9
France	0.9	−2.6	10.2	14.5	5.6	4.4	17.7	116.6
Germany	0.3	1.7	9.1	−11.3	2.9	10.4	59.9	102.2

Notes: Real GNP percentage deviation from historical values: GM, current gold inflow
(difference from historical values) in tens of millions of dollars for the UK and USA,
hundreds of millions of francs for France and tens of millions of marks for Germany.
UK actual gold inflow 30.12 −3.5, 31.12 −1.56, 32.12 −2.9, 33.12 +7.9
USA   +3.3,   +5.7   +10.1   −0.9

lost 45 per cent of its 1929 value. Yet opinions have been divided as to how
far trade controls were warranted. Had Britain followed Keynes' suggestion
and adopted a temporary revenue tariff at the beginning of 1930, subsequent
concern about the trade balances and foreign exchange rate depreciation
would have been alleviated. That would have removed at least one source of
contraction in international trade because Britain could have remained on
the gold standard. Retaliation on any scale was unlikely, and domestic output and employment would have been boosted before the worst of the
depression struck.

Free trade was obsolete in a world where major monetary players mis-
understood the game. But stable and convertible exchange rates were a form
of international co-operation that was worth keeping. They allowed the
securing of some gains from trade even when cross-border movement of
goods was taxed. An open world economy was not threatened by a 10 or 15
per cent tariff, but it was by exchange controls and erratic or persistently
misaligned exchange rates. Britain's departure from gold meant precisely that
in the 1930s.

APPENDIX A: BILATERAL TRADE MONTHLY
EQUATIONS 1927–1936

Notes

LX $= \log(X)$
DX $= X - X_{-1}$
BDC $=$ floating rate dummy
LM(k): $=$ LM – test for k^{th} order residual autocorrelation, distributed as $X^2(k)$, asymptotically.
ARCH(k) $=$ ARCH–test for k^{th} order squared residual autocorrelation, distributed as $X^2(k)$, asymptotically.
NOB $=$ no. of observations (estimation period is also given).
       t statistics in parentheses
       All R^2 are adjusted for degrees of freedom.

(1) Imports to USA from UK

$$\text{LMMUSUK} - \text{LPUS} = 2.45 + 0.36 \, (\text{LMMUSUK} - \text{LPUS})_{-1}$$
$$(2.41) \quad (3.88)$$

$$+ \, 0.09 \, (\text{LMMUSUK} - \text{LPUS})_{-4} + 0.49 \, \text{LIPUS} + 0.30 \, \text{LIPUS}_{-1} - 0.01$$
$$\text{Smoot}$$
$$(1.32) \qquad\qquad (1.84) \qquad (0.98) \qquad (1.45)$$

$$+ \, 1.41 \, \text{D(LPUS} - \text{LPUK} + \text{LDSTEXR})_{-11} + \text{seasonals}$$
$$(2.91)$$

$R^2 = 0.86$, NOB $= 108$, 28:1 – 36:12, LM(1) $= 9.17$, LM(9) $= 15.83$, ARCH(1) $= 0.11$

(2) Imports to UK from USA

$$\text{LXMUSUK} - \text{LPUK} = 0.22 + 0.44 \, (\text{LXMUSUK} - \text{LPUK})_{-1}$$
$$(1.68) \quad (4.53)$$

$$- \, 0.34 \, (\text{LXMUSUK} - \text{LPUK})_{-2} + 1.47 \, \text{DLIPUK}_{-3}$$
$$(3.63) \qquad\qquad (1.60)$$

$$+ \, 0.27 \, (1 + \text{BDC}) . \, \text{D(LPUK} - \text{LPUS} - \text{LDSTEXR})_{-1} - 0.07 \, \text{Tariff} +$$
$$\text{seasonals}$$
$$(2.32) \qquad\qquad (3.15)$$

$R^2 = 0.87$, NOB $= 108$, 28:1 – 36:12, LM(1) $= 0.07$, LM(2) $= 0.78$, LM(6) $= 3.37$, ARCH(1) $= 0.22$

(3) *Imports to USA from France*

$$\text{LMMUSFR} - \text{LPUS} = 1.06 + 0.27\ (\text{LMMUSFR} - \text{LPUS})_{-1}$$
$$\qquad\qquad\qquad\quad (1.82)\ \ (2.70)$$

$$+\ 0.19\ (\text{LMMUSFR} - \text{LPUS})_{-2} + 0.04\ (\text{LMMUSFR} - \text{LPUS})_{-4}$$
$$\quad (2.01) \qquad\qquad\qquad\quad (0.49)$$

$$+\ 1.13\ (\text{LPUS} - \text{LPFR} + \text{LDFEXR}) - 1.64\ (\text{LPUS} - \text{LPFR} + \text{LDFESR})_{-1}$$
$$\quad (1.59) \qquad\qquad\qquad\qquad\qquad (2.91)$$

$$+\ 0.45\ \text{LIPUS} - 0.075\ \text{Smoot} + \text{seasonals}$$
$$\quad (3.60) \qquad\quad (1.33)$$

$R^2 = 0.82$, NOB $= 108$, $28:1 - 36:12$, LM(1) $= 0.96$, LM(2) $= 1.34$, LM(6) $= 5.80$, ARCH(1) 0.32

(4) *Imports to France from USA*

$$\text{LXMUSFR} - \text{LPFR} = 7.80 + 0.62\ (\text{LXMUSFR} - \text{LPFR})_{-1}$$
$$\qquad\qquad\qquad\quad (2.87)\ \ (7.02)$$

$$+\ 0.02\ (\text{LXMUSFR} - \text{LPFR})_{-4} - 0.06\ (\text{LXMUSFR} - \text{LPFR})_{-12} + 0.10$$
$$\qquad\qquad\qquad\qquad\qquad\qquad\qquad\qquad\qquad\qquad\qquad \text{LIPFR}_{-1}$$
$$\quad (0.19) \qquad\qquad\qquad\qquad (0.58) \qquad\qquad\qquad (0.23)$$

$$-\ 0.20\ \text{Dumfr} + \text{seasonals} - 1.67\ \text{D(LPUS} - \text{LPFR} + \text{LDFEXR})_{-1}$$
$$\quad (2.15) \qquad\qquad\qquad\quad (3.09)$$

$R^2 = 0.80$, NOB $= 108$, $28:1 - 36:12$, LM(1) $= 0.039$, LM(2) $= 2.01$, LM(6) $= 10.00$, ARCH(1) $= 0.68$

(5) *Imports to USA from Germany*

$$\text{LMMUSG} - \text{LPUS} = 4.43 + 0.262\ (\text{LMMUSG} - \text{LPUS})_{-4} + 0.72\ \text{LIPUS}_{-1}$$
$$\qquad\qquad\qquad\quad (4.59)\ \ (3.66) \qquad\qquad\qquad\qquad\quad (6.56)$$

$$+\ 1.14\ (\text{LPUS} - \text{LPG} - \text{LRMDEXR})_{-4} - 0.008\ \text{Smoot} + \text{seasonals}$$
$$\quad (8.28) \qquad\qquad\qquad\qquad\qquad (2.00)$$

$R^2 = 0.57$, $1927:5 - 1936:12$, NOB $= 116$, LM(1) $= 1.17$, LM(6) $= 6.87$, ARCH(1) $= 0.0043$

(6) *Imports to France from UK*

$$\text{LMMFRUK} - \text{LPFR} = 2.03 + 0.45 \, (\text{LMMFRUK} - \text{LPFR})_{-1}$$
$$(1.71) \quad (3.75)$$

$$+ 0.32 \, (\text{LMMFRUK} - \text{LPFR})_{-2} + 1.21 \, \text{D}(\text{LPFR} - \text{LPUK} - \text{LSTFREXR})_{-7}$$
$$(2.70) \qquad\qquad\qquad\qquad (2.19)$$

$$+ 0.01 \, \text{LIPFR}_{-9} - 0.13 \, \text{DUMFR} + \text{seasonals}$$
$$(0.10) \qquad\quad (2.25)$$

$R^2 = 0.85$, NOB $= 80$, $27\!:\!10 - 34\!:\!5$, LM(1) $= 1.44$, LM(2) $= 2.04$, LM(6) $=$ 8.60, ARCH(1) $= 0.035$

(7) *Imports to UK from France*

$$\text{LXMFRUK} - \text{LPUK} = 8.19 + 0.20 \, (\text{LXMFRUK} - \text{LPUK})_{-1}$$
$$(3.09) \quad (1.74)$$
$$- 0.04 \, (\text{LXMFRUK} - \text{LPUK})_{-10} - 0.81 \, (\text{LPFR} - \text{LPUK} - \text{LSTFREXR})_{-1}$$
$$(0.76) \qquad\qquad\qquad\qquad (2.28)$$

$$+ 1.63 \, \text{LIPUK} + \text{seasonals} - 1.78 \, \text{LIPUK}_{-2} + 0.17 \, \text{LIPUK}_{-12}$$
$$(2.32) \qquad\qquad\qquad\qquad (2.58) \qquad\qquad (0.31)$$
$$- 0.10 \, \text{Tariff}$$
$$(4.77)$$

$R^2 = 0.95$, $28\!:\!1 - 34\!:\!5$, NOB $= 77$, LM(1) $= 0.48$, LM(2) $= 0.72$, LM(4) $=$ 3.23, ARCH(1) $= 0.04$

(8) *Imports to France from Germany*

$$\text{LMMFRG} - \text{LPFR} = 0.73 + 0.40 \, (\text{LMMFRG} - \text{LPFR}) + 0.30$$
$$(\text{LMMFRG} - \text{LPFR})_{-2}$$
$$(0.71) \quad (4.05) \qquad\qquad\qquad\qquad (3.38)$$

$$+ 0.20 \, (\text{LPFR} - \text{LRMFREXR})_{-5} + 0.24 \, \text{LIPFR}_{-2} - 0.006 \, \text{Dumfr}$$
$$(0.76) \qquad\qquad\qquad\qquad (1.21) \qquad\qquad (0.16)$$

$+ \text{seasonals}$

$R^2 = 0.93$, $28\!:\!1 - 34\!:\!5$, NOB $= 77$, LM(1) $= 0.10$, LM(2) $= 1.08$, LM(6) $=$ 2.79, ARCH(1) $= 0.36$

(9) *Imports to Germany from France*

$$LXMFRG - LPG = 0.47 + 0.45 \ (LXMFRG - LPG)_{-1} + 0.2 \ (LXMFRG - LPG)_{-9}$$
$$(1.46) \ (3.41) \qquad\qquad (2.03)$$

$$- \ 0.13 \ (LXMFRG - LPG)_{-12} + 0.4 \ (LPG - LPFR + LRMFREXR)_{-12}$$
$$(1.60) \qquad\qquad (1.30)$$

$$+ \ 0.43 \ LIPG - 0.04 \ Dumg + seasonals$$
$$(4.02) \qquad (0.94)$$

$R^2 = 0.95$, $28:1 - 33:12$, NOB $= 72$, LM(1) $= 1.15$, LM(2) $= 1.17$, LM(6) $= 5.7$, ARCH(1) $= 0.01$

(10) *Imports to UK from Germany*

$$LMTUKG - LPUK = 9.41 + 0.18 \ LMTUKG - LPUK)_{-3}$$
$$(7.32) \ (1.94)$$

$$+ \ 0.01 \ (1 + BDC).(LPUK - LPG - LRMSTEXR)_{-1} + 0.47 \ LIPUK$$
$$(0.60) \qquad\qquad\qquad (5.22)$$
$$- \ 0.029 \ Tariff + seasonals$$
$$(5.0)$$

$R^2 = 0.80$, NOB $= 117$, $27:4 - 36:12$, LM(1) $= 0.32$, LM(2) $= 0.80$, LM(6) $= 4.12$, ARCH(1) $= 1.41$ (5.11)

(11) *Imports to Germany from UK*

$$LXTUKG - LPG = 2.06 + 0.71 \ (LXTUKG - LPG)_{-1} - 0.11 \ (LXTUKG - LPG)_{-2}$$
$$(2.03) \ (6.34) \qquad\qquad (1.60)$$

$$+ \ 1.37 \ DLPG_{-3} - 0.16 \ (LPUK - LRMSTEXR)_{-12} + 0.11 \ LIPG - 0.002 \ DumG$$
$$(2.86) \qquad (1.72) \qquad\qquad (1.15) \qquad (0.04)$$

$$+ \ 0.023 \ BDC + seasonals$$
$$(0.49)$$

$R^2 = 0.97$, NOB $= 88$, $28:9 - 35:12$, LM(1) $= 0.04$, LM(2) $= 1.01$, LM(9) $= 14.5$, ARCH(1) $= 1.96$

(12) Imports to Germany from USA

$$\text{LXMUSG} - \text{LPG} = 3.34 + 0.51\,(\text{LXMUSG} - \text{LPG})_{-1} + 0.96\,\text{LPG}_{-12}$$
$$\quad\quad (1.88)\ \ (12.73) \quad\quad\quad\quad\quad\quad (2.22)$$

$$- 1.56\,\text{D}(\text{LPUS} - \text{LRMDEXR}) + 0.80\,\text{DLIPG}_{-4} + 0.029$$
$$\text{DUMG}.\text{LMMUSG}$$
$$(1.21) \quad\quad\quad\quad\quad\quad\quad (0.99) \quad\quad (1.01)$$

+ seasonals

$R^2 = 0.90$, NOB = 89, $28:6 - 35:12$, LM(1) = 0.28, LM(2) = 0.79, LM(6) = 5.47, ARCH(1) = 0.048

APPENDIX B: DATA SOURCES AND VARIABLE LIST

Bilateral merchandise trade

MMUSFR, MMUSUK, MMUKG

Imports to USA from France, UK and Germany, respectively (*US and General Import of Merchandise*, USA)

XMUSFR, XMUSUK, XMMSG

Exports from USA to France, UK and Germany, respectively (source as above)

MMFRG, XMFRG

Imports and exports of France from/to Germany, respectively (*Commerce Spécial*, France)

MMFRUK, XMFRUK

Imports and exports of France from/to UK (CSO, UK)

MRUKG, XTUKG

Imports and exports of UK from/to Germany, respectively (*Trade and Navigation Accounts of UK*, monthly figures are interpolated from quarterly data)

XUK, XWUK, IMUK, MWUK

UK total merchandise exports, exports to the rest of the world (ROW), total merchandise imports, imports from the ROW, respectively

XUKH, XWUKH, IMUKH, MWUKH

UK historical values of XUK, XWUK, IMUK, MWUK (similar definitions for France, USA, Germany)

Spot and forward exchange rates

DSTEXR	Spot rate	£/$
DSTEXR1	Forward rate	£/$
RMDEXR	Spot rate	£/M
RMDEXR1	Forward rate	£/M
DFEXR	Spot rate	FFr/$
DFEXR1	Forward rate	FFr/$
STFREXR	Spot rate	FFr/£
RMSFEXR	Spot rate	£/M
RMFREXR	Spot rate	FFr/M

Source: P. Einzig, The Theory of the Forward Exchange Rate, (Macmillan, London, 1937).

UK

PPUK

General wholesale price, 200 commodities, Board of Trade (LCES).

PUK

Ministry of Labour retail price index (cost of living) (cost of maintaining an unchanged standard of living for a working class household before 1914).

PMUK

Board of Trade wholesale price index for materials.

IPUK

GNP index (Feinstein GNP annual series in 1938 prices in Mitchell interpolated from 'Index of Business Activity', Economist Supplement 25 July 1936 for method of construction.
First published in October 1933, this seasonally adjusted index was, according to The Economist, 'widely accepted as a measuring rod of Britain's economic activity . . . designed to give an approximate idea of fluctuations in "real" national income.' It is a weighted average of bank clearings (0.119), foreign trade and shipping movements (0.167), employment (0.238), power consumption (0.143), freight transport movement (0.143), postal receipts (0.071), building activity (0.048), consumption of iron and steel and cotton (0.071).

PRW

Rest of world prices (LNM). Quarterly price index of seventy-five states or territories in sterling interpolated by monthly world trade series.

USA

PPUS

Price index of finished product (FED/LNM).

PRMUS

Raw materials prices (FED/LNM).

IPUS

GNP Index (GNP in 1958 prices; *Historical Statistics* (1975) interpolated from industrial output index, IA).

France

PPFR

Wholesale price, forty items, LCES.

PFR

Paris Retail Price Index, thirteen items, LCES.

PRMFR

Raw materials prices.

IPFR

GNP index (annual NNP in 1938 prices in *Annuaire Statistique* in Mitchell interpolated from monthly industrial production index, LCES/LNM) 18 series covering one-half of total industrial production. For details *Indices Generaux du Mouvement Economique en France de 1901 a 1931* (Statistique Générale de la France).

Germany

PPG

Index of wholesale prices – all items, *Statistiches Reichsamt Index*, average for middle of month (LCES).

PG

Cost of Living, Reichs Index, *Eiledienst des statischischen Reichsamtes*, middle of month (LCES).

THE END OF FREE TRADE

GNP index (Hoffman's NNP series in 1913 prices from Mitchell interpolated from industrial output index (coverage 30 per cent before 1931 and 60 per cent after 1931), Institut für Konjuncturforschung, LNM). For details *Vierieljahrshefte zur Konjunkturforschung* 4 4 A 1930 , 6 1 A 1931, 7 4 A 1933.

Dummy variables

BDC	Dummy variable to capture move from Gold Standard to managed exchange rates in September 1931 (= 1 from $31:9$ onwards) in UK.
Gold	Dummy variable to capture gold/asset build up between 1928 and 1930 in France as a consequence of regulations governing Bank of France.
Seasonals	Seasonal dummies (monthly).
Smoot	For Smoot–Hawley tariff (= 1 from $30:6$ onwards) in USA.
Tariff	For the effects of increasing duties of all imports in UK (= 1 from 31:11 onwards).
dumfr	Trade prohibitions from 31:9 in France.
dumFRK	France–UK bilateral trade tariffs effects.
dumG	All duties increased in Jan. 1932 in Germany.
D294	Young Reparations, effects of the fears of French capital withdrawals from Germany.

Source abbreviations

FED	*Federal Reserve Monthly Bulletin*
LCES	*London and Cambridge Economic Service*
LNA	League of Nations, *Annual Statistical Bulletin*
LNM	League of Nations, *Monthly Statistical Bulletin*
F/S	M. Friedman and A. Schwartz, *A Monetary History of the United States*, (Princeton, NJ, 1963).
IA	International Abstracts (J. Tinbergen (ed.) *International Abstract of Economic Statistics 1919–30* (International Conference of Economic Services, Brussels, 1934); J.B.D. Derksen, *International Abstract of Economic Statistics 1931–36* Permanent Office of the International Statistics and Institute (The Hague, 1938).

Notes

1 This work was supported by ESRC grant number R000231534.
2 J. Foreman-Peck, A. Hughes Hallett, and Y. Ma, 'Optimum Policies for the World Depression', *Economie et Sociétés* 4–5, 1996, pp. 219–42.

3 J. Conybeare, 'Trade Wars: A Comparative Study of Anglo-Hanse, Franco-Italian and Hawley–Smoot Conflicts', *World Politics* 38, 1985, pp. 147–72.

4 K.A. Oye, *Economic Discrimination and Political Exchange: World Political Economy in the 1930s and 1980s* (Princeton, NJ, Princeton University Press, 1992).

5 B. Simmons, *Who Adjusts? Domestic Sources of Foreign Economic Policy during the Interwar Years,* Princeton Studies in International History and Politics (Princeton, NJ, Princeton University Press, 1994).

6 M. Kitson and S. Solomou, *Protectionism and Economic Revival: The British Interwar Economy* (Cambridge, 1990).

7 League of Nations, *Commercial Policy in the Interwar Period: International Proposals and National Policies* (Geneva, 1942).

8 J. Conybeare, 'Trade Wars'.

9 Department of Overseas Trade, *France* (London, HMSO, 1934), pp. 670–3.

10 League of Nations, *Commercial Policy in the Interwar Period*, p. 37.

11 K.A. Oye, *Economic Discrimination and Political Exchange*, p. 71.

12 League of Nations, *Commercial Policy in the Interwar Period*, p. 52.

13 B.J. Eichengreen, 'The Political Economy of the Smoot Hawley Tariff', NBER Working Paper 2001, 1986.

14 K.A. Oye, *Economic Discrimination and Political Exchange*.

15 F. Capie, *Tariffs and Growth* (Manchester, Manchester University Press, 1994), p. 60.

16 As the Banque de France told the Bank of England. A Bank official reported, 'Officials at the Bank of France were not hostile over the tariff. They thought it natural if Great Britain were to get a proper hearing on proper terms.' Bank of England Archives, OV45/82, 17 December 1931, memo re Moret from F.R. Rodd.

17 T. Rooth, *British Protectionism and the International Economy: Overseas Commercial Policy in the 1930s* (Cambridge, Cambridge University Press, 1993), pp. 49–50.

18 M. Kitson and S. Solomou, *Protectionism and Economic Revival*, p. 66.

19 Sir Percy Ashley, 'An Experiment in Tariff Making', *Transactions of the Manchester Statistical Society*, Session 1939–40, pp. 1–35.

20 J.H. Richardson, *British Economic Foreign Policy* (London, Allen & Unwin, 1936), pp. 110–12.

21 H.K. Heusser, *Control of International Trade,* (London, Routledge, 1939), p. 43.

22 League of Nations, *World Economic Survey 1932–3* (Geneva, 1933), p. 194.

23 F. Capie, *Tariffs and Growth*, p. 63.

24 League of Nations, *World Economic Survey 1933–4* (Geneva, 1934), p. 206; A. Predohl, 'Memorandum of the Experiences of Countries applying Foreign Exchange Control', in International Chambers of Commerce, *The Improvement of Commercial Relations between Nations: The Problem of Monetary Stabilisation* (Paris, 1936).

25 M. Kitson and S. Solomou, *Protectionism and Economic Revival*, p. 53–4.

26 F. Capie, *Depression and Protectionism: Britain between the Wars* (London, Allen & Unwin, 1983).

27 J. Williamson and C. Milner, *The World Economy: A Textbook in International Economics*, 2nd edn (London: Harvester Wheatsheaf, 1991), pp. 250–254.

28 J. Foreman-Peck, A. Hughes Hallett, and Y. Ma, 'The Transmission of the Great Depression in the United States, Britain, France and Germany', *European Economic Review* 36, 1992, pp. 685–94.

29 G.C. Chow and A. Lin, ' Best Linear Unbiased Interpolation, Distribution and Extrapolation of Time-series by Related Series', *Review of Economics and Statistics*, 53, 1971, pp. 372–5.

30 J.M. Keynes, in *New Statesman and Nation*, 7 March 1930, pp. 53–4.

22

SHAPING THE LESSONS OF HISTORY

Britain and the rhetoric of American trade
policy, 1930–1960

Patricia Clavin

In October 1945 the US State Department prepared an 'information programme' to educate the American public, and therefore Congress too, as to
the benefits of the United States' new commitment to multilateral tariff
reductions. A central theme of the numerous speeches delivered, in particular, by Assistant Secretary of State William Clayton, was the importance of a
strong Anglo-American partnership to support the American commitment
to 'Good Neighbourliness'. 'No other country', the American public was
told, was 'as important to our international trade, or indeed, the international trade of the world as Great Britain.'[1] Anxious to educate the American public as to the 'economic realities' which demanded an unequivocal
American commitment to the international economy, the State Department
worried whether the subject of economics was sufficiently 'sexy' to engage
the interest of the American public. So rather than dwell on the subtleties of
multilateral trade negotiation, particular stress was placed on the importance of
Anglo-American co-operation. Historical examples livened up the innumer-
able speeches and interviews given across the United States of America. In particular, the history of British 'responsibility' toward the world economy in the
nineteenth century was contrasted with the 'irresponsibility' of American protectionism during the Depression and the new enlightened thinking which
prevailed throughout the United States' policies in the new world order. The
information programme soon ran into trouble, however, as Anglo-American
negotiations foundered once again on the issue of regional (imperial) protection. By 1948 State Department efforts to educate key protectionist lobby
groups, notably the agricultural community, as to the benefits of tariff liberalisation no longer dwelt on Anglo-American partnership – the message now
was that the United States must show leadership in the world economy.

The issue of leadership was taken up by American scholars writing in the 1950s and 1960s. They charted the development of American economic foreign policy as a linear history maturing progressively from the 'blinkered, irresponsible and selfish' protectionism, exemplified by the Hawley–Smoot tariff of 1930, to its conversion into the new champion of the drive to lower international trade barriers with the Reciprocal Trade Agreements Act (RTA) of 1934. The RTA was seen as the precursor to the United States' ultimately unsuccessful attempt to create an International Trade Organisation (ITO) during and immediately after the Second World War, after which, of course, the capitalist 'free world' settled for the General Agreement on Tariffs and Trade (GATT). According to Calleo and Rowland, the legislation of 1934 determined that 'free trade was not dead, it had simply moved to America.'[2]

Of the recurrent themes in historians' and more particularly international relations theorists' accounts of the United States' changing approach to world trade, the question of whether the United States demonstrated 'responsibility' and 'leadership' in its trade policy became the most prevalent; in other words whether the United States had acted as a true hegemon in the world economy. The, now classic, statement of hegemonic responsibility is that of Charles Kindleberger: the stability of the world economy and open liberal relations are best provided and secured by the world's dominant economic power. Kindleberger's definition of American power was characterised not so much by the changing pattern of world trade after the First World War – in the 1920s Britain continued to be the most important importer and second only to the United States in terms of the volume of goods exported – as by the changing pattern of monetary power.[3] The emergence of the United States as the 'world's banker' and the dramatic redistribution of assets and liabilities which provoked this change, coupled with the huge growth in short-term credits during and after the Great War, made the global economy more vulnerable to monetary and economic shocks. So, too, did the composition and operation of the international gold exchange standard. It also made the debtor nations, which now included Britain and France, dependent on export earnings, particularly to the United States, to pay off their debts. Yet American monetary and trade policy failed to reflect these changes.

Central to accounts of America's failure as hegemon was its adoption of the Hawley–Smoot tariff in 1930, which increased American tariffs to, on average, around 40 per cent, making it, as Germany and others repeatedly alleged, impossible for foreign creditors to earn sufficient dollars to pay their debts, triggering a retaliatory flight to protectionism around the world and further impeding the already troubled operation of the gold standard.[4] Given the United States' position as the world's pre-eminent economy, the Hawley–Smoot tariff, more than any other protectionist act, came to symbolise the failure of the United States to recognise its *responsibilities* as the world's economic hegemon. (Conybeare, in contrast, takes American behaviour as evidence that the United States abused its market size to implement optimal tariffs, which he sees as a more likely outcome of hegemonic power than attempts to liberalise international trade.)[5]

More recent research, however, suggests that the victory of regionalism over globalism during the Great Depression owes more to the failure of multilateral co-operation in an increasingly complex world than to the failure of the United States to exert leadership in the world economy. The regionalism which gripped Europe, in particular, after 1930 was not triggered primarily as a retaliatory response to American protectionism, but was conditioned largely by internal/domestic political and economic elements which, for a variety of reasons, were able to exert a particularly strong influence over international trade.[6] Moreover, when it came to a question of retaliation against foreign tariff walls, countries like France and Germany were as, if not more, influenced by Britain's resort to protectionism in 1931 and 1932 as by that of the United States two years earlier because of the perceived contribution of free trade to the expansion of British power and the fact that, throughout the interwar period, Britain remained the world's largest import market.[7] Indeed, while internal and external economic considerations had the greatest impact in shaping American trading policy as well as the conception of American power in the interwar period, it is worth remembering that the US government, as well as the American public, overestimated British power in all aspects of international relations. True, Britain was superior to the United States when it came to the size and strategic superiority of the Royal Navy and to British dominance of that institution of ill-repute, the League of Nations, but the American public, coupled with the legislative and executive arms of government, exaggerated the strength of the British economy in relation to their own in most, if not all, aspects of economic policy too. It was a perception of British power firmly rooted in the nineteenth century.[8]

There is now a considerable body of scholarship detailing how the structural changes within the American economy, coupled with the new constellation of interest group politics and the profound desire to avert another Great Depression, generated policies to fundamentally reform international economic relations in order to restore world trade. The American drive to liberalise international tariffs took shape during the Second World War in order to free both its national and the international economy from the desultory performance in the 1930s. But while the war and then the Cold War added much to the rhetoric of 'freedom and liberty' which framed American efforts to secure first bilateral and then multilateral tariff reductions, the early leg-work for the American tariff initiative was done during the 1930s. By 1941 the White House and the State Department had reflected long and hard on their policy errors in the recent past and sought to learn from them – as a White House speech writer put it, the ghost of Woodrow Wilson was often at Roosevelt's shoulder.

During the war British and American negotiators shared the same desire to establish an open economic system at war's end, provided that safeguards for national economic policies could be established. As is well known, this did not prove easy and negotiators struggled with incompatible domestic priorities and the cumbersome machinery of tariff negotiation. What is less well known is that the United States sought a tariff-cutting partnership with Britain as early as 1933. As will be demonstrated in the first section of this chapter, the history of Anglo-American negotiations in the 1930s offered important lessons for future co-operation which went unheeded. At the same time, however, the rhetoric of the United States' move to free trade was intimately connected with the American perception of British power in the nineteenth century and by Britain's attitude towards American tariff legislation in the first half of the twentieth century.

The interaction was not accidental. As the subsequent two sections of the chapter demonstrate, the British government consistently sought to define American responsibilities to the rest of the world. The ineffective, contradictory but usually selfish foreign policy of the United States was repeatedly contrasted with the incisive and global orientation of British power in the nineteenth century. After the outbreak of war, the historical models of '*Pax Britannica*' implicit in Foreign Office and Treasury criticisms of the United States became explicit as the British government employed a large number of historians to shape American policy in Britain's interests, and so did the tension between 'freedom' and 'responsibility' which subsequently resulted. Britain could not prevent the transition of power to the United States, but the way it sought to shape that transition also had unforeseen and undesirable consequences for British policy on trade after 1945.[9]

The 'lessons of history', coupled with though distinct from the legacy of history, and the creation of an axiomatic link between the promotion of free trade and political freedom, were central to the American rhetoric on, first, the ITO and then the GATT. Historians have studied how statesmen employed readings of history (often highly selective or just plain erroneous ones) to make crucial decisions, but less attention has been paid to the role of historians in the evolution of policy. The chapter will explore, although by no means offer a comprehensive account of, how the lessons of the past were defined by the US government and the roles played by professional and amateur historians in shaping contemporary policy, as well as their later historical accounts of American foreign policy in general and its trading policy in particular.

The ghost of trade negotiations past

A southern Democrat who was a key ally in Roosevelt's management of the Democrat party, Cordell Hull, professed that, from the outbreak of the First World War, he had come to believe that 'if we could increase commercial exchanges over lowered trade and tariff barriers . . . we would go a long way to eliminating war itself.' Implicit in his somewhat eccentric account of the origins of the war was a vision of British free-trading history in the nineteenth century, which, so Hull believed, had brought stability to the world at a time when the United States 'had no permanent policies to deal with the international economic situation and its relations to tariffs.'[10] Like most of the American political elite, Hull was proud of his 'pure Anglo-Saxon [but] revolutionary background', and coupled with his strong interest in history, his formal and political education was imbued with a view of British history which identified free trade with the growth of British power in the nineteenth century and imperialism and protectionism with the origins of the First World War. In this he was also strongly influenced by the Woodrow Wilson and Democratic party debates on the style and content of American internationalism around the time of the Paris Peace Conference.[11]

Much of Hull's argument was unoriginal. Manufacturing and trade had long been cornerstones of American foreign policy, although the determination to safeguard the continued growth of American trade was closely tied to a concept of national interest which also provided ready encouragement to protectionist lobby groups. The contradiction was apparent throughout Herbert Hoover's tenure as Secretary of Commerce and as President. His trade policies reflected both the American desire to trade overseas and to incorporate its economic interests into the prosecution of foreign policy, alongside the contradictory impulse to protect the domestic market. The ambiguity encouraged a 'schizophrenic' American position on tariffs which advocated the expansion of American trade through the 'Open Door' policy at the same time as encouraging high protective duties – a tension underlined by the imposition of the notorious Hawley–Smoot tariff.[12]

By 1932 many, both inside the Commerce and State Departments and without, began to argue that the United States should move away from the inconsistent, 'double-edged' Open Door and adopt a reciprocal trading policy. The State Department, in particular, was stung by repeated European criticism (Britain was included in America's conception of Europe) that American protectionism compromised its investments in Europe, that it had prompted Britain and France to abandon the collection of reparations, and was forcing countries like Germany from the international economy.[13] The shift in official sentiment was supported by the increasingly free-trade position of the largely capital-intensive industries like banking, and the oil and electricity companies – Ferguson's 'multinational bloc', which fared rather better than most in the Depression. Once Republican supporters, they were now increasingly drawn toward the professed low-tariff position of the Democratic party.[14]

In the new Democratic administration Cordell Hull was the undoubted champion of such a strategy, intent on liberating world trade as 'the basis of friendship and confidence in which permanent peace can be built.' Once dismissed by scholars, Hull's contribution to successive Roosevelt administrations has been reappraised, most recently by Irwin Gellman, stressing his long-term influence on American economic diplomacy and Roosevelt's internationalism.[15] After his appointment as Secretary of State in March 1933, he took every opportunity to publicise the administration's resolve to secure Congressional authority to negotiate reciprocal tariff agreements based on a flat rate reduction of 10 per cent of existing barriers, a corresponding percentage enlargement of quotas, and bilateral agreements within unconditional MFN treatment.

The State Department's competition with the nationalist-orientated 'bright, young things' responsible for devising and implementing the New Deal is well known and certainly worked to delay Roosevelt's support for the RTA until 1934, whereupon the United States concluded reciprocal agreements with countries in Central and South America – the region where they were most successfully implemented (by 1945, twenty-nine RTA treaties had been secured), reducing the United States tariff by almost three-quarters.[16] Hull's initiative had important consequences for pan-American commerce and diplomacy, which have been well documented. Less well known is the fact that Hull sought to conclude his very first reciprocal tariff agreement with the British government. From December 1932 (the initiative is more typically dated from 1934 or 1936), Hull's overtures for an agreement to halt the escalation of, in the words of those who mimicked his lisp, 'twade baa-yuhs' were directed, in particular, at the British government. In January 1933, three months before he was fully installed as Secretary of State, Hull already had adopted the Republican-sponsored tariff truce for the World Economic Conference scheduled for June 1933. He planned to use it to secure the first reciprocal tariff agreement with the British government. The State and Commerce Departments even harboured hopes that an Anglo-American agreement would provide the basis for initiating multilateral tariff reductions throughout the world through the operation of unconditional most-favoured-nation treatment. The fact that Britain's commitment to unconditional MFN had been compromised by the Ottawa agreements was largely ignored by the American administration, although it troubled the British Foreign Office greatly.[17] Indeed, from February until early June 1933 both the German Foreign Ministry and the new National Socialist economics minister, Hjalmar Schacht, repeatedly expressed a profound concern that Britain and the United States were 'very likely to sign a trade agreement in the near future' heralding a new era in Anglo-American co-operation.[18]

The fact that most historians date American overtures to Britain after 1936 is hardly surprising given that it was only then that a politically motivated British interest in the treaty awoke – the National Government belatedly hoping that this evidence of Anglo-American solidarity would discourage German imperial ambitions.[19] Accounts of the Anglo-American tariff negotiations emphasise both the Act's shortcomings as a means of demonstrating transatlantic solidarity to the Germans and its failure to reduce international protectionism. However, in many ways, the year 1933 provided a window of opportunity to pursue an Anglo-American *rapprochement* on economic and monetary issues. With the flotation of the US dollar in April, membership of the gold standard was no longer a source of tension in Anglo-American relations, and much has been made of the failure of Britain and the United States to launch a joint initiative to reflate the world economy and break the stranglehold of gold standard orthodoxy.[20] There was also an opportunity to make progress on the question of intergovernmental indebtedness.

Of course, it is exercising the historians' privilege of hindsight, which makes the first two years of Roosevelt's presidency seem like a lost opportunity in Anglo-American economic relations. Back in 1933 the timing of Secretary Hull's tariff overture appeared particularly poor – the Abnormal, General and Imperial tariffs had only just passed into law and it remained unclear how far Hull enjoyed the support of a president apparently torn between the nationalist and internationalist elements in his government. As the chief British economic adviser Frederick Leith Ross put it, Britain should eschew co-operation because 'no-one can foretell which of these two horses he is likely to be riding at any particular moment.'[21] Equally unconvincing from the British perspective was the way that the State Department skirted over the sticky question of whether Congressional support for the RTA could be secured.

The Department preferred to side-step such awkward questions and instead concentrate its efforts on selling the political advantages of the agreement to the British government. The internationalists in Roosevelt's administration were encouraged by what they perceived to be 'positive' features in British economic foreign policy. Officials in the State Department from Ray Atherton, the influential chargé based at the US Embassy in London, up to Hull all believed that the reports of the death of British internationalism, reflected in Britain's departure from gold and by the imperial tariff agreements, were greatly exaggerated. This erroneous perception was shaped, in part, by a misreading of the likely long-term impact of the Ottawa agreements and by an underestimation of the depth and breadth of support for protectionism in Britain.[22] Perturbed by the fact that the imperial agreements introduced quotas into Britain's protective arsenal and the imperial rhetoric which accompanied the agreements, the White House and the State Department none the less paid greater heed to intelligence reports underlining Dominion, and to a lesser extent British, dissatisfaction with the agreements, observing 'an extra-ordinary amount of sympathetic interest manifested in the [Canadian] Conservative and Liberal press favouring reciprocity with the United States.'[23]

But it was the State Department's conviction that British power was founded on free trade and that Britain would, with American support, return to free trade which was the most influential on American preparations for negotiations with the British. The determination of men like Hull, and of like-minded advisers William Phillips, Herbert Feis, Leo Pasvolsky and later Dean Acheson, came from the lessons of history as they perceived them. History demonstrated the dependence of the British economy on the world export market, and, moreover, Britain's reputation and experience in the field of free trade would enhance that of the United States. As the financier, James Warburg, put it, 'the idea for a bilateral trade treaty with the British' arose because: 'they would probably be the easiest person [sic] to do it with . . . the British . . . and then see what kind of animal that would be and how wide its application would be to others.'[24]

The State Department also took a selective interpretation of recent developments in British policy to bolster a reading of history which underlined the British commitment to free trade: the National Government's desire to secure agreement on its war debts to the United States; and the devaluation of both sterling and the US dollar, which removed the gold standard, albeit temporarily, as a source of tension in their relations and whose beneficial effects were, so Herbert Feis, international economic adviser in the State Department, rightly argued, impeded by protectionism. Finally, there was Britain's promotion of a World Economic Conference ostensibly to tackle the breakdown of international economic co-operation. To the Americans this was all evidence that Britain's departure from internationalism was temporary. More troubling signals, like Britain's new bilateral trade treaties with Denmark, Sweden, Norway and most significantly, Argentina, were played down by the internationalists (some argued that an Anglo-American agreement was now more likely as the United States imported a larger volume of British goods than either Argentina or Denmark, taking 7.6 per cent of British exports while Argentina and Denmark imported 5.3 and 4.9 per cent respectively), although there is no doubt that it was hoped a bilateral RTA treaty with Britain would limit the impact of these agreements. American farmers, in particular, were enraged by what they saw as their increasing exclusion from a charmed circle of European and imperial producers and their determination grew to secure agricultural concessions from Britain at the same time as isolating the United States from international 'entanglements'.[25]

It was the clash between nationalist and international elements in the early New Deal, both in terms of policy and personalities, which pulled the rug from under Hull's feet. In June 1933 the presidential support needed to get the RTA legislation through Congress evaporated, and Roosevelt embarked on a (superficially) radical policy of dollar devaluation which soured the climate of international co-operation. The drama over co-operation on monetary issues (incidentally now increasingly seen by scholars as a failure of multilateral co-operation rather than hegemonic leadership) dramatically overshadowed Hull's pleas at the World Conference for international and especially British support for his planned tariff-cutting initiative. The unpredictable character of the American administration and the contradiction between Hull's plans to reduce the American tariff and the policies of the new Agriculture Administration gave Britain a ready excuse, as did the increasingly turbulent international climate. The American administration and press, in their turn, accused the British of exaggerating and playing upon the differences within the administration.[26] By 1934 the State Department, strongly supported by the new Tariff Division created within it, was able to claim that Roosevelt had acted to quash British criticism of his 'ambiguous' position on American tariff reductions by overseeing the passage of the RTA into law.[27]

What the British government failed to make clear to the Americans was its conviction that a reciprocal tariff agreement with the United States was not in the interests of the British economy. The fundamental problem for the British government was that, as Chamberlain explained to French Prime Minister, Georges Bonnet, 'the United States sells to us five or six times what she takes from us. We thought that it was for America to first lower its tariffs, not very substantially, so that we could increase our trade with her.'[28] Britain's £70 million trading deficit to the United States was a genuine obstacle to the conclusion of an Anglo-American trading agreement, as well as a source of great embarrassment to successive British governments.[29] Until Anglo-American negotiations on a trade agreement officially reopened in 1936, the British preferred to skirt over the embarrassing reality of its trading deficit to the United States to assert its continued interest in international tariff reductions and that imperial preference was motivated by the obligations of 'historic kinship' not naked protectionism. The State Department was not insensitive to the issue of the trade deficit, but argued, when it was given the opportunity, that 'if trade between the United States and the whole of the British Empire was considered – and not merely trade between the United States and the United Kingdom – we bought as much from the empire as the empire bought from us.'[30]

Nor, the National Government repeatedly declared, although not usually to the Americans, was it interested in joining any regional low-tariff groups, exemplified by the 1932 Ouchy Convention between the Benelux states, even one which centred on the United States. Despite its professed interest in securing a reduction of national protectionism, and ignoring the complication that Britain was itself a member of an imperial low-tariff group, the National Government expressed the view that such groups were divisive to international relations and impeded global economic recovery.

Throughout 1933 Britain made it clear by political and, to a lesser extent, economic arguments that it was unimpressed by American overtures and uninterested in an Anglo-American trade agreement. Indeed, the Treasury and Foreign Office were confident that unless the British government indicated that 'the plan can be developed in any form at all, it will probably be dropped.'[31] But they were wrong. In the United States, criticism of the

National Government's position was swift and harsh. The *New York Times* condemned Britain for advocating 'the abolition or reduction of all barriers to its commerce, except of the kinds which it itself is practising', while, more significantly, Herbert Feis, economic adviser to the State Department, complained that though American statesmen 'were no angels', the British were behaving with 'a diminished sense of international responsibility' which was 'very likely to stand in the way of any about turn in the whole course of international relations.'[32] His assessment reflected a view which was widespread in the State Department and echoes the findings of international relations theorist David Lake that Britain now acted as a 'spoiler' in international trading relations.[33]

To Britain's critics in the United States, not only did British opposition to low-tariff groups seem hypocritical, but the direct percentage comparison of tariff values had also become misleading. Primary prices had collapsed dramatically since 1929 and after 1931 the variable of currency depreciation now had to be added to the equation, although most American observers concluded the trading advantage which nations like Britain, Denmark and Norway had accrued since devaluation was transitory. Moreover, British 'mistrust of American ability' to provide the lead on international trade not only fostered American 'mistrust of Europe's ability to receive and act upon our advice', but also lessened the authority of internationalists in the American administration in their power struggles with those increasingly determined to isolate the United States from world events.[34]

The British change of heart came in July 1936 when Neville Chamberlain, then still Chancellor of the Exchequer, and Walter Runciman, President of the Board of Trade, signalled Britain's new determination to open trade negotiations with the United States. Politics took precedence over economics for Chamberlain was now determined to secure an Anglo-American trade agreement to present Europe's dictators with 'the possibility of these two great powers working together.'[35] The bruising battle over British agricultural concessions to the United States – since 1932 inter-imperial trade had grown stronger and American farmers more vociferous in their demands for access to the British market – lasted twenty-seven months and left the German government in little doubt as to the true character of Anglo-American relations.[36] London's new willingness to explore the possibility of an agreement could disguise neither the incompatibility of British and American tariff structures, which had grown more acute since 1933, nor the cumbersome machinery of the RTA. Nevertheless, the primacy of politics prevailed and the final Anglo-American Reciprocal Trading Agreement was finally signed on 17 November 1938. The agreement did little to liberalise Anglo-American trade, never mind trigger a global move to reduce international protectionism. Nor did it cause Germany to overestimate the extent of genuine co-operation in Anglo-American relations. Although Hull was right to argue that the global crisis triggered the move to nationalist

economic and political systems with concomitant difficulties for international stability, by 1938 the crisis could no longer be resolved by a piecemeal return to economic internationalism. What concerns us here, however,
are not the Anglo-American agreement's economic or diplomatic limitations
– these have been fully explored elsewhere – but how history and historians,
particularly British ones, shaped the American administration's growing
conviction that it now had fully taken up the role of 'champion of trade
liberalisation' apparently discarded by Britain in 1931.

Pax Britannica as role model

The myriad of individuals who had opinions on, though intermittent influence over, American foreign policy in the 1930s has always made it difficult
to trace precisely who influenced the development of American foreign policy, and when. So, too, did the dramatic pace of events and the tremendous
growth of the American economy at war, but it is clear that by 1941 the
administration had developed a much more critical view of its foreign policy
efforts in the interwar period, in general, and its efforts to reduce international protectionism in particular. The lessons of recent history, alongside
structural changes in the American economy and the changing composition
and constellation of interest groups which this economic change helped to
stimulate, were instrumental in shaping the Atlantic Charter in June 1941.
In it the United States made clear its determination to rectify the errors of
the last peace. According to Roosevelt, 'the well-intentioned but ill-fated
experiments of former years did not work. . . . It is my intention to do all
that I humanly can as President and Commander in Chief to see that these
tragic mistakes shall not be made again.'[37] Errors in regard to the treatment
of Germany were uppermost in the minds of the audience of this fireside
chat, but for Roosevelt the lessons went further. Although he was determined to 'strip Germany of its military might', the destructive power of
economic depression had had a far greater impact than German aggression on
both domestic and international politics in the 1930s.

The efficacy of the American 'system' over those of the European powers
was demonstrated by the way it recovered from the Depression and waged
war. It was also clear to Roosevelt that Woodrow Wilson had been right.
Economic stability and national security could be achieved only on a world-
wide scale and America had to take the lead now that European leadership
had failed.[38] American reflections on the ineffectiveness and irresponsibility
of its foreign policy in the interwar period echoed earlier stinging British
criticisms of American foreign policy. This was no accident. John Lewis
Gaddis has described the evolution of American policy thus: 'like the British,
from whom they *inherited* the tendency, Americans had traditionally associated their security with balancing the power of the world.'[39] But the transfer
of a sense of global responsibility was not genetic. My contention is that as

the United States sought to define the *Pax Americana* to govern international relations in the postwar period, it was not a question of 'inheriting tendencies', but a process of conscious (and unconscious) adoption of the rhetoric and perceived history of British power in the nineteenth century. As the State Department and the White House drew up their plans for peace, British history and British historians played an important, if subtle, role.

Britain could not define all the 'lessons of history' drawn by the US government. The anti-imperialism rooted in the founding of the United States was reinforced by blunt lessons drawn from the 1930s. Profoundly impressed by the strategic advantages that Germany had accrued through its economic nationalism in its preparations for war, and, more importantly, the conviction that British and French imperialism fuelled the drive for similar advantages by the 'have not' powers, the American administration grew increasingly hostile to British imperialism. Particularly influential was the American observation that it was easier 'for the dictators to handle the crisis [provoked by rearmament] than for liberal capitalistic governments whose free market economies leave them open in times of international tension.'[40] Imperial agreements, it was concluded, damaged the world economy and American interests with them, and strong American leadership was now vital to secure viable and truly multilateral trade agreements.

Historians as propagandists

British efforts to 'publicise' and to 'educate' the American elite and, to a lesser extent, public opinion as to the benefits of strong Anglo-American co-operation both during the war and in the new international order to be created in its wake, engaged the energies of the Foreign Office, the Ministry of Information and subsidiary departments overseas like the British Library of Information and the newly created British Press Service with offices in New York, Washington, San Francisco and Chicago. As part of the initiative, the Ministry of Information (MOI) also mobilised personnel skilled at research and persuasive argument, who became leading lights in Britain's postwar historical establishment (if establishment is the right term). E.H. Carr was head of section at the MOI; Harold Nicolson acted first as Parliamentary Secretary to the MOI, before becoming head of III Section in the American Division of the MOI responsible for briefing British visitors to the United States in 1941. John Wheeler-Bennet, head of research at the British Press Service, enjoyed highly prized, direct contact with Franklin D. Roosevelt because he had taught the president's son history at the University of Virginia, while Denis Brogan worked first in the MOI and then, when his personality and forthright views proved too abrasive, as the BBC's intelligence expert on the United States. The task of the historians employed in the British government was not to educate the American public as to the 'facts of history' (uncomfortable facts like the First World War were left out), but to use historical example to add validity and appeal to their propaganda message.

At the heart of the MOI's 'target audience' (to borrow the parlance of modern advertising) were members of the executive and legislative branches of the American administration – history had demonstrated the risk of ignoring Congress – and, whenever possible, the British government sought to use Americans to deliver their message. 'Friendly contacts' (today's 'agents of influence') like Herbert Feis, now in the War Department, journalist Walter Lippmann, Hamilton Armstrong Fish, Director of the Council of Foreign Relations, and Roosevelt's old friend Justice Felix Frankfurter were cultivated and exploited to disseminate the British view on waging the war and determining the peace. Although the MOI's strategies for disseminating information in the United States grew more sophisticated as the war went on, the story remained much the same. At the heart of Britain's propaganda message lay what the Foreign Office and the MOI called the 'doctrine of responsibility', in other words that the United States recognise and act on its 'responsibilities to the world', with the aspiration that, in so doing, the United States would adopt policies favourable to Britain. History played a big part in British propaganda as a means to stress the kinship and 'common cultural and political values' which Britain and the United States were fighting to protect. More particularly, the MOI encouraged friendly American journalists, broadcasters and statesmen visiting or based in London (in what E.H. Carr called 'the strategy of truth') to characterise the nineteenth century as one in which the British had taken the responsibility for maintaining world peace and the stability of the international economy. Now it was the turn of the United States.[41] Not that such an acceptance of American global dominance was easy, even for those members of the British government who were 'friendly' towards the United States. It was often reflected in private that the United States was not worthy of inheriting Britain's world role. The widely held desire to encourage American internationalism was coupled with the conviction that American power was to be kept 'within proper limits'.[42]

The great difficulty for the MOI was that while the British government supported the Foreign Office goal articulated in 1940 of creating an American belief in Britain's military, economic and moral strength, the reality of British dependence on the United States for supplies, coupled with its inability to defend its Pacific bases, undermined its best efforts.[43] The goal of the Foreign Office was to encourage and to shape American internationalism based on a strong Anglo-American partnership. It presented Anglo-American relations in a global context, and a history whose recurrent theme was one of shared interests and co-operation. This was true, particularly when it came to strategic and defence issues, but the history of their peacetime and, to a lesser extent, their wartime relations was a history peppered with rivalries and conflict when it came to economic issues. Moreover, the

299

reality of Britain's diminishing power base, the questioned future of the empire, coupled with American hostility towards it, presented Britain with an insuperable problem.

In its efforts to 'educate' American opinion as to the responsibilities of *Pax Americana*, the MOI did not explicitly draw parallels between British free trade in the nineteenth century and the new American determination to promote trade liberalisation. However, for all that the MOI tried not to emphasise the fact that British power in the nineteenth century was intimately connected with overseas trade in general, and free trade in particular, the White House, the State Department and the Department of Agriculture did. Indeed, the unwillingness of the MOI to dwell on Britain's past commitment to trade liberalisation rested uneasily with past British demands for a 'responsible' American policy towards international trade after 1918. Earlier British criticism of US trade policy continued to resonate for two reasons, despite the reluctance of British wartime Treasury officials to commit Britain to a complete removal of its protective barriers at the war's end. The first was the American conviction that the prevalence of protectionism throughout the 1930s was responsible for the persistence of the global depression in general, and the low levels of international trade in particular. That the link between British criticisms of American 'irresponsibility' and tariffs remained so strong reflected the second reason why the US administration was determined to reduce protectionism as low and as soon as possible: a strong continuity of personnel within the US administration between 1933 and 1945.

Throughout the war the British propaganda message in the United States was a 'partnership on equal terms', yet the bitter and persistent Anglo-American dispute over the terms and character of lend-lease, in particular, demonstrated the true gulf between British and American ambitions for the economics of the postwar order. The British government argued long and hard before accepting 'the Consideration', as Article 7 of the Master Lend-Lease Agreement of 1942 became known, which sought to remove the ambiguity of the British commitment to a liberal economic order enshrined in the Atlantic Charter a year earlier.[44] The gulf between the rhetoric of an Anglo-American partnership and the reality of Britain's power-base became acute. Anglo-American negotiations over the arguably more important monetary negotiations were facilitated by a common economic language and a shared view on the technicalities of monetary co-operation. As Ikenberry has demonstrated, agreement on the monetary order needed to promote growth, stability and a relatively open, multilateral system of trade and payments grew out of an 'expert consensus' inspired by the Keynesianism embraced by a group of well-placed British and American economists.[45]

Harry White and Adolf Berle, responsible for the twenty-one sub-committees of the wartime Committee for Economic Foreign Policy, made the American prosecution of international tariff reductions an essential corollary of its plans for postwar global monetary relations. Yet expert and political consensus on trade policy was difficult to establish. This was, in part, because of a tension between the US Treasury's emphasis on internal stability and the State Department's determination to effect free trade. It was also because the war had reinforced the appeal and, to an important extent, the necessity of imperial preference to the British economy, if anything strengthening the link between British global power and the empire.

The central role of the sterling bloc and inter-imperial trade to Britain's war efforts and the problems which were destined to face British interests at home and in the empire after the war's end made all but a select few in the British government deeply hostile to American proposals for direct action to eliminate forms of discriminatory treatment, including tariffs and quotas. The select few favouring a renewed British commitment to free trade were to be found, unsurprisingly, in the Board of Trade. The most hostile to such proposals were Conservative cabinet ministers, who believed that the future of the British economy lay in imperial preference. Holding the middle ground was Treasury and Foreign Office opinion, dominated by John Maynard Keynes. This, the largest group, wanted to co-operate with the United States but wished to define that co-operation, as far as possible, to reflect British interests. As well as harbouring a grim determination to protect Britain's global power which seemed predicated on the continued vitality of the empire, the government also (rightly as it turned out) calculated that Britain would need currency controls and discriminatory trading practices to rebuild its economy.

When Keynes was first presented with American plans for postwar Anglo-American economic relations in Washington in the summer of 1941 he vehemently attacked the American 'imposition of an ironclad formula [for *laissez-faire*] from the Nineteenth Century.'[46] Although he later apologised for the strength of his language, the British government stalled until February 1942 before it gave up its option to use discriminatory trading practices after its military position had greatly weakened through Japanese advances in the Pacific. In the end, British dependence on the United States in war determined an apparent British commitment to the American drive for free trade. As Keynes put it, the alternative to co-operation was a trade war with the United States, and it were a war Britain was bound to lose.[47] Thus satisfied the US government continued to underestimate British hostility to American demands for the abolition of imperial preference. This was in part because the State Department believed that opposition to American economic demands was coming from reprobate imperialists in London, and not, as was in fact the case, from the majority of the Cabinet and Parliament, supported, in turn, by the Treasury and the Foreign Office.[48]

But poor intelligence from the US Ambassador in London for this error offers only part of the explanation. Equally, if not more important, was British propaganda, which, though it sought to avoid explicit reference to questions of trade, drew parallels between British power founded on free trade in the nineteenth century and the global power of the United States in the twentieth. The hitherto ignored role of British propaganda in the United States helps to explain why the State Department misread Keynes' early thoughts on postwar economic policy, which stressed national measures to ensure employment and social welfare.[49] Indeed, in the past Keynes himself had helped to popularise the call to, in some way, resurrect the economic *Pax Britannica* which had facilitated growth and prosperity in the nineteenth century.[50] The British propaganda message also made repeated reference to the need for a strong Anglo-American partnership in international relations. Where better to start, so the State Department argued (as it had in 1933), than in a clear Anglo-American commitment to liberalise international trade?

Other lessons of history had a further influence on the character of American policies towards Britain. The 1930s had demonstrated the power of the American Congress to limit the ability of the executive to conclude even bilateral tariff reductions, and Congress's growing antipathy to British imperial preference (generated, in part, by vociferous lobbying from agricultural pressure groups) also strengthened Hull's determination to make Britain give up imperial preference. Equally problematic for the British was the fact that the American public continued to be obsessed by Britain's failure to pay its war debts incurred in the First World War to the United States. When Truman abruptly cancelled lend-lease at the war's end and negotiations opened for an American loan to Britain as part of the final lend-lease settlement, the British government was forced to reiterate its commitment to abolishing imperial preference (despite the huge scale of the sterling balances). The United States public continued to harbour suspicions about Britain's commitment to American postwar objectives. When questioned by opinion poll, the American public revealed its conviction that Britain was far less likely to pay back its wartime loans than either Russia or China. Yet despite the public's opposition, Truman and the US Congress granted Britain a generous lend-lease settlement because they believed the MOI's portrayal of Britain as a 'sturdy ally with temporary economic difficulties' and its government's commitment to the liberalisation of international trade.[51]

Conclusion

On the question of trade, the work of British propagandists was not necessarily in Britain's favour as it led the United States to underestimate the depth and scale of British opposition to its calls to set up an International Trade Organisation dedicated to the promotion of global free trade. Seeking to shape the American definition of its responsibilities to global stability by likening American power to that of Britain in the nineteenth century also may have led the State Department to underestimate the depth of opposition to free trade among the American public. Certainly, when representatives acting on instructions from Secretary of State William Clayton gave a series of public lectures to educate American farmers as to 'US Commercial Policy in World Economic Leadership', American 'responsibility' was the watchword. The speeches contrasted American irresponsibility in the Depression against the effectiveness of the RTA and the administration's new recognition of its responsibilities to leadership.[52] Where once 'freedom' was associated with the freedom of the United States to pursue American economic interests as it saw fit, now 'freedom' meant adopting responsible policies towards promoting free trade in the international economy and was strongly associated with the protection of political freedom.

History, as it unfolded after 1946, however, made it clear that the rhetoric of America's commitment to free trade differed greatly from a reality which saw the protectionist impulse of Congress destroy the ITO at birth and limit the effectiveness of GATT until the 1960s. It was the logic of Cold War confrontation, coupled with new tariff initiatives on the part of the European Community on international trade, which persuaded American public opinion in general, and Congress in particular, of the value of multilateral trade agreements.[53]

A further demonstration of the power of the historical motif employed by the British to influence the development of American internationalism can be found in the impact of British history and historians on policies advocated by key individuals in the US administration and academia. Take, for example, Herbert Feis, a prominent adviser to the State Department and the War Department until 1946, who became a Pulitzer Prize-winning historian in the Cold War. Writing in 1934, he argued that the disintegration of the international economy could only be halted 'when Great Britain, the United States and France [have] faced their responsibilities fully in both their currency and political relations.' By 1950 this multilateral account of international relations in the 1930s became one in which the United States failed to realise an economic potential that would 'have made the difference between peace and war.'[54] Feis's change of heart, in part but only in part, reflected a disillusionment with European politics which was widespread in the United States in the war and the bi-polar world of the Cold War. But equally influential were ideas drawn from his writing on the nineteenth-century economy and his prolonged contact with a number of leading British historians and economists throughout his career both as a government employee and as an historian. In turn, just as these historians influenced Feis, so he, in his long and active career as a professional historian after the Second World War, helped to shape the writings of the next generation of American historians, the majority of whom depict the history of American foreign policy as one which matured 'in a stream of responsibility that [ran] from Wilson to Truman, from Hughes to Acheson.'[55]

303

PATRICIA CLAVIN

The use of historical example to explain, justify or criticise the present is nothing new. However, the employment of historians in government both in peace and war to shape government policy poses important questions about the social responsibilities of historians. One of the fundamental difficulties is that while many historians now believe that to study history is to become increasingly aware of the subjectivity of their outlook, the employment of historical example to inform and justify government policy pulls history in the opposite direction – politicians, social scientists and 'the plain interested' want historians to find 'lessons' or 'laws'. It is not the case, and it seems fitting to end with Hegel, where the 'process' of history began, to argue that 'we learn from history that we do not learn from history', but that a particular conception of the past does help to determine the way that politicans and the public conceive of, and plan for, the future.[56]

Notes

1 Lot Files on International Trade, National Archives, Washington, DC (hereafter NA RG43), RG43, box 3, memorandum on the information programme of the United States, 4 Oct. 1945.
2 Calleo, D. and Rowland, B., *America and the World Political Economy: Atlantic Dreams and National Realities*, Bloomington, Indiana University Press, 1973, p. 33.
3 Kindleberger, C.P., *The World in Depression, 1929–1939*, Harmondsworth, Penguin Books, 1979, *passim*.
4 Schuker, S., *American 'Reparations' to Germany 1919–1933: Implications for the Third World Debt Crisis*, Princeton NJ, Princeton Studies in International Finance, 61, 1988, pp. 47–69; Kindleberger, C.P., *The World in Depression, 1929–1939*, London, Penguin, 1987 (2nd edn), pp. 64–5; Capie, F., *Trade Wars: A Repetition of the Inter-War Years?*, London, George Allen & Unwin, 1992, pp. 10–15; Simons, J., *Who Adjusts? Domestic Sources of Foreign Economic Policy during the Inter-War Years*, Princeton, NJ, Princeton University Press, pp. 5–6; Kent, B., *The Spoils of War: The Politics, Economics, and Diplomacy of Reparations, 1918–1932*, Oxford, Oxford University Press, 1989, pp. 373–87.
5 Conybeare, J.A.C., *Trade Wars: The Theory and Practice of International Commercial Rivalry*, New York, Columbia University Press, 1987, ch. 3.
6 Simons, *Who Adjusts?*, pp. 11–19.
7 At the time the National Government and the Foreign Office argued that the adoption of protection was likely to increase British diplomatic power as it now had a weapon with which to secure economic and political concessions. See Records of Cabinet Office Committees, Public Record Office, London (hereafter PRO Cab 27), PRO Cab 27/475, Foreign Office memorandum II: Europe, United Kingdom Tariff Policy, 24 March 1932.
8 McKercher, B., 'Wealth, Power and the International Order: Britain and the American Challenge', *Diplomatic History*, 12, 1988, *passim*.
9 The 'compare and contrast' approach to the historical examples of British and American hegemony over the past two centuries continues to provide fuel for speculation as to the prospect of future American decline. See Lake, D.A., 'British and American Hegemony Compared: Lessons for the Current Era of Decline', in Jeffry A. Frieden and David A. Lake (eds) *International Political Economy:*

Perspectives on Global Power and Wealth, London, Unwin Hyman, 1995, pp. 120–33.

10 Hull, C., *The Memoirs of Cordell Hull*, vol. 1, London, Hodder and Stoughton, 1948, pp. 83–4.

11 Knock, T., *To End All Wars: Woodrow Wilson and the Quest for a New World Order*, New York, Oxford University Press, 1992, pp. 20–2, 40–4.

12 Gardner, L.G., *Economic Aspects of New Deal Diplomacy*, Madison, University of Wisconsin Press, 1963, p. 3; Records of the State Department (hereafter NA SD), NA SD 550.S1 Agenda/104, memorandum by Durand and Wallace, October 1932.

13 Records of the Department of Commerce (hereafter NA DC), NA DC 400 US General 1918–US General 1934, Trade Promotion, Jones to Lamont, 3 Aug. 1932; NA SD 550.S1/231, memorandum by Feis, 29 Sept. 1932; NA SD 611.003/2650, memorandum by Division of Western European Affairs, 8 Dec. 1931; Harris, S.R.S., *Germany's Foreign Indebtedness*, London, Oxford University Press, 1935, *passim*.

14 Ferguson, T., 'Industrial Conflict and the Coming of the New Deal: The Triumph of Multinational Liberalism in America', in G. Gerstle and S. Fraser (eds) *The Rise and Fall of the New Deal Order, 1930–1980*, Princeton, NJ, Princeton University Press, 1989, pp. 17–18.

15 Gellman, I., *Secret Affairs: Franklin D. Roosevelt, Cordell Hull, and Sumner Welles*, Baltimore, MD, Johns Hopkins University Press, 1995.

16 Steward, D., *Trade and Hemisphere: The Good Neighbour Policy and Reciprocal Trade*, Columbia, University of Missouri Press, 1975, pp. 208–20.

17 NA SD 641.003/303, Cox to Boal, 15 January 1933; Records of the Lausanne Conference (hereafter PRO Cab 29), PRO Cab 29/142(i), memorandum by the Board of Trade and Dominions Office, ME(B)21, Annex 1, May 1933.

18 Records of the German Foreign Ministry (hereafter PRO GFM), PRO GFM 33:1231, 3177/D684107, Neurath to Ritter, 3 April 1933.

19 Schatz, A.W., 'The Anglo-American Trade Agreement and Cordell Hull's Search for Peace, 1936–38', *Journal of American History*, 57, 1970/1.

20 Eichengreen, B., 'The Origins and Nature of the Great Slump Revisited', *Economic History Review*, 45, 2, 1992, *passim*.

21 General Correspondence of the Foreign Office (hereafter PRO FO 371), PRO FO 371/16606, A45874 W/45, Leith-Ross to Ashton-Gwatkin, 13 June 1933.

22 Clavin, P.M., *The Failure of Economic Diplomacy 1931–36: Britain, Germany, France and the United States*, London, Macmillan, 1996, pp. 72–83.

23 NA SD 611.423/205, Bickers to Stimson, 9 April 1932; NA DC 400 Trade Promotion US-Canada, Report by commercial consul Toronto, 18 August 1932; NA SD 611.423/215, Heinzelman to Hull, 18 Nov. 1932; NA SD 811.00/328, Jackson to Hull, 10 Nov. 1932. In the Canadian parliament Prime Minister Bennett indicated a softening of the Conservative party's previously uncompromising position on tariffs: *Debates of the House of Commons, Ottawa, Canadian Parliament*, vol. 2, 1933, speech by Bennett, 20 Feb. 1933, pp. 2264–7. In Whitehall the Foreign Office was consistently the greatest advocate of an Anglo-American trade agreement and the most sceptical regarding the long-term viability of the empire. See Ikenberry, G.J., 'A World Economy Restored: Expert Consensus and the Anglo-American Postwar Settlement', *International Organisation*, 46, 1992, p. 307.

24 Diaries and papers of James Warburg, Butler Library, Columbia University, New York (hereafter BL Warburg) BL Warburg: vol. 3, diary entry, 7 April 1933.

25 For an example of agricultural support for 'radical' isolationists see Smith, G.S.,

To Save a Nation. American 'Extremism', the New Deal and the Coming of World War II, Chicago, Elephant Paperbacks, 1992, pp. 24–7.

26 Gardner, R.N., *Sterling–Dollar Diplomacy*, New York, McGraw-Hill (2nd edn), 1969, pp. 39–47; NA SD 611.0031, Exec Cttee/40, memorandum by the drafting committee, 18 Nov. 1933. The Germans were delighted by the public display of antagonism between the remaining democratic powers. See records of the German Finance Ministry, Bundesarchiv, Koblenz (hereafter BA R2), BA R2/21674, Deutsche Führerbriefe, 58, 28 July 1933.

27 The American claim was only partially true. The nationalist George Peek's appointment as Chairman of the Executive Committee on Commercial Policy was charged with drafting the bill, but the British were well aware that the State Department did most of the work.

28 Private Papers of Frederick Leith-Ross (hereafter, PRO T188), PRO T188/63, W3292/5/50, notes on meeting held in the Treasury between Chamberlain and Bonnet, 17 March 1933.

29 Britain earned £31 million from its exports to the USA in 1936 while importing £114 million. Drummond, I. and Hillmer, N., *Negotiating Freer Trade: The United Kingdom, the United States, Canada and the Free Trade Agreements of 1938*, Waterloo, Wilfred Laurier University Press, pp. 42–3.

30 Private papers of Herbert Feis, Library of Congress, Washington, DC (hereafter LC Feis), LC Feis:14, Feis to Frankfurter, 6 Oct. 1937.

31 PRO F0371, W4450/5/50, minute by Nicholls, 25 April 1933 and W4507/5/50, minute by Craigie, 25 April 1933.

32 LC Feis:123, Feis to Frankfurter, 8 Nov. 1933; Franklin D. Roosevelt, Presidential Library, Hyde Park, New York (hereafter FDR), FDR:PPF 744, Kent to Roosevelt, 19 Jan. 1934.

33 Lake, D., 'International Economic Structures and American Foreign Policy', *World Politics*, 35, 1983, p. 540.

34 NA SD 550.S1/1376, Washburn-Child to Hull, June 1934.

35 Schatz, A.W.,'The Anglo-American Trade Areement and Cordell Hull's Search for Peace', *Journal of American History*, 57, 1970/1, p. 100; Drummond and Hillmer, *Negotiating Freer Trade*, p. 157; Parker, R.A.C., 'Pound Sterling, the American Treasury and British Preparations for War, 1938–39', *English Historical Review*, 98, 1983, p. 263.

36 Since 1932 British primary imports from its Ottawa and bilateral trade treaty partners had grown while America's share had fallen from 16.5 per cent of total imports in 1929 to 11.1 per cent in 1936. See Hillmer and Drummond, *Negotiating Freer Trade*, p. 26–34; Rooth, T., *British Protectionism and the International Economy: Overseas Commercial Policy in the 1930s*, Cambridge, Cambridge University Press, 1992, pp. 303–4.

37 May, E., *'Lessons' of the Past: The Use and Misuse of History in American Foreign Policy*, New York, Oxford University Press, 1973, pp. 4–5.

38 Kimball, W., *The Juggler: Franklin Roosevelt as Wartime Statesman*, Princeton, NJ, Princeton University Press, 1991, pp. 186–7.

39 My italics. Gaddis, J.L., *The End of the Cold War: Implications, Reconsiderations, Provocations*, New York, Oxford University Press, 1992, p. 9.

40 LC Feis:125, memorandum by Feis on French financial crisis, 3 March 1937.

41 Carr, E.H., *The Conditions of Peace*, London, Macmillan, 1942, pp. 170–86.

42 Harold Butler quoted in Brewer, *Creating the Special Relationship*, p. 265.

43 PRO FO371/25174, W3839/3839/49, Carr to Balfour, 2 Jan. 1940; Brewer, *Creating the Special Relationship*, pp. 71–3.

44 The American Open-Door principle was the fourth point of the Atlantic Charter,

but Churchill had added the qualifying phrase, 'with due respect for our existing obligations', in other words Britain's imperial preference system.

45 Ikenberry, 'A world economy restored', pp. 289–321.
46 Keynes, quoted in Dobson, A.P. , *The Politics of the Anglo-American Economic Special Relationship*, Brighton, Wheatsheaf Books, 1988, p. 28.
47 Kimball, W., *The Juggler*, pp. 43–62.
48 Hull believed he needed a British commitment to dissolve imperial preference in order to secure Congressional support for his tariff initiative – another lesson drawn from 1933. Reynolds, D., *The Creation of the Anglo-American Alliance*, London, Europa, p. 270.
49 Though he spoke of restoring European trade he believed imperial preference would continue. See Harrod, R., *The Life of John Maynard Keynes*, London, Macmillan, pp. 503–4; Gardner, *Economic Aspects of New Deal Diplomacy*, p. 276.
50 Keynes, J.M., *The Economic Consequences of the Peace*, New York, Harcourt, Brace and Howe, 1920, pp. 10–12.
51 Brewer, S., *Creating the Special Relationship*, Ithaca, NY, Cornell University Press, forthcoming, p. 363.
52 For examples of the public relations offensives, see NA RG 43, box 1.
53 Stiles, K.W., 'The Ambivalent Hegemon: Explaining the 'Lost Decade' in Multilateral Talks', *Review of the International Political Economy*, 2, 1995, p. 19.
54 LC Feis:16, Feis to Frankfurter, 29 March 1934; LC Feis:83, essay for *Issues in American Life*, 1953, pp. 12–13. For futher details see Clavin, P. and Wilhelm, C., 'History as Propaganda: The Role of German and British Historians in "educating" the United States, 1933–1955', European Union Human Capital and Mobility Programme project, *History and Historians in European and American Societies and Cultures*, 1996.
55 Feis, 'Is the United States Imperialist?', *Yale Review*, 1950, p. 2. Among them were William L. Langer, S. Everett Gleason, Jeanette Nichols, Robert Divine, William Adams Brown, Richard Gardner and Raymond Mikesell.
56 Hegel, quoted in May, *'Lessons' of the Past*, p. 179; Thorne, C., *Border Crossings: Studies in International History*, Oxford, Basil Blackwell, 1988, pp. 26–7.

23

COMMENTS ON FOREMAN-PECK, HUGHES HALLET AND MA AND ON CLAVIN

Tim Rooth

Although other writers have calculated that protection benefited British GNP in the early 1930s, James Foreman-Peck, Andrew Hughes Hallett and Yue Ma present a model which indicates an even more dramatic rise than previous estimates. In this, they reinforce an emerging orthodoxy. However, they now take the case much further with the surprising argument that Britain's best contribution to alleviating the international depression would have been by introducing tariffs earlier in the slump. An earlier adoption of protection, by improving the balance of payments and perhaps bolstering confidence, would have enabled Britain to stay on gold, thus averting the catastrophic consequences that followed the breakdown of the international exchange rate regime. Moreover, British tariffs, with stable exchange rates preserved among the major industrial economies, would have provided a powerful bargaining counter for trade liberalisation.

This is an intriguing argument, clearly presented and supported by sophisticated modelling. By emphasising the destructive instability that followed Britain's abandonment of gold, Foreman-Peck *et al.* tilt at the arguments of recent American writers who have emphasised the liberalising effects of early devaluation and the heavy costs of clinging to overvalued exchange rates.

Although the counterfactual case is powerfully argued, this commentator harbours some lingering doubts. Given the immense complexity and variety of deflationary forces at work, could a single timely step have averted the financial crash? Were the exchange rate parities of the major powers really sustainable? To what extent was the British financial crisis of 1931 a liquidity problem arising from pressures on the reserves of a nascent sterling area? In this sense it was partly a product of the difficulties of the periphery, caused by a collapse of primary prices and the cessation of international lending. Inappropriate exchange rates and the drying up of international capital flows

308

contributed to a gross maldistribution of world liquidity, especially the clot of gold accumulated in New York and Paris.

The second reservation centres on whether Britain could have used its new tariffs, even in a stable exchange rate regime, to encourage international tariff disarmament. There is little doubt that exchange instability of sterling and the dollar underlined the refusal of the French to countenance tariff liberalisation during the World Economic Conference (WEC) of 1933. But would the UK government have been able to override the great hostility of business and Conservative backbench opinion to any erosion of its newly won tariffs in negotiation with industrial countries?

While this is a well-argued and authoritative examination of the impact of tariffs on GNP and the balance of payments of the major countries, it leaves some doubts about both the practicalities of implementing such policies and whether the break-up of the gold standard could have been avoided. Meanwhile the literature on the impact of tariffs has been considerably enriched.

Patricia Clavin's chapter provides a fresh and unusual account of the lessons of history and the role of historians in influencing policy. How often have historians been recruited to engage in explicit propaganda?

The dangers of emphasising continuity in history are clearly brought out. One consequence was the Americans' continual underestimation of the strength of British protectionist sentiment because this was seen merely as an aberration from the internationalism that had characterised British policy in the nineteenth century. An influential exponent of this view was diplomat and historian Herbert Feis, whose study of *Europe: The World's Banker, 1870–1914* had been published in 1930. In reality, if British internationalism was not dead by the 1930s, it was deeply comatose. UK business interests, which had become fiercely protectionist by the early 1930s, were pressing Whitehall for a more aggressive international economic diplomacy, and the government backbenches were packed with members of the protectionist Empire Industries Association. Even Board of Trade officials, normally a moderating influence on the more extreme protectionist demands, were producing unyielding memoranda on British commercial policy for the forthcoming WEC.

Underestimating the strength of British protectionism, Hull persisted with his free-trade campaign during the conference. US overtures for tariff liberalisation were rejected. Tariff concessions might easily have been outweighed by currency movements, and thus the refusal of the USA to stabilise the dollar (Roosevelt's bombshell message) provided a legitimate reason to hold back on tariff cuts. Yet it is very doubtful that the Americans could have delivered anyway. The delegation itself was violently divided: Feis recollected an episode when Senator Key Pitman, apparently blaming him for proposed tariff reductions, drunkenly pursued him along the corridors of Claridges with a hunting knife (H. Feis, *1933: Characters in Crisis,* Boston, MA, 1966, pp. 188–9). Moreover, it is extremely unlikely that an increasingly nationalistic Administration, let alone Congress, would have backed its delegation over tariff cuts.

Nor, of course, were disagreements between the Americans and British restricted to commercial policy. Although Clavin suggests that 1933 'provided a window of opportunity to pursue an Anglo-American rapprochement', in part because the devaluation of the dollar removed a source of tension over membership of the gold standard, the refusal of the USA to contemplate stabilisation raised instead the spectre of intensified American trade competition. Thus US departure from gold changed the nature of the argument rather than removing it. Currency issues featured prominently at the WEC. There is clear evidence that lessons were drawn from history. Kindleberger's later analysis of the stabilising role of a hegemon was partly foreshadowed by Harvard professor John Willams, who argued the real cause of the breakdown of the international gold standard was that 'since the war there has been no centre, such as London used to be before the war, in which debtor countries can be certain of disposing of their goods and obtaining temporary financial assistance if required' (PRO CAB 58/183, Report on the Work of the Preparatory Committee for the World Economic Conference, 31 October to 9 November 1932, F. Leith-Ross and F. Phillips, 10 November 1932).

There were few if any signs of British internationalism reviving later in the 1930s. As Clavin emphasises, Britain was drawn into trade negotiations with the Americans from 1936 for political reasons, not by economic conviction. The Reciprocal Trade Agreements Act, however, does appear to suggest a move towards liberalism in Washington. The USA was able to respond to the overtures that Canada had been making since early 1933, and also signed a number of treaties with Latin American neighbours. Perhaps this was a form of regionalism rather than internationalism. Certainly there was nothing for Australia or New Zealand, a fact that later contributed to their jaundiced view of American planning for the postwar international order. The illiberal nature of the Anglo-American trade treaty, characterised by its striving for narrow bilateral advantage, is powerful evidence against the view that the USA was preparing to assume the mantle of a liberalising hegemon (T. Rooth, *British Protectionism and the International Economy: Overseas Commercial Policy in the 1930s*, Cambridge, 1993, pp. 283–306).

US trade policy, however, continued to demonstrate considerable ambivalence. Although US tariff levels fell after 1934, American efforts during and immediately after the war – as illustrated, for instance, at Bretton Woods – were concentrated more on eliminating discrimination in international trade (a return to the open door policy of the 1920s?) than on liberalisation of domestic tariffs: multilateralism yes, free trade no. Even if the Administration was prepared to move, Congress was often reluctant, and hence the rejection of the ITO and the inclusion of the protectionist 'peril points' in 1948 when Truman sought renewal of the RTA legislation (R.E. Baldwin and A.O. Krueger, *The Structure and Evolution of Recent US Trade Policy*, Chicago, 1984, p. 9).

The role of British historians in moulding American opinion was fraught with contradictions. What and whose message were they pushing? There might be consensus that the USA should assume international responsibilities and not retreat into isolationism after the peace. Yet as Clavin points out, the implications of this for international economic policy were dangerous for Britain. Perhaps the concentration on emphasising British strength backfired to the extent that it contributed to American perceptions of the UK as a postwar rival. This was reinforced by the necessity for Britain to operate discriminatory trade and currency controls and the suspicion that Britain was planning a 'two-world' international economy. As Clavin suggests, imperial relations had probably become more important during the war, not less, and the UK, fiercely resisting any winding down of imperial preferences, was supported by Commonwealth suspicions of US economic policy.

INDEX

INDEX

oversaving 210, 212, 215–16, 218
Owens, John 88–9, 91
Owen Owens and Co. 88–9
Oxford, University of 168
Oxford University Press 1

Paine, Tom 207
Pall Mall Gazette 176
Palmer, Sarah 170
Palmerston, Viscount 97, 135, 170, 172–3
Paris 152
Paris Economic Conference (1916) 250, 255
Paris Peace Conference (1919) 291
Parrish, Richard 108
Parker, C.S. 166
Parkes, Joseph 100
Parnell, Sir Henry 166
Parry, J.P. 171
Pasvolsky, Leo 294
paternalism 83
Patterson, Wilson MP 94
pauperism, pauper settlement 111, 116–17, 121
Payne–Aldrich tariff (1909) 229, 234
Pax Americana 297–8, 300
Pax Britannica 290, 297–8, 302
Pearson, C.H. 212–14
Peel, George 166
Peel, (Sir) Robert 2, 5, 6, 7, 8, 18, 28–9, 32–42, 44–5, 48, 50, 52, 54–61, 76, 82–5, 93, 99,100, 102, 133, 137–8, 141, 164–9, 171–4, 203, 204; and manufacturing 83–4
Peelites 3, 5, 76, 164–9, 173, 176, 203
Pennington, James 133
perfect competition 162
Persia 234
Philadelphia 89
philanthropy 154
Phillips, William 294
physiocrats, physiocracy 18, 150, 151
Pickering and Chatto 1
pig rearing 54
Pigot's Directory (1825) 89
Pigou, Arthur C. 226–7
Pitman, Senator Key 309
Pitt, William 85, 166
Plato 246
'Plug plot' riots 101

Political Economy Club 147–8, 172, 175
Polizei (Hamburg) 109–24
Poor Law (Amendment) Act, 1834 83
poor rates 92
poor relief 111
Portugal 171, 173–4, 229
potatoes 51–61
potato blight and famine (Ireland) 6, 50, 52, 54–61, 84–5; Scientific Commissioners 54, 57
poultry 59
poverty 8, 16, 116, 119, 153–4, 184, 194, 208–9, 211–12
Prest, John 82–3
price level 129–42
Produktplakatet 152
prohibitions 154, 272
protection, return to (1932) 5, 246–58, 262–77
Protestantism 55, 56
providence 20, 39, 54–5, 60–1, 84–5
Prussia 74
'public choice' analysis 6–7, 9, 246–9, 258, 260

Quesnay, François 150

Rabenius, Lars Georg 151–4
railways 118, 155–6, 237
Rainbow Circle 214
Raleigh, Sir Walter 51
'rational choice' analysis 6–7, 9, 246–9, 258, 260
Reciprocal Trade Agreements Act (1934) 270, 288, 292–6, 303, 310
reciprocity 3, 22, 43–4, 129–42, 148, 152, 165–6, 185, 203, 224–38, 263, 265–7, 269–70, 288, 291–6, 303, 310
Redford, Arthur 91
Reform Act: 1832 21, 73; 1867 73, 175; 1884 73, 208
Reichstag 75, 227
reparations 291
Repeal Association (Ireland) 51
retaliation 8–9, 28, 43, 75, 134, 174, 185, 187–8, 192, 197, 224–38, 244–5, 262, 265, 267–70, 289
Reveille programme 195
revenue duties *see* tariffs, revenue
revolutions (1848–9) 110, 171
Rhodes, Cecil 215

320

Ricardo, David 22, 40, 41, 42, 129–31,
133, 137, 141, 147–8, 161, 220;
Ricardianism 6, 37, 40, 99, 130–1,
247
Ricardo, John Lewis 40, 43–4, 132–5,
141, 161, 168
Richthofen, Baron von 227
Ripon, Lord 32, 33, 34
Ritchie, C.T. 185
Robinson, Joan 162, 243
Robertson, J.M. 178, 214, 229, 244
Rochdale 16
Roebuck, John Arthur MP 139–40
Rooke, John 18–19
Roosevelt, Franklin D. 289–95, 297–8,
309
Rooth, Tim 310
Rosebery, Lord 208
Roß, Edgar 114
Rotherham 87
Rothermere, Lord 250
Rothstein, Morton 237
Routh, Randolph 52, 56
Rowland, B. 288
Royal Academy 94
Royal College of Surgeons 94
Royal Commission on Occupation of
Land in Ireland (1843–5) 56
Runciman, Walter 296
Ruperti, Julius 105, 108, 111, 114,
120–1
Ruskin, John 190
Russell, Lord John 35–6, 40, 41, 59, 60,
138, 168
Russel, Odo 176
Russia 37, 209, 233–4, 238, 302
Rutland 15
Rye 237

Sadler Committee 93–5
'Safeguarding Committee' (UK) 250
'safeguarding' of industry 193
Safeguarding of Industry Act
(1921) 206, 251–2, 256, 260, 265
Salford 15
Salisbury, Lord 85, 191
Salomons, David 21
Samuel, Herbert 214
Samuelson, Paul 39–40
Sandars, J.S. 193
Sandford, Benjamin 94
Sandon, Viscount 133

Sartori, Giovanni 68–9, 76
Sartorius, G. 150
Saul, S.B. 233–6, 238
Say, Jean Baptiste 151–3, 162; Say's
Law 8, 210, 218, 243
Scammell, William 4
Scheffer, Carl Gustav 150
scientific instruments 256
Schacht, Hjalmar 266, 270, 292
Schleswig-Holstein 108–9
Schofield 94
Schonhardt-Bailey, Cheryl 1, 6–7,
82–4, 121
Schulze-Gaevernitz, G. von 98
Schulzenheim, David von 150–1
Schutzverwandschaft 110
Scoby-Smith, G. 251
Scott, Gilbert 108
Scottish Secession Church 22
Searle, Geoffrey R. 3
Seed, John 91
Select Committee on Import Duties
(1840) 166
Senate (Hamburg) 109–10, 113
Senior, Nassau 95, 131, 133
Sharpe, Thomas 91
Sharpe and Roberts 91
Sheffield 187, 197, 225
shipbuilding 117, 119
shipping 53, 170–1, 198
Sidgwick, Henry 213
Simmons, Beth A. 263–4
Sinclair, John 151
slavery 169
Smith, Adam 4, 22, 40, 41,42, 52, 129,
137, 141, 146–8, 150–4, 156, 158,
161–2, 165, 170–1, 177, 198
Smith, J.B. 21
Smith, Roland 89
'Social-Darwinism' 8, 184, 198, 214
'Social-Imperialism' 5
social-market economy 83, 84
social reform 186, 190, 193–198,
205–6, 208, 212–4, 216, 218, 302
Solomou, Solomos 272
Somerville, Revd Andrew 22
soup kitchens 60
South Africa 185, 191, 198, 214–5
Sozialdemokratische Partei (Germany)
75–8
Spain 171, 173–4, 234, 266, 267
Specie-flow mechanism 130–1, 140–1

227, 293; Uppsala, University of 149
utilitarianism 164

vested interests *see* economic interests
Villiers, Charles Pelham 21, 166, 168, 173
Vincent, John 169
Virginia, University of 298

Wadensjö, Eskil 153
wage boards 194–5
wages 6, 14–26, 28, 41, 43, 48, 83–4, 94–5, 98, 100, 105, 119, 127, 136–7, 139, 177, 186, 189–90, 194, 210–11, 257–8, 264; wages fund, 'iron law of wages' 14, 22
Wallace, Robert 40
Wallenberg, A.O. 155–6
Wallerstein, Emanuel 220
Walsall 49
Wappengren, Anders 150
Warburg, James 294
Ward, J.T. 93
Webb, Sidney 178, 210
Welcker, Theodor 113
Wellington, Duke of 50, 55
Westminster Hospital 94
Westminster Review 24
West Indies 169, 177
wheat cultivation 52–3, 61, 85, 237

Wheeeler-Bennet, John 298
Whig party 2, 8, 18, 20, 36, 48, 51, 56, 59, 60, 73, 85, 99, 100, 167–73, 203
White, Harry 300–1
Wicksell, Knut 158
Williams, John 310
Williamson, J. 273
Williamson, Jeffrey G. 237
Wilson, Woodrow 289–90, 297, 303
wines 134, 174
Wise, B.R. 177
Wood, (Sir) Charles 59, 140, 168–9, 172
Wood, G.W. 100
Wood, Henry George MP 99
woollen and worsted industry 253
workhouse system 60
working classes 3, 14–26, 87, 94–5, 101, 127, 168, 171, 184, 186, 204, 207, 210–11, 213, 216, 264
World Economic Conference; 1927 266; 1933 270, 292, 294–5, 309–10
Wyndham, George 190–2

York 15
'Yorkshire manufacturer' 22
Young, G.M. 164
Young, John 59

Zollverein 7, 75, 96–8, 113, 115, 171; trade treaties of 113